CONTENTS

PUBLISHER'S NOTE

A word is necessary about three of the plays in this volume.

"Parnell" is of course the famous "banned" play which was the occasion of a leading article in *The Times* of 29th April 1936. It has now been licensed for public performance, and we understand that it is shortly to be presented in the West End.

"Till the Day I Die" is one of the three plays which have made the reputation of Clifford Odets in the United States. This dramatist is considered by many American critics as the most important since Eugene O'Neill.

"Bury the Dead" was recently produced at the Ethel Barrymore Theatre in New York, and can be said without exaggeration to have "made a sensation" with the critics.

FAMOUS PLAYS
of 1936

UNIFORM: EACH 7/6

FAMOUS PLAYS OF 1935-6:

St. Helena	*Call it a Day*	*After October*
Red Night	*Awake and Sing*	*Katie Roche*

FAMOUS PLAYS OF 1935:

Night Must Fall	*Accent on Youth*	*Close Quarters*
Grief Goes Over	*The Mask of Virtue*	*Youth at the Helm*

FAMOUS PLAYS OF 1934-5:

Viceroy Sarah	*The Dominant Sex*	*Frolic Wind*
The Old Ladies	*Flowers of the Forest*	*Lovers' Leap*

FAMOUS PLAYS OF 1934:

Touch Wood	*Men in White*	*The Maitlands*
Queen of Scots	*Old Folks at Home*	*Family Affairs*

FAMOUS PLAYS OF 1933-4:

Clive of India	*The Wind and the Rain*	*Reunion in Vienna*
The Laughing Woman	*Sixteen*	*The Distaff Side*

FAMOUS PLAYS OF 1933:

The Late Christopher Bean	*Richard of Bordeaux*
Ten-Minute Alibi	*Sometimes Even Now*
Alien Corn	*Of Thee I Sing*

FAMOUS PLAYS OF 1932-3:

Children in Uniform	*Miracle at Verdun*	*Service*
Strange Orchestra	*Behold, We Live*	*Counsellor-at-Law*

FAMOUS PLAYS OF 1932:

Musical Chairs	*Somebody Knows*	*See Naples and Die*
The Rose Without a Thorn		*There's Always Juliet*
	Once in a Lifetime	

FAMOUS PLAYS OF 1931:

The Barretts of Wimpole Street

	The Improper Duchess	*To See Ourselves*
After All	*London Wall*	*Autumn Crocus*

SIX PLAYS:

The Green Pastures	*Street Scene*	*Badger's Green*
Down our Street	*Socrates*	*Alison's House*

FAMOUS PLAYS OF TO-DAY

Journey's End	*Young Woodley*	*Many Waters*
The Lady with a Lamp	*Such Men are Dangerous*	*Mrs. Moonlight*

FAMOUS PLAYS OF 1936

PROFESSOR BERNHARDI
ARTHUR SCHNITZLER

PARNELL
ELSIE T. SCHAUFFLER

THE TWO BOUQUETS
ELEANOR AND HERBERT FARJEON

BURY THE DEAD
IRWIN SHAW

BOY MEETS GIRL
BELLA AND SAMUEL SPEWACK

TILL THE DAY I DIE
CLIFFORD ODETS

LONDON
VICTOR GOLLANCZ LTD
1936

Printed in Great Britain by
The Camelot Press Ltd., London and Southampton

PROFESSOR BERNHARDI

Arthur Schnitzler

PROFESSOR BERNHARDI

A Play
In Three Acts

English version by
LOUIS BORELL and RONALD ADAM

Professor Bernhardi was first presented publicly in London at the Embassy Theatre, June 15th, 1936, and transferred to the Phœnix Theatre, July 14th, 1936, with the following cast:

Characters in order of their appearance:

Nurse Ludmilla	ANNE COTTON
Pointner	DUDLEY RELTON
Dr. Oskar Bernhardi	LEONARD SACHS
Professor Bernhardi	ABRAHAM SOFAER
Dr. Kurt Felder	JOHN STOBART
Professor Ebenwald	EARLE GREY
Professor Tugend	ARTHUR SEATON
Dr. Adler	DON GEMMELL
Professor Cyprian	JOHN GARSIDE
Father Reder	BERNARD MEREFIELD
Servant to Professor Bernhardi	DAVID DUNCAN
Dr. Feuermann	PETER ASHMORE
Professor Filitz	NOEL HOWLETT
Dr. Lowenstein	RICHARD WARNER
Attendant at the Institute	NOEL WOOLF
Dr. Flint	RONALD ADAM
Dr. Schreimann	REGINALD JARMAN
Dr. Wenger	RAF DE LA TORRE
Professor Felder	CHARLES MAUNSELL
Councillor Winkler	ALAN WHEATLEY
Commissionaire at the Ministry of Education	
	WILL LEIGHTON

The Play Produced by HEINRICH SCHNITZLER

CHARACTERS

PROFESSOR BERNHARDI – Director of the Elizabeth Institute.

DR. EBENWALD – Vice-Director of the Elizabeth Institute.

DR. CYPRIAN
DR. FELDER
DR. FILITZ
DR. TUGEND
DR. LOWENSTEIN
DR. SCHREIMANN
DR. ADLER
DR. OSKAR BERNHARDI
DR. KURT FELDER
DR. WENGER
POINTNER
NURSE LUDMILLA

All of the Elizabeth Institute.

DR. FLINT – The Minister of Education.
FATHER REDER – A priest.
DR. FEUERMANN – A country practitioner.
COUNCILLOR WINKLER
MANSERVANT TO BERNHARDI
ATTENDANT AT ELIZABETH INSTITUTE
COMMISSIONAIRE AT MINISTRY OF
EDUCATION

SCENES
The action of the play takes place in Vienna

ACT I

SCENE I: An ante-room to a ward of the Elizabeth Institute.

SCENE II: A room in Professor Bernhardi's house.

ACT II

Committee Room of the Elizabeth Institute.

ACT III

SCENE I: A room in Professor Bernhardi's house.
SCENE II: A room at the Ministry of Education.

ACT I

SCENE I

An ante-room of moderate size all in white, leading to a hospital ward. On the right and left doors leading to corridors. At the back a door leading into the ward. On the left a rather broad window. In the centre of the room towards the left an oblong table on which lie a thick register, files containing records of patients and various papers and documents. Beside the ward door a wash-basin in a white stand. On the other side a glass case containing medical instruments, etc. On the clothes-stand a white overall. Some chairs as required.

Nurse Ludmilla, about twenty, rather pretty, pale, is busy at the glass instrument-case.

Pointner enters—a young man of twenty-five, medium height, pince-nez, pale, busy-body type.

Pointner: Professor not here yet? They're taking a long time. (*Looking into one of the files on the table*) That makes the third post-mortem in a week. Pretty high for a ward of twenty beds. And to-morrow there will be another one.

Nurse: You think so, doctor? The sepsis case?

Pointner: Yes. By the way, have the authorities been informed?

Nurse: Of course, doctor.

Pointner: Nothing can be proved, of course. But it was certainly an illegal operation. Yes, nurse, all sorts of things happen in the world outside. (*Sees an opened packet on the table*) Why, those are the invitation cards for our ball. (*Reads*) " Under the patronage of Princess Stixenstein." Well, nurse, are you coming to the ball?

NURSE (*smiling*): Oh, no, I don't think so, doctor.

POINTNER: Are you forbidden to dance?

NURSE: Oh, no, we are not a religious order; we are not forbidden anything.

POINTNER: Not anything?

NURSE: It would hardly be proper. And besides, one does not feel like it in our profession.

POINTNER: But why, what about us doctors? Look at Dr. Adler, for instance. He is a noted pathological anatomist, but a very gay fellow all the same. Personally I'm always at my best in the dissecting-room.

[DR. OSKAR BERNHARDI *enters, on the right, twenty-five years old, very well dressed, with amiable but somewhat uncertain manner.*

OSKAR: Good morning.

POINTNER }
NURSE } Good morning, doctor.

OSKAR: My father will be here in a moment.

POINTNER: Have they finished below? What was the finding, if one may ask?

OSKAR: The tumour started in the kidney and was quite sharply defined.

POINTNER: Then it might still have been possible to operate?

OSKAR: Yes, it might have been. . . .

POINTNER: If Professor Ebenwald had thought that too . . .

OSKAR: . . . there would have been a post-mortem a week earlier. (*At the table*) Why, these are the invitations for our ball. What are they doing here?

POINTNER: It looks as if it's going to be one of the most brilliant events of the season. It's in the papers already. I hear you have dedicated a new waltz to the committee. . . .

OSKAR: Oh, a trifle. (*Nodding towards the ward*) Anything new in there?

POINTNER: It's nearly over with the sepsis girl.

OSKAR: Pity. (*Regretfully*) There was nothing we could do.

POINTNER: I have given her a camphor injection.

OSKAR: Yes, we certainly know the art of prolonging life.

[PROFESSOR BERNHARDI *enters from the right; over fifty. Beard a little grey, distinguished face; more a man of the world than a savant.*

DR. KURT FELDER, *his first assistant, twenty-seven, moustache, pince-nez, vivacious but at the same time somewhat reserved character, enters with him.* NURSE *takes his coat, hangs it on a peg.*

KURT: Professor, I can assure you Dr. Adler would have preferred Professor Ebenwald's diagnosis to have been right.

BERNHARDI: My dear Felder, you suspect everybody. Where will all these suspicions lead you?

POINTNER: Good morning, professor.

BERNHARDI: Good morning.

POINTNER: Dr. Oskar told me we were right after all.

BERNHARDI: Yes; but " we " were wrong at the same time. Or don't you attend Professor Ebenwald's lectures any more?

OSKAR: Dr. Pointner attends lectures in every section.

BERNHARDI: Then you must side with a great number of opinions.

[POINTNER *bites his lip.*

All right. Is there anything new? (*Lays his hand good-naturedly on* POINTNER'S *shoulder.*)

POINTNER: The girl is in a very bad way.

BERNHARDI: The poor child is still alive, then?

POINTNER: What shall we state as the cause of death?

OSKAR: Sepsis, of course.

POINTNER: And the cause of the sepsis? After all, it was an illegal operation. . . .

BERNHARDI (*who has been busy signing papers which the* NURSE *gave to him*): We could not prove it. There was no injury. The matter has been notified and that is the end of it for us. For the poor creature in there—it was the end before she came here. (*He makes for the ward.*)

[PROFESSOR EBENWALD *enters; about forty; tall and slim; overcoat thrown over shoulders; small beard, monocle; speaks in an assured manner.*

EBENWALD: Good morning. Do you know——Oh, there you are, professor.

BERNHARDI: Good morning, Ebenwald.

EBENWALD: Could you spare me a moment?

BERNHARDI: Now?

EBENWALD (*close to him*): If it is possible. You see, it is about the new appointment for Tugend's section.

BERNHARDI (*considering a moment*): I shall not be long in there. Could you wait here a moment?

EBENWALD: Of course, of course.

BERNHARDI (*to* OSKAR): Have you given Dr. Pointner the report of the post-mortem?

OSKAR: Oh, yes. (*Takes it from his pocket*) Would you be good enough to enter it right away?

POINTNER: Certainly.

[BERNHARDI, OSKAR, KURT *and the* NURSE *go into the ward.*

POINTNER *sits down and prepares to write.* EBENWALD *has gone over to the window; looks out, wipes his monocle.*

(*Attentively*) Won't you take a seat, professor?

EBENWALD: Don't disturb yourself, Pointner. Well, how are you getting on?

POINTNER (*rising*): Thank you, professor, as well as I can hope, a few weeks before the final.

EBENWALD: Why, you needn't worry—with your keenness.

POINTNER: On the practical side I feel pretty safe, but that grim theory. . . .

EBENWALD: Well, it was never my strong point either. (*Closer to him*) If it's any comfort to you, I can tell you that I failed in physiology myself. As you see, it hasn't made much difference to my career.

[POINTNER *sits down, laughs flatteringly.*

(*Looking over his shoulders*) Post-mortem report?

POINTNER: Yes, professor.

EBENWALD: Great rejoicing in Israel, what?

POINTNER (*uncertain*): What d'you mean, professor?

EBENWALD: Well, because Bernhardi's section has triumphed.

POINTNER: Oh, you mean because the tumour was quite sharply defined?

EBENWALD: And actually originated in the kidney.

POINTNER: But surely one could not say that with certainty. It was more, I should say, a matter of guesswork.

EBENWALD: Guesswork? Pointner, how dare you! We call that intuition. Diagnostic clairvoyancy.

POINTER: And in any case it was too late to operate.

EBENWALD: But you'd better go on with your writing.

[POINTNER *begins to write.*

Oh, by the way—I'm sorry to interrupt again. You attend the lectures in Tugend's section too, don't you?

POINTNER: Yes, indeed, professor.

EBENWALD: Now, in confidence, what is your opinion of Dr. Wenger's lectures?

POINTNER: Dr. Wenger?

EBENWALD: Yes. He often deputises for the old man. Well, then, how does he lecture?

POINTNER (*hesitating*): I should say—quite well.

EBENWALD: Oh!

POINTNER: Perhaps a little too—too erudite. But very vital; but I think I ought not to criticise a future chief . . .

EBENWALD: What do you mean by a future chief? That is not decided yet. There are others as well. Don't hesitate. What have you against Dr. Wenger? Vox populi, vox dei.

POINTNER: Well, I really have nothing against his lectures, but it's just his way. If I may say so, professor, he is a little flashy in his manner.

EBENWALD: Oho! As my Parliamentary cousin calls it: " The Labour jack-in-office."

POINTNER: Ha, ha, very good. The Labour jack-in-office.

[BERNHARDI, OSKAR, KURT *and* NURSE *come out of the ward.*

BERNHARDI: Well, here I am, Ebenwald.

[NURSE *lays a paper before him for signature.*

What, something else? Oh, yes. Excuse me a moment. (*While writing*) Astonishing how it always works. (*To* EBENWALD) We have a case of sepsis in there, you know. Eighteen-year-old girl. Completely conscious. Would like to get up and go for a walk. Believes herself to be perfectly well; and you can hardly feel her pulse. Within an hour it may be all over.

EBENWALD (*professionally*): We often find that.

POINTNER (*eagerly*): Shall I give her another camphor injection?

BERNHARDI (*looking at him steadily*): You might have saved yourself the trouble before. (*Reassuring him*) But perhaps you gave her the happiest hour of her life. Though I don't suppose you intended that.

POINTNER (*annoyed*): Why not, professor? After all, we are not butchers.

BERNHARDI: I don't remember suggesting anything of the kind. (*Goes to basin to wash his hands.*)

[POINTNER *and* EBENWALD *exchange glances.*

(*To* NURSE) Has she any relations?

NURSE: No one has been here since she came.

BERNHARDI: Not her lover either?

KURT: He'd see to that.

OSKAR: She has not mentioned him once. Maybe she does not even know his name.

BERNHARDI: And that's what they call love. (*To* EBENWALD) Well, now I am at your service, Ebenwald.

OSKAR: You will be coming in again, father, won't you? Remember she begged for you.

BERNHARDI: Yes, I shall be round again.

[KURT *has gone over to the shelves and is busying himself with two test-tubes.* OSKAR *goes over to him, they talk together and soon re-enter the ward.*

NURSE (*to* POINTNER): I will go and fetch the priest.

POINTNER: All right, And if you're late, it doesn't much matter.

[NURSE *goes out.* POINTNER *selects a few patient records from the file and goes into the ward.*

EBENWALD (*who has become very impatient*): Well, Bernhardi, it's this. I have heard from Professor Hell in Graz that he is quite ready to be nominated as Tugend's successor.

BERNHARDI: Oh, quite ready, is he?

EBENWALD: Yes.

BERNHARDI: Has anybody asked him?

EBENWALD: Yes, I took the liberty—as an old friend and fellow student.

BERNHARDI: But you wrote him privately, I presume?

EBENWALD: Of course, as no decision has yet been taken.

[PROFESSOR TUGEND *enters from the right; about fifty; grey hair, jovial in manner, intentionally humorous, but at the same time somewhat unsteady and eager for applause; on the whole looks more like a stockbroker than a professor.*

TUGEND: Good morning, Bernhardi, good morning, Ebenwald.

EBENWALD: Am I in the way, Tugend?

TUGEND: What an idea! No secrets here.

BERNHARDI: Well, what is it, Tugend? You want to speak to me?

TUGEND: Yes. The Minister of Education has just enquired whether I can take over the clinic at once.

BERNHARDI: At once?

TUGEND: As soon as possible.

BERNHARDI: I thought you weren't wanted until the beginning of the summer.

TUGEND: The other man has applied for leave. Poor devil! Six per cent sugar. Last days of Pompeii. What?

[*He has the habit of adding a thoughtlessly questioning " What ? " to some sentences, especially quotations.*

I was in the Ministry yesterday, you know. He sent his regards, by the way.

BERNHARDI: Who did?

TUGEND: Flint. We talked a lot about you. He thinks a great deal of you. Looks back with pleasure to the time when you were assistants together. Some career, what? The first time that a clinical professor has become Minister of Education.

BERNHARDI: Your new friend Flint was always a good politician.

TUGEND: He takes a great interest in our— in your—no, for the present still—in our institute.

BERNHARDI: I know—so much interest that he very nearly ruined it.

TUGEND: That wasn't his doing. It was the whole Medical Board. The fight of the old men against the young. But that is all long past. I can assure you, Bernhardi, that Flint regards the Elizabeth Institute with the greatest sympathy. . . .

BERNHARDI: And we can do without it. Thank heaven !

TUGEND: Proud as a peacock. What ?

BERNHARDI: We shall, of course, not keep you a day longer than you wish. Fortunately you have a very able assistant who can carry on the section for the present.

TUGEND: Young Wenger ? Yes. Clever lad. Yes. But you won't let him deputise for long, will you ?

EBENWALD: I had just been saying that in general I do not approve of temporary appointments and took the liberty of referring to a letter I have received from Professor Hell in Graz who would be prepared . . .

TUGEND: Oh. I had a letter from him too.

BERNHARDI: He seems to spend a lot of money on postage.

TUGEND (*with a quick glance at* EBENWALD): You know, Bernhardi, Hell would be an excellent acquisition to the institute.

BERNHARDI: Then he must have developed wonderfully in Graz. When he was in Vienna he was not considered too capable.

TUGEND: Excuse me. I think I can answer that. He has published some excellent theses. Wenger is too young. I am sure he's not expecting it himself.

BERNHARDI: He ought to. His latest work on serums has created a lot of attention.

EBENWALD: Created a sensation. That is not the same thing.

BERNHARDI: The day you start your work at the hospital, your present assistant will take charge.

EBENWALD: Then I ask you to hold the meeting to decide the appointment within the next few days.

BERNHARDI: Will you please leave everything to me, Ebenwald. I think you will agree that nothing so far has been unnecessarily delayed in our institute, but also nothing undertaken with undue haste.

EBENWALD: I deny that I have ever advocated undue haste.

BERNHARDI (*smiling*): I accept your statement.

EBENWALD (*looking at his watch*): I must get back to my section. Good morning, gentlemen.

BERNHARDI: It's time I went too. (*Stands aside for* EBENWALD.) Lead the way, Ebenwald; your students will be waiting.

TUGEND: Can I make a third? What?

EBENWALD (*meets* DR. ADLER *at the door*): How are you?

[*Exit* EBENWALD. DR. ADLER *enters; short, dark, fresh, vivacious, keen eyes, about thirty; in white overall.*

ADLER: Hello!

BERNHARDI: What brings you here, Adler?

ADLER: I wanted to look up the case-sheet with regard to your patient, professor.

BERNHARDI: It is at your disposal.

[TUGEND *and* BERNHARDI *go out.* POINTNER *enters from the ward.*

POINTNER: Morning, Dr. Adler.

ADLER: Good morning. I wanted to ask you if you could let me have a look at the case-sheets.

POINTNER: Certainly. (*Takes a sheet from the file.*)

[KURT *enters from the ward.*

ADLER (*to* KURT, *studying the record*): So the patient was only eight days with you?

POINTNER: Yes. Before that he was with Professor Ebenwald. But as the case could not be operated . . .

ADLER: Your chief is first rate at diagnosis at least.

KURT: How do you mean—at least?

ADLER: Why jump on me, Dr. Felder? I just meant that your section's strength is in diagnosis, not so much in therapy, where in my humble opinion you do a damn sight too much experimenting.

KURT: We feel bound to try everything. Especially where all else fails.

ADLER: I am the last to belittle his services. And he has been able to get almost to the top—in spite of existing tendencies. . . . I have some right to mention this—as I have never concealed my Jewish descent, although on my mother's side I come from a very old Viennese family. During my student days I even had to suffer for the other strain.

KURT: We know, doctor.

ADLER: I am glad to find that you too do our director full justice.

KURT: Why glad, doctor?

ADLER: Because you were in the German-Nationalist Students' Movement.

KURT: And anti-Semitic. Yes. On the whole, I am still. But I have become anti-Aryan as well. I find that mankind in general is a rather inferior species and I cling to the few exceptions.

[PROFESSOR CYPRIAN *enters from the right; elderly, short, with long hair, still almost blond, somewhat drawling sing-song manner of speaking; is continually lapsing unintentionally into lecturing, speaking as if to an audience.*

CYPRIAN: Good day, gentlemen. (*Greetings.*) Ah, there you are, Dr. Adler. I've been looking for you downstairs. Can you assure me, doctor, that they will not remove my new skull? My recent paralytic one disappeared recently.

ADLER: The attendant has had instructions, professor.

CYPRIAN: The attendant is not to be found. Probably having a drink. You will be having the same experience as I had when I was working in Prague. We had an attendant in the pathological-anatomical institute who was always inebriated. The rascal gradually consumed all the spirit in the test-bottles.

[*They laugh.*

ADLER: You needn't worry, professor; our man still prefers beer.

CYPRIAN: I would like to come down and see you to-night. Will you be in?

ADLER: I am usually working till midnight.

CYPRIAN: I see. Then I'll come after ten.

[BERNHARDI *enters from the right.*

BERNHARDI: Good day. Glad to see you, Cyprian. Are you looking for me?

CYPRIAN: I really had to see Dr. Adler about a skull. But I am very glad to find you here. I wanted to ask you, if you could make time, to come with me to the Ministry of Education.

BERNHARDI: Why, what's the matter?

[*They stand alone together. The others apart in conversation, inspecting X-ray photographs.*

CYPRIAN: It's the most favourable moment now for getting something out of them for our institute—when a doctor, a clinical professor, is Minister of Education. It's an opportunity we should not miss.

BERNHARDI: You've forgotten one thing. Flint is our bitterest enemy.

CYPRIAN: That's all over long ago. To-day he is most sympathetic towards our institute. Only yesterday Councillor Winkler said so. Quite spontaneously.

BERNHARDI: M'phm !

[OSKAR *comes out of the ward and goes quickly over to* BERNHARDI.

OSKAR: Father, I think if you want to speak to her again . . .

BERNHARDI: Excuse me, Cyprian. Will you be good enough to wait five minutes ? (*Exit.*)

OSKAR (*to* CYPRIAN): A girl, dying, professor. (*Follows his father.*)

KURT (*casually*): A sepsis case. Young girl. Abortion.

POINTNER (*to* ADLER): A pathological dissection for you to-morrow, doctor.

CYPRIAN (*in his monotonous drawling manner*): When I was an assistant under Skoda, we had a chief at the hospital—mentioning no names— who begged us assistants to call him whenever possible in case of a death. He wanted to write a psychology of dying.

[*The* PRIEST *enters, calm and intelligent face.*

ADLER (*assiduously*): Good day, your reverence.

PRIEST: Good day, gentlemen. I do hope I am not too late ?

KURT: No, your reverence. The professor is with the patient now. (*Introduces himself*) I am Dr. Felder.

PRIEST: Hope has not yet been given up altogether, then?

OSKAR (*from the ward*): Good day, your reverence.

KURT: I'm afraid so; it is quite a hopeless case.

OSKAR: Will your reverence, please . . . ?

PRIEST: Perhaps I'd better wait until the professor has left the patient.

[POINTNER *offers the* PRIEST *a chair.*

Thank you, thank you. (*Does not sit down.*)

CYPRIAN: Yes, your reverence, our job is not only to attend to them while there is still hope. . . . Sometimes we cannot do anything else but comfort them.

KURT: And tell them lies.

PRIEST (*sits down*): That's a very hard expression, doctor.

KURT: Excuse me, your reverence. I was referring to us doctors only. But sometimes lying is just the most difficult and praiseworthy part of our profession.

[BERNHARDI *is in the door. The* PRIEST *rises.* NURSE *follows* BERNHARDI.

BERNHARDI (*somewhat disagreeably surprised*): Oh, your reverence . . .

PRIEST: We relieve one another, professor. (*Offers his hand.*) I do hope to find the patient still conscious.

BERNHARDI: Yes. I might, in fact, say intensely conscious. (*More to the others*) She is in a state of absolute euphoria. (*As if explaining to the* PRIEST) In a way she's never been better.

PRIEST: Why, that's excellent. Who knows——
Quite recently I had the pleasure of meeting a

young man in the best of health, to whom I had given the last sacrament a few weeks before in full expectation of death.

BERNHARDI (*to* ADLER): His reverence has misunderstood me. (*To the* PRIEST) I meant to say that the patient is completely unaware of her condition. She is dying, but she believes herself cured.

PRIEST: Really.

BERNHARDI: I'm very much afraid, your reverence, that the sight of *you* . . .

PRIEST (*very gently*): Don't fear for your patient, professor. I am not here to pronounce a death-sentence.

BERNHARDI: Of course not. . . .

PRIEST: Perhaps someone could prepare the patient.

[NURSE, *on a hardly noticeable glance from* POINTNER, *goes into the ward, unnoticed by* BERN-HARDI.

BERNHARDI: That wouldn't make matters any better. As I've said already, the patient is quite unaware of her real condition. On the contrary, she is under the happy delusion that in an hour or so someone very dear to her will come and fetch her back to life and happiness. Is it fair to disillusion her? I feel that God himself would disapprove of that.

PRIEST (*first hesitatingly, then decidedly*): Is there a possibility, professor, that I could unfavourably affect the course of the illness?

BERNHARDI (*quickly interposing*): It is possible that the end might be hastened, perhaps only by a few minutes, but still . . .

PRIEST (*still more decidedly*): Once more! Can your patient be saved? Does my appearance mean a danger in that sense? In that case I would be willing to withdraw at once.

[ADLER *nods approvingly.*

BERNHARDI: There is no hope at all for her. The end is certain.

PRIEST: Then, professor, I see no reason whatsoever . . .

BERNHARDI: Excuse me. I am still in charge here as the doctor. And it is part of my duty to see that my patients have a happy death—as far as may be possible.

[CYPRIAN *shows signs of slight impatience and disapproval.*

PRIEST: A happy death. It is probable, professor, that we have different opinions on that subject. And according to what the nurse told me your patient is more in need of absolution than many others,

BERNHARDI (*with an ironical smile*): Aren't we all of us sinners, your reverence?

PRIEST: That is not the question here, professor. You cannot know whether somewhere in the depths of her soul, which God alone sees, there is a longing in these last few moments to be freed of all sin by confession.

BERNHARDI: Must I repeat, your reverence? The patient does not know she is dying. She is cheerful, happy and—without regret.

PRIEST: Then my fault would be all the greater if I left here without having given the dying girl the consolations of our holy religion.

BERNHARDI: From that fault, your reverence, God and every earthly judge would absolve you. (*Seeing the* PRIEST *move*) Yes, your reverence. As her doctor, I cannot permit you to approach the bed of this patient.

PRIEST: I was summoned here. I must therefore request . . .

BERNHARDI: Not with my consent, your reverence. I repeat that as the doctor I am responsible for my patients to their last moments, and I must unfortunately—forbid you to enter that door.

PRIEST (*advancing*): You forbid me?

BERNHARDI (*touching his shoulder lightly*): Yes, your reverence.

NURSE (*coming hurriedly out of the ward*): Your reverence . . .

BERNHARDI: You were in there?

NURSE: It will be too late, your reverence.

[KURT *hurries into the ward.*

BERNHARDI (*to* NURSE): You told the patient that the priest was here?

NURSE: Yes, professor.

BERNHARDI: Oh! And—tell me quite calmly—how did the patient take it? Did she say anything? Speak! Well?

NURSE: She said——

BERNHARDI: Well?

NURSE: Well, she was a little frightened.

BERNHARDI (*not angrily*): Go on. What did she say?

NURSE: " Must I really die? "

[KURT *comes out of the ward.*

KURT: It's all over.

[*Small pause.*

BERNHARDI: Don't worry, your reverence. It's not your fault. You wished to do your duty. I wanted to do mine. I'm sorry I didn't succeed.

PRIEST: It is not for you, professor, to give me

absolution. It is the poor creature in there who has passed away as a sinner without the consolations of religion. And that is your fault.

BERNHARDI: I accept the blame.

PRIEST: It remains to be seen, professor, whether you will be in a position to do so. Good day to you, gentlemen.

[*The* PRIEST *goes out. The others remain behind; in some of them there is obvious embarrassment.* BERNHARDI *regards them one after another.*

BERNHARDI: Well ! A post-mortem to-morrow morning, Dr. Adler.

CYPRIAN (*to* BERNHARDI, *unheard by the others*): That was not right of you, Bernhardi.

BERNHARDI: Why not right ?

CYPRIAN: You can't raise a point like this in an individual case. You won't be able to change anything in matters like these.

BERNHARDI: As between the clergy and doctors ? That was never my intention.

ADLER: I should consider it dishonest, professor, if I did not declare to you at once that I shall not be able to associate myself with your attitude in this affair.

BERNHARDI: It would not be honest of me, doctor, if I did not assure you that I should hardly have expected otherwise.

[*Exit* CYPRIAN *and* ADLER. OSKAR *bites his lip.*

Well, my son, I hope this won't damage your career.

OSKAR: Oh, dad.

BERNHARDI (*laying his hand on* OSKAR'S *shoulder, tenderly*): Well, well. I don't want to put you in a difficult position.

NURSE: I thought, professor . . .

B

BERNHARDI (*sternly*) : What did you think ? However, it's all over now.

NURSE : But it's always the custom—and besides —(*glancing at* POINTNER)—Mr. Pointner, there . . .

POINTNER : Yes, and of course I did not forbid her.

BERNHARDI : Of course, Pointner. You probably attend Sunday School as well. What ?

POINTNER : We are living in a Christian State, professor.

BERNHARDI : Yes. (*Regards him steadily for a moment*) May the Lord forgive you . . . you know damned well what you are doing.

[*Exit with* KURT *and* OSKAR.

POINTNER : My dear girl, what are you so apologetic about ? You only did your duty. Why are you crying ? Don't be so hysterical.

NURSE : But the director was so angry.

POINTNER : And what if he was angry ! The director ! He won't remain director for long now. This will finish him.

CURTAIN

SCENE II

PROFESSOR BERNHARDI'S *well-furnished study in his private house. General entrance R. L. a door to another room. Books on shelves up stage. Writing desk with chairs. Photos of famous doctors on the walls.*

DR. OSKAR BERNHARDI *is sitting at the desk, writing in register. The bell rings.* SERVANT *enters and brings card to* OSKAR.

OSKAR: He wants to speak to me?

SERVANT: The gentleman asked first if the Professor was in, but . . .

OSKAR: But it seems to satisfy him that I'm in—all right, show him in.

[SERVANT *exits.* FEUERMANN *enters; young, nervous, shy little man with spectacles; hat and gloves in hand.* OSKAR *goes to him.*

FEUERMANN: I don't know whether you will remember me?

OSKAR: But—Feuermann? Do I *not* remember you? (*Shakes hands.*)

FEUERMANN (*glad*): But it's more than eight years ago since . . .

OSKAR: Well, how are you getting on? You haven't come as a patient? . . . Where are *you* practising?

FEUERMANN: In Linz.

OSKAR: Of course. Well, what brings you here? Do you want to open a sanatorium or become a beauty specialist? Or do you want to turn Linz into a health resort?

FEUERMANN: No—nothing like that. It's a terrible matter. Don't you know anything about it yet?

[OSKAR *signifies* " *no.*"

I've written to your father about it already.

OSKAR: He gets so many letters.

FEUERMANN: If you could only put in a word for me . . .

OSKAR: Sit down and tell me all about it.

FEUERMANN: You know me, Bernhardi. We've studied together. You know I was always very conscientious and keen. Such an accident could happen to anyone who has to go straight from the university to practice. I hadn't opportunities like you for further practical study.

OSKAR: Well, to be the son of a famous father also has its drawbacks.

FEUERMANN: Excuse me, I did not mean it that way. But it's grand to be able to continue one's studies in a hospital and to attend lectures. . . .

OSKAR (*slightly impatient*): Well, what has actually happened?

FEUERMANN: I am charged with professional misconduct endangering human life. I may be struck off the register. A so-called professional blunder. I won't say I am entirely without blame. If I had been able to practise my obstetrics for another year, I should probably have been able to pull the woman through. Imagine what practising is like in such a remote place, out of touch with expert assistance. You fellows in the city here have no idea. Nobody counts the lives I have saved. Then one accident happens, and I can go and hang myself.

OSKAR: Oh come, Feuermann, you're looking on the gloomy side. You have not been convicted yet. We've still got to hear what the experts say.

FEUERMANN: Yes, the experts. That is just it. . . . Professor Filitz has been appointed to act in the case. So I wanted to ask your father whether he could perhaps put in a good word. . . . Oh, I don't want any favouritism, you know, but. . . .

OSKAR: Yes, yes, Feuermann, I understand; but whether the influence of my father could be of any help to you. . . . He is not on such good terms with Filitz as you imagine.

FEUERMANN: But your father is Director of the Elizabeth Institute. . . .

OSKAR: Yes, Feuermann, but things have happened since that make it not quite so simple. But that's a long story. I am not sure whether my father's intervention would not have just the opposite effect . . .

[SERVANT *enters with a visiting card.*

(*Looking at the card*) Oh, Fili—(*Rising, to* FEUERMANN) You must excuse me. (*To the servant*) Ask him in.

[SERVANT *goes out.*

FEUERMANN: Didn't I hear you say Filitz?

OSKAR: Filitz. . . .

FEUERMANN: Yes, that's what you said.

OSKAR: You can't talk to him here . . . in fact I'd rather if you don't mind—that you went through this door. . . .

FEUERMANN: No, no. You can't expect that of me. This is the hand of fate.

[FILITZ *enters; forty, incisive, tall, fair, pince-nez.*

FILITZ: Good morning.

FEUERMANN: Please introduce me to the professor, Bernhardi.

OSKAR (*with an embarrassed smile*): But the professor has come to talk to me . . .

FEUERMANN (*introducing himself*): I am Dr. Feuermann. I look upon it as a sign from heaven, professor, that you should appear at this moment . . . that I am so lucky—I am a general practitioner at Linz—Dr. Feuermann. A charge has been made against me.

FILITZ: Feuermann! Oh yes. I remember. (*Amiably*) You've sent somebody into the next world . . . the wife of a teacher. . . .

FEUERMANN (*shocked*): You have been badly misinformed, professor. If you knew the facts of the case. . . . I mean, if you would have the great kindness to look into it. . . . I was the victim of most unfortunate coincidences.

FILITZ: Yes, it always happens like that. But such accidents and coincidences would not happen if young people would avoid rushing into practice without the necessary experience. They manage to scrape through a few exams, and think providence will do the rest. But it does not always, and with very good reasons.

FEUERMANN: Professor, if you will allow me. I passed all my examinations with distinction, including obstetrics. And I was obliged to go into practice or starve. And that this woman should have bled to death—I do not hesitate to say—could have happened to any specialist.

FILITZ: There are all kinds of specialists.

FEUERMANN: But had it been a specialist, he would not have been charged. It would have been called the—the inscrutable will of God.

FILITZ: You think so? Well, who knows. (*Stands in front of him and regards him fixedly.*) Are you by any chance one of these young men who consider it due to their scientific dignity to side with the atheists?

FEUERMANN: Really, professor, I had not the slightest. . . .

FILITZ: Just as you like, doctor. But I can assure you that science and religion agree very well together. There are plenty of examples of the results of agnostic arrogance. And I hope it is not your ambition, Dr. Feuerstein . . .

FEUERMANN (*diffidently*): Feuermann——

FILITZ: . . . to present an astonished world with a further illustration. As a matter of fact I have the papers relating to your case at home. If you could come and see me to-morrow morning (*consults diary*) at nine, we will go into the matter further.

FEUERMANN (*jubilant at this turn of events*): So you will really allow me, professor? I am extremely grateful to you. If you will permit me to give you the material . . . my existence is at stake, you know. I have a wife and two children. There would be nothing left for me but to destroy myself.

FILITZ: I should be much obliged to you, doctor, if you would kindly spare me sentimental remarks of that kind. If you have really nothing to reproach yourself with, there is no need for such nonsense, at least not with me. Well, I will see you to-morrow then, doctor.

OSKAR: You will excuse me if I don't accompany you, Feuermann.

FEUERMANN: Oh, don't mention it.

[*He goes out.*

OSKAR: I must apologise on his behalf, professor, for his somewhat tactless remarks. But he was in a state of some excitement, as you can understand.

FILITZ: Fellow-student?

OSKAR: Yes. And I would like to add, professor, a very industrious and conscientious one. I know he had to live on a miserable pittance which he earned by giving lessons.

FILITZ: Well, that proves nothing. My father was a millionaire and I managed to become a capable fellow all the same. Well, well. Is your father out of town?

OSKAR: Not out of town, professor, only at Baden attending Prince Constantine.

FILITZ: Oh.

OSKAR: He intended to be back in time for his rounds.

FILITZ (*looking at his watch*): Well, I'm afraid I shan't be able to wait very long. Perhaps you will be kind enough to tell your father that my wife was not received by Princess Stixenstein to-day.

[SERVANT *as before enters with a visiting card.*

OSKAR: Excuse me, professor. Dr. Lowenstein is here. Show the doctor in.

FILITZ: Don't let me disturb you. I must be going in any case.

[FILITZ *prepares to go.* LOWENSTEIN *enters; about thirty, medium height, somewhat hurried and restless in manner; forceful and direct.*

LOWENSTEIN: Good day. Oh, Professor Filitz, Going already? Stay a minute, won't you. The matter will interest you. Here, Oskar, read. (*He gives him a letter.*) Excuse me, Professor Filitz, he must read it first, as a member of the Ball Committee. Princess Stixenstein has withdrawn her patronage.

OSKAR (*after running through the letter hurriedly, hands it to Professor Filitz*): Without giving any reason?

LOWENSTEIN: She did not consider it necessary.

FILITZ: Especially as the reasons are so obvious to everyone.

OSKAR: Has the—affair—become so public already? Within a week?

LOWENSTEIN: My dear Oskar. I never expected otherwise. When the matter was reported to me

I said to myself at once: " That will be a feast for certain people. The story will be enlarged and distorted."

FILITZ: Excuse me, Lowenstein. There has been no distortion at all, and there was no need for it. The whole incident in its plain, simple truth. . . . But I prefer to say what I think about it to my friend Bernhardi personally.

OSKAR: I need hardly tell you, professor, that I support my father absolutely in this affair.

FILITZ: Oh, of course, quite naturally, that is only your duty.

OSKAR: It's not only a matter of duty, but of conviction, professor.

LOWENSTEIN: And it is also mine, professor. And I declare most definitely that only ill will could make an affair out of a perfectly harmless incident. And, to be quite frank, no one would attempt to do so if Bernhardi did not happen to be a Jew.

FILITZ: There you are again, back at your old fixed idea. Do you call me anti-semitic, when I always have at least one Jewish assistant? There is no antagonism against decent Jews.

LOWENSTEIN: Oh, indeed. I affirm just the contrary. . . .

FILITZ: If a Christian had behaved in the same way as Bernhardi, there would have been just as much fuss. You know that very well, Lowenstein.

LOWENSTEIN: Possibly. But in that case millions of people would have stood behind that Christian who now wouldn't raise a little finger.

FILITZ: Who?

LOWENSTEIN: The Nationalists, and of course the Jews—a certain kind of Jew, I mean, who neglect no opportunity of placing themselves in favour with the ruling powers.

FILITZ: Excuse me saying so, my dear Lowenstein, but this is becoming a positive persecution mania. And it is just people like you with their eternal anti-semitic suspicions who aggravate these racial antagonisms. And it would be a thousand times better . . .

[*In the middle of these shouted arguments* BERNHARDI *enters.*

BERNHARDI (*obviously in a good mood, with his slightly ironical smile, greeting and shaking hands with everybody*): Hallo, gentlemen. What's the matter? Are we broke or has somebody left us a million?

OSKAR (*handing him the letter*): The Princess has withdrawn her patronage from our Ball.

BERNHARDI (*running through the letter*): Oh well, then you will have to look for another patroness. (*Jokingly to* OSKAR) Or are you going to resign your presidency too?

OSKAR (*somewhat offended*): Father!

BERNHARDI (*touching* OSKAR's *arm affectionately*): Why, of course not. Don't mind my little joke. And Lowenstein, I needn't apologise to you. But what is the matter with you, Filitz? *You* look as if we really *were* broke.

OSKAR: I must be going now. (*Smiling*) At six o'clock we have a meeting of the Ball Committee. Good day, professor, good day, doctor. (*Shakes hands with both.*) Oh yes, father, I forgot. Dr. Feuermann was here. He said he had written to you.

BERNHARDI: Oh, yes.

FILITZ: You needn't worry about this Feuermann. If it's at all possible I will get him out of it—(*with a triumphant glance at* LOWENSTEIN) although he *is* a Jew.

OSKAR: I feel certain, professor, he is not unworthy of . . .

FILITZ: To be sure. To be sure. Good-bye, doctor.

[OSKAR *goes out.*

BERNHARDI: Was it Feuermann you came to see me about?

FILITZ: Oh, no. I only happened to meet him here by chance. I came here to tell you that my wife was not received by Princess Stixenstein to-day.

BERNHARDI: Really. And you came to tell me that?

FILITZ: Why play the innocent, my dear Bernhardi? You know very well that, however insignificant in itself, it shows the view taken in higher quarters of a certain incident of which you are not wholly unaware.

BERNHARDI (*very cheerfully*): Well, I can give you an example from still higher up. I have just come from Prince Constantine, who's heard the story, and who takes a very different view from Her Highness the Princess.

FILITZ: For goodness' sake, Bernhardi, don't talk to me about your Prince Constantine. To him liberalism is a sport, like hunting to others of his class.

[CYPRIAN *enters.*

CYPRIAN: Good morning, gentlemen. Excuse me for intruding like this . . . but I can guess . . . (*Shakes hands with everybody.*)

BERNHARDI: Have you also come to tell me that Princess Stixenstein has withdrawn her patronage?

CYPRIAN: The ball is a secondary affair.

FILITZ (*looking at his watch*) : I have unfortunately no more time. You will excuse me, Cyprian. I ask you again, Bernhardi, what are you going to do to give satisfaction to my wife (*with a glance at* CYPRIAN) for not being received by Princess Stixenstein.

[LOWENSTEIN *looks at* CYPRIAN.

BERNHARDI (*very calmly*) : Tell your wife, my dear Filitz, that I consider her much too sensible a woman to be worried for one moment by such an exalted cuckoo.

FILITZ : The manner of your reply certainly relieves me from any necessity of discussing the matter further. Good day to you, gentlemen.

[*He goes out quickly.*

CYPRIAN : You should not have said that, Bernhardi.

LOWENSTEIN : Why shouldn't he ?

CYPRIAN : Quite apart from the fact that one should not needlessly upset certain people, the statement was incorrect. Princess Stixenstein is by no means a cuckoo. On the contrary, she is a very clever woman.

BERNHARDI : Clever ? Babette Stixenstein ?

LOWENSTEIN : She's narrow-minded, petty, bigoted.

CYPRIAN : We must understand these people ; that is part of *our* job. They need not under-understand us at all ; that again is part of *their* job. Besides, this is only the beginning. The Prince will naturally take action as well—that is to say, the trustees of the institute will probably resign in a body.

LOWENSTEIN : Why, that would be monstrous.

BERNHARDI : Excuse me, Cyprian. The trustees

consist of Prince Constantine, Bishop Lieben-berg, Prince Stixenstein, the bank manager, Veith, and Councillor Winkler. And apart from the Prince I can assure you . . .

CYPRIAN: Don't be too sure of anything.

BERNHARDI: I spoke to the Prince an hour ago.

CYPRIAN: And I suppose he expressed his appreciation?

BERNHARDI: He couldn't have been more friendly.

CYPRIAN: Did he start the subject?

BERNHARDI: Of course.

LOWENSTEIN: What did he say?

BERNHARDI (*smiling, somewhat flattered*): He said that a few hundred years ago I should probably have been burned at the stake.

CYPRIAN: And you considered that as showing his approval?

BERNHARDI: But you don't know what he added. He said: " And I as well ! "

LOWENSTEIN: Ha !

CYPRIAN: And did you ask the Prince what the other trustees thought of the matter?

BERNHARDI: Of his own accord, he repeated to me a remark of the Bishop's.

LOWENSTEIN: Well?

BERNHARDI: " I like that man."

LOWENSTEIN: *You* like the Bishop?

BERNHARDI: No, no, the Bishop likes me. Any-way, Cyprian, Councillor Winkler is on the Board and he surely will not desert us.

CYPRIAN: And what good would that do, if Winkler alone took your part? You cannot expect him, for your sake.

BERNHARDI: It is not a question of myself, you know that very well.

CYPRIAN: To be sure, Bernhardi. It is not. It is a question of the institute. Our institute. And if the Board of Trustees resigns, we are finished.

BERNHARDI: Come, come, Cyprian!

LOWENSTEIN: Well, isn't it so? Your Prince and His Eminence have never been particularly generous in their support.

CYPRIAN: And I could name to you a dozen Jews who have only contributed because a prince and a bishop are on the Board. And if money stops coming in, we simply have to close down.

BERNHARDI: And all this happens just because I did my duty as a doctor. . . .

LOWENSTEIN: It is monstrous, monstrous.

CYPRIAN: There might be a way of avoiding these resignations, and Winkler, who you admit is a very clever, far-sighted man, and who is thoroughly well disposed towards you, is also of opinion . . . that you would lose nothing in dignity or prestige if you made some suitable statement . . .

LOWENSTEIN (interrupting): You want him to apologise?

CYPRIAN: Who's talking of apology? There is no need for him to do penance. (To BERNHARDI) It would be quite sufficient if you expressed your regret. . . .

BERNHARDI: I have nothing to regret.

LOWENSTEIN: On the contrary.

CYPRIAN: Well then, not your regret. We won't quarrel about words. But you could declare, without in any way retreating from your position, that you had no intention of hurting any religious feelings—which you certainly had not.

BERNHARDI: But everybody knows that already.

CYPRIAN: Of course, everybody knows it, and especially those people who want to break you for it. But nevertheless I foresee, and there are already signs, that an attempt will be made to represent you as a disturber of religion and to accuse you of contempt of the holy sacraments.

BERNHARDI: Oh!

CYPRIAN: And of course, it will also be said that you in particular should have been more careful to avoid giving offence in this manner, since in your position you fail to understand the inner meaning of the Catholic sacraments.

BERNHARDI: Oh!

CYPRIAN: I have heard it all already. And from people who like you. So you can imagine what you may expect from the others.

LOWENSTEIN: And for the sake of such a rabble. . . .

CYPRIAN: Yes, people are a rabble . . . but you have to reckon with that fact.

LOWENSTEIN: If you do, I will take the thing on my shoulders. I will fight the matter out on my own, as if *I* had refused his precious holiness. . . .

CYPRIAN: Don't let him work you up, Bernhardi. You have something better to do than waste your strength in a fruitless and rather ridiculous fight. You are a doctor, and the saving of one human life is of greater value than holding up a banner.

LOWENSTEIN: Sophistry!

CYPRIAN: We stand at the cross-roads, Bernhardi. And a brilliant future for our institute depends on you alone.

[BERNHARDI *stops, astonished.*

I have not told you yet the most important thing. I had the opportunity of talking with Flint about the matter.

BERNHARDI: Did you seek that opportunity?

CYPRIAN: No. I purposely avoided the subject and so did he. But of course we came to discuss the Elizabeth Institute, and I can assure you, Bernhardi, that he has completely changed his attitude towards us. He realises to-day what the Elizabeth Institute means, and would be a friend to us, Bernhardi. Believe me. Well, that's the position. The future depends upon you. Now, don't do anything foolish.

BERNHARDI (*after a short pause*): We shall have to meet again to-day in any case, in regard to the new appointment.

CYPRIAN: Yes, of course. I will ring up Tugend.

LOWENSTEIN: He won't be coming.

BERNHARDI: If you agree, then, we'll meet at half past nine at the Riedhof, and we can also discuss the so-called declaration. . . .

LOWENSTEIN: Bernhardi !——

BERNHARDI: I have really no desire to be a hero at any price. You know that in serious matters I stand by my convictions. And so perhaps we may be able to find a suitable form. . . .

LOWENSTEIN: You're a nice set of people !

CYPRIAN: Be quiet, Lowenstein. You are only a looker-on at the game, no stakes are too high for you.

LOWENSTEIN: I am not a looker-on, but I am playing a lone hand.

CYPRIAN: Well, *au revoir*, Bernhardi, till half

past nine. And bring a draft of your statement along with you.

BERNHARDI: Yes, one that will not offend even *your* religious feelings, Lowenstein.

LOWENSTEIN: Well, I like that.

[BERNHARDI *shakes hands with both and they go out.*

BERNHARDI, *left alone, paces up and down a few times, then looks at his watch, shakes his head, takes his note-book from his pocket, looks at it, puts it away with a gesture as if to say, " That can wait " ; then sits at the writing-table, takes a sheet of paper from the folder and begins to write, at first with a serious expression then with an ironical smile on his lips. He continues to write; the* SERVANT *enters and hands him a visiting card.*

BERNHARDI (*displeased, hesitates, then*) : Show the professor in.

[EBENWALD *enters.*

EBENWALD: Good morning.

BERNHARDI (*going towards him and shaking hands*) : Good morning, professor. To what do I owe the pleasure ?

EBENWALD: If you will allow me, director, I will come to the point at once.

BERNHARDI: Of course. At your service. (*Offers him a seat.*)

[EBENWALD *sits down on a chair beside the writing-desk.* BERNHARDI *sits down at the writing-desk.*

EBENWALD: I think it is my duty to inform you that a certain action is contemplated against you and our institute. I learn from a parliamentary source that a question is to be raised in the House with regard to a certain incident that you know about.

BERNHARDI: We must wait and see what happens.

EBENWALD: That is certainly one way of looking at it. But it is not a question of you alone, director, but also of our institute.

BERNHARDI: I am aware of that.

EBENWALD: And it appears to me advisable to think of a means of preventing this question in the House.

BERNHARDI: That doesn't seem so easy to me. Those who intend to raise the question will no doubt be acting from strong conviction—and in the name of the religion I am supposed to have offended. And what on earth would induce such men to withdraw from a course which they think is proper and necessary?

EBENWALD: What could induce these people to renounce their intention? Well, the realisation that there was no offence, or at least not to the extent at first supposed, and the conviction that no deliberate—how shall I express it—anti-Catholic tendency is being pursued. . . .

BERNHARDI: Is it really necessary to tell these people all that?

EBENWALD: No, not to tell them. Telling is too easy. It should be proved.

BERNHARDI: This is becoming quite interesting. And how do you propose to furnish the proof?

EBENWALD: By a concrete case from which the desired conclusion could be unmistakably deduced.

BERNHARDI (impatiently): Why, such a case would have to be specially constructed.

EBENWALD: That's unnecessary. The case lies ready to hand.

BERNHARDI: What case?

EBENWALD: To-morrow the new appointment in Tugend's department will be decided.

BERNHARDI: Ah !

EBENWALD (*coolly*): Yes. There are two candidates for the position.

BERNHARDI (*very decidedly*): One who deserves it and one who does not.

EBENWALD: Possibly both candidates deserve it. And I do not know whether you have sufficiently studied dermatology to be able, in this case, to——

BERNHARDI (*growing more and more impatient*): It is not I who will decide, but the meeting.

EBENWALD: But in case of an equal vote, your vote will decide. And an equal vote may be certainly expected.

BERNHARDI: How ?

EBENWALD: For Wenger there will be Cyprian, Lowenstein, Adler, and of course the old liberal, Felder. . . .

BERNHARDI: And Tugend.

EBENWALD: You don't think that yourself, do you ?

BERNHARDI: Has he promised you his vote already ?

EBENWALD: It wouldn't prove anything if he had. But you know as well as I do, Bernhardi, that he will *not* vote for Wenger. And the fact that his own teacher will not vote for him should give you some cause for thought. . . .

BERNHARDI (*pacing up and down, according to his habit*): You know very well, Professor Ebenwald, why Tugend is against his pupil. Simply because he is afraid that his private practice might suffer through him.

EBENWALD: You should tell that to Professor Tugend personally, professor.

BERNHARDI: Leave that to me, professor. It has always been my custom to tell people what I think to their faces. And so I tell you now that the only reason why you are agitating for Hell is because he is not—a Jew.

EBENWALD (*very calmly*): With equal right I might reply that your reason for supporting Wenger . . .

BERNHARDI: You forget, Professor Ebenwald, that three years ago I voted for you.

EBENWALD: But against your inclination, didn't you? And that is how I should feel with Wenger. And that is why I shall not vote for him. (*Rises.*) It is really deplorable that with us in Austria every question of personnel should eventually become a question of politics. But we must adapt ourselves to the fact. Now, director, if Hell were an idiot I naturally should not vote for him or expect you to do so. But actually he cures people just as well as Wenger. But it would in any case be well worth while for you, director, to consider the matter, and we could discuss it again to-morrow before the meeting.

BERNHARDI: That will be unnecessary.

EBENWALD: Just as you think, director. But if I may say so, you should not allow false pride . . . of course all this is in confidence.

BERNHARDI: I have no reason to ask for your discretion, Professor Ebenwald. Tell the gentlemen who sent you here . . .

EBENWALD: Oh ! Oh !

BERNHARDI: . . . that I do not deal in business of that kind.

EBENWALD: Pardon me, but nobody sent me

here. I am therefore unable to take messages. My visit, director, was entirely unofficial. Please remember that. I did not come here either as a delegate, or in my own interest, but solely in the interests of our institute, as well as in yours, director. You have scorned the proffered hand of a friend——

BERNHARDI: And you leave as an enemy. I prefer it. It is the more honest rôle.

EBENWALD: As you wish, director. Good morning.

BERNHARDI: Good morning.

[*He accompanies* EBENWALD *to the door.* EBENWALD *goes out.* BERNHARDI, *alone, takes the sheet on which he had written before, reads it through and then tears it up. Looks at his watch again and gets ready to go.* SERVANT *enters.*

What is it?

[SERVANT *gives him a card.*

What? His Excellency is here himself?

SERVANT: Yes, sir.

BERNHARDI: Ask him to be good enough to come in.

[SERVANT *goes out. Immediately afterwards* FLINT *enters; tall, a persuasive and dominant personality, well dressed, a not quite unstudied diplomat's expression, very amiable, often with genuine warmth of feeling.*

(*Still at the door*) Your Excellency? (*With his mildly ironical smile.*)

FLINT (*offering his hand*): We have not seen each other for a long while, Bernhardi.

BERNHARDI: Not so long ago—in the Medical Society.

FLINT: I mean privately, together.

BERNHARDI: Yes, that is so. Won't you sit down?

FLINT: Thank you, thank you.

[*He sits down, and* BERNHARDI *soon after.*

(*Purposely lightly*) You are surprised to see me here?

BERNHARDI: I am—agreeably surprised, and let me take this opportunity of wishing you good fortune in your new official dignity.

FLINT: Dignity? You know I don't look upon my new post in that light. But thank you for your good wishes, Bernhardi, they give me special satisfaction. To be sure I have not come here only to collect good wishes, as you can imagine.

BERNHARDI: No . . .

FLINT (*interposing*): Let me say at the outset, I don't intend to use my cabinet portfolio as a pillow for my head, but that I am determined to use the period of my office, however short, to carry out a number of reforms which, as you may remember, I have had in mind since my young days. Reforms in the field of medical training, public hygiene, education of the people and so on. There is no lack of able officials in Austria, especially in the Ministry of Education; but what I require for the execution of my plans are men. And I have come to ask you, my dear Bernhardi, if I can count on your co-operation.

BERNHARDI (*after a moment's hesitation*): Perhaps you could be a little more precise. I must know first in what direction you want me to help . . . (*With his ironical smile*) in regard to medical instruction, public hygiene, education of the people. . . . Have I forgotten anything?

FLINT (*laughing*): Just the same as ever. And just

for that reason I place special hopes in you. Perhaps there are still certain things dividing us, although I really don't quite know . . .

BERNHARDI (*seriously*): I will tell you, Flint; the friendship of our youth—and what became of it.

FLINT: Do you bear old grudges, Bernhardi?

BERNHARDI: No. Only—I happen to have a good memory.

FLINT: That may be a defect, Bernhardi, if it prevents a clear understanding of present circumstances. I thought, you know, that the old fighting years were forgotten.

BERNHARDI: Fighting? That is rather a noble word for a very ignoble business.

FLINT: Bernhardi!

BERNHARDI: No, my friend, it was not nice, and I should be unfaithful to my own past if I glossed it over lightly. (*Has got up.*) When I think what weapons you used against us—by what methods you tried to ruin our young undertaking—the things you brought up to discredit us in the eyes of the public—how we were suspected, persecuted, hounded! It was said that we were founding an institute to deprive the ordinary practitioner of his livelihood, that we were spreading disease in the town, that we wanted to found a medical faculty of our own . . .

FLINT (*interrupting him*): My dear Bernhardi, all these reproaches might still be justified to-day if the good you have been doing had not long since outweighed the less positive sides of your institute. And you can believe me when I say that the Elizabeth Institute has no better friend to-day than I—besides which, my attitude towards the institute was never dictated by personal motives but was purely a matter of conviction.

BERNHARDI: Conviction !

FLINT: Bernhardi, we all have our faults. You probably also, as well as I. But if there is anything I can affirm with certainty it is this: that never, not even in the smallest thing, have I acted against my conviction.

BERNHARDI: You are certain of that ?

FLINT: Bernhardi !

BERNHARDI: Think a moment.

FLINT (*somewhat uncertain*): Of course, I may have done wrong in my life—we all have. But as to acting against my convictions . . . no !

BERNHARDI: Well, I know of a case in which you quite definitely did act against your conviction.

FLINT: Then I must really ask you . . .

BERNHARDI: And your action resulted in the death of a man.

FLINT: That is going too far, Bernhardi. Now I really must insist . . .

BERNHARDI: All right then; I will tell you. (*Paces up and down the room a few times, then suddenly stops.*) We were assistants at the time under Rappenweiler. There was a labourer in the clinic—I can see him now—and our chief and all of us had made a wrong diagnosis. At the post-mortem it was found that the patient could have been saved by another treatment. And as we stood there you whispered to me: " I knew it ! " Do you remember ? *You* had known what was wrong with the patient, *you* had made the correct diagnosis. . . .

FLINT: The only one who had.

BERNHARDI: Yes, the only one. But you carefully avoided saying anything about it while the patient was alive. And why you did that is a question you can answer yourself. It can hardly have been from conviction.

FLINT (*after pause*): Good gracious, Bernhardi, what a memory you have. Yes, I remember the case, and it is true that I kept my opinion to myself that another treatment was likely to be more successful—in fact was essential. And I also frankly admit that the reason for my silence was in order not to upset Rappenweiler's susceptibilities, who, as you know, did not like his assistants to know more than he did. So you may perhaps rightly accuse me of having sacrificed a human life. But you are wrong as to the reasons, the deeper reasons, to which you attribute my action. This one sacrifice had to be made, Bernhardi, for the sake of the hundreds of other human lives which were later to be entrusted to my medical care. Rappenweiler's good will and recommendation were still necessary to me, and the professorship in Prague was in immediate prospect.

BERNHARDI: You think Rappenweiler would have dropped you if you had . . . ?

FLINT: Probably. You have too high an opinion of mankind, Bernhardi. You do not realise how small-minded people are. Of course it would not have ruined my career, but it might certainly have delayed it. For that reason, I allowed the labourer to die, and I do not repent it. To act in an unimportant matter true to one's convictions is not so significant as to follow the deep inner purpose of one's life. You, Bernhardi, are perhaps—and more so than I— a man of acute feeling. In any case you are more sentimental. What you lack, Bernhardi, is a sense of the essential, without which, fidelity to conviction remains after all mere opinionatedness.

What matters is not to be in the right but to do great work for big things. And to throw over the possibility of such work for the rather poor satisfaction of having done the right thing in some insignificant case appears to me not only small-minded, but in a higher sense actually immoral.

BERNHARDI: What?

FLINT: Yes, immoral, my dear Bernhardi.

BERNHARDI (*reflecting slowly*): If I understand you rightly, you have now some definite case in mind.

FLINT: It has come into my mind while speaking.

BERNHARDI: And may we not have come quite unconsciously to the actual purpose of your visit?

FLINT: Not the real reason, but still not an unimportant one.

BERNHARDI: And for that you take the trouble . . .

FLINT: Yes, for that too. In your usual good-natured though sometimes unfortunate manner, and in the exaltation of the moment, you failed to look farther ahead, and so forgot one small fact in your behaviour towards the priest— the fact that we are living in a Christian State. I don't know what there is to smile about in that.

BERNHARDI: You will be surprised again at my good memory. I remember a certain article you wanted to write as a young man. The title was to be: " Churches or Hospitals."

FLINT (*angrily*): H'm.

BERNHARDI: You wished to point out that

instead of so many new churches one should build more hospitals.

FLINT: Oh ! Just one of the many articles which I meant to write but never did.

BERNHARDI: And never will.

FLINT: Certainly not that one. To-day I know that churches and hospitals can exist very well side by side, and that some ills are cured in the churches which are still beyond our reach in the hospitals. But we don't want to lose ourselves in political discussions, do we ?

BERNHARDI: I could hardly compete with you in that field.

FLINT: I sincerely wish, for your sake as well as for the institute, that the whole affair could be ended as soon as possible.

BERNHARDI: So do I.

FLINT: Why ?

BERNHARDI: I have many more important things to do than to waste more time with this affair.

FLINT: Do you mean that seriously ?

BERNHARDI: Can you doubt it ? Hardly an hour ago I discussed a declaration with Cyprian and Lowenstein which would certainly have satisfied the people I am supposed to have offended.

FLINT: Why that would be—that would be excellent. But I'm afraid it would hardly suffice in the present circumstances.

BERNHARDI: Why ? What do you want me to do then ?

FLINT: If you could perhaps . . . you would not, in my opinion, be giving away your position in the least, especially as no official notification of the incident has yet been made to my knowledge, if you could, by a personal visit to the priest . . .

BERNHARDI: What?

FLINT: It would make an excellent impression. Since you actually committed, shall we say, the indiscretion of preventing him more or less by force . . .

BERNHARDI: By force? I hardly touched him. Whoever suggests that I used violence is a deliberate liar. Oh, I know who the people are. But they shall not get away with that. . . .

FLINT: Calm yourself, Bernhardi. Officially nothing has been notified against you. If you have decided to make a declaration anyway, it would be best to take the opportunity of declaring that all these rumours . . .

BERNHARDI: Excuse me, Flint, you are mistaken. I certainly intended to make a declaration at to-morrow's meeting, but circumstances have arisen now which make it absolutely impossible for me to do so.

FLINT: What circumstances?

BERNHARDI: Compelling ones, you may be sure.

FLINT: H'm. And you can't tell me anything more about it? I should really be very interested to know. . . .

BERNHARDI (*smiling*): Tell me, Flint, did you really only come here to help me out of this dilemma?

FLINT: You have behaved in such an indiscreet manner, to say the least, that I should not feel any compunction whatever in letting you clear up the mess yourself, if I did not feel sorry for you and your institute.

BERNHARDI: Actually you want me, for *my* sake—to spare *you* the awkward business of a question in Parliament.

FLINT: Well, that is so. Not much good could come of it, anyway.

BERNHARDI: An hour ago I had it in my power to avoid the danger for us both.

FLINT (*rising*): You had it in your power? . . .

BERNHARDI: In the simplest manner. As you know, there is a vacancy to be filled to-morrow in Tugend's department. If I had promised, in case of an equally divided vote, to give the deciding vote, not for Wenger but for Hell, everything would have been in order.

FLINT: Promised? How do you mean? To whom?

BERNHARDI: Ebenwald just came to see me about it. *He* made the proposal to me.

FLINT (*pacing up and down*): Ebenwald is on very friendly terms with his cousin, the member of Parliament, who is a leader of the Clerical Party, and if he did not want the question to be raised it would no doubt be withdrawn. Well, how did you receive the proposal?

BERNHARDI: Flint!

FLINT: Well, yes, no doubt you consider Wenger the more capable dermatologist.

BERNHARDI: And so do you. You know as well as I do that Hell is a nonentity. In any case, Ebenwald's proposal would have made it impossible for me to vote for anyone else but Wenger.

FLINT: Yes, he certainly did not go about it very cleverly.

BERNHARDI: Not cleverly——! And is that all you have to say about it?

FLINT: My dear Bernhardi, in politics . . .

BERNHARDI: What have I to do with politics?

FLINT: They concern us all.

BERNHARDI (*warmly*): Flint, even though you are a Cabinet Minister to-day, you are after all, still a doctor—a man of science, a man of truth. What was it you said to me just now, about following one's conviction for the essential in things? Well, what is the essential thing here? Don't you see? It is that the department should be entrusted to the most capable man, who will then have an opportunity of doing good work for sick people and for science. That is what matters here, isn't it? That is the essential in this case. Not that you and I will be spared the inconvenience of a question in Parliament to which a reply could easily be found.

FLINT: H'm. The reply certainly doesn't worry me much.

BERNHARDI: I am sure it doesn't.

FLINT: I say, Bernhardi, wouldn't it be possible for you to put in writing . . . I mean for you to write me a letter in which the whole affair is briefly and clearly described, so that I could, if necessary——

BERNHARDI: If necessary?

FLINT: In any case I would like to have it in black and white. It might not be necessary to read the letter, you know. The reply to the question, if raised, could at first be somewhat reserved. Only if they continued to give trouble, I could then produce your letter. (*Makes a gesture as if taking the letter from his pocket.*)

BERNHARDI: No doubt your parliamentary experience would guide you.

FLINT: Experience? In this case it is more intuition. But I don't think it would come to that—the reading of your letter, I mean. My first words and the whole tone of my remarks would tell them that I had something in reserve. They would all notice it. For I have them, Bernhardi, as soon as I start to speak. Just as I had my pupils in my hand at the clinic, so I have the people in Parliament—and although you may think me vain for saying so, I am beginning almost to wish that the fellows *would* ask their question.

BERHARDI: Flint !

FLINT: For I could take that opportunity to lead into general matters. This particular case appears to me a symbol of our political conditions.

BERNHARDI: Aha. " Churches and Hospitals."

FLINT: You smile. Unfortunately I can't treat such matters so lightly.

BERNHARDI: Well, it almost appears that you are inclined to side with me in this affair.

FLINT: It's not very difficult to see that. I will admit that at first I was not altogether—I still think your conduct towards the priest was not particularly correct—but this Ebenwald proposal certainly does put everything in a different light.

BERNHARDI: Of course, it is most gratifying to me, Flint—that you should be willing to do all this for me, but—I warn you—the party you would oppose is very strong and very ruthless, and it is doubtful whether you could get along without them.

FLINT: It would have to be put to the test.

BERNHARDI: Are you really *quite* convinced, Flint, that this insignificant affair is worth the risk ?

FLINT: Insignificant affair ? Bernhardi !——

Don't you realise that much higher things are at stake than appear at first sight? That in a sense, the eternal fight between the powers of light and darkness is involved? . . . But that sounds high-flown, maybe.

BERNHARDI: In any case, Flint, it is a fight, in which the issue is pretty uncertain and in which your whole ministerial prestige . . .

FLINT: Don't worry about that, Bernhardi. Let that be my look-out. Whatever may happen, I cannot wish for a better end than fighting for a good cause, and for one who—admit it frankly—was my enemy an hour ago.

BERNHARDI: I have never been your enemy. I shall be glad to apologise if I've been unjust to you. But I tell you, Flint—if this matter does not end well for you, I shall feel no compunction. For *you* know on which side right is, and I refuse to admire you in advance for doing your duty in a serious case.

FLINT: I wouldn't want you to, Bernhardi. (*Gives his hand.*) Good-bye. (*As lightly as possible*) I was looking for a real man, and I have found one. Good-bye.

BERNHARDI: Good-bye, Flint. (*Hesitating*) Thank you.

FLINT: No, you mustn't do that. Our sympathies must rest on firmer foundations.

[FLINT *goes out.*

BERNHARDI (*stands reflecting for a moment*): Well, we shall see.

CURTAIN

ACT II

Committee-room of the Elizabeth Institute. Furnished in the usual way: long green table in the centre, two windows rear centre, photographs of famous doctors on the walls, green-shaded lights over table. On the right against the wall a smaller table.

POINTNER *sits at a table copying from a sheet of paper into a large minute-book.*

DR. SCHREIMANN *enters: Tall, black military moustache, duel scar over forehead, spectacles, very well-fed voice.*

POINTNER (*springs up*): Good evening, sir—er—doctor.

SCHREIMANN: How do you do, Pointner. Well, have you slept off the effects of the ball?

POINTNER: I did not go to bed at all, doctor. It wasn't worth while.

SCHREIMANN (*as* POINTNER *is still standing*): Make yourself comfortable.

POINTNER (*in easier position*): I danced until seven o'clock, at eight I was in the internal department; at ten in the surgical; at twelve...

SCHREIMANN (*interrupting him*): All right, that's enough, I know you are all over the place. And have you copied out the minutes?

POINTNER: I did not get a chance to do it sooner, doctor.

SCHREIMANN: That's quite all right, it is not really your job at all, you know. As secretary—I thank you. Could you manage to read everything? (*Moving over to him and reading in the minutes, muttering*) "Voting . . . four votes for Professor Hell of the University of Graz, four for Dr. S. Wenger." (*Reading further*) "The Director made use of his right under the bye-laws to decide in case of an equal vote and

C

decided for Dr. Wenger, whereby the latter is considered elected head of the department for dermatology." (*Small pause*) Well, are you satisfied with your new chief?

POINTNER (*bowing*): Certainly.

SCHREIMANN (*laughing, laying his hand on* POINTNER'S *shoulder*): What are you doing, man? You are no longer a medical assistant under me.

POINTNER: No, worse luck. They were good days.

SCHREIMANN: Yes, we were younger. But tell me, Pointner, now that we are on the subject, when do you intend taking your final?

[EBENWALD *enters*.

EBENWALD: Yes, that is what I am always asking him.

POINTNER: Good day, professor.

EBENWALD: Good evening, Schreimann.

SCHREIMANN: Good evening.

EBENWALD: By the way, what are you doing in the Committee-room?

SCHREIMANN: He was kind enough to copy out the minutes for me.

EBENWALD: What, that too? Whatever would the institute do without Pointner? . . . And last night you were the first on the dance floor, weren't you?

POINTNER: Yes, professor, and the last off it.

SCHREIMANN: And he has not even been to bed.

EBENWALD: Well, well, these young people. . . . Well, and how was it?

POINTNER: Very full. Very cheerful.

EBENWALD (*to* POINTNER): Do you realise you were dancing on a volcano?

POINTNER: It was certainly very hot, professor.

EBENWALD (*laughing*): Ha, ha. Well, remember, make the most of it, finish your exams, and don't dance on any more volcanoes. Not even on dead ones. Good-bye.

> [*Gives his hand.*
> SCHREIMANN *does the same.*
> POINTNER *bows again and goes out.*

So His Excellency the Minister of Education was there as well?

SCHREIMANN: Yes, and was talking for at least half an hour with Bernhardi.

EBENWALD: Strange.

SCHREIMANN: At a ball?

EBENWALD: But he must have known that the Board of Trustees had resigned. Presumably the meeting to-day has been called about these resignations. Well (*hesitating*)—can I rely on you, Schreimann?

SCHREIMANN (*lightly*): That's rather an extraordinary question.

EBENWALD: All the same, there might be questions that would cause you some hesitation in placing yourself on my side.

SCHREIMANN: My dear Ebenwald, I have already told you that in my opinion this affair should not be be considered from a religious or denominational standpoint, but from a tactical aspect only. So that, whatever my Jewish sympathies may be, I would still be opposed to Bernhardi in this matter. Apart from that, however, I am as good an Austrian as you are. And it requires more courage nowadays, I can assure you, for one of my race to declare himself

an Austrian and a Christian than to remain
what he was born as. Had I been a Zionist, I
should have had an easier time.

EBENWALD: Possibly. You could have been sure
of a professorship in Jerusalem.

SCHREIMANN: Nonsense.

[PROFESSOR FELDER *enters:* KURT's *father; firm,
kindly.*

FELDER: Good evening, gentlemen. Have you
heard that the Board of Trustees has resigned?

EBENWALD: You appear to be surprised. But
it was generally expected, you know.

FELDER: Surprised? Not at all. I have long
since lost my capacity for surprise, but unfortunately not for disgust. No. And disgust is
the only word to describe what I feel about it.

EBENWALD: Disgust?

FELDER: I think you will admit, gentlemen,
that all this agitation against Bernhardi has
not the slightest moral justification.

EBENWALD: I am not aware of any agitation.

FELDER: Oh, indeed—you are not aware, eh?
Really . . . and I suppose you are also not aware
that your cousin, Ottokar Ebenwald, is the chief
man behind it?

EBENWALD: I must ask you . . .

FELDER: But of course, I am not identifying
you with your cousin. You are an old German
student. And what are the German virtues,
Ebenwald? Courage, loyalty and a faithfulness
to principles. Have I forgotten one? Well, it
does not matter. These will suffice. And so I
hope you agree with me that we should to-day
express to Bernhardi our entire approval and
satisfaction.

EBENWALD: Satisfaction? What about? What has happened to him?

FELDER: Oh, I see . . . well, well. You are what you are, Ebenwald. All the same, if I needed an operation I'd go to you. For you know your job. But Schreimann? You are silent? Are you also against Bernhardi? Also indignant that he asked the priest to allow a poor sick child to die undisturbed? Well, well, we can quite understand. Such newly acquired religious feelings must be treated with special care.

EBENWALD (*calmly*): Don't let him work you up, Schreimann.

[FILITZ enters.

FILITZ: Good evening, gentlemen. I may as well tell you at once what I intend to do. You can, of course, do what you like. But I for my part intend to follow the good example of the trustees and resign.

EBENWALD: What?

FELDER: What?

FILITZ: I do not know what other course it is possible to take, unless I declare my approval of the conduct of our director and . . .

[ADLER *enters*.

ADLER: Good evening, gentlemen. Have you heard about it yet?

EBENWALD: About what?

ADLER: The question in Parliament.

SCHREIMANN: In the Bernhardi affair?

FILITZ: Has it been put already?

ADLER: It is in the evening papers.

EBENWALD (*rings the bell*): We have read nothing. (*To* FILITZ) I thought it was to be to-morrow.

SCHREIMANN: We doctors have no time to sit about in cafés in the afternoon.

[ATTENDANT *enters*.

EBENWALD: Will you please get an evening paper.

FILITZ: Bring two.

SCHREIMANN: Six.

EBENWALD (*to* ATTENDANT): Better bring a dozen.

SCHREIMANN (*to* ADLER): Is the question very strongly worded ?

FELDER: Doesn't anyone here know what it says ?

[DR. WENGER *enters: the junior, undecided in manner, not definite*.

WENGER: Good evening, gentlemen.

SCHREIMANN: He's got one. Give it to me, Dr. Wenger. (*Takes the evening paper out of his pocket*.)

WENGER: Well, doctor. . . .

EBENWALD: It's nice of you to have brought one along with you.

WENGER: What have I brought along ? Oh, that. Is it usual for the junior to bring an evening paper to the meeting ?

EBENWALD (*with the paper*): Here it is.

FELDER: Let Filitz read it.

[*The others with the exception of* ADLER *and* WENGER *try to read the paper over* EBENWALD's *shoulder*.

EBENWALD: Filitz reads better. Go on then, Filitz.

FILITZ (*reads*): " The attention of the Government is drawn to the following incident which occurred in the Elizabeth Institute on the 4th of February," etc., etc. " His reverence, Father Reder, priest at the church of St. Florian, was summoned by Nurse Ludmilla to the dying woman, Philomena Beier, for the purpose of administering the last sacrament. His reverence found several doctors assembled in the ante-room in front of the ward, among them being Professor Bernhardi, head of the ward in question and director of the institute, who roughly ordered his reverence not to proceed with the execution of his intention, giving as a reason that the condition of the patient might be damaged by the excitement."

FELDER (*pacing up and down*): No, no !

THE OTHERS: Keep quiet !

FILITZ (*reads on*): " His reverence called the attention of Professor Bernhardi, who is a Jew, to the fact that he had come to fulfil a sacred duty, which was all the more necessary in the present case, as the patient was suffering from the consequences of an illegal operation ; where-upon Professor Bernhardi sneeringly referred to his rights as occupier of the premises, these premises being built and maintained by the subscriptions of generous patrons. When his reverence, declining further discussion, wished to enter the ward, Professor Bernhardi pushed him back . . .

ADLER: An absolute lie !

FELDER: Infamous !

SCHREIMANN: Were you there then ?

FILITZ: As if it were the push that mattered.

EBENWALD: There are witnesses.

FELDER: I know your witnesses.

ADLER: I was there too.

FELDER: But you were not examined.

WENGER: Examined?

FELDER: By a certain commission. Or perhaps you have heard nothing of this commission either, Professor Ebenwald?

SCHREIMANN: Read on.

FILITZ (*reads*): " In bringing this incident to the notice of the Government, we ask the Government, and in particular, the Minister of Education, if the Minister does not think it advisable, when making such public appointments in future, to exclude once for all such persons who by their descent, education and character are incapable of showing the necessary understanding for the religious feelings of the native population."

EBENWALD: Well, now we are in a nice position.

WENGER: Why we? There is not a word said against the institute.

SCHREIMANN: True.

EBENWALD: Hear, hear, Wenger.

WENGER (*encouraged*): The institute is unaffected. It remains spotless.

FELDER: And the director?

WENGER: I don't doubt for one moment that he can refute the allegations.

FELDER: Allegations? . . . You call them allegations. . . . But my dear Wenger, this question is nothing but a political manœuvre.

FILITZ: Nonsense!

EBENWALD: The old dodge!

WENGER: Religious and national differences do not exist for me. I am a man of science. I abhor . . .

SCHREIMANN: We all abhor . . .

[BERNHARDI *and* CYPRIAN *enter.* BERNHARDI *is in good humour, manner of speaking more ironically humorous than usual. He takes the evening papers from the* SERVANT *who opens the door for him.*

BERNHARDI: Good evening, gentlemen. Here, help yourself. Please excuse me for being a little late, but I am sure you've been amusing your-selves meanwhile.

[*General greeting.* BERNHARDI *at once takes his place at the head of the table, the others gradually sit down; some smoke.*

I declare the meeting opened. Dr. Wenger, in the name of us all, I welcome you to the insti-tute. You all know why I have summoned this meeting. It is, however, my duty to read to you a letter I received this morning by registered post.

FILITZ: Read it !

BERNHARDI (*reads*): " Dear Sir, I have the honour to inform you that the members of the Board of Trustees have unanimously decided to resign their honorary positions. In communi-cating to you this decision I request you to inform the members of the directorate and teaching staff accordingly. I have the honour to remain, etc., Councillor Winkler, Honorary Secretary."

[EBENWALD *bends over the letter.*

Professor Ebenwald desires to address the meeting.

EBENWALD: I beg to ask the director whether he is aware of the reason which led to the resignation of the trustees, a question which appears the more justified as their letter is so thoroughly silent about it.

FELDER (*disgusted*): Bah !

BERNHARDI: I might reply with another question; whether the reason is not already known to Professor Ebenwald and the other gentlemen. But as we all have other work to do elsewhere . . .

CYPRIAN: True.

BERNHARDI: . . . and the meeting should therefore not be unnecessarily prolonged, I will reply to the question of the vice-president, Professor Ebenwald; yes, I do know the reason. The reason is to be found in the incident of which you have just read, with more or less pleasure, an account in the evening paper in the form of a parliamentary question.

SCHREIMANN: The question is not under discussion here.

BERNHARDI: Quite right. And in my opinion it should not have been brought before Parliament either. . . .

FELDER: Certainly not.

BERNHARDI: I have not come here to justify myself to anyone, but to ask the meeting as director of this institute what attitude we should take with regard to the resignation of the trustees. I call upon Professor Cyprian to address the meeting.

CYPRIAN (*beginning in his monotonous voice*): A few years ago when I was on holiday in Holland, I was standing in the picture gallery . . . (*Signs of impatience.*) What is the matter, gentlemen?

SCHREIMANN: In view of the late hour I would like to request Professor Cyprian most urgently not to tell us any anecdotes to-day, but to come to the point as quickly as possible.

CYPRIAN: It was not going to be an anecdote but was in the deepest sense . . . but have your own way, gentlemen. Well, the Board of

Trustees has resigned. The reason or rather the pretext we all know. For we know that in forbidding the priest to enter the ward, Bernhardi acted solely in accordance with, and in fulfilment of, his duty as a doctor. We should all have acted in the same way in a similar situation.

FILITZ: Really!

EBENWALD: But you never *have* done it, all the same.

SCHREIMANN: And as far as we know Bernhardi's only done it once.

FILITZ: Very true.

CYPRIAN: If we have never done it ourselves, gentlemen, the reason is simply because such a sharply defined situation as that in which Professor Bernhardi found himself the other day very rarely presents itself. Nobody wishes to deny for one moment that countless believers—and even doubters—have found comfort and strength from the administration of the last sacrament; but the appearance of the priest at the sick bed against the will of the patient or against the judgment of those responsible for his welfare in his last hours must be considered at least as an unwarrantable encroachment of clerical—er—care, which it may in certain cases become a duty to prevent. Bernhardi's only fault, if such it can be called, thus consisted in obeying the inner voice of his conscience as a doctor and man and in following a course of which all of us, as doctors and—er—men, must approve. There can therefore only be one reply from us to the letter of the Board of Trustees, and that is to express unanimously our entire and fullest confidence in our director, Professor Bernhardi.

FELDER: Bravo!

[ADLER *nods assent, but somewhat half-heartedly.*
WENGER *looks to* ADLER *and then to the others.*

BERNHARDI: Our vice-president, Professor Ebenwald, will now address the meeting.

EBENWALD: Gentlemen, do not let us deceive
ourselves. The resignation of the Board of
Trustees is, under present conditions, about the
worst thing that could happen to our institute.
I do not hesitate to call it a catastrophe.

SOME: Hear, hear !

EBENWALD: Yes, gentlemen, a catastrophe. And
I consider that it would not only be in the
highest degree ungrateful towards the trustees,
but also a crime towards our institute, if at a
time when our director, no doubt without any
bad intentions, but nevertheless in a highly
imprudent manner, has brought us to the verge
of ruin—if at such a moment, we declare ourselves in agreement with his conduct.

[*Corresponding commotion.*

I am therefore not only opposed to the vote of
confidence proposed by Professor Cyprian, but
propose that we should express our regret in
suitable terms with regard to the incident in
question and emphasise that we disapprove in
the strongest manner of the conduct of our
director towards his reverence.

[*He shouts down the growing disturbance.*

I further propose that this resolution be com-
municated to the trustees in a suitable manner,
with the request, in view of this resolution on our
part, to withdraw their resignation.

[*Great disturbance.*

BERNHARDI: Gentlemen . . .

[*Disturbance. He begins again.*

Gentlemen—to avoid any misunderstanding I would like to remark that votes of censure do not affect me—I foresaw them; and I am also in the fortunate position of being able to dispense with an official vote of confidence. And in order to save you from taking steps which you might later regret, I will confide to you that we shall probably no longer need a Board of Trustees. A considerable State subsidy for our institute in the immediate future is already pretty certain, as I was again given to understand only yesterday by the Minister of Education.

EBENWALD: Ballroom whispers.

SCHREIMANN: Air castles of the future.

EBENWALD: A State subsidy after this affair !

FILITZ: After this question !

[*Great disturbance.*

LOWENSTEIN *enters.*

LOWENSTEIN: I have just come from Parliament, gentlemen.

[*Movement.*

The question has been answered. . . . A criminal inquiry is to be instituted against you on a charge of religious obstruction.

[*Corresponding sensation.*

FELDER: Impossible !

CYPRIAN: Lowenstein !

SCHREIMANN: Oh !

ADLER: Religious obstruction ?

CYPRIAN: Well, tell us about it.

EBENWALD: Lowenstein will perhaps be so kind as to give us a little fuller information.

[BERNHARDI *remains motionless.*

LOWENSTEIN: What more do you want to know. A criminal investigation is to be instituted. A humiliation ! You have got what you wanted.

FILITZ: No abuse, my dear Lowenstein.

CYPRIAN: Speak, man !

LOWENSTEIN: I don't know anything further that may be of interest to you. You will find all the details to-morrow morning in the papers. The vital part of the speech was the end. At the beginning of the speech, one obtained the distinct impression that the people behind the question were going to suffer a humiliating defeat. The Minister spoke of the great services of our director and specially emphasised that there could be no question of any ulterior motives on his part, that Professor Bernhardi stood completely aloof from all political controversy. At this stage there were interruptions, such as " If only it were so ! " " Universities over-run with Jews," etc., and the Minister was somehow led away from his subject and became, it seemed, annoyed and confused, and he ended suddenly with the announcement—I am sure to his own surprise—that he would get into touch with the Minister of Justice—(*scornfully*)— with a view to ascertaining whether he did not consider it advisable to institute a criminal inquiry against Professor Bernhardi on a charge of religious obstruction.

FELDER: Shameful.

FILITZ: Oh, oh.

CYPRIAN: And how did the House take it ?

LOWENSTEIN: The speaker was congratulated on all sides.

BERNHARDI (*calmly*): I believe I am expressing the general desire of those present in thanking Dr. Lowenstein for his information. I request you, gentlemen, to calm yourselves. Gentlemen, as I previously remarked, the question is not under discussion here, and neither is the reply. Two resolutions have been proposed.

EBENWALD: I withdraw mine.

[*Commotion.* ADLER *whispers to* LOWENSTEIN, *explaining.*

Or rather I include it in another, which appears to me necessary in the interests of the institute in view of the new situation created by the Minister's reply.

CYPRIAN: The Minister's reply is irrelevant to the meeting.

FELDER: It does not concern us at all.

EBENWALD: I therefore move: that Professor Bernhardi be suspended as director of the Elizabeth Institute until the conclusion of the criminal inquiry instituted against him.

[*Great disturbance.*

FELDER: Aren't you ashamed of yourself, Ebenwald?

CYPRIAN: You don't even know yet whether the charge will be made.

LOWENSTEIN: Monstrous! Professor Bernhardi is and remains our director. No one has the power to remove him.

FILITZ: For me he has ceased to be director from to-day.

ADLER (*very excited*): Gentlemen, allow me to say a few words. If the inquiry instituted by the Minister of Education should lead to a trial, my evidence cannot be ignored, as I saw the incident in question. But just because I am so deeply and utterly convinced of the innocence of Professor Bernhardi and can testify to that effect . . .

BERNHARDI: Thank you.

ADLER: . . . just because of that I welcome—and we all without distinction of party should welcome . . .

SCHREIMANN: There are no party distinctions here.

ADLER: . . . the fact that this whole affair will be publicly clarified by means of a proper investigation. If, therefore, I support the motion of the vice-director, Professor Ebenwald, for the suspension of the director . . .

[*Commotion.*

FILITZ: Bravo !

ADLER: . . . I beg you all, and in particular Professor Bernhardi, to consider it a proof of my confidence in him—and also of my conviction that the inquiry will completely clear Professor Bernhardi from all blame in the matter.

CYPRIAN: But, Dr. Adler, you are thereby admitting the justification for the inquiry.

FILITZ: Who does not admit it ?

LOWENSTEIN: On the strength of such an infamous denunciation ?

FILITZ: That remains to be seen.

FELDER: Boot-licking to the Minister. Crawling before the Clericals !

LOWENSTEIN: It is not the first time.

CYPRIAN (*to* BERNHARDI): Take the vote on my motion.

BERNHARDI: Gentlemen . . .

[*Commotion.*

SCHREIMANN (*shouting in order to be heard*): Is this a meeting or a pot-house gathering ?

[*Nobody heeds him.*

FILITZ: The motion of Professor Ebenwald is more far-reaching. It must be voted on first.

BERNHARDI: Gentlemen, I wish to ask a question of the vice-director, Professor Ebenwald.

EBENWALD: At your service.

BERNHARDI: I ask you, Professor Ebenwald, whether you are aware that the question—the reply to which has been taken by you as a reason for moving my suspension—whether you are aware that this question could have been prevented by me ?

LOWENSTEIN: Oh !

SCHREIMANN: Do not reply.

BERNHARDI: If you are a man, Professor Ebenwald, you will reply.

[*Commotion.*

EBENWALD: Gentlemen, the question put by Professor Bernhardi comes as no surprise. You will excuse me, however, if, in view of the singular tone the director thinks fit to adopt towards me, I prefer not to reply to him direct, but explain to you the meaning of this somewhat—insinuating—question.

[*Unrest; expectant tension.*

Well, the question recently arose, as you know, as to who should succeed Professor Tugend as head of his department. Professor Hell of Graz or Dr. Wenger. Now imagine, gentlemen, that a good friend comes to you . . .

FELDER: Or a cousin. . . .

EBENWALD: . . . or it might be a cousin—and says to you: It will make rather a bad impression, you know, if another Jew is elected at the Elizabeth Institute, especially after the unfortunate incident about which all Vienna is

talking at the moment. And it is quite likely that
the whole affair may be brought up against
you in Parliament. Well, gentlemen, do you
think it so very wrong if in such circumstances
one goes to the director, as I did, and suggests
that it would be better to choose Professor Hell,
who after all is no fool either, in order to avoid
possible trouble ?

WENGER : Quite right.

[*Laughter.*

EBENWALD : You hear that, gentlemen ? Perhaps
it would have been better if I had gone to
Dr. Wenger instead and asked him to withdraw
his candidature. But I don't like backstairs
manœuvres. And so I went to Professor Bernhardi direct. And it is perfectly correct that the
question might have been avoided if Hell were
here to-day instead of Wenger. However, the
fates willed it otherwise. And now we are—
vulgarly—in the soup.

FELDER : Well done, Bernhardi.

BERNHARDI : Gentlemen, Professor Ebenwald
has answered my question, in a way which he
has made famous by now, but every one of you
will know what to think of the matter. To defend
myself for not having entertained the crooked
bargain proposed to me . . .

SCHREIMANN : Oh, oh.

BERNHARDI : I call it a crooked bargain, more
accurately than my behaviour towards the
priest is called religious obstruction.

FELDER : Very true.

BERNHARDI : But in any case I confess myself
guilty—guilty of not having done my utmost, as
director of this institute, to prevent a parliamentary question calculated to discredit the

institute in the eyes of all hypocrites and block-heads. And in order to accept the consequences of my action and avoid any further delay, I hereby resign my position as director of the institute.

[*Great commotion.*

CYPRIAN: What are you dreaming of?

LOWENSTEIN: You must not do it, Bernhardi.

FELDER: The question must be put to the vote.

BERNHARDI: What for? Professor Ebenwald, Professor Filitz, Drs. Schreimann and Adler are in favour of my suspension. . . .

LOWENSTEIN: That is only four.

BERNHARDI: And I would like to spare Dr. Wenger any inner conflict. He might vote for me out of gratitude, because I recently decided for him, and I do not wish to be indebted to such a motive for the somewhat doubtful honour of remaining your director.

SCHREIMANN: Oh, oh.

FILITZ: That is going too far.

CYPRIAN: What are you doing, Bernhardi?

FELDER: This is your fault, Adler.

LOWENSTEIN: The question must be put to the vote.

BERNHARDI: No, I will not have the vote. I will not submit myself to judgment.

FILITZ: Especially as judgment has already been pronounced.

SCHREIMANN: Might I ask whether Professor Bernhardi has resigned his position as director of the Elizabeth Institute or not?

BERNHARDI: Yes!

SCHREIMANN: Then, according to the statutes of

the institute, the directorship passes to the vice-President, Professor Ebenwald, and Professor Ebenwald at the same time assumes the chairmanship of this meeting.

LOWENSTEIN: Scandalous.

FILITZ: Naturally.

FELDER: And we have to submit to that?

CYPRIAN: Bernhardi! Bernhardi!

EBENWALD (*walks quickly round to* BERNHARDI'S *vacated chair, and rings the bell for silence*): Professor Bernhardi having, to our regret, resigned his position as director of the Elizabeth Institute, I take over that position and the chairmanship of this meeting in accordance with paragraph 7 of the statutes of our institute. I request you, gentlemen, to show me the same confidence as the late director enjoyed in such full measure, and I hope to prove myself worthy of it. I call upon Professor Filitz to address the meeting.

LOWENSTEIN: Infamous!

FELDER: You are not the director, Professor Ebenwald, not yet.

[*Commotion.*

FILITZ: We are now confronted with the question as to who is to take charge of Professor Bernhardi's department.

CYPRIAN: What do you mean?

BERNHARDI: Gentlemen, though I am no longer director, I am still a member of the institute, like all of you, and head of my department.

ADLER: Why, of course!

WENGER: Certainly.

CYPRIAN: There can be no discussion on that point.

SCHREIMANN: It might lead to disagreeable complications if the suspended director of the institute . . .

LOWENSTEIN: He is not suspended.

CYPRIAN: He has resigned from the directorship.

FILITZ: Not quite voluntarily.

FELDER: He has flung it in your face.

EBENWALD: Order, order, gentlemen.

BERNHARDI (*who has now quite lost his temper*): No one has any right to remove me as head of my department, but I will take leave until the settlement of the affair.

CYPRIAN: What are you doing?

BERNHARDI: Taking leave . . .

EBENWALD: It is granted.

BERNHARDI: Thank you. And during the period of my absence I appoint my present assistants, Dr. Kurt Felder and Dr. Oskar Bernhardi, to take charge of my department.

EBENWALD: I see no reason to object to that proposal.

BERNHARDI: And now, gentlemen, I begin my leave and wish you all good day.

LOWENSTEIN: I also.

[CYPRIAN *takes his hat to go.*

BERNHARDI: That would just suit these gentlemen. I beg you to stay.

FELDER: And you stay too, above all.

BERNHARDI: What, here?

ADLER (*to* BERNHARDI): I should feel very unhappy, professor, if you should misconstrue my behaviour. And I would like at this moment to express, before all, my very high esteem for you.

BERNHARDI: Thank you. Whoever is not for me is against me. Good evening, gentlemen.

[*Goes out.*

FELDER (*speaks during growing commotion, which he sometimes has to shout down*) : And you let him go, gentlemen ? I beg you for the last time to come to your senses. You must not let Bernhardi go. Consider for a moment, calmly, how all this unhappy affair arose—and you must come to your senses. Where is the person whose religious feelings could possibly have been offended by Bernhardi's action ? And if there is such a one, the fault lies with those who have deliberately spread a distorted account of the affair. And if it were not for place hunting, parliamentarism and human rascality and baseness—in short, for politics—is it conceivable that this incident could have been made into a public affair ? Well, it has happened, gentlemen, for unfortunately there is no lack of place hunters, scoundrels and fools. But we do not wish to belong to any of these categories, gentlemen. What blindness can lead us, lead you, doctors, men accustomed to attend to dying men and women and with opportunities for gaining insight into realities behind appearances, what blindness, what madness can induce you to go through with this wretched sham, playing a ridiculous parliamentary comedy, and for miserable reasons of party politics deserting a man who has done nothing else but what was right and natural ? And I do not ask anything of you, gentlemen, but to show yourselves worthy of that same modest title by considering as null and void all the decisions taken at this meeting and requesting Professor Bernhardi to re-accept and resume his position for which there is none more worthy. Call him back at once, gentlemen, I implore you, call him back.

EBENWALD: May I ask whether Professor Felder

has finished his recitation? It appears so. We will therefore proceed with the agenda, gentlemen.

FELDER: Good evening to you, gentlemen.

CYPRIAN: Good evening.

LOWENSTEIN: You no longer constitute a quorum, gentlemen.

SCHREIMANN: We shall not desert the institute.

FILITZ: We shall take the responsibility of voting decisions without you.

FELDER (*opening the door*): Oh. Why, you have come just at the right time, Dr. Pointner. Come in, please.

LOWENSTEIN: Carry on with your little party, vice-president.

FELDER: Now you can all be happy, gentlemen. I wish you all a pleasant time.

[CYPRIAN, FELDER, LOWENSTEIN *go out*.

EBENWALD: Do you want anything, Dr. Pointner?

POINTNER: Oh! (*Remains standing at the door.*)

EBENWALD: Well, get out and close the door. (*Door is closed.*) The meeting will now continue, gentlemen.

CURTAIN

ACT III

SCENE I

Same as Act I, Scene II. FELDER *enters from the right followed immediately by* LOWENSTEIN.

LOWENSTEIN (*while still behind the scenes*): Professor Felder.

[LOWENSTEIN *enters.*

FELDER: Ah, Lowenstein ... Why, you are quite out of breath.

LOWENSTEIN: I ran after you from the street. (*Questioning*) Well, what is the result ?

FELDER: Guilty ! Two months.

LOWENSTEIN: Guilty ! Two months, in spite of the priest's evidence ?

FELDER: That evidence ? It turned out to be only to the priest's advantage and did not benefit Bernhardi in the least.

LOWENSTEIN: But that is ... why of advantage to the priest ?

FELDER: Didn't you hear the prosecutor's speech ?

LOWENSTEIN: Only the beginning. I was called away four times during the trial. At other times I can wait for days before a patient takes it into his head ...

FELDER: Well, well. You can't complain, you know. . . .

LOWENSTEIN: Well, now, what about the prosecutor ?

FELDER: The statement of the priest that he was not pushed, but only felt a light touch on the shoulder, was seized on by the prosecutor to represent his reverence as a shining example of Christian forbearance and gentleness.

LOWENSTEIN: Then Bernhardi was actually condemned on the evidence of this hysterical Nurse Ludmilla and that fine fellow Pointner? For all the other witnesses were absolutely in his favour. I must really apologise to Adler. He behaved wonderfully. And Cyprian! Not to mention your son!

[CYPRIAN *enters. Mutual greetings.*

CYPRIAN: Good evening, gentlemen.

FELDER: Where is Bernhardi?

LOWENSTEIN: They didn't keep him there, did they?

CYPRIAN: He will be coming with his counsel, Dr. Goldenthal, I expect, before giving himself up.

LOWENSTEIN: Goldenthal behaved like a toady. It could hardly be expected otherwise.

CYPRIAN: Why do you say that?

LOWENSTEIN: A converted Jew. His wife wears one of those crosses. Sends his son to be educated at a Christian college. Those are the worst kind.

CYPRIAN: You make one tired with your fixed idea.

LOWENSTEIN: The trial would have ended differently if we had had another lawyer.

CYPRIAN: I doubt it. Perhaps it would have ended differently if there had been another defendant.

FELDER: How do you mean?

CYPRIAN: We don't want to blame Bernhardi now, especially not to-day. But his most ardent admirers can't pretend that he behaved very cleverly.

LOWENSTEIN: Why ? I thought him wonderful. To have remained calm even during the evidence of that rascal Pointner . . .

CYPRIAN: You call that calm ? It was defiant.

LOWENSTEIN: Defiant ? What do you mean ?

FELDER (*to* CYPRIAN): He probably wasn't there when Bernhardi asked for Ebenwald to be called as a witness.

CYPRIAN: Yes. He wanted to have the Minister, Flint, called too. It was sensation-mongering.

[KURT *enters.*

FELDER: Kurt ! (*Goes up to him and embraces him.*)

LOWENSTEIN (*to* CYPRIAN): Why this touching family scene !

CYPRIAN: Don't you know ? Kurt called Pointner a liar in court . . .

LOWENSTEIN: How . . .

CYPRIAN . . . and was fined two hundred schillings for it.

LOWENSTEIN: My dear Dr. Felder, can I give you a kiss ?

KURT: Thank you, professor. We will take that as read.

LOWENSTEIN: Well, at least let me contribute to the two hundred schillings.

FELDER: We shall pay that all right. (*To* KURT) But I tell you, Kurt, that if you're thinking of letting yourself in for a duel with this person . . .

KURT: Let him try it on. But in any case the Pointner affair is not finished by any means, even if the Bernhardi affair is.

CYPRIAN: And we hope it is not.

LOWENSTEIN: What do you intend to do, Kurt?

[BERNHARDI *and* OSKAR *enter.*

BERNHARDI (*in excellent spirits, as he has heard the others laughing*): Forgive me for keeping you waiting.

[*Handshakes.*

CYPRIAN: Well, did you succeed in escaping from the ovations?

BERNHARDI: Not quite. A few—" gentlemen "—waited at the side door, and gave me an appropriate reception.

LOWENSTEIN: Did they offer to draw you through the streets?

BERNHARDI: " Down with the Jews ! " they shouted.

LOWENSTEIN: Did you really hear that?

BERNHARDI: Do me the pleasure, gentlemen, of staying to dinner, won't you? Oskar, go and see if there's enough? My housekeeper has given notice, you know. Her confessor told her that it would be impossible for her to remain in this house without the gravest danger to her soul.

[OSKAR *goes out.*
ADLER *enters.*

Greetings, Adler! A repentant sinner is more pleasing in my sight than ten just men.

ADLER (*lightly*): I was never a sinner, professor. I was convinced, as you know, from the first that the trial was a necessity. But I anticipated that the court would attach less weight to the evidence of Mr. Pointner than to that of Professor Cyprian and myself.

CYPRIAN: We can't complain. Even the priest himself did not fare any better.

[MANSERVANT *enters and whispers something to*
BERNHARDI. BERNHARDI, *very surprised and
perplexed, hesitates a while, about to consult* CYPRIAN,
then decides otherwise.

BERNHARDI: Excuse me, gentlemen, a visitor
whom I cannot possibly refuse to see. I hope I
shall not be detained too long—please get on
with dinner. (*Calls*) Oskar. Be so kind, gentlemen. . . .

[OSKAR *appears in dining-room doorway, and shows
them all in.*

CYPRIAN (*to* BERNHARDI): Well! What is it?

BERNHARDI: I will tell you later.

[CYPRIAN *follows the others into the dining-room.*

BERNHARDI (*to the* SERVANT): Ask him in.

[SERVANT *goes out.* BERNHARDI *closes the door
into the dining-room. The* PRIEST *enters.*

BERNHARDI (*receiving him at the door*): Come in.

PRIEST: Good evening, professor.

BERNHARDI: A visit of condolence, your
reverence?

PRIEST: Not exactly that. But I felt compelled to
come and speak to you to-day.

BERNHARDI: I am at your service.

[*He offers him a chair and they both sit down.*

PRIEST: In spite of the unfavourable result of the
trial, you will realise, I think, professor, that I
was not to blame for your sentence.

BERNHARDI: If I were to thank you for speaking
the truth in your evidence, I should be merely
offensive.

PRIEST (*already somewhat put out*): I have not
come here, professor, to obtain your thanks,

although I did *more* than simply reply to the question to which it was my duty as a witness to answer. But you will understand, professor, that I have not come here to repeat to you in private my public evidence. What moved me to see you at this late hour is the fact that I wish to make you—a still more important admission.

BERNHARDI: A still more important admission?

PRIEST: Yes. Before the court I expressed my conviction that you had not acted with any hostile intentions against me—or against that which I represent. But now I feel compelled to admit to you further that in this particular case —I wish you to understand me rightly, professor —that in this particular case you acted perfectly correctly in your capacity as doctor, and that in fulfilment of your duty as such, as I in fulfilment of mine, you could not have acted otherwise.

BERNHARDI: Have I understood you rightly? You admit that I acted perfectly correctly— that I could not have acted otherwise?

PRIEST: That as a *doctor* you could not have acted otherwise.

BERNHARDI (*after a pause*): If that is your opinion, then I must say that there was a better occasion, perhaps the only proper occasion, for making the admission a few hours ago.

PRIEST: It was not lack of courage that kept me silent. Otherwise should I be here?

BERNHARDI: What then . . . ?

PRIEST: I will tell you, professor. What kept me silent in court was the realisation that came upon me suddenly with the power of divine inspiration, that by saying one word more I should do immeasurable harm to something really sacred —to me the most sacred of all.

BERNHARDI: I cannot imagine that for a man of

your courage there can be a more sacred thing than the truth.

PRIEST: What? No more sacred thing than the relatively insignificant truth which I might have followed up to the end in this particular case? You can hardly mean that, professor. If I had not only publicly admitted your good intentions—and I already went further than many good people will forgive me for—but also admitted your *right* to keep me away from the bedside of a dying Christian sinner, the enemies of our holy Church would have exploited such a declaration in a manner for which I could not make myself responsible. For we have not only honest enemies, as no doubt *you* know, professor. And the relatively insignificant truth, which I should have spoken would have thereby become in a higher sense, a lie. That is why I did not speak, professor.

BERNHARDI: And why do you do so now?

PRIEST: Because at the moment of that divine revelation I vowed to make to you personally, as the only one to whom perhaps it was due, a confession which would have been misunderstood and misconstrued by the public.

BERNHARDI: Thank you, your reverence. And let's hope you will never be called upon to give public evidence in a matter where more is at stake than my own insignificant fate. At such a time you might consider as divine revelation what seems to be only a personal scruple—and so do wrong to a higher truth than that which you claim to represent.

PRIEST: I cannot recognise a higher one than that of my Church, professor. And the highest law of my Church is discipline, order, and obedience. If I were ever expelled from that community which radiates such infinite blessings throughout the world—unlike men in private professions as yourself, professor—I should lose all possibility of further work, and the whole meaning and foundation of my existence would be destroyed.

BERNHARDI: And yet I believe there have been priests whose real work only began when they severed their connection with the Church—and preached to the world with a total disregard of consequences, what they believed to be right and true.

PRIEST: If I were of such, professor . . .

BERNHARDI: Well?

PRIEST: . . . then doubtless God would have moved me to say before the court what you now hear from me in private.

BERNHARDI: So it was God who kept you silent? And now God sends you to me to confess to me in private what you were not allowed to express in court? I must say your God makes things easy for you!

PRIEST (rising): You must excuse me, professor. I have nothing to add to the admission I have made to you and which you strangely enough consider as a confession of a wrong done to you. It was certainly not a part of my vow to enter into a discussion with you upon matters about which we can hardly hope to understand one another.

BERNHARDI: And so you shut the door in my face, your reverence? I cannot take that as proof that you are within and I without. I regret that you have troubled to come here in vain.

PRIEST (not without irony): In vain?

BERNHARDI: . . . As I cannot give you such complete absolution as you expected.

PRIEST: Absolution? I did not come here for that, professor. Perhaps to reassure myself and set my mind at rest. And *that* I have been able to do—to a greater extent than I could have hoped for. For only now, professor, am I beginning to see the whole matter in the proper light. The real reason for my coming—my being sent to you—is gradually becoming clear to me.

BERNHARDI: Oh!

PRIEST: I had no confession to make to you, as I at first believed, but I was sent to deliver myself from a doubt. A doubt, professor, of which I was not even fully conscious when I entered this room. Now, however, the doubt has been removed; I see clearly; and what I have but now admitted to you, professor, I regret to say I must withdraw.

BERNHARDI: You withdraw it? But I have already accepted it, your reverence.

PRIEST: It no longer counts. For now I know, professor, that you were *not* in the right in turning me away from the bedside of the dying girl.

BERNHARDI: Ah!

PRIEST: Not you. Others in similar circumstances might perhaps have been in the right. But you do not belong to such. I know that now. It was at best a self-delusion on your part to think that your reason for refusing me admission to the ward was care for your patient, or pity. Such pity, such care, were but pretexts; the real reason lay deeper—in the roots of your nature. Yes, professor, the real reason was—how shall I express it—an antipathy against me . . . an uncontrollable antipathy—or rather hostility . . .

BERNHARDI: Hostility?

PRIEST: . . . against all that which this robe signifies to you—and men like you.

BERNHARDI: And what if it were so? Would not what I have suffered during the past few weeks—all this lying agitation against me, which you yourself condemn and despise— justify what you call hostility? But to this I can swear, your reverence. At the moment when I refused you admission to the ward there was no trace of hostile feeling in me. I stood before you as doctor with as pure a heart as any priest at the altar. With no less pure a heart than your own when you wished to give my dying patient the consolations of religion. You knew that when you came here—you admitted it. You should not deny it because you feel—as I also feel, and have never felt more strongly than now—that something separates us—something which we can never hope to conceal even from ourselves.

PRIEST: And you never felt it more strongly than now?

BERNHARDI: Yes, now, when I am face to face with one who is the most open-minded of his kind. For that which separates us—and probably will for all time—for that, " hostility " seems too small a word. It is something greater . . . and more hopeless.

PRIEST: There you are probably right, professor. Hopeless. When there is such an unbridgeable gulf—such an abyss—between two men like you and me, who both of us perhaps are . . . without (*smiling*) hostility—there must be some deeper cause. And that cause appears to me to be that, while an understanding is possible between belief and doubt, there is no understanding possible between humility and—you will I hope, not misunderstand the word, in view of some of your previous utterances— between humility and arrogance.

D

BERNHARDI: Arrogance? And you, your reverence, who can find no milder word for what you believe to be at the bottom of my soul, you think yourself free from hostility to . . . men of my kind?

PRIEST (*about to become more vehement, but checks and composes himself; after a brief pause, with hardly noticeable smile*): I know myself to be free. My religion teaches me, professor, to love even those that hate me.

BERNHARDI (*strongly*): And mine—or that which is within me in its place—to understand even where I am misunderstood.

PRIEST: I do not doubt your good intentions. But there are limits to understanding, professor. Where the human intellect alone is concerned—you will have experienced it often enough yourself—there is deception and error. But that which does not deceive—which cannot deceive men of my calling—is (*hesitates*)—I will use a word, professor, to which even you can have no objection—is . . . our inner feeling.

BERNHARDI: Let us call it that then, your reverence. And this inner feeling, even though it may flow from other sources in my soul—I also try to follow and trust. And if it is . . . not so easy for one of us, as for men of your calling, your reverence, God who made you so humble, and me so arrogant, this . . . incomprehensible God no doubt has his reasons for it.

[PRIEST *looks at him for a long time, then with sudden decision stretches out his hand.*

(*Hesitating, smiling very slightly*) Across—the abyss, your reverence?

PRIEST: Do not let us look down—for a moment.

[BERNHARDI *clasps his hand.*

PRIEST: Good-bye, professor.

[*He goes out.*

BERNHARDI, *alone, stands undecided for a while, reflecting, puckered brow, then smooth again; movement as if shaking off something, then pushes aside the partition and opens the door to the dining-room.*

CURTAIN

SCENE II

An office apartment at the Ministry. Furnished accordingly. COUNCILLOR WINKLER, *youngish, fresh complexion, sparkling blue eyes, is alone. Telephone rings. As curtain rises he is humming a Viennese tune.*

COUNCILLOR (*speaks into the telephone*): Ministry of Education speaking—No. Councillor Winkler. Oh, Professor Ebenwald. . . . He has not arrived yet. . . . Perhaps in half an hour. . . . I am afraid I am not in a position to give any information on the subject, at any rate not by telephone. . . . Yes, with pleasure. Good day, professor.

[*He rings off, continues humming same tune. Telephone rings again.*

Ministry of Education speaking. . . . Councillor Winkler, yes. . . . Oh. Good morning, my dear lady. . . . This evening ? . . . Yes, if I possibly can, with pleasure. . . . What do I think about the elections ? Nothing. . . . No. . . . Because I don't like to see pretty women mixed up in politics. . . . Nobody understands anything about politics. You have got the next twenty years to do that in. . . . Au revoir . . . (*an after thought*) kind regards to your husb . . . (*But he is already cut off.*)

[COMMISSIONAIRE *enters with card.*

Well, what is it ? Oh, Dr. Feuermann. . . . Show him in.

[COMMISSIONAIRE *goes out.* DR. FEUERMANN *enters. He makes a deep bow.*

Good day to you, doctor. To what do we owe the pleasure ?

FEUERMANN: I've come on a very serious matter, councillor.

COUNCILLOR: Oh, doctor, not another unfortunate accident, I hope.

FEUERMANN: To be sure I was acquitted. But what is the use of that to me ? No patient comes near me now. If I remain as a doctor in Linz I shall simply have to starve. That is why I have taken the liberty of applying for another post. . . .

[*Telephone rings.*

COUNCILLOR: Excuse me, doctor. (*Into the telephone*) Yes, Councillor Winkler. . . . Oh, good morning—What's that? What? (*Very surprised*) You don't say so—Really? Nurse Ludmilla? That would be a strange coincidence—Because he is coming out to-day—Of course, Professor Bernhardi—To-day, yes—You're coming yourself ? . . . Yes. Of course I won't mention anything to His Excellency yet if you wish. . . . Good-bye. (*Rings off. Totally oblivious of* FEUERMANN'S *presence, he commences to hum again.* FEUERMANN *makes a little movement.*) Well . . . Oh, I beg your pardon. And then ?

FEUERMANN: And I wanted to ask you, councillor, to support my application . . . as you are always . . .

[FLINT *enters*.

FLINT: Good morning, Winkler. (*Notices* FEUERMANN.) Ah——

FEUERMANN (*bowing deeply*): Your Excellency, my name is Feuermann.

FLINT: Oh yes, of course. I have already . . . from the *Monday Chronicle* . . . ?

COUNCILLOR (*aside to him*): Not a journalist for once, your Excellency. Dr. Feuermann of Linz.

FLINT: Oh yes—Dr. Feuermann.

COUNCILLOR (*as before*): Who was recently charged in connection with a so-called professional blunder and acquitted.

FLINT: Oh, I know. Professor Filitz gave a very favourable expert opinion. Ten votes against two . . .

FEUERMANN: Nine against . . .

[COUNCILLOR *makes a deprecating sign to him*.

FLINT: I congratulate you, my dear Dr. Feuermann.

FEUERMANN: I am very touched that your Excellency should have taken such an interest in my insignificant affair.

FLINT: Insignificant affair ! For me there is no insignificant matter. And there should not be for men in my position. In a higher sense everything is equally important.

[*He casts a brief glance at the* COUNCILLOR, *seeking approval*.

FEUERMANN: I took the liberty, your Excellency . . .

COUNCILLOR: I presume, doctor, that you have mentioned everything in your application.

FEUERMANN: I would only like to point out . . .

COUNCILLOR: That is probably also included. . . .

FEUERMANN: Yes.

COUNCILLOR: Well, give it to me, doctor, and we will have it attended to as quickly as possible. Good morning, doctor.

FLINT (*who has in the meantime commenced to read a paper given him by the attendant*): Good day to you, doctor.

[FEUERMANN *goes out.*

(*Looking at the paper*) What is it he wants?

COUNCILLOR: Application for another post. The poor devil is of course being boycotted in Linz, in spite of his acquittal. . . .

FLINT: Well, I suppose that's natural. You probably wouldn't let yourself be treated by him either.

COUNCILLOR: Certainly not if I were expecting a baby.

FLINT (*throwing down the paper angrily*): What's the news?

COUNCILLOR: Professor Ebenwald has telephoned. He will be calling in the course of the morning.

FLINT: What, again? Why, he was here the day before yesterday.

COUNCILLOR: They need money badly at the Elizabeth Institute. The debts are beginning to sink them. . . .

FLINT: But the Board of Trustees withdrew their resignation after Bernhardi's removal.

COUNCILLOR: Yes, but it appears that Bernhardi was the only one able to keep the trustees up to scratch. Since he has gone, they're all asleep. Even I myself . . .

FLINT: They must have a subsidy. I promised it to Bernhardi at the time. By the way, I must congratulate you on the result of yesterday's elections. Ten new Socialist gains. That was not to be expected.

COUNCILLOR: I shall not be in a position to accept congratulations until after the final returns, your Excellency.

FLINT: Those may show different results. The majorities yesterday were not so overwhelming. So don't jubilate too soon, my dear anarchist.

COUNCILLOR: You are giving me quick promotion, your Excellency. I have only just been decorated with the title of a Social-Democrat.

FLINT: Not such a difference.

COUNCILLOR: For my part, I must not omit to congratulate you on your yesterday's speech.

FLINT: Speech? . . . What! Those few improvised words? They worked well.

COUNCILLOR: Did they express your private opinions, your Excellency?

FLINT: My dear Winkler, my own private attitude towards questions is quite another matter. It is only political amateurs who blurt out their private opinions in public. The tone of mere crude conviction sounds hollow. What is effective in politics is counterpoint.

COUNCILLOR: Until someone comes along, your Excellency, who thinks of a new tune.

FLINT: Quite so. But—to drop this metaphorical dialogue and come down to realities—do you really think that the people are ripe, or ever will be ripe, for doing without religion?

COUNCILLOR: What I understand by religion, your Excellency, can be better learnt in any other lesson than the so-called religious lesson.

FLINT (*chaffingly*) : Well, are you an anarchist, Winkler, or aren't you ?

COUNCILLOR : Yes, it appears I am. But as a government official one has no other choice but to be an anarchist or an idiot. . . .

FLINT (*laughing*) : Oh come, allow a few intermediate stages. But believe me, anarchism is an unproductive state of mind. I have been through such a stage myself, but it is past. *Now*, my view of life can be summed up in two words : work, results. And since I can only carry out a number of things with the co-operation of Parliament, I am obliged to make what are called concessions. Even anarchists have to make concessions, otherwise they could not be councillors. . . . Well, I won't say any more . . . but it will be seen that I am not a Minister of Culture and Catholicism, as some scribbler has chosen to call me in a so-called leading article.

COUNCILLOR : Ah.

FLINT : Just after your own heart, what ? But it is not even his own phrase. It was coined by the gallant Felder at an election meeting the other day during which he brought up the Bernhardi affair. . . . Always this Bernhardi affair ! It seems these people will not allow it to rest. Have you read the article in this morning's paper ? A positively festive welcome to Bernhardi on the occasion of his release from prison. It is really going too far.

COUNCILLOR : Bernhardi is certainly not to blame for it.

FLINT : Not altogether blameless, I think. He appears to rather like his new rôle. Well, anyway, it would be regrettable if Bernhardi allowed himself to be egged on by his friends to engage himself further in a matter in which he can only be a loser. . . . We are confronted with a question of law, and we are determined to employ the strongest measures, if necessary, to uphold the authority of the law and the Government. And yet, however much trouble Bernhardi may have caused me, there still remains here—(*pointing to his heart*)—a certain sympathy for him. It seems one can never quite lose that.

COUNCILLOR: Friendships of one's youth. . . .

FLINT: Yes, that's it. But men in our position should be free from sentimentalities of that kind.

[COMMISSIONAIRE *enters with card.*

COUNCILLOR: Professor Ebenwald.

FLINT: Show him in.

[COMMISSIONAIRE *goes out.*

How much did you say we could ask for the Elizabeth Institute?

COUNCILLOR: Three thousand . . .

[EBENWALD *enters; he bows.*

FLINT: Good morning, my dear professor, or rather I should say director.

EBENWALD: Not yet, your Excellency, only deputising. It is by no means unlikely that Professor Bernhardi may be re-elected during the next few days. He was only suspended, you know.

COUNCILLOR: There would be difficulties about such re-election. For as things stand at the moment Bernhardi is neither professor nor doctor.

EBENWALD: No doubt he will soon be let off the legal consequences of his imprisonment. Your Excellency probably knows already that Bernhardi has just been led in triumph from the prison to his home.

FLINT: What?

EBENWALD: Yes, my students just told me.

FLINT: In triumph? What do you mean by that?

EBENWALD: Well, a number of students are said to have waited for him at the prison gates and welcomed him with cheers.

FLINT: It only needs a torchlight procession now.

COUNCILLOR: If your Excellency desires instructions to be given to that effect . . .

FLINT (*half angrily at* WINKLER's *deliberate misunderstanding*): Well, well, well. (*Dropping the subject*) You have come about the subsidy, professor?

EBENWALD: Yes, your Excellency.

FLINT: We shall unfortunately only be able to place a fraction of what we had intended at your disposal. But you must not forget that we have not only to deal here with the Elizabeth Institute and not only with the medical faculty, but with the entire immense field of culture and Catholi—and education.

[COMMISSIONAIRE *enters again with a card.*

COUNCILLOR: Professor Tugend.

FLINT: I leave him to you, Winkler. Will you come with me, professor?

[FLINT *and* EBENWALD *go out.*
Enter TUGEND.

TUGEND: Good morning, councillor. I shan't keep you waiting long. Stand up, speak up, shut up, what? Well, I come to ask you again how my little affair is progressing.

COUNCILLOR: It is proceeding favourably.

TUGEND: I need not tell you, councillor, that

I personally am not much concerned about the title. But you know what women are. . . .

COUNCILLOR: How should I know, professor?

TUGEND: Oh yes, of course. Not lonely, but alone—what? Well, we are by ourselves. My wife is really crazy for this title. She simply can't wait for it. And if it could possibly be arranged to be conferred by the 1st of June— that being my wife's birthday, you know . . . I would like to bring her the title as a birthday present.

COUNCILLOR: Certainly a cheap and practical present.

TUGEND: So if you can possibly do anything to hasten my affair, councillor . . .

COUNCILLOR (*in an assumed official tone*): The Ministry of Education is unfortunately unable to take into consideration private or family circumstances of professors or their wives in connection with the conferring of titles.

[COMMISSIONAIRE *enters, bringing card.*

(*Surprised*) Ah.

COMMISSIONAIRE: The gentleman wishes to speak to His Excellency personally.

COUNCILLOR: Tell the professor that it will no doubt be possible, but that I should be very pleased indeed to be able to welcome him in my office first.

[COMMISSIONAIRE *goes out.*

TUGEND: Do I intrude?

COUNCILLOR: He is an old friend.

[BERNHARDI *enters.* TUGEND *is rather astonished.*

BERNHARDI: Oh, you are not alone, councillor.

TUGEND: Bernhardi!

COUNCILLOR (*shaking his hand very cordially*) : I am very happy to see you again, professor.

BERNHARDI : I also am very glad.

TUGEND : My greetings to you, Bernhardi. (*Stretches out his hand.*)

BERNHARDI (*gives his own hand coolly*) : Is His Excellency not free ?

COUNCILLOR : He won't be long. Won't you sit down, professor ?

BERNHARDI : Thank you.

TUGEND : I say, Bernhardi, you're looking wonderful. I—I—do you know I had entirely forgotten—— How quickly two months pass.

BERNHARDI : Especially when you're free.

TUGEND : But you really look wonderful. Isn't it so, councillor ? If you had been to the Riviera you could not be looking better. Positively recuperated.

COUNCILLOR : If you would care to indulge in a little blasphemy, professor, I could guarantee you a cheap holiday of the same kind.

TUGEND (*laughing*) : Thank you, thank you.

BERNHARDI : I really have not had a bad time. A good angel watched over me : the bad conscience of the people who put me there.

TUGEND : Do you know what I heard the other day ? That you intend to write a history of the whole affair.

BERNHARDI : Indeed. Is that what they say ?

COUNCILLOR : That should make an interesting book. You have had an opportunity of getting to know people.

BERNHARDI : One knew most of them already, councillor. Only one sort of person has remained a riddle to me. . . .

TUGEND: Namely?

BERNHARDI: The people with unselfish rascality. Those who behave in a sorry way without the least advantage to themselves, merely for the pleasure of the thing, so to speak.

[FLINT and EBENWALD *enter*.

FLINT (*quickly under control*): Oh, Bernhardi !

EBENWALD (*the same*): How do you do, professor.

BERNHARDI: Good morning. No doubt the professor is here with reference to the Elizabeth Institute.

EBENWALD: Yes.

FLINT: It is with regard to the subsidy . . .

BERNHARDI: I have always thought that the interests of my work would be well looked after by you—during my absence.

EBENWALD: I thank you for your kind appreciation, professor.

FLINT (*to* BERNHARDI) : You wish to speak to me, Bernhardi ?

BERNHARDI: I shall not keep you long.

COUNCILLOR (*to* EBENWALD *and* TUGEND): May I ask you gentlemen . . .

[*He goes out with both.*

FLINT (*quickly decided*): My dear Bernhardi, I am glad to be able to congratulate you on your release. In my official position it was unfortunately impossible to let you know in a suitable manner how painfully surprised I was at the issue of your case; and I shall be all the more pleased for an opportunity of being of any service to you now that the affair is over.

BERNHARDI: You are really very kind, Flint. I have come, in fact, to ask you a favour.

FLINT: Which is?

BERNHARDI: It is this. Prince Constantine is seriously ill and has sent for me.

FLINT: Oh yes. But I do not see . . .

BERNHARDI: Has sent for me as a doctor. I am to resume his treatment.

FLINT: Well, what prevents you?

BERNHARDI: I do not wish to make myself guilty of another offence.

FLINT: Offence?

BERNHARDI: I should be considered a quack if I resumed treatment of Prince Constantine. Having been sentenced for the offence of religious obstruction, I have lost my diploma and the right to practise. I now bring you a petition to give me back my professional privileges. I came to you because you are an old friend who has already shown that he has great influence with the Minister of Justice. If the petition is to be granted, I beg you to hasten the matter so as not to keep the Prince waiting too long.

FLINT (*after a pause*): Oh, I see. You come here to have a little joke at my expense.

BERNHARDI: Not at all. I am acting in the properly prescribed manner. I have absolutely no desire to go to jail again, although I had a relatively good time. So if you will be so kind . . . (*Hands him the petition.*)

FLINT: It's granted. I take full responsibility. I give you my word that no consequences of a criminal nature will result for you. Does that satisfy you?

BERNHARDI: I think it should suffice; as in this case the keeping of your word does not involve any disagreeable consequences for yourself.

FLINT: Bernhardi!

BERNHARDI: Your Excellency?

FLINT (*regaining his composure immediately*): Well, I understand. I knew at once that you did not come here for the sake of Prince Constantine. But it is just as well. We will talk about the matter you're alluding to. I should have had to tell you anyway. So you accuse me of breaking my word to you?

BERNHARDI: Yes, Flint.

FLINT: And do you know what I reply to you? There is something higher in public life than keeping one's word, or what you call by that name. And that is to keep one's end in view and not to allow one's work to be jeopardised. I had no other choice, as I realised in a flash at the moment, but of casting myself with you into the abyss and committing thereby what would have amounted to a crime against myself, my mission and perhaps the State, or of surrendering a man who was lost already, and of being in a position thereby to build new scientific institutes, re-organise on modern lines the systems of instruction of the various faculties, improve public health, and carry out, or at least prepare the way for, reforms in various fields of our cultural life, all of which you yourself will admit were not too dearly paid for by two months of not very strict imprisonment. For I hope you don't imagine that I am particularly impressed by your martyrdom. If you had borne all the various annoyances for the sake of something big, some idea, for your country or your religion, I could have felt some respect for you. But your whole behaviour as I see it—and as an old friend you will allow me to say so—appears to be nothing else but a tragi-comedy of obstinacy, and I also venture to doubt whether you would have carried it through with such persistence if burning at the stake had still been in vogue in Austria.

[BERNHARDI *looks at him a while and then begins to clap.*

What do you mean by that ?

BERNHARDI : I thought you might miss it.

FLINT : And you can find nothing else to reply to me but that rather second-rate foolery ?

BERNHARDI : What there is to reply, you know as well as I do ; so what's the sense of replying to you, here between ourselves.

FLINT : Oh, I see. That's it, is it ? Well, you need not suppose that your intentions are unknown at the Ministry. Only it is not clear to me why, in such circumstances, you honoured me with a personal visit. For it could not have been only about Prince Constantine. . . .

BERNHARDI : Perhaps I was unnecessarily thorough about that. But I was naturally interested to know what you would say to explain yourself. This conversation between His Excellency and the ex-convict would make a very effective closing chapter to a certain book, if it were worth while writing it.

FLINT : Oh, I hope you will not let yourself be prevented from doing so. It should make a very good election address.

BERNHARDI : Election address ?

FLINT : Oh, well, it is only a question of days or hours no doubt, before you will be offered a seat.

BERNHARDI : My dear Flint, as hitherto, I intend to leave politics entirely to you.

FLINT : Politics ! Politics ! If you would only let me get away from that word. To the devil with politics. I only accepted the portfolio because I believed that there is no one else to do what must be done. But even if I may be destined to introduce a new legislative era, these few years—or months—at the Ministry will always be merely an episode for me. I am doctor, a teacher, and I long for patients and students. . . .

[COUNCILLOR *enters*.

COUNCILLOR: Excuse me, your Excellency, for intruding . . . but I have just received an extremely important communication from the Ministry of Justice . . . and since it concerns the professor's affair . . .

BERNHARDI: Mine ?

COUNCILLOR: Yes. Nurse Ludmilla, the State witness, has just made a declaration accusing herself of giving false evidence at your trial.

BERNHARDI: Accusing herself . . .

COUNCILLOR: Berman, from the Ministry of Justice, will be here shortly to report to you fully about it. There is no doubt about the matter at all. The nurse's declaration has been actually received.

FLINT: Received ?

COUNCILLOR: And you, professor, will of course demand a new trial at once.

BERNHARDI: A new trial ?

COUNCILLOR: Of course.

BERNHARDI: I wouldn't dream of it.

FLINT: What !

BERNHARDI: What for ? Am I to go through the whole business again ? All sensible people know I was imprisoned for nothing, and no one can give me back the two months, anyway.

FLINT: The two months ! Always harping on the two months ! As if that's the thing that mattered here ! You have no sense of justice, Bernhardi.

BERNHARDI: Obviously.

FLINT: Do you know any further details yet, councillor ?

COUNCILLOR: Not much. The most curious thing about the matter is—as Berman telephoned me —that Nurse Ludmilla states in her declaration that her confession of perjury was first made to her confessor, who enjoined her to make good her grave sin as far as lay in her power.

FLINT: The confessor ?

COUNCILLOR: Obviously he had no idea of the case involved.

FLINT: How do you know that ?

BERNHARDI: Must I go before the court again ? I would rather certify Nurse Ludmilla as highly hysterical and irresponsible.

FLINT: That would be like you.

BERNHARDI: What good will it do me if *she* is imprisoned ?

FLINT (*who has been pacing to and fro*): In the confessional. That ought to give some people food for thought. It will be seen, perhaps, that *some* of the Catholic usages can have very salutary effects for those of other denominations.

BERNHARDI: I don't want the salutary effects. I want to be left in peace.

FLINT: I would like to point out to you, Bernhardi, that it is not your convenience alone that is concerned.

BERNHARDI: For me, the matter is at an end.

FLINT: Oh !

BERNHARDI: Absolutely at an end. And should a new trial be ordered, my evidence in the first is available, and I have nothing to add to it. And I shall not require your Excellency's evidence.

FLINT: Oh. But you will not be able to prevent me from appearing before the court if I think it desirable. The first trial was a necessity. . . . How else could we come to the second one, which will bring full light and justice ? And it is perhaps just as well, Bernhardi, not to use all one's power too soon. (*Pointing to his breast pocket.*)

BERNHARDI: What is that ?

FLINT: A letter, a certain letter which will still perhaps do good service in the fight that lies before us—your letter.

BERNHARDI: Oh, my letter. I thought perhaps it was—your article.

FLINT: What article ?

BERNHARDI: You know, the famous one from our assistant days—" Churches and Hospitals."

FLINT: Oh, that one.

[COUNCILLOR *makes questioning gesture.*

FLINT: Yes, Winkler. One written during my revolutionary days. I must hunt it up for you some time. . . .

BERNHARDI: It exists, then ?

FLINT (*passing his hand to his brow*): Dear, dear, what tricks one's memory plays—why, no, I never wrote it . . . but perhaps I shall have an opportunity of—speaking it before long.

[COMMISSIONAIRE *enters.*

COMMISSIONAIRE: Mr. Berman would like to speak to His Excellency personally.

FLINT: Ah. (*To* BERNHARDI) Would you mind waiting a few minutes, Bernhardi?

BERNHARDI: Well, Prince Constantine, you know . . .

FLINT: Has been waiting two months for you. Half an hour more or less won't matter. Keep him for me, Winkler. It might be necessary to discuss together the combined line of action to be taken. I think I can ask this small favour of you, Bernhardi.

[*He goes out.*

COUNCILLOR: You have been called to Prince Constantine, professor? To-day already? That's just like him.

BERNHARDI: I shall ask him to do without my services for a while. These new developments will simply make me run away.

COUNCILLOR: I am only afraid, professor, you will have to stay away longer than your numerous patients will like. For now the thing is just beginning to start . . . and it will probably last a long time.

BERNHARDI: What am I to do, then?

COUNCILLOR: One gets used to it in time. One even becomes proud of it.

BERNHARDI: Proud? And now this affair of Nurse Ludmilla . . . and the prospect of a retrial, you will understand, councillor, that in order to come to myself again and get back my self-respect, I must get away from all this noise, and people will gradually come to realise that I was in the right.

COUNCILLOR: But, my dear professor! Nobody yet became popular by being in the right—unless his being right happened to suit the game of some political party. . . . And besides, you know, professor, that it is only your imagination that you were in the right.

BERNHARDI: You think so? In your opinion I should have allowed his reverence . . .

COUNCILLOR: Certainly you ought, my dear professor. For I don't suppose you feel yourself born to be a reformer.

BERNHARDI: Reformer——? Good heavens ! . . .

COUNCILLOR: As little as I do. . . . That is probably due to the fact that we do not feel inwardly prepared to go to the ultimate limit— and if need be to lay down our lives for a conviction. And so it is best for men like us—in fact, the only right and decent thing to do—not to meddle in such . . . things.

BERNHARDI: But . . .

COUNCILLOR: No good comes of it. What would you have accomplished after all, my dear professor, had you spared that poor young person a last fright on her death-bed? It appears to me just as if someone tried to solve the whole social question by giving some poor devil a villa as a present. . . .

BERNHARDI: You forget, councillor, like most other people—that I have been far from meaning to solve any social question whatsoever. I have only, in a very special case, done what I thought was right.

COUNCILLOR: That was just the mistake. If we always did the right thing, or let us say, if you woke up in the morning and, without thinking of it, tried to do the right thing the whole day long, you would certainly be in jail the same night.

[*They laugh.*

BERNHARDI: And may I tell you something,

councillor? In my place, you would have acted exactly as I did.

COUNCILLOR: Possibly. But then—excuse me, professor—I would have been just as big a damn fool—as you.

CURTAIN

PARNELL

Elsie T. Schauffler

PARNELL

A Play
in Three Acts

Revised for the English stage by
MARGARET RAWLINGS

The terms for the professional and amateur performances of this
play may be obtained from J. B. Pinker & Son, Talbot House,
Arundel Street, Strand, London, W.C.2, to whom all applications
for permission must be made.

CHARACTERS

(in order of their appearance)

KATHARINE O'SHEA

MRS. HAMISH ("AUNT CAROLINE")

PHYLLIS	A parlourmaid.
MRS. BRIDGET BLAIR	A friend.
MRS. ANNA STEELE	Katie's sister.
CAPTAIN W. H. O'SHEA	"Willie," Katie's husband.
GENERAL THE O'GORMAN MAHON	His friend.
TIMOTHY HEALY	
THOMAS MURPHY	Members of the Irish Party.
MICHAEL DAVITT	
MONTAGU HARRISON	Secretary to Parnell.
CHARLES STEWART PARNELL	Leader of the Irish Party.
GLADSTONE	
STANLEY	His secretary.
JOHN REDMOND	
1ST LEADER	
2ND LEADER	Members of the Irish Party.
3RD LEADER	

SCENES

ACT I

ACT II

ACT III

TIME: *England, 1880–1890.*

PROGRAMME NOTE

N.B.—Parnell actually died in 1891, at Brighton after months of illness, and after marrying Katie as soon as her decree became absolute. For the sake of dramatic cohesion, the author has advanced the date of his death by several months.

Parnell was first produced in England at The Gate Theatre Studio, in Villiers Street, on the 23rd April, 1936, with the following cast:

Characters in the order of their appearance :

Katharine O'Shea	MARGARET RAWLINGS
Mrs. Benjamin Wood	MARDA VANNE
Phyllis	DIANA MORGAN
Mrs. Steele	TOSKA BISSING
Clara Wood	CLARE BROCKLEBANK
Captain William Henry O'Shea	JAMES MASON
	(by permission of Fox Films)
General The O'Gorman Mahon	E. J. KENNEDY
Thomas Murphy	J. A. O'ROURKE
Timothy Healy	DAVID HOFMAN
Michael Davitt	HARRY HUTCHINSON
Montagu Harrison	LAURIER LISTER
Charles Parnell	WYNDHAM GOLDIE
William Ewart Gladstone	ARTHUR YOUNG
Mr. Stanley	DAVID READ
John Redmond	MICHAEL MORICE

Produced by NORMAN MARSHALL

ACT I

SCENE: KATHARINE O'SHEA'S *drawing-room at Eltham, nine miles from London, May, 1880.*

Late afternoon.

It is a charming room, for in spite of the occasional fussiness of the period, it is Georgian in mood. At the back are windows opening on to the terrace. A door L. opens into the hall, piano above, and R. is a fireplace. MRS. HAMISH (" AUNT CAROLINE ") *is seated, her gold-headed, rubber-tipped cane by her side.* KATHARINE O'SHEA *is standing, a newspaper in her hands, from which she has been reading aloud. She is extraordinarily graceful. Her face sensitive, vivid, passionate.*

KATIE (*reading from a newspaper*): " The two successful candidates elected to represent County Clare, were the O'Gorman Mahon and Captain William Henry O'Shea." (*Looking up from the paper*) There is no mistake. It is true.

AUNT CAROLINE: I never doubted it.

KATIE: Willie a Member of Parliament ! Aunt Caroline, he will want a bigger allowance.

AUNT CAROLINE (*dryly*): Undoubtedly.

KATIE: Yes, as a Member of Parliament he'll have new ways to spend money.

AUNT CAROLINE: At any rate, politics will at least keep him busy.

KATIE: I hope so.

AUNT CAROLINE: Don't let it disturb you too much.

KATIE: I'll try.

AUNT CAROLINE: You mustn't. You're much too young, and much too attractive. Have you forgotten " To the beautiful and young Mrs. William O'Shea " ?

KATIE: Oh, Aunt Caroline, don't.

AUNT CAROLINE: You are disturbed. What about?

KATIE: Oh, nothing. I'm tired, I think.

AUNT CAROLINE: Of what?

KATIE: Getting up, going to bed, dressing, undressing—hearing the clock tick. Oh, Aunt Caroline, why does anyone marry anyone?

AUNT CAROLINE: You probably married Willie for his yellow curls.

KATIE: Probably. But why should I marry him —want to marry him—live with him—and then suddenly find him so—so unattractive that when he comes near me—when he so much as touches me——

AUNT CAROLINE: I don't know, my dear. (KATIE *rises and crosses to window.*) Katie, are you in love?

KATIE: No, I wish I were.

AUNT CAROLINE: Heaven forbid. What is the matter with you, then?

KATIE: Restless. Life is blowing by outside, and it doesn't even touch me. My hair is not even ruffled.

AUNT CAROLINE: That wind blows dust and dirt, Katie.

KATIE: Yes, and the smell of earth, and trees, and sea. Oh, I'm ungrateful, Aunt Caroline. The room is beautiful—but—(*with a smile*) just a little stuffy. (*With a change of tone, picking up newspapers from the floor*) Well, Willie arrives by the five-two, and I've decided one thing.

AUNT CAROLINE: What?

KATIE (*crosses up to piano and places the papers*

there): I simply will not give him any more of Aunt Ben's money.

AUNT CAROLINE: He will expect you to give him something.

KATIE: Why?

AUNT CAROLINE: He isn't coming for a cup of tea. My dear, you know he is not indifferent to you.

KATIE: "The holy bonds of matrimony," ridiculous, isn't it? "These twain"; oh, Aunt Caroline, some day I am afraid I shall kick over the traces.

AUNT CAROLINE: You can't, Katie.

KATIE: Why not?

AUNT CAROLINE: Because you were born Katharine Wood.

KATIE: I wish I'd been born Katie Jones.

AUNT CAROLINE: Well, you weren't, and it's only in the Bible that people are born again. Somebody doubted it then. Besides, my dear, what could you do? You can't divorce Willie. Of course, he has provided you with grounds for divorce—about the only thing he has provided—but the law demands more than adultery. Personal violence added thereunto.

KATIE: Yes, he hasn't knocked me down yet. I wish he would.

AUNT CAROLINE: Yes—if you had witnesses. Remember, the law is on his side. You'll have to let him come here occasionally——

KATIE: I don't mind his coming here if——

AUNT CAROLINE: I know, my dear—but he doesn't—does he?

KATIE: No. Not now.

E

AUNT CAROLINE: Be tactful. All we have is
money. Useful—but not always successful.

KATIE: I suppose you mean be liberal.

AUNT CAROLINE: Oh no, you can screw down
the sum total if you like.

[*Enter* PHYLLIS, *a parlourmaid.*

PHYLLIS: Excuse me, ma'am. But Mrs. Blair is
calling.

KATIE (*looking at* AUNT CAROLINE): Bridget !
Show her in, please, Phyllis.

PHYLLIS: Yes, ma'am. (*She goes out.*)

AUNT CAROLINE: We are honoured. When
Bridget leaves London on a beautiful afternoon
in the midst of the season she must be fonder
of us than I thought, Katie.

PHYLLIS (*at the door*): Mrs. Blair.

KATIE (*standing*): Bridget, how nice of you.

BRIDGET (*crossing to* KATIE, *kisses her on both
cheeks*): I am fortunate to find you at home.
How do you do, Aunt Caroline ? How are you ?

AUNT CAROLINE: Fairly well, for an old woman
deprived of all the things she likes to eat.

BRIDGET (*solicitously*): Another twinge of gout ?

AUNT CAROLINE: Bridget, when you have gout,
as you undoubtedly will, you will not allude to
it as a " twinge."

BRIDGET: So sorry, dear.

AUNT CAROLINE: How's Herbert ?

BRIDGET: Like all husbands—stodgy and busy.
Where's Anna ? Don't tell me she's visiting the
poor on such an afternoon as this.

AUNT CAROLINE: The admirable Anna is sure
to be reading to Aunt Ben.

BRIDGET: Really? I thought she employed that what's his name? Wrote *Harry Feveral*—or was it *Richard Richmond*?

AUNT CAROLINE: Yes, dear, Mr. Meredith. She still pays him to read to her—anything but his own works.

BRIDGET: Isn't this news about Willie perfectly entrancing? Such fun for him. Seems incredible, though.

AUNT CAROLINE: Ridiculous, but not incredible. How did you hear it, Bridget?

BRIDGET (*hesitates just the fraction of a second*): Why—— (*She notices the newspapers.*) Why, it's in the papers, isn't it? General Election?

AUNT CAROLINE: You so seldom read anything, Bridget.

KATIE: Yes, it is in the papers, and I've had a note from Willie. He is coming down here this afternoon.

BRIDGET: How pleased you must be. Since Willie sold his commission in the Hussars he really hasn't known what to do.

AUNT CAROLINE: " Satan finds mischief," etc., etc.

BRIDGET: Fancy Willie being addressed as the Honourable Member. Too amusing. He is so boyish looking. And fancy his running into the old O'Gorman Mahon!

AUNT CAROLINE: Was that in the papers, too?

[BRIDGET *hesitates more obviously this time.* KATIE *perceives that* AUNT CAROLINE *is baiting her, breaks in, smiling.*

KATIE: Aunt Caroline, I read it to you.

AUNT CAROLINE (*with a look at* KATIE, *acknowledging the checkmate*): So you did, my dear.

KATIE: The O'Gorman was an old beau of Aunt Caroline's.

AUNT CAROLINE: One of them.

BRIDGET: Too thrilling.

AUNT CAROLINE: Too conceited. I never did like handsome men. Preferred having the looks myself.

ANNA (*calling from outside the French windows*): Where are you, Katie?

AUNT CAROLINE (*annoyed*): Anna! Oh, Katie, I do wish you would not invite your dear Aunt Ben to tea *every* day. I can put up with her, but as for your sister Anna—once a week is quite sufficient.

ANNA (*outside*): Katie, where are you?

AUNT CAROLINE: Don't you ask her to stay for dinner!

ANNA: Katie!

KATIE (*rising*): Here we are, Anna.

ANNA (*entering by the window, crosses to the centre, in an injured tone*): You said you would be in the garden, Aunt Caroline. (*To* KATIE) Dear Aunt Ben wishes me to tell you that she will be unable to come over to tea this afternoon.

AUNT CAROLINE: Dear me! Is she indisposed?

ANNA: Well, when one is over ninety, you know, one mustn't over-exert oneself, as you should know, dear Aunt Caroline.

AUNT CAROLINE: I'm not over ninety. And I shall over-exert myself, as much as I please.

ANNA: I'm sure I was only trying to be kind.

AUNT CAROLINE: Well, you have been. I am a cross old woman, so don't mind me. Here's Bridget.

ANNA: Oh, Bridget, I didn't see you. Have you just come?

BRIDGET: Yes. I drove down. How are you, Anna?

ANNA: Can't complain.

PHYLLIS (*at the door*): Excuse me, ma'am. Will you be having tea in the garden, or in here, ma'am?

KATIE: Aunt Caroline, what about the garden? Too cool?

ANNA: Very imprudent, Aunt Caroline. The ground is damp.

AUNT CAROLINE: The sunshine isn't.

KATIE (*to* PHYLLIS): In the garden, please, Phyllis. Take out plenty of rugs.

PHYLLIS: Yes, ma'am. (*She goes out.*)

AUNT CAROLINE: Katie has the loveliest garden this year. She has worked like a slave. What have you been doing with yourself, Bridget?

BRIDGET: Oh, the usual thing. London is a frightful crush this season. Saw Irving and Terry in *Hamlet* the other night.

KATIE: Oh, I must go up and see them.

BRIDGET: I like something funnier myself.

AUNT CAROLINE: It shouldn't be hard to find something funnier than *Hamlet*.

BRIDGET: Of course, Irving is wonderful.

AUNT CAROLINE: Can't compare with Macready.

KATIE: I love Ellen Terry.

AUNT CAROLINE (*rising*): Too " weepy."

KATIE: Aunt Caroline, no! She walks in beauty.

AUNT CAROLINE: Well, well, well. Come and pour out my tea, Katie. (*To* ANNA'S *proffered arm*) No, thank you. And then you can finish admiring Miss Terry.

KATIE: You're teasing me. I won't have it. I have heard you admiring her many and many a time. . . .

BRIDGET (*moving towards the window, pauses before a bowl of white roses*): What lovely white roses, Katie !

KATIE: Aren't they ? It's an Irish rose. Lady Londonderry's gardener told me they couldn't be grown out of Ireland, but I've done it. I sent her a box this morning.

BRIDGET: I should go in for flowers, too, if I were not so busy. Simply haven't the time.

KATIE (*without irony*): I have so much.

BRIDGET: My dear, it's ridiculous at your age, shutting yourself up in the country. I can't think why you do it. We must arrange a party —you and Willie——

KATIE: Oh, no. No, thank you.

BRIDGET: Why not ?

KATIE: I'd rather not.

BRIDGET: Nonsense. We'll dine, and go to the play. Irving and Terry, if you like. You're much too young——

[*The voices die away. After a pause,* PHYLLIS *shows in* CAPT. O'SHEA *and the* O'GORMAN MAHON. O'SHEA *is a very smart ex-cavalry officer. Speaks English without a trace of brogue. The* O'GORMAN *is a tall, silver-haired old soldier of fortune. His mane is long, and he has a roving eye for the ladies. His manner is reminiscent of the days of Louis Philippe.*

O'SHEA (*on entering*): Tell your mistress, Captain O'Shea.

[PHYLLIS *starts for the window.*

O'GORMAN: Why not the O'Gorman Mahon and Captain O'Shea? It's proud she'll be to hear the name O'Gorman Mahon.

O'SHEA: The O'Gorman Mahon and Captain O'Shea.

PHYLLIS: Yes, sir.

O'SHEA: Is your mistress alone?

PHYLLIS: Mrs. O'Shea is in the garden with Mrs. Hamish, Mrs. Steele, and Mrs. Blair, sir. (*She goes out.*)

O'GORMAN: Pretty wench. Is it a harem you've got, Willie? And you concealing it from me?

O'SHEA: Well, it's not as simple as it sounds, General. Mrs. Hamish is an old friend of the family. Dotes on Katie; spends most of her time here. We all call her Aunt Caroline. Mrs. Steele is Katie's sister. She lives across the Park with Aunt Ben. You know, famous old party, Mrs. Benjamin Wood—owns half the countryside. She gave Katie this place.

O'GORMAN: And who is the other one? There were three names, were there not?

O'SHEA: What? Oh, the other one? She is a regular dazzler; wait till you see her. A distant cousin of Katie's.

O'GORMAN: And it's a cosy little place ye have here, Willie. Nice, very nice, indeed.

O'SHEA: Not my place, my wife's.

O'GORMAN (*sentimentally*): Ah, happy wife. A beautiful home, and a brave and handsome husband.

O'SHEA: She may like the happy home, but the brave and handsome husband—that's another story.

O'GORMAN: You were always the modest one, Captain. I'll warrant Mrs. O'Shea would tell me differently.

O'SHEA: Your faith is touching, General, but please believe me, this isn't going to be any too easy.

O'GORMAN: Ah, Willie, what woman that ever lived could resist you and me together? Have you so soon forgot the girls of County Clare?

O'SHEA: My wife isn't exactly that type.

PHYLLIS (re-entering): Mrs. O'Shea will be here directly, sir. She says will you be making yourselves comfortable.

O'GORMAN: And what with, me dear?

O'SHEA (to PHYLLIS): Bring whiskey and soda.

PHYLLIS: Yes, sir. (She goes out.)

O'GORMAN: Willie, Willie, why did you stop me? Another minute and I'd have kissed her.

O'SHEA: So I inferred. Look here, General, we want to get on the good side of my wife. Do you think flirting with her parlourmaid the best method?

O'GORMAN: You're right, my boy. You're right.

[PHYLLIS enters with tray on which is decanter, syphon of soda and glasses, and places them on a table down R.

PHYLLIS: Will that be all, sir?

O'SHEA: Thank you, yes. (PHYLLIS goes out.)

O'GORMAN (with a magnificent gesture, as if the house were his): Have a drink, my boy.

O'SHEA: Not now, thanks.

KATIE (coming in through the windows): Good afternoon, Willie.

O'SHEA: Ah, there you are, Katie! This is my colleague from County Clare, General the O'Gorman Mahon. General, my wife.

O'GORMAN (*bowing with a flourish*): This is more happiness than I'd dared dream of. Madam, I now understand why Captain O'Shea was ever lonely.

KATIE (*smiling*): Was he? Really?

O'GORMAN (*warming to the tale*): He was that lonely . . .

KATIE (*interrupting*): But Willie is so brave. Once, when he was in Spain, he was lonely for eighteen months, and only wrote to me twice to mention it.

O'SHEA: There was nothing to write about.

KATIE: I know. And the Spanish mails are so uncertain. I won't tease you. Shame to me. Won't you sit down? Did you have a nice time in Ireland?

O'GORMAN: We kissed every pretty girl and drank with all the men.

O'SHEA: Ugh!

KATIE: And Willie loves Irish whiskey so.

O'SHEA: It makes me ill to mention it.

O'GORMAN: But he drank it for the good of the State, and the old County rewarded him. It's proud and glad ye are, ma'am, I'll warrant.

KATIE: Yes, very glad.

O'GORMAN: What did I tell you, Willie?

O'SHEA: Are you? Really, Katie?

KATIE: Yes—I'm glad—if you're interested. How did you manage it? To get elected, I mean?

O'GORMAN: Through me. I hold the County

Clare like that ! (*Raises a clenched right hand.*) It was through me.

KATIE: How nice of you, General.

O'GORMAN: I said to Willie, " Would ye like to stand for Parliament ? " Willie said, " Yes." " 'Twill cost ye a pretty penny," I said to Willie. " That I haven't got," says Willie. " Me boy," says I, " we'll not deprive Ireland of your services for the mere matter of a—*couple of thousand pounds.*"

KATIE: How very generous of you.

O'GORMAN: I said to Willie, " As for me—I haven't got a penny to bless myself with—not a penny, not a penny." But, I said to Willie, " There be plenty to open wide their purses in such a cause, and proud of the chance." That's what I said to Willie—" Proud of the chance. Sure no one would deprive Ireland of your services for the mere matter of money."

KATIE: Can Willie be worth two thousand pounds to Ireland ?

O'GORMAN: It's a bargain she's got this day in Willie.

O'SHEA: May I suggest, General, that you let me handle this ?

O'GORMAN: Oh, certainly. (*He rises.*) Mrs. O'Shea, with your kind permission I'll light a cigar and smoke it on your beautiful terrace. Good luck, my boy. (*Exits up R.*)

KATIE: What does he mean ?

O'SHEA (*confidentially*): He means I'm let in for two thousand pounds.

KATIE: You.

O'SHEA: My election expenses—and his.

KATIE: Willie, where will you get it ?

O'SHEA: Why do you suppose I have come to you?

KATIE: I have nothing. You know that.

O'SHEA: You can get plenty.

KATIE: I can't ask Aunt Ben again. She paid your debts only a few months ago. You promised then——

O'SHEA: Could I tell then that I should be going into Parliament?

KATIE: Oh, Willie!

O'SHEA: I've won political honour and distinction, and all I get is " Oh, Willie."

KATIE: Aunt Ben has done enough for me.

O'SHEA: You have done plenty for her.

KATIE: I've done nothing.

O'SHEA: You're at her beck and call.

KATIE: She gave me this house. She wants me near her. She likes me living just across the Park.

O'SHEA: You earn your keep.

KATIE (rising): Do you earn your keep, Willie?

O'SHEA: Yes, I do. I stay away from you, don't I?

KATIE: Yes, because you prefer your steeplechasing.

O'SHEA: Well, you've never been interested in my pursuits, have you?

KATIE: That's what makes me so unhappy. That's why I've begged you for a divorce, but you won't give it to me. Now you only come to see me when you want money from Aunt Ben. I understand you, Willie, but do you expect me to welcome you with open arms?

O'SHEA: Well, what about me? What do you

think I am ? " Thanks for the election, but you can whistle for the money." (*Crosses to her.*) That's what I'm to say, is it ? I'll be the laughing-stock of London. Talk of ashamed—I tell you I won't have it.

KATIE (*sits*): It's no use, Willie. I've made up my mind.

O'SHEA (*looks at* KATIE. *Sits*): Have you ? I'm too good-natured. Most husbands wouldn't stand being without their wives for two years. I don't know how I have. I have rights——

KATIE: Willie—wait. I'm sorry.

O'SHEA: Will you get the money, Dick ? Be a sport over this. You always have been. I'm rather looking forward to being an M.P.

KATIE: Well, I'll try.

O'SHEA: Come on, darling. You can if you want to. Say: Yes or No.

KATIE (*giving in*): Yes.

O'SHEA: Thank you. (*Kisses her hand.*) That's my Katie. Well, will you send it to me in town, or would you prefer me to come down here for it ?

BRIDGET (*outside*): Katie. (*Coming in from the garden*) Katie, Aunt Caroline wants to know why you don't give the gentlemen tea ?

KATIE: Of course. How stupid of me.

O'SHEA: Bridget.

BRIDGET: How do you do, Willie ?

KATIE (*at the window*): General ! (*He enters.*) Let me introduce you. This is General the O'Gorman Mahon—Mrs. Blair.

O'GORMAN (*bowing*): Your servant, Madam.

KATIE: Do have some tea, General.

O'GORMAN: No tea, thank you.

BRIDGET (*speaking*): But you must come and speak to Mrs. Hamish. She knew you, I believe, when she was Caroline O'Farrell.

O'GORMAN: Caroline O'Farrell! The toast of London and of Dublin!

KATIE (*leading him into the garden*): She is in the garden, General. She will be delighted to see you, I am sure.

O'GORMAN (*he goes out with* KATIE, *reminiscing*): The beautiful Caroline O'Farrell. It was in the year . . . (*They both exit.*)

O'SHEA (*eagerly crossing to* BRIDGET): What luck —finding you here!

BRIDGET: Luck? When I had your letter I decided to drive down.

O'SHEA: You angel.

BRIDGET: And—I'll drive you back.

O'SHEA: Marvellous! I'll get rid of the O'Gorman.

BRIDGET: No. Better not. Aunt Caroline has eyes like gimlets. Have you talked to Katie about entertaining for you yet?

O'SHEA: No.

BRIDGET: You must. It's more important than ever, Willie, politically—and it will look so much better for us.

O'SHEA: Having Katie about, you mean?

BRIDGET: Of course.

O'SHEA: I'll make her. By God, if Katie were only like you—I wouldn't——

BRIDGET: Yes, you would, Willie. You're no husband. Of *course* she doesn't understand you and all that sort of thing——

O'SHEA: Are you making fun of me?

BRIDGET: But *I* do. I don't expect the model of all the virtues wrapped in the same package with curly blond hair, blue eyes——

O'SHEA (*seizing her and kissing her*): And *this*.

BRIDGET: Willie! Be careful! (*Disengaging herself*) Suppose Aunt Caroline, or Katie——

O'SHEA (*crosses to her*): When can I see you alone then?

BRIDGET: Don't be foolish, Willie.

O'SHEA: I tell you I won't be kept on toast like this. Herbert's away. I know he is. Let me come to-night.

BRIDGET (*turns to him*): Come to the house? Are you crazy? You know it's a hot-bed of governesses—children—servants—it isn't safe.

O'SHEA: You've got your feet firmly on the ground, haven't you, Bridget?

BRIDGET: I don't count the world well lost for love if that's what you mean—and you don't, either—so let's be sensible.

O'SHEA: When am I to see you alone, then?

BRIDGET (*after a pause*): Are you invited to the Seymour Bellocs' the week-end of the twelfth?

O'SHEA: No—but I can get a bid. I know young Belloc.

BRIDGET: You needn't. I'll ask Fannie to invite you. She will. I've been nice to her on occasions.

O'SHEA: One good turn deserves another? All right, then. It's a promise? You won't fail me? (BRIDGET *moves to him, and puts her hand against his cheek. He tries to kiss her, but the same hand warns him back.*) Bridget. . . .

BRIDGET: Hush!

[AUNT CAROLINE, *leaning on the* O'GORMAN'S *arm, and followed by* ANNA *and* KATIE, *comes in from the garden.*

ANNA (*outside, and in triumphantly righteous tones*): I said the garden would be too damp, and I was quite right.

AUNT CAROLINE: It isn't too damp, it's too cold.

O'GORMAN: Mrs. Hamish should have a drop of whiskey. Nothing so good for a chill.

AUNT CAROLINE: Thank you, General, no. But *you* must have some.

O'GORMAN: You are most kind.

AUNT CAROLINE (*sitting*): Willie——

O'SHEA: How do you do, Aunt Caroline?

AUNT CAROLINE: Do give the General some whiskey.

O'SHEA: Of course—let me——

AUNT CAROLINE: Anna, since you find the garden so damp, don't you think you had better go home and change your shoes? Oh, and Aunt Ben will be waiting for you.

O'SHEA (*pouring*): Say when.

O'GORMAN (*with a loud laugh*): Fill it up, man, and pour the rest of it over me. To high hopes! May they never fail us!

O'SHEA: Aunt Caroline, you haven't congratulated me.

AUNT CAROLINE: I do, Willie, I do.

O'SHEA: I mean really to go in for politics. I think I have a future.

AUNT CAROLINE: Maybe, maybe.

O'SHEA: Some day I shall be Leader of the Irish Party. Who knows?

O'GORMAN: Are you forgetting Parnell?

O'Shea: Forget? I voted for him, didn't I? And he never even thanked me.

O'Gorman: Listen, Willie. Parnell doesn't have to thank anybody.

O'Shea: If he thinks that because he's the leader of the Irish Party . . .

Katie: He *is* the Irish Party.

O'Gorman (*with quickening interest*): Do you know him, Mrs. O'Shea?

Katie: No.

Bridget (*laughing*): I met him once in the lobby of the House. The " Irish Messiah " impressed me as being decidedly English.

Aunt Caroline: He isn't. He was born in Ireland, but educated here.

Bridget: He is very reserved. I don't think he has much time for women.

O'Gorman: That's because he has never laid eyes on Mrs. O'Shea.

Katie (*surprised*): Thank you.

O'Shea: We should entertain him, I think.

Katie: But that's absurd, Willie. He can't be got by the most powerful political hostesses in London. Isn't that true, Bridget?

Bridget: You might try, Katie.

O'Gorman: He'd not refuse you, my dear.

Katie: That's very nice of you, General, but Bridget's impression doesn't give me very much hope.

Bridget: Don't be ridiculous. He is not invulnerable.

O'Shea: Katie, it's important that we at least try. I ought to give some political dinners.

BRIDGET: He should, if he wants to get on.

O'GORMAN: Indeed, you should cut a figure, Willie.

O'SHEA: Will you help me, Katie? Invite Parnell to dine—act as hostess? It isn't much to ask.

O'GORMAN: I was wrong. You have a future, Willie.

O'SHEA: Well, Katie——

KATIE: But, Willie, don't you see he never accepts invitations and——

O'GORMAN: Mrs. O'Shea, won't you plead the cause of two unworthies—that's you and me, Willie——

BRIDGET: Hurry up and say yes, Katie. I must go, and I want to hear the end of the story.

KATIE: What do you say, Aunt Caroline?

AUNT CAROLINE: Willie shouldn't be left cutting a figure alone.

O'SHEA: Will you, Katie?

KATIE: Very well, I'll ask him. Shall we set a time?

O'SHEA: I'll send you word immediately I get back to town. Thank you.

BRIDGET: How delightful! (*Rising*) Now, I simply must go. Willie, can I give you and the General a lift to town?

[AUNT CAROLINE *and* KATIE *exchange a look.*

O'SHEA: That's uncommonly kind of you, Bridget.

O'GORMAN: It's delighted we'll be, ma'am.

BRIDGET: I'll have to hurry you off, I fear. (*Crosses to* AUNT CAROLINE *and kisses her.*) I am dining early. Good-bye, Aunt Caroline, so lovely seeing you.

O'SHEA (*crossing to* AUNT CAROLINE *and kissing her*): Good afternoon, Aunt Caroline.

AUNT CAROLINE: Good-bye, Willie.

O'GORMAN (*bowing over* AUNT CAROLINE'S *hand*): More beautiful now as the evening star than ever she was. . . .

AUNT CAROLINE: You had better go, General, before that metaphor gets you into trouble.

O'GORMAN: Madam, as ever your servant.

BRIDGET (*to* KATIE): Don't forget, you and Willie are going to dine with me. What about the tenth? Well—I'll see if Willie is free—and I'll ask Herbert to get tickets for the Lyceum. You'll come, won't you?

KATIE: Yes. I should like to. Thank you. Good-bye.

BRIDGET: Good-bye. General, I'm so glad you are driving back with me. The country is so lovely . . . (*She is away down the hall with* O'GORMAN.)

O'SHEA (*at the door*): About that other little matter. You had better send it to me in town. Make it soon. Good-bye. (*He clicks his heels, bows, and exits.*)

AUNT CAROLINE (*after a pause*): Well—how much does he want?

KATIE: Two thousand pounds.

AUNT CAROLINE: What!

KATIE: Election expenses. His, and the O'Gorman's.

AUNT CAROLINE: Willie's is not a timid nature.

KATIE: Oh, Aunt Caroline, I am so ashamed. So bitterly ashamed of giving in so easily. I ought to be able to manage Willie alone.

AUNT CAROLINE: You leave that to those who love you, my dear. With your Aunt Ben's money, and my tongue . . . (*Pause.*) Katie, I'm not leaving to-morrow after all.

KATIE: How adorable of you.

AUNT CAROLINE: Not at all. The weather is just beginning to turn pleasant.

KATIE: Darling !

AUNT CAROLINE: " Cutting a figure " ! Humph ! I am not so sure it won't be worth two thousand pounds after all.

CURTAIN

SCENE II

SCENE: *Committee Room Number 15, House of Commons.*

Doors R. and L. leading to small inner rooms. Door centre to the corridor. Fireplace L.

Two men are seated at a table.

TIMOTHY HEALY *has a book containing the names of members of the Irish Party, arranged by County.*

THOMAS MURPHY *has a similar book, the names arranged alphabetically.*

MURPHY (*reading*): Severn—S-e-v-e-r-n, Patrick, County Limerick.

HEALY (*turning to his County Book*): Limerick— Limerick. (*Finds the page.*) Mr. Patrick Severn. (*Consults a small notebook and reads*) " Good in a fight but no brains. One hundred pounds to Party funds. Can be trusted." (*He writes this in the County Book then looks up at* MURPHY)—" can be trusted "—all right—next.

MURPHY (*looking in his own book*): Shand, S-h-a-n-d, Mr. Timothy, County Mayo. (MURPHY *watching little book.*)

HEALY: Mayo—here it is—County Mayo. "Fifty pounds to Party Funds. Obstinate as a mule. Brains. Can be trusted." (*Writes in the County Book.*)

MURPHY (*slowly*): How does he know? That's what I can't get through my head.

HEALY (*disturbed in his writing*): What?

MURPHY: Mr. Parnell. How does he know Severn and Shand can be trusted?

HEALY (*writing*): He knows. You can stake your last quid.

MURPHY: He said of George Cobbe, "Wouldn't trust him with a bad sixpence."

HEALY: And did you?

MURPHY: No.

HEALY: You were lucky, Murphy.

MURPHY: But how does he know so much?

HEALY: He can see right through to the back buttons on your braces. That's how. (*Writes rapidly.*) Go on.

MURPHY (*referring again to his list*): Shea—S-h-e-a—County Clare.

HEALY (*looking in the County Book*): Clare, County Clare—it's O'Shea, Murphy.

MURPHY: Mr. Healy, I took the liberty of discardin' the O's entirely. They filled the book. I alphabetted by the second letter for convenience.

HEALY: Damned inconvenient, if you ask me. Oh, well—let's get on. "O'Shea, William Henry——

MURPHY (*with a grin*): "Willie" O'Shea.

[DAVITT *enters.*

HEALY: Evening, Michael.

DAVITT: Evening. Where's Mr. Parnell?

HEALY: In the House, I suppose.

DAVITT: He told me to meet him here.

HEALY: Late—of course.

MURPHY (*smiling*): Sure, it's important business he's got.

DAVITT: Of course, it's important.

MURPHY: And didn't I just *say* important.

[DAVITT *walks R.*

HEALY: Shut up, Murphy.

MURPHY (*smothering his feelings and resuming the thread of conversation*): William O'Shea.

HEALY (*looking at his notes*): The Chief has no comment on him.

DAVITT (*stops and turns*): Well, I have.

MURPHY (*imitating*): Oh, I say, me good man, have you seen me top hat? (*His tone changing*) And him by the name of O'Shea.

DAVITT (*crosses back*): To hell with him.

MURPHY (*eagerly*): To hell with him—write it down.

HEALY: Nothing goes in this book except on orders from the Chief.

MURPHY: Well, if he can see through to the back of yer pants it's eager I am for his word on O'Shea.

DAVITT (*looking at his watch*): Before the sitting Mr. Parnell was trying to see Gladstone—but he won't.

MURPHY: And why not?

DAVITT: Because the old dog-fox won't be caught—until he can't help himself.

MURPHY: Sure, he's no fox—it's a spider he is—waitin' to devour the Irish.

DAVITT: He'll be waitin' a long time, I'm thinkin'.

MURPHY: Why should Mr. Parnell lower himself hangin' around the English? " No traffic with the enemy." That's my motto.

DAVITT (*turning on him*): *Your* motto—burnin' an' outrage is your motto. An' how far have ye got with it? How near has Ireland been to gettin' Home Rule until now—*now*? This Party, that Party. It's all one to us if they'll give us what we want.

MURPHY: Why should they? They never have.

HEALY: Why should they? Are ye blind, man?

DAVITT: Count the new names, ye have the lists. Who'll be namin' the next Prime Minister? The Queen likely? I'll tell ye. Just one man.

MURPHY (*awed*): Charles Stewart Parnell.

DAVITT: God love him.

HEALY (*to* MURPHY. *Balancing imaginary scales*): That Party—that Party—Parnell calls the tune.

DAVITT (*steps up. Hotly*): It's hangin' round the English we are, is it? Well—the English'll be doin' the hangin' before long, or my name's not Michael Davitt.

HEALY: Never a word of this, Murphy. Mr. Parnell does his own talking.

MURPHY: Never a word.

[*The door from the corridor is flung wide by a young man, blue-eyed and with a boyish smile, but he is not smiling at the moment. He is* MONTAGU HARRISON, PARNELL'S *secretary, called* " MONTY."

MONTY: Gentlemen—the Irish Members are being suspended from the House.

HEALY: Suspended? For what?

MONTY: For moving that Mr. Gladstone be no longer heard.

MURPHY (*overjoyed. To* HEALY): Holy Mither! Tellin' the Old Spider to shut up.

MONTY: Gentlemen, Mr. Parnell says, will you please, all of you, go down and get suspended at once.

MURPHY (*jumping to his feet*): Will I get suspended! (DAVITT *stands back.*) I'll get suspended —an' as soon as that's done—I'll refuse to be suspended. (*Crosses to R. door.*)

MONTY (*stops him*): Mr. Parnell says no violence, please.

MURPHY (*dejected*): An' did he that? Well— sittin' still's no violence. Devil a foot will I stir from the place till they get the police after me.

HEALY: Murphy—you put your motion—get suspended—and *come right back to these books.*

MURPHY (*sadly*): Yes, sir. (*He goes out.*)

DAVITT (*crosses to end of table. To* MONTY): Mr. Parnell started this, of course?

MONTY: Oh, yes, sir. He was suspended over an hour ago.

DAVITT: We'd better be followin' Murphy, Mr. Healy. (*To* MONTY. *Finishing off writing*) If Mr. Parnell comes, tell him where we are, will ye, Mr. Harrison?

MONTY: Yes, Mr. Davitt. He'll be here any minute. (HEALY *rises.*) He's in a great hurry for those lists.

HEALY: We won't be long.

[*The door from the corridor opens and* PARNELL *comes in. He is tall, dark-haired, slender, a man between thirty and thirty-five. Very pale, curiously burning dark eyes. His manner, unconsciously aloof, is very quiet. The relation between himself and his Party workers is almost that of a schoolmaster, adored yet feared by his pupils.*

PARNELL: Good evening, gentlemen.

HEALY: Good evening, Chief.

DAVITT (*jubilant*): We're on our way to get suspended, Mr. Parnell.

PARNELL (*with his grave smile*): That won't take you long, Michael.

DAVITT: Not if you're an Irish Member, it won't.

PARNELL: Good luck.

[HEALY *and* DAVITT *exit.*

MONTY: Murphy's gone too. Mr. Parnell, when all our Members have been suspended, what will happen, sir?

PARNELL: Nothing. They'll take us all back in a day or two.

MONTY: But before they do—they'll pass the Coercion Bill, won't they, sir?

PARNELL: Yes. In any case we can't stop that—now. But we can show them our strength—and unity.

MONTY (*with enthusiasm*): "Sit together, act together, VOTE together."

PARNELL (*nods. He walks over to the table and glances at the books*): When the Grand Old Man sees us walking out "together," I think perhaps he will condescend to notice me.

MONTY: The Party's with you to a man, sir.

PARNELL (*sits*): There are no men in politics, Monty. Only votes—and secretaries.

MONTY: I'm a vote too, sir, if I can vote for you. (*Mechanically*) Oh, Mr. Parnell, may I remind you of your appointment with Mr. Clarke at eleven o'clock to-night. To-morrow morning at nine-thirty you are to see Mr. McLeanore and Mr. Martin to discuss Irish export. Lunch with——

PARNELL (*he has been talking to* MONTY, *but his*

inner mind has been concerning itself with a different train of thought) : Monty——

MONTY : Yes, sir.

PARNELL : Did you ever hear of a rose called the Queen's Messenger ? It's white. Perhaps that isn't the real name—with a strange scent—heavy and white.

MONTY (*amazed*) : Yes, sir. We used to grow them at home in Ireland.

PARNELL : I have not suddenly gone mad, Monty. I merely happened to—remember a rose. I'm still the Leader of the Irish Party—and I still intend to get a Parliament for Ireland. Don't be alarmed.

[*The door opens and* MURPHY *comes in.*

MURPHY : Good evenin', sir.

PARNELL : Well, Murphy, how did it go ?

[MONTY *makes notes in his book.*

MURPHY : Very peaceful, sir. When I took me seat the old gentleman was speakin'. Pretty soon he thumps the table, so I thumps the bench and moves the Honourable Member be no longer heard, an' he says I'm suspended—an' I was. All very peaceful.

PARNELL : Good. Thank you, Murphy.

MURPHY : When I left Mr. Healy was on his feet. He'll be baptised and back agin before you can say Jack Robinson. (*Sits.*)

PARNELL : How are the lists coming on ?

MURPHY : We're nearly done, sir. Just a few things Mr. Healy has to ask you, sir. Sure it's wonderful, Mr. Parnell, all ye know about the members. It's afraid I am to read what's written under the name of Thomas Moonlight Murphy.

PARNELL : Turn to his name, Monty.

MURPHY (*hastily, scared*) : You needn't put yourself to that bother, Mr. Harrison.

MONTY (*turning the pages*): Here it is. (*Looks up.*) " To be trusted."

MURPHY (*smiles, then his face falls a little*): And is there any word about " Brains " ?

MONTY (*reading*): " Some brains—will learn." (*Puts down book.*)

[DAVITT *and* HEALY *come in from the corridor.*

HEALY (*crosses to former seat*): Twenty have been suspended already, Mr. Parnell.

PARNELL: About fifty more to come. It will take them all night.

HEALY (*sits. With a smile*): It will that.

PARNELL: Nice breathing spell for work.

DAVITT: Well—did you see the old man ? Did ye see Gladstone ?

PARNELL: No.

DAVITT (*indignantly*): What word did he send ye ?

PARNELL: None. I gather he's afraid to be seen with me publicly. Wants to be sure first what I can do for him. Well—I'm showing him.

DAVITT: He's the old spider.

PARNELL: But he'll not get any of my flies into his parlour unless——

DAVITT: There's no unless.

PARNELL (*lightly*): It's a very pretty parlour, Michael.

HEALY: I beg your pardon, Mr. Parnell. We've come to the name of O'Shea. You've nothing down for him.

PARNELL (*definitely*): No.

HEALY: He voted for you.

DAVITT (*at table*): If he did less he'd be out of his wits.

HEALY: He ought to have influence.

DAVITT: He ought to be in prison. They say he's a friend of Chamberlain's.

PARNELL: He can't be imprisoned for that.

DAVITT: Some have for less.

PARNELL: I know that, Michael.

MONTY (*breaking in quite casually*): You've accepted several dinner invitations from the O'Sheas, sir.

PARNELL: What !

MONTY: Oh, you've never gone, sir.

PARNELL: Not unless I walked in my sleep.

DAVITT: And might I ask who told you to accept anything from the O'Sheas ?

MONTY (*defensively*): I always accept invitations from the Party for Mr. Parnell. They know he won't come, but it pleases the women. They can say he accepted and was—prevented.

PARNELL: I hadn't thought of O'Shea as being in the Party yet.

DAVITT: He's not. He doesn't belong.

PARNELL: His vote does.

HEALY (*reading*): " O'Shea. Captain William Henry." (*There is a knock at the door.* MONTY *crosses to answer it.*) No comment. But he'll vote with the boys, I'm thinking.

DAVITT: Are ye now ?

USHER (*outside*): Someone to see Mr. Parnell.

DAVITT: He can't be seen. He's busy.

MONTY: Just a moment, please. (MONTY *crosses few steps into room.*) *Mrs.* William Henry O'Shea.

DAVITT: Speak of the devil——

HEALY: What can she want?

MURPHY: To invite him to dinner, " old top " !

MONTY: Do you want to see her, Mr. Parnell?

PARNELL: No. (MONTY *starts for door.*) Monty ! She's a friend of Gladstone's, isn't she?

MONTY: Yes, sir.

PARNELL (*crossing before* DAVITT *to R. end of table*): Will you ask Mrs. O'Shea to come in?

DAVITT: You're never going to see her, the wife of that——

PARNELL (*turning to* DAVITT): I don't often ask advice. When I do, I take it. Murphy and Mr. Healy, supposing you take the books into the next room.

[HEALY *exits.* MURPHY *rises.*

MURPHY: Yes. Mr. Parnell. I'd like to say, sir, when you wrote the words " Can be trusted " under Tom Murphy's name, ye were writing God's truth.

PARNELL (*with one of his grave smiles*): Thank you, Murphy.

[MURPHY *exits up L.*

DAVITT: Mr. Parnell—— (PARNELL *glares at him.*) Oh, very well. (DAVITT *exits up L.*)

[PARNELL *walks a few steps L. He has his back to the door.* MRS. O'SHEA *enters door R. She is wearing a white evening dress. Her cloak is white and she wears white roses.*

KATIE (*hesitating a moment*): Mr. Parnell?

[PARNELL *turns to her. For a moment they look at each other as people might in a dream.* PARNELL *crosses to her without speaking.*

PARNELL: Yes—and you?

KATIE: I sent in my card.

PARNELL (*he looks at her as though only by an effort of will could he look away*): *You* are—Mrs. O'Shea?

KATIE: Katharine O'Shea.

[PARNELL *holds out his hand almost mechanically, not the usual social gesture. She puts her hand in his.*

PARNELL: You——! (*She withdraws her hand.*) I—I beg your pardon. But I have seen you before—— You were with some people in a carriage in Palace Yard. You were wearing those roses. Do you remember?

KATIE: Yes.

PARNELL: The other night, too, in the lobby. There was a crowd and I lost you. Then to-night—while I was speaking—you came into the gallery.

KATIE: Yes. (*Then turning toward him in surprise*) You can't see into the gallery from the floor of the House.

PARNELL: No—but I knew. I was speaking and suddenly—I knew you were there. Don't think me mad.

KATIE: You are a little—aren't you?

PARNELL: Perhaps. Do you always wear white roses?

KATIE: They only bloom at this time of year.

PARNELL: I shall have them grown all the year round for you.

KATIE: Mr. Parnell——

PARNELL: I have been trying to find out for days who you were.

KATIE: Couldn't you? I'm not at all mysterious.

PARNELL: I found it difficult.—Could you tell me the name of a woman with dark hair—grey eyes—— (*He can only look into them.*) Wearing white roses. (*He breaks off.*) I found it difficult.

KATIE (*summoning resolution*): Mr. Parnell, you are quite mad——

PARNELL: Yes, if you like.

KATIE: I think I had better go. (*She turns to go.*)

PARNELL: Don't go—please—have I offended you? I swear I won't again. I can be quite sane. You'll see I—— I'll talk about the weather.

KATIE: Good night.

PARNELL: Did you see the Irish suspensions?

KATIE: I saw yours.

PARNELL: Amusing—wasn't it?

KATIE: No—I wanted to kill Gladstone.

PARNELL: Did you? How kind of you! Don't, though. I hope he'll prove useful.

KATIE: I had a talk with him the other day. I met him with my beloved Mrs. Hamish. They are old friends. I asked him outright if he was a friend of yours—and of Ireland's. He said—— (*She pauses.*) At great length and with much elaboration—nothing at all.

PARNELL (*gaily*): He does it so well, too.

KATIE: Doesn't he?

PARNELL: In the House last night he made an impassioned speech—whether for or against us, God knows.

KATIE: How disappointing!

PARNELL: Oh, no. I told the Irish members to cheer loudly—so everyone thought he was for us.

KATIE (*eagerly, but with dread in her voice*): Oh, Mr. Parnell—I do hope *you* will never prove useful to him.

PARNELL: I assure you, if he does swallow me up, I shall be a very nasty mouthful.

KATIE: It has been suggested that I should invite——

PARNELL: Yes?

KATIE: It—it doesn't matter. Good night.

PARNELL (*crosses and takes her hand*): I shall see you again.

KATIE: No.

PARNELL: When shall I see you again?

KATIE: Mr. Parnell, my husband is one of the new members of your Party.

PARNELL: Yes, I know.

KATIE (*quietly*): I shall not see you again.

PARNELL (*levelly*): You know that is not true. It can never be true in this world.

KATIE: Don't.

PARNELL: I have known you always.

KATIE (*steadily*): We have met to-night—for the first time.

PARNELL: In a Committee Room of the House of Commons—but not for the first time.

KATIE: I should never have come here.

PARNELL: Why did you come?

KATIE (*pause*): It doesn't matter.

PARNELL: No—not now.

[KATIE *crosses to the door. He watches her quietly. He knows he has found her.*

KATIE: Good night. (KATIE *exits.*)

[PARNELL *stands looking after her.* DAVITT *enters door up L.*

DAVITT: Excuse me. She's gone?

PARNELL: Yes.

DAVITT: She didn't stay long.

PARNELL: No.

DAVITT: I don't suppose she asked you again for dinner.

PARNELL: No (*he crosses back to table, and sits in former seat*), but I'm going.

DAVITT: You're going?

PARNELL: If God lets me.

DAVITT: You're daft, I'm thinkin'.

PARNELL: I'm thinking so, too. (*He rings bell.*) Monty. (MONTY *enters door R.*)

CURTAIN

SCENE III

SCENE: *Drawing-room at Eltham.*

   A lamp is burning. The stage is empty. Laughter is heard from across the hall. KATIE *enters from door on R., goes up to the French windows and flings them open. Walks across to the fireplace.* O'SHEA *enters.*

O'SHEA: Well, Katie!

KATIE: Was everything as you liked it?

O'SHEA: Yes. Your dinners are always perfect, Mrs. O'Shea.

KATIE: I'm glad this one was. Cook has been in a trance for days at the prospect, and Phyllis and Delia are both struck dumb with joy at being in the actual *presence*.

O'SHEA: Is that what's the matter with you?

KATIE: Why? Was I dumb?

O'SHEA: Yes. What's wrong with you? You can be gay enough when you want to be. Not a word to say for yourself. What's the matter? Doesn't he pay you enough compliments? Well —he's interested, I can tell you that. Why did you clear out?

KATIE: It's usual to leave the gentlemen to their wine, isn't it?

O'SHEA: Don't make stupid evasions. I begged you to stay. We all did; but no, you swept out like a Siddons.

KATIE: You asked me to entertain Mr. Parnell as part of your political programme. Well, I have. If the result is not as you hoped, I'm sorry, but I can't help it.

O'SHEA: Oh, so far so good, Katie. But do try to take an interest. We must see more of him.

[PHYLLIS *enters.*

KATIE: Don't you think you should return to your guests?

O'SHEA: Not a bad idea. (O'SHEA *exits.*)

[KATIE *sits down at the piano and begins to play the "Londonderry Air."* PHYLLIS *crosses to draw curtains on window up* L., *after putting down decanter and glasses on table behind settee down* R.

KATIE: Don't draw the curtains, Phyllis.

PHYLLIS: Yes, ma'am; but it's dark outside.

KATIE: Is the twilight all gone?

PHYLLIS (*crosses to* R. *window*): It's dark as hope, and the moon not up till late.

KATIE: Very well. (PHYLLIS *pulls the curtains. She crosses to* R. *door.*) Dinner was nice, Phyllis. Please tell cook.

PHYLLIS: Yes, ma'am. I never thought to see the day I'd wait on Mr. Parnell. Delia and me is both writin' home about it. Delia's doin' the writin' for us both, mine bein' what it is. That is unless—— (*Closer*) You'll excuse me, ma'am——

KATIE: What is it, Phyllis?

PHYLLIS: I thought, ma'am—if it wouldn't be

F

puttin' ye to too much trouble—— It's yourself might be afther writin' to me mither for me
—makin' the letters very plain, please, ma'am
—as it's Mr. Parnell I'm tellin' her about.

KATIE: Is your mother one of Mr. Parnell's
admirers?

PHYLLIS: It's to worship the ground he walks
on, she does. Sure, he's the uncrowned king of
Ireland. And if you'll be afther makin' the
letters very plain. Delia's writin' is not what
she thinks it is, if you're askin' me.

KATIE: I'll make them very plain, Phyllis.

PHYLLIS: Thank you, ma'am. (*She crosses down
R. to sofa.* PARNELL *enters.* KATIE *stops playing.*)

PARNELL: Don't stop.

KATIE: Phyllis, will you tell Captain O'Shea
and the O'Gorman Mahon that I should be
glad to see them in the drawing-room?

PHYLLIS: Yes, ma'am.

KATIE: I think a game of whist might be
pleasant—will you tell the Captain?

PHYLLIS: Yes, ma'am. (PHYLLIS *exits.*)

PARNELL: Why did you stop? Please go on.

KATIE (*rises*): It's too sad.

PARNELL: A wail for the dead?

KATIE: Don't say that. It's a bad omen.

PARNELL: Do you believe in omens?

KATIE: Do you?

PARNELL: Yes.

KATIE: They can't have any influence—really.
They can't change things.

PARNELL: Nothing can change Fate.

KATIE: They can point to it?

PARNELL: The Ides of March, you know.

KATIE: I don't believe in destiny—or predestined Fate.

PARNELL: Yet you try to escape it. You wouldn't drive with me yesterday. Why?

KATIE (*crosses to settee down R.*): I had another engagement.

PARNELL (*following down*): You're avoiding me.

KATIE: That's absurd.

PARNELL: Is it?

KATIE: Why should I avoid you?

PARNELL: Shall I tell you?

KATIE: No.

PARNELL: Then will you tell me why you wouldn't drive with me?

KATIE: The reason's obvious, isn't it?

PARNELL: You didn't care to?

KATIE: Is that obvious? I should have said that was merely conventional.

PARNELL: Do conventions mean so much to you?

KATIE: They mean nothing at all to me. But they do to other people. I hoped you wouldn't come here to-night.

PARNELL: You knew that I would.

KATIE: I hoped that you would see that it was——

PARNELL: Unwise? Oh, yes—I saw that— perfectly—with my House of Commons vision.

KATIE: And yet—you came.

PARNELL: There is another vision. It only comes once—sometimes never—that moment when the heavens open—and there is light. I've seen it.

KATIE: Don't.

PARNELL (*sits in chair*): Can we not at least be honest with each other?

KATIE: No.

PARNELL: I will have nothing else.

KATIE: Very well, then. He may not know it himself, but I imagine Willie invited you here to-night hoping that you would find me attractive. Attractive enough to pull down some political plums into Willie's mouth. It was a trap—and you've fallen into it.

PARNELL: Not fallen—jumped. O'Shea is fairly transparent. But what has that to do with you and me?

O'GORMAN (*from outside*): When I was in France they used to tell me I was the only man who knew where and when to finesse.

[*The door opens and* O'SHEA *and* O'GORMAN *come in.* PHYLLIS *follows and waits to see if she is wanted further.*

O'SHEA: Now, General, here's a chance to prove your game.

O'GORMAN: How much a point?

O'SHEA: Shall we play in the library? It's cosier.

O'GORMAN: And a shorter reach for the glass, I'm thinking.

KATIE: In the library, please, Phyllis.

PHYLLIS: Yes, ma'am. (PHYLLIS *goes out.*)

PARNELL (*smiling*): I'm very sorry, but I've never played a hand in my life.

O'SHEA (*staring at* KATIE): A joke of Katie's, perhaps.

KATIE: I beg your pardon. I—misunderstood Mr. Parnell.

O'SHEA: Quite so. A chat will be pleasanter all round, I think. Will you sit here, General?

PARNELL (*rises*): It is getting late. I must say good night.

O'GORMAN: Sure the shank of the evenin's still to come.

PARNELL: I speak in the House to-morrow, and still have some preparations to make.

O'SHEA: Mr. Parnell, will Ireland ever really get a Parliament?

PARNELL: Yes. Sooner or later.

KATIE: If anything happened to you, it would be later. Perhaps too late.

PARNELL: Perhaps, but it is already written.

KATIE: Not yet. We are writing it now.

PARNELL: The book is shut.

O'GORMAN: Faith, I'd like to look ahead a page or two. It's a bomb I'd put under old Gladstone and all his shilly-shally-shenanigan—off again— on again—gone again Finnegan.

O'SHEA: He's a hard one to pin down.

PARNELL: I'll pin him down or——

O'SHEA (*too eagerly*): Or what?

PARNELL: Or—I won't——

O'SHEA: What does he say?

PARNELL: Nothing. I can't reach him.

O'SHEA: I know one who could.

O'GORMAN: Is it yourself you're meanin', Willie?

O'SHEA: I'm not pious enough for that old bird. But Katie—he dotes on Katie.

KATIE: Oh, no. I'm not pious either, Willie.

O'SHEA: He hasn't found that out yet. Katie's your bet, Mr. Parnell.

PARNELL (*to* KATIE): Will you, Mrs. O'Shea?

KATIE: I know nothing of politics.

PARNELL: I need someone whose discretion is absolute. Someone I can trust.

KATIE: Can you trust me?

PARNELL: Utterly.

O'GORMAN: With such a teacher as Mr. Parnell, you will go far. We ought to be goin'. We're for ever catching boats or trains.

O'SHEA (*looking at his watch*): We have just time to catch the last one.

PARNELL: Sorry my trap only holds two.

O'SHEA: So you drove down?

PARNELL: I dislike trains.

O'SHEA: Will you allow me to make my excuses and leave first, Mr. Parnell?

[KATIE *rises, crosses up.*

PARNELL: Certainly.

O'SHEA: You were very good to come to us for so informal an evening.

PARNELL: Not at all. I go nowhere for formal ones.

O'SHEA: Good night. I shall see you to-morrow at the House.

PARNELL: Good night, and thank you.

KATIE (*to* O'GORMAN): Good night, General.

O'GORMAN: Good night, Mrs. O'Shea. A delightful evening. I kiss your hand.

KATIE: Perhaps Mr. Parnell would drive you up to London, even if he hasn't room for Willie.

O'GORMAN: County Clare sticks together. I'll

not be desertin' Willie. (*Crosses to* PARNELL) Good night to ye, Mr. Parnell.

[O'GORMAN *exits.*

O'SHEA: Good night, Katie. Good night, Parnell. See you to-morrow. (O'SHEA *exits.*)

PARNELL: I bless their departure. (*Crosses a step to her.*)

KATIE: Please go.

PARNELL: Are you afraid of the truth? I love you.

KATIE: No—no, it's not true.

PARNELL: I love you.

KATIE: You shall not say it. I ask you not to.

PARNELL: A man sees a woman for a moment— and he loves her. Is there anything more to be said?

KATIE: So much.

PARNELL: What?

KATIE: Ireland. Will she live or die?

PARNELL: Ireland will live. My part in her life is settled. I love you. That is settled too. I'm not asking you to start a flirtation, or even an affair. I want you before the world—my wife.

KATIE: You would have no world.

PARNELL: You're not living with O'Shea—all London knows that. He will divorce you.

KATIE: I'm—I'm afraid not. Don't you suppose I have begged for a divorce? But if he should —then what of you? The Irish Messiah married to a divorced woman. . . .

PARNELL: You are free—— You are living apart——

KATIE: Oh, don't under-estimate facts. Every peasant from Ulster to Galway would be told that you had stolen his wife. They would weep with him and turn on you and curse you.

PARNELL: All you say may be true—but it doesn't matter.

KATIE: Don't.

PARNELL: My darling, you are coming with me.

KATIE: No.

PARNELL: That night when I first saw you, and the scent of the roses you wore swept over me—from that moment you were in my arms, my lips on yours. I knew I would never let you go. You are so beautiful—so beautiful. (*Taking her in his arms*) I love you. (*Kisses her.*)

KATIE: I should break your life.

PARNELL: Then it's already broken.

KATIE: Your life, for a passing moment, a woman——

PARNELL: The scent of a rose. Oh, my sweet—my sweet—can you leave me now? (*Kiss.*)

KATIE (*on his shoulder*): Don't let me go. Never let me go.

PARNELL: You will come with me?

KATIE: I can't—because I love you—but I can't let you go. You must come to me. Oh, my darling, will you come to me?

PARNELL: I shall come where you are—always.

CURTAIN

ACT II

SCENE: *The drawing-room at Eltham, 1886. A woman's writing-table and also a large desk-table have been added to the room. Both are littered with documents, blue books, etc.*

MONTAGU HARRISON *is at the desk sorting letters.* ANNA STEELE *is sitting on the sofa, knitting.*

ANNA: It is pleasant to work in the country, is it not, Mr. Harrison?

MONTY: Yes, Mrs. Steele.

ANNA: Mr. Parnell seems to find it so, doesn't he?

[MONTY *takes no notice.* MRS. HAMISH *enters from library.*

AUNT CAROLINE: Oh, I forgot you were working here, Monty. Shall I be disturbing you?

MONTY: Not at all, Mrs. Hamish. Please stay.

AUNT CAROLINE: You are quite sure we shall not be interrupting your work?

MONTY: No, thank you. I am working in my office this afternoon.

ANNA (*glancing at the larger desk*): And we shall not be keeping Mr. Parnell from his desk?

MONTY: Mr. Parnell is in town this afternoon.

ANNA: Ah! I saw him this morning taking his usual canter. He is keeping his horses here now, isn't he?

MONTY (*briefly*): Yes.

ANNA: He keeps himself fit in spite of the pressure of political life. So wise!

MONTY: If you will excuse me, I shall get back to my work. (*Crosses to the door.*)

ANNA: You must be very busy. Fancy being secretary to the man who made Gladstone Prime Minister. Something to remember all one's life.

MONTY: Yes. Excuse me. (*He bows and goes out.*)

ANNA: Nice, chatty boy.

AUNT CAROLINE: You didn't expect him to burst into confidences, did you? Your methods are so obvious, Anna. To lure political secrets requires finesse—not a frontal attack.

ANNA: I am not interested in political secrets.

AUNT CAROLINE: Nor am I.

ANNA: But I am interested in other aspects of this affair which are neither political nor secret.

AUNT CAROLINE: Anna, will you be kind enough to open a window? This room seems warm. (ANNA *crosses to open a window.*) Fancy a fire on a day like this.

ANNA: Mr. Parnell, no doubt, likes warm rooms.

AUNT CAROLINE: And will you oblige me by not making any further allusions to Mr. Parnell? I am tired of the subject.

ANNA: So am I.

AUNT CAROLINE: You have a strange way of showing it.

ANNA: Tired of the whispers—the underground rumours——

AUNT CAROLINE (*shutting her up*): Very unusual weather for March. I can scarcely remember a season like it.

ANNA: Oh, Aunt Caroline, why will you always put me off?

AUNT CAROLINE: The state of the weather is of great interest to me, Anna. I can only get out when it is fine.

ANNA: I should think what people are saying about Katie would be of interest to you.

AUNT CAROLINE: Not in the least.

ANNA: It is some time since you were last here. Doubtless rumours have not reached you. But you will have to hear it—sooner or later, and I feel that I should prepare you.

AUNT CAROLINE: You need not trouble yourself. I am in full possession of my wits, though aged.

ANNA: Parnell practically lives here.

AUNT CAROLINE: At Willie's invitation—as Willie's guest.

ANNA: They have pulled the wool over Willie's eyes, too. Can't you see? Why, you have only to look at them together. . . .

AUNT CAROLINE: I have heard enough.

ANNA: You have heard nothing because you won't. Not just London, but all Ireland, is seething with it. What would happen if it came to dear Aunt Ben's ears I tremble to think.

AUNT CAROLINE: I tell you I have heard enough.

ANNA: And I tell you I insist on speaking to Katie. Where is she? She has become most elusive. I have been here two days, and not one occasion have I had to speak to her like an elder sister.

[KATIE *enters, followed by* PHYLLIS, *who is carrying a black bag.*

KATIE: Oh, you are in here. Phyllis, will you put that bag on Mr. Parnell's desk, please. (*After a pause.*) I have just been cutting out the leaders on Mr. Parnell's last speech.

AUNT CAROLINE: The papers are full of it.

KATIE : Wasn't it wonderful ? Wasn't he wonderful, I mean ? Yes, that was a hostile audience at first, too. Do you know, he has a way when the odds are against him, of throwing back his head, and straightening his shoulders. Monty tells me the boys at Headquarters call it " shoot and be damned."

ANNA : Asking for trouble. I wonder he has time to bother with Home Rule for the Irish, with his many duties here.

KATIE : Mr. Parnell came here, Anna, at Willie's request, after his serious illness nine months ago. We thought that the country would be better for him, and that he needed personal attention.

ANNA : I am sure he got it. It was something to do with his heart, no doubt.

KATIE : Yes.

ANNA : You hear it on all sides.

AUNT CAROLINE : Be quiet.

KATIE (crossing to desk down R.) : Let her speak, Aunt Caroline. She's been bursting with it for days.

ANNA : I am not the only one, I can tell you. Do you suppose others have not commented on Mr. Parnell's prolonged visits to Eltham these last few months ?

KATIE : You are forgetting that Willie and I are also working with Mr. Parnell politically. Everyone knows that. Willie has just been re-elected to Parliament through Mr. Parnell's influence.

ANNA : And would you like to hear what Ireland has to say about that ? What they are openly shouting at political meetings ? Did you think you could have this man here most of the time—why, he is even stabling his horses here, all the village knows that—yet you dare to sit there and tell me that he is nothing to you?

KATIE: I am not obliged to tell you anything, Anna. I am not accountable to you.

ANNA: You can hedge if you want to, but you can't fool me. I am not a child——

AUNT CAROLINE: No, indeed.

ANNA: —or a doting old woman.

KATIE (*rising*): How dare you!

ANNA: I don't pretend to be the favourite here. Oh, dear, no—but I have never brought scandal on the family name——

AUNT CAROLINE (*rising*): No. You have been more than discreet, Anna, whether from choice or necessity, I am not prepared to say. But since you seem so anxious to shake from your skirts the contaminating dust of this house perhaps you had better go.

ANNA: Certainly. I have no desire to stay here a day longer.

AUNT CAROLINE: And as you are so particular about dust, perhaps you will not find it necessary to visit Katie quite so often.

ANNA: Aunt Caroline!

AUNT CAROLINE: Oblige me by asking Morton to pack your boxes as quickly as possible. Good-bye.

ANNA: I might have known this would happen.

AUNT CAROLINE: Yes, the wicked flourish, Anna. That always seemed to surprise King David too. Good-bye.

ANNA (*to* KATIE): I hope you are satisfied. (*She goes out.* AUNT CAROLINE *sits.*)

KATIE: Oh, Aunt Caroline, I am sorry. I am sorry this happened.

AUNT CAROLINE: I have seen it coming. No one can stop Anna once her tongue begins to clack. It is all a pack of lies.

KATIE: Aunt Caroline—it's all true.

AUNT CAROLINE: I have known that for a long time, my dear.

KATIE: You have known? Oh, Aunt Caroline, Aunt Caroline! (*She flings herself on her knees beside* AUNT CAROLINE.)

AUNT CAROLINE (*sighs, then after a pause*): I told you that the wind outside would blow plenty of stones and dirt.

KATIE: Yes.

AUNT CAROLINE: I hope that the smell of earth and sea makes up for it. Does it?

KATIE (*with a radiant smile*): Yes.

AUNT CAROLINE: Katie—I'm afraid—for you.

KATIE: You mean because of Willie. I know. But he's been indifferent up till now. He doesn't know; I believe that he doesn't know, and in a little while he won't matter. Charles and I are going away.

AUNT CAROLINE: In the next world, thank God, there will be neither marrying nor giving in marriage. The Lord Himself sees that it is a mistake. Well, well, well. I suppose I must see that the sun doesn't go down upon poor Anna's wrath. (*She moves toward the door.*) But not enough to make her change her mind about leaving.

[*There is a knock at the door.*

KATIE: Come in.

MONTY (*entering*): I am so sorry, Mrs. O'Shea, but this telegram has just come for you.

KATIE (*taking the envelope and tearing it open*): Thank you. Excuse me, Aunt Caroline. It's from Willie ! He is coming down here this afternoon.

MONTY : Mr. Parnell had a message from him too. Captain O'Shea crossed from Ireland last night.

AUNT CAROLINE : I hear he's been re-elected.

KATIE : By a small majority, unfortunately.

MONTY : But Mr. Parnell got him in. Did you know, the other night after the sitting, there was an Irishman waiting to kill him ?

KATIE : To kill Willie ?

AUNT CAROLINE (*without emphasis*) : Who stopped him ? (*She exits.*)

MONTY : Nobody. He was too drunk to kill anyone. He said the Captain had mocked him.

KATIE : Monty, I am going to ask you something, and I want a straight answer, please.

MONTY : Yes ?

KATIE : Was there any trouble at the last Election ?

MONTY : Did you ever hear of a peaceful Irish Election ?

KATIE : No, I didn't mean that. I meant special trouble—about—Captain O'Shea.

MONTY (*evading*) : Well, you know how unpopular he is in Ireland.

KATIE : I am not going to get that straight answer, am I ?

MONTY : Well . . .

KATIE : Oh, never mind. It doesn't matter. I am being awkward. Has the post come yet ?

MONTY : I put the letters on the desk.

KATIE : Thank you.

[Monty *exits*. Katie *crosses up to* Parnell's *desk, and begins to look through two heaps of letters.* Parnell *enters through window from the garden.*

Parnell (*kissing her*) : Queenie !

Katie : Husband ! (*They kiss.*) What brings you home so early—a guilty conscience ?

Parnell : A what ?

Katie (*pointing to the black bag*) : Now, don't try to look injured. I am seriously annoyed.

Parnell : Where did you find it ?

Katie : Where you hid it.

Parnell : You shouldn't pry.

Katie : Why didn't you take it with you ?

Parnell : Because, my beloved, the papers feared that it might contain dynamite to blow up the Liberals, should they fail to support Home Rule. I didn't want to worry them.

Katie : This is no joke. What is the use of going to a doctor if you won't obey him ?

Parnell : He never mentioned black bags.

Katie : But he did mention dry boots. Sir Harvey Wilson warned you . . .

Parnell : I cannot see the connection between a heart attack, and getting one's feet wet.

Katie : He said that when you caught cold, it affected your heart.

Parnell : So I have to carry dry boots wherever I go. Ridiculous.

Katie : It wasn't so ridiculous a year ago when you were so shockingly ill. (*Crosses to him.*) My darling, do we have to go over this all over again ? Will you promise me always to take them with you ? And if you won't do it for me, will you do it for Ireland ? And if you won't do it for Ireland, will you do it for me ? And if you won't do it for either of us, will you move out of my house ?

PARNELL : I don't want to move—so I promise.

KATIE : Sweet. (*She kisses him.*)

PARNELL : You know, darling, only two things affect my heart—Home Rule and Katie.

KATIE (*crossing to sofa*) : Darling, I am so glad you are back.

PARNELL (*follows, and sits on the sofa beside her*) : Anything wrong ?

KATIE : No. Just glad. Why are you home so early ? Did you talk with Mr. Gladstone ?

PARNELL : Yes, Katie. There can be little doubt now that he is converted.

KATIE : To Home Rule ? Darling !

PARNELL : What remains to be seen is what *his* Home Rule Bill will be like. However—he has promised to introduce the first reading this session.

KATIE : And I am the first to know !

PARNELL : Oh, no ! I couldn't keep a secret like that. I told the butler as I came out, and the policeman who was on point duty. They were delighted, and sent you their love. Darling, I could never have done it without your help. The Old Spider said as much to-day. He spoke of your " invaluable services." And, he has invited us all down to Hawarden, too.

KATIE : Me ?

PARNELL (*quickly*) : Why not ?

KATIE : Well—of course he knows—he must know—about—us. Or, doesn't he ? Anyhow, it is rather nice of him.

PARNELL : Nice ! God !

KATIE: Oh, very well, darling. He'll probably put down a red carpet for me. Think of it—to Hawarden ! At any rate, this means he is going through with it, doesn't it ?

PARNELL: I suppose so.

KATIE: Even Gladstone would hardly arrange a house party, unless . . .

PARNELL: Somehow I have the feeling that he is—waiting . . .

KATIE: For what ?

PARNELL: To find the Ace of Trumps up his sleeve. I don't mind his finding the Ace of Trumps up his sleeve, if only he wouldn't proclaim that God Almighty put it there.

KATIE (*with a little laugh*): Did he congratulate you on your speech ?

PARNELL: Soft soap.

KATIE: You were wonderful.

PARNELL: Was I ?

KATIE (*quoting*): " The British Government has wept over the sorrows of the Bulgars—will it never weep for the starving agony of Ireland ? " —that was fine ! (*She breaks off, smiling.*)

PARNELL: He was chief mourner for the Bulgars too. Rather decent of him to congratulate me.

KATIE: I was so proud of you.

PARNELL: I had one terrible moment, Katie. Complete panic.

KATIE (*softly*): Yes, I know you did.

PARNELL: I couldn't find you in the crowd. I thought, " If I never find her." Utterly foolish, I know. Then your eyes looked into mine, and I could go on. I love you so. I wish I could find a new way of saying it.

KATIE: I shouldn't like a new way. I should simply hate it.

PARNELL: Katie—as soon as Home Rule is safe——

KATIE: It is safe, darling.

PARNELL: Then—you and I together—no more fencing, no more evasions—just you and I——

KATIE: Where there's sunshine !

PARNELL: We shall soak in it.

KATIE: Italy—or Spain.

PARNELL: Algiers—or Carcassonne. Soon— soon. (*He takes her in his arms and kisses her.*)

KATIE: Oh, God, give us that day !

PARNELL: And millions more.

KATIE: No, not millions. I should be tottering, and horrible to look upon by then.

PARNELL: I don't insist on having them all in this world.

KATIE: It is the only one we're sure of.

PARNELL (*romantic*): Don't be so local, darling ! There are æons and æons of worlds. With you in each one.

KATIE: " Æons "—no, that's a lonely word.

PARNELL: Not if you are there. (*There is a knock at the door.* PARNELL *kisses and releases her.*) Come in.

[*It is* MONTY, *and he is obviously worried.*

MONTY: Oh, I didn't know you were back, sir. But—Michael Davitt is here.

PARNELL (*absolutely still*): What ?

MONTY: I gave him no appointment, Mr. Parnell.

PARNELL: Send him away. You know I never see the Party here.

MONTY: Yes, sir—but he seems a good deal upset. (*He and* KATIE *exchange a look.*)

KATIE: Perhaps you'd better see him.

PARNELL: Certainly not.

KATIE (*anxiously*): Michael Davitt would never have come down here unless his business were urgent. Won't you see him?

PARNELL: No.

KATIE (*in a little rush of emotion*): Please.

PARNELL (*after a pause*): Monty—you may ask him to come in. (MONTY *goes.* PARNELL *turns to* KATIE.) What is it?

KATIE (*crosses to him. Hurriedly*): Anna made a scene this afternoon.

PARNELL: A scene?

KATIE: She said all Ireland was talking about you and me.

PARNELL: I am sorry you had to know.

KATIE: It's true then. Is that why you went to Ireland?

PARNELL: Yes. Healy and Davitt refused to support O'Shea. I forced him down their throats.

KATIE: Willie's coming down to see you this afternoon, too. I have just had a telegram.

PARNELL (*reads it, folds it, and hands it back to* KATIE. *Definitely*): I'm done with him, Katie.

KATIE: Darling, do be careful.

PARNELL: I ran him for Galway because you begged it of me.

KATIE: Yes, I know. Willie is ambitious. I was afraid.

PARNELL: He can never again say that I have

promised and not performed. But there comes
an end to all things, and I have done with
him.

KATIE: Whatever you do, don't anger him.

MONTY (*entering*): Mr. Michael Davitt.

[DAVITT *is ill at ease. Strides in—awkward before*
KATIE, *he stands twirling his hat.*

PARNELL: Come in, Michael. You know Mrs.
O'Shea. (MONTY *exits, shutting the door.*)

KATIE (*crossing to him*): How do you do, Mr.
Davitt ? (*She holds out her hand to him, but he does
not take it.*)

DAVITT: Your servant, ma'am.

KATIE: I hope you'll ask Mr. Davitt to stay to
tea, Charles.

DAVITT: Thank you kindly, ma'am, but I'll be
going.

KATIE: I am sorry. Good afternoon, then.

DAVITT: Good afternoon, ma'am.

KATIE (*to* PARNELL): I shall be in the study,
dear, if you want me.

[*She goes out. The two men look at each other for a
moment.* MICHAEL'S *face is distressed yet stubbornly
obstinate.*

PARNELL (*coldly*): Well ? I suppose you have
good reason for coming down here.

DAVITT: I have that.

PARNELL: Entirely against orders.

DAVITT (*anxiously*): Mr. Parnell, haven't I
always obeyed orders ?

PARNELL: Yes.

DAVITT: Didn't I obey orders in this last
election when I'd sooner cut my hand off ?

PARNELL: You were absolutely loyal, Michael.

DAVITT: And so I am now, but I have come to tell you there will be no more obeying orders if—what is going on isn't brought to an end.

PARNELL (*rises. His eyes blazing*): What do you mean?

DAVITT (*doggedly*): I mean if there's any more favours going to Captain O'Shea.

PARNELL: That is for me to say.

DAVITT (*pleadingly*): I know that. All I ask is that you hear me before it comes to the saying.

PARNELL: Go on.

DAVITT: You know what they're saying. You know what they were like. We have got things calmed down now—but you faced the mob when you got off the train at Galway.

PARNELL: Mob? They were very mild.

DAVITT: But before you came they had sticks and stones—and they meant to use them. They let out such a roar when they saw you there, quiet and smiling, I thought they meant to kill you. But thank God they were only cheering. But it can't be done again. I have come here in love and loyalty to tell you it can't be done again. It's not just the voters. It's the boys at headquarters. Oh, Mr. Parnell—for the sake of the Party—for the sake of Ireland—I tell you the bridge will not stand another load.

PARNELL: Michael, Home Rule is here. To-day Mr. Gladstone told me he would move the first reading of the Bill this session.

DAVITT: Thank God.

PARNELL: Mrs. O'Shea carries my views to Gladstone, and his to me. Neither of us would have trusted them to paper. Now he is arranging a house party at Hawarden to celebrate our

Irish Party in the recent Election it would seem that we are in for a time of peace and quiet. However (*rising and pacing about*), I find the temper of the people to be exactly the opposite. You will perhaps pardon me if I suggest to you " . . . It won't do any good, Katie.

KATIE (*looking up*): Go on. (*Taking his hand*) Go on. " If I suggest to you——"

PARNELL (*dictating*): No. " If I once more emphasise the fact that the immediate introduction of the Home Rule Bill might have a calming effect, not only upon the members of the Irish Party, but on the people as a whole."

[*His voice trails off, and* KATIE *stops writing.*

CURTAIN

SCENE II

SCENE: *The drawing-room at Eltham.*

WILLIE O'SHEA *alone. His nerves are at tension. He paces up and down. Pauses at the table, opens a book, puts it down again. Walks to the fire and stands with his back to the room when the door opens and* AUNT CAROLINE *enters. He turns round, startled. Everyone in this scene is in deep mourning with the exception of* BRIDGET.

O'SHEA: Aunt Caroline !

AUNT CAROLINE (*crossing to chair and sitting down*): You didn't expect to see me, did you, Willie ?

O'SHEA: Well, I did—rather.

AUNT CAROLINE: You tried to hope against hope ?

O'SHEA: I came to see Katie, of course.

AUNT CAROLINE: You'll see her. Have you rung for whiskey?

O'SHEA: There's some on the table, thanks. (*Crosses to table.*) I own I could do with a spot. (*Pours one for himself.*)

AUNT CAROLINE: I could myself. These last few days have not been easy.

O'SHEA (*pouring her a drink*): May I?

AUNT CAROLINE: No, thank you. I'll compromise on brandy. (*He crosses to her with a glass.*) Thank you.

O'SHEA: Aunt Caroline, is there any truth in this rumour that Katie means to fight the divorce?

AUNT CAROLINE: Why shouldn't she?

O'SHEA: Why, she can't. She hasn't got a leg to stand on.

AUNT CAROLINE: Really?

O'SHEA: She has begged for a divorce often enough.

AUNT CAROLINE: But you wouldn't give it to her—now—she has changed her mind.

O'SHEA: It's too late, I'm afraid. If only everyone didn't know of her relations with Parnell. That's what hurts me so desperately. Everybody!

AUNT CAROLINE: Quite so. Everybody! (*Giving him back her glass.*)

O'SHEA: Look here, Aunt Caroline, you're not suddenly turning against me after all these years, are you? What do you mean? You're not suggesting that I knew that Katie and Parnell . . .

AUNT CAROLINE: You are away so much, aren't you, Willie?

O'SHEA: Aunt Caroline, if you're shooting at me, I won't stand it even from you. My honour has been tarnished.

AUNT CAROLINE: The only person who has tarnished your honour, Willie, is yourself.

O'SHEA: I think you'll regret your attitude to me, Aunt Caroline.

AUNT CAROLINE: Well, if I don't have more than that to regret, the Lord is kind.

O'SHEA: May I see Katie?

AUNT CAROLINE: She will be down in a minute. What made you think she would defend the case, Willie?

O'SHEA: My solicitor told me. He said that she was naming Bridget co-respondent.

AUNT CAROLINE: Has Bridget heard this too?

O'SHEA: Yes. I told her.

AUNT CAROLINE: Dear! Dear! You're braver than I thought you were, Willie. (WILLIE *turns away impatiently. He has a vivid recollection of his interview with* BRIDGET.) How did she take it?

O'SHEA: She wasn't exactly pleased.

AUNT CAROLINE: So far Bridget has always been able to eat her cake and have it too.

O'SHEA: The thing is impossible. Katie can't accuse . . . one of her own circle of adultery! It's simply not done!

AUNT CAROLINE: There's nothing like establishing a precedent. Just why did you bring this suit for divorce?

O'SHEA: Why does any man? The usual reasons.

AUNT CAROLINE: I express myself badly. I mean, why did you choose this particular moment to become aware of the usual reasons?

O'SHEA: Aunt Caroline, I simply can't allow you to insinuate that this shocking . . . well, that this has been happening. Why, it's monstrous, intolerable ! Here is a man everyone looks up to for his integrity of character. I like him, and get on well with him. Then he comes down here——

AUNT CAROLINE: Under your very nose, Willie?

O'SHEA: Yes, of course, under my very nose. I trusted him. Staying under my roof——

AUNT CAROLINE: Your roof, Willie ?

O'SHEA: Oh, what does it matter whose roof ? In the world's eyes he was my guest; I was his host, and he calmly steals my wife.

AUNT CAROLINE: Did he steal anything that had not ceased to belong to you years ago, Willie ?

O'SHEA: Well—whose fault was that ?

AUNT CAROLINE: Yours, Willie. Be honest.

O'SHEA: Oh, I know the man always gets the blame for the wreck of a marriage.

AUNT CAROLINE: I'm afraid it is too late to talk about that now. Let us keep to the present facts. You naturally want to do what is best for yourself. Perhaps we might come to an agreement after all. The highest bidder usually wins, doesn't he ?

O'SHEA: Certainly not in the present circumstances. This is a matter of principle.

[*The door is opened by* PHYLLIS.

PHYLLIS (*announcing*) : Mrs. Blair and Mrs. Steele, ma'am.

[BRIDGET *and* ANNA *come in.* BRIDGET *sweeps by* O'SHEA *with a bare look, goes up to* AUNT CAROLINE *and kisses her.*

O'SHEA: Bridget !

BRIDGET: Aunt Caroline !

AUNT CAROLINE: How do you do, Bridget ? Phyllis, will you ask Mrs. O'Shea to come down ?

PHYLLIS: Yes, ma'am. (*She exits.*)

AUNT CAROLINE: I thought we should be seeing you. I did not foresee Anna, however.

ANNA: Naturally Bridget came straight to me for advice. I have come with her because I thought that under these shocking circumstances she needed——

AUNT CAROLINE: The support of virtue ? Quite so. Very prudent of you, Bridget. I should have foreseen, Anna.

ANNA: Aunt Caroline ! (*She flutters over to* WILLIE.) How do you do, Willie ?

O'SHEA: Rotten, thanks.

AUNT CAROLINE: Quite a family gathering.

ANNA: But regrettably different from the last occasion of our meeting.

AUNT CAROLINE: Oh, do you prefer funerals ?

ANNA: They at least are respectable. But dear Aunt Ben, God be praised, has been spared the knowledge of Katie's disgrace. Very fortunate for Katie.

AUNT CAROLINE: Regretting your discretion, Anna ?

ANNA: What do you mean ?

AUNT CAROLINE: Well, you are trying to tell us, are you not, that had you taken the trouble to enlighten Aunt Ben while she was with us, she would not have left Katie her fortune ? Is that it ?

G

ANNA: Of course not.

AUNT CAROLINE (*sweetly*): Do lay aside your wraps.

BRIDGET: No, thank you, Aunt Caroline.

ANNA: We can't stay long.

AUNT CAROLINE: Bridget, did you give orders for them to feed and water your horses?

BRIDGET: I sent the carriage to the inn in the village.

AUNT CAROLINE: As you please. But Mr. Parnell tells me the grooms there are exceedingly careless.

[*At the mention of* PARNELL'S *name they look at each other, and away. The door opens and* KATIE *comes in. She closes the door, keeping her face to the room, and for a moment she gives the impression of standing with her back to the wall.*

KATIE: How do you do, everybody? (*A pause.*) Well—who'll begin? I suppose you don't want to waste time enquiring how I am, or talking about the weather?

BRIDGET: Not in the least. I'll begin. Yesterday, Willie came to me with some cock-and-bull story that my name was to be dragged into this disgraceful mess you have got yourself into. I couldn't believe it, but decided to come down and find out. Is it true?

ANNA: I cannot believe it.

[AUNT CAROLINE *looks at* ANNA, *and she relapses into silence.*

O'SHEA: Bridget, I suggest that you let me talk to Katie first.

BRIDGET: You've done enough talking, I think.

O'SHEA: If you'll let me see her—alone—that's what I came down here for——

BRIDGET: I tell you, you and Katie have talked enough. Between you you are starting a hideous scandal, and I am to be the victim.

O'SHEA: If you'll only let me see her alone, I can arrange things. I can manage her.

KATIE: You always have, haven't you, Willie?

O'SHEA: Katie, you surely cannot mean to bring Bridget into this—you wouldn't——

BRIDGET (to KATIE): My name has never been dragged in the mud.

AUNT CAROLINE: You've been very lucky, Bridget.

BRIDGET: What do you mean?

AUNT CAROLINE: Lucky? Means favoured by chance.

BRIDGET: The fact remains, however, that my name has not been bandied about in the public prints.

O'SHEA: What about my name?

BRIDGET: Willie, for once forget yourself and think of someone else.

AUNT CAROLINE: Don't ask the impossible, Bridget.

BRIDGET (to KATIE): I have come here to find out the truth. Are you going to drag me into this?

ANNA: Katie—you wouldn't—you couldn't—— Remember who you are—think——

BRIDGET: Is it true?

ANNA (desperately, a squealing mouse): I am sure it isn't.

KATIE: It is perfectly true.

BRIDGET: Well—I won't have it. I won't be treated in this way. What have I ever done to you ? When I heard the talk about you and Parnell—what did I do ? Invited you to the Opera.

ANNA: But, Bridget, Mr. Parnell wouldn't go.

BRIDGET: Be quiet ! (*Crosses to* KATIE.) I didn't care. I was glad you were amusing yourself. It seemed more normal. You could have had an affair with a crossing-sweeper, and I would have——

KATIE: Invited him to the Opera ?

BRIDGET: I won't be treated in this way. You haven't the slightest shred of evidence against me——

O'SHEA: You have absolutely nothing to go on—— You can't prove a thing——

KATIE (*to* BRIDGET): Willie is your lover. Can you deny it ? (BRIDGET *turns away.*) You don't suppose I want to prove it, do you ? But I can. And unless Willie withdraws this suit, I shall.

ANNA: I never would have believed it.

AUNT CAROLINE: Oh, wouldn't you, Anna ?

ANNA (*with injured dignity*): I mean that Katie would do such a thing. I am shocked beyond words. (*Crossing to* KATIE) If you care anything for the family name—if you have the slightest consideration for——

KATIE: I care nothing for the family name—or for your name, Bridget—or for my own name —nothing at all.

BRIDGET (*stares at* KATIE *for a second. There is something here she is curious to understand. Then she turns to Willie*): You got me into this ! Now— you can get me out.

O'SHEA: What can I do ?

BRIDGET: You can withdraw your suit.

O'SHEA: Bridget—I—I can't.

BRIDGET: Can't?

O'SHEA: It's impossible. You don't understand.

BRIDGET: Oh, yes, I do. Quite. You kept silent as long as it suited you. Now it doesn't, God knows why. . . .

AUNT CAROLINE: It is not necessary to invoke the Deity, Bridget, to discover Willie's reasons.

BRIDGET: And you've decided to talk. You never dreamed Katie would talk back. You think now you can manage her, because you always have. You're wrong. Katie has her back to the wall, and Aunt Caroline is beside her. Perhaps you think you can fight Aunt Caroline.

AUNT CAROLINE: Ha!

BRIDGET: You haven't known her as long as I have. Take my advice, get out of this, and get out now.

O'SHEA: She is only trying to blacken us to save him. That's the size of it. But you can't do it, Katie. If you think you can explain away Parnell——

KATIE: I have no intention of explaining away Parnell. (ANNA and BRIDGET both stare at KATIE.)

O'SHEA: What are you going to do, then?

KATIE: I intend to explain you, Willie.

BRIDGET: Do you mean you're not going to deny your relations with that man? Is that what you are saying?

KATIE: Just that.

BRIDGET: You're a fool! You don't even play the game.

KATIE: I don't play your game, Bridget.

BRIDGET: Well, if you want to save your skin

alive you had better begin. I don't care in the least whom you flirt with—or sleep with—but for God's sake don't shriek it aloud in Piccadilly Circus.

ANNA: Oh ! This is becoming too painful ! Can't somebody stop it ?

KATIE: Yes, Willie.

O'SHEA: I tell you I can't. It's too late.

BRIDGET: Katie—I'm warning you——

AUNT CAROLINE: Bridget ! Don't you think the best thing for you to do is to return home, and let me talk to Willie ?

ANNA: You had better talk to Katie too, while you are about it.

AUNT CAROLINE (to BRIDGET): And take Anna with you.

BRIDGET: Yes, I shall go. Katie has lost her senses. Perhaps if we give her time she may get some of them back again. Come along, Anna.

ANNA: Good-bye, Aunt Caroline.

AUNT CAROLINE: Good-bye, Anna.

ANNA (to KATIE, on her way to the door): The innocent always suffer with the guilty.

AUNT CAROLINE: A little vicarious suffering won't hurt you, Anna. (Exit ANNA.)

BRIDGET: Aunt Caroline, if you have any influence over either of them, make them drop this. (To KATIE) If there is to be any public washing of dirty linen, you will be sorry to your dying day.

KATIE (slowly): Yes. If there is to be any public washing—I shall be sorry to my dying day.

[BRIDGET exits.

AUNT CAROLINE: You had better give it up, Willie.

KATIE: Now that you know that Bridget's name will be brought into this, surely you won't go on.

O'SHEA: You're afraid if this scandal breaks, Parnell will be ruined. You are quite right. He will. You are only using Bridget to frighten me off.

KATIE: Willie, for years I have begged you to let me go—to divorce me. Now, I beg you—I implore you—not to.

O'SHEA: How can I do anything but divorce you now?

AUNT CAROLINE: Katie, let me talk to him. Better give it up, Willie.

O'SHEA: Aunt Caroline, you are a wonderful woman. You should have been a man. By George, you would have cracked a whip, and given them hell.

AUNT CAROLINE: I can crack a pretty good whip as it is, Willie.

O'SHEA: Only I am not afraid of it. You can't prove anything against me, and you can't prove anything against Bridget. I know that well enough.

AUNT CAROLINE: Legal proof is difficult.

O'SHEA: I think you'll find it so.

AUNT CAROLINE: Merely a relative term, however.

O'SHEA: Well, whatever it is, you have to have it in a Court of Law. Suspicion is one thing, proof is another.

AUNT CAROLINE: How true. I suspected you and Bridget long before I had proof.

O'SHEA: Had—proof?

AUNT CAROLINE: Willie, you and Bridget and I have been guests at various country houses simultaneously. My maid, Morton—you remember her?—she will make an excellent witness. (*Pause.*) You had better give it up, Willie.

O'SHEA (*to* KATIE): You're going to sacrifice your own family to save him?

KATIE: Won't you ever understand? I will sacrifice anything to save him.

O'SHEA: You won't sacrifice me. I'll tell you that. I have never set myself up on a pedestal of leadership and virtue. I am sorry for Bridget, of course——

AUNT CAROLINE: Somehow I didn't think Bridget's sorrow would affect you sufficiently. (*Rises.*) Your own sorrows are what I am really counting on. When you see yourself as all England will see you—the *mari complaisant*—the consenting husband——

O'SHEA: It isn't true.

AUNT CAROLINE: The facts are against you, Willie.

O'SHEA: I can't help that.

AUNT CAROLINE: Posterity will not believe you.

O'SHEA: Whether it believe me or not I must stand by the present truth. I may have been a fool, but I have not been a villain.

AUNT CAROLINE: I warn you, Katie intends to defend the suit.

O'SHEA: You will never make out a case. I trusted my wife, and was deceived.

AUNT CAROLINE: You never dreamed that Parnell was your wife's lover?

O'SHEA: No.

AUNT CAROLINE: Even when London was agog?

O'SHEA: No.

AUNT CAROLINE: And when the papers began to hint at the story, even then, you still trusted—— ?

O'SHEA: Yes.

KATIE: Can you really mean that, Willie?

AUNT CAROLINE: Katie, please! Then, why, after an article appeared in a London paper, did you write a letter to Katie, begging her to be more careful about being seen in public so much with Mr. Parnell?

O'SHEA: I didn't.

AUNT CAROLINE: After that article appeared, you remember coming down here to see her?

O'SHEA: Yes.

AUNT CAROLINE: But she was out—so you wrote a note——

O'SHEA: Yes, by Jove, I did! I thought she was being a bit indiscreet. But I tore it up.

AUNT CAROLINE: And threw it in the wastepaper basket. Imprudent, Willie, very.

O'SHEA: But look here—you can't use a thing like that! You can't twist facts.

AUNT CAROLINE: Facts or necks, Willie! It's all the same to me! There's an easy way out, Willie.

O'SHEA: Easy?

AUNT CAROLINE: Withdraw the suit.

O'SHEA: My God, you think that's easy?

AUNT CAROLINE: Willie! Katie has offered to make you a substantial settlement. Ten thousand pounds.

O'SHEA: Aunt Caroline, for God's sake let us
keep our heads. I told you this is a matter of
principle. No one could withdraw a suit that's
gone as far as this one. If I did—then I should
look as if——

AUNT CAROLINE: Willie—on the day you withdraw your suit—we will give you twenty
thousand pounds !

O'SHEA: Aunt Caroline, I cannot tolerate these
insults even from you ! I am a man of honour.
Allow me to take my leave. (*He walks to the door.*)

KATIE: Don't you forget, Willie, I'll stop at
nothing. I will do anything—anything.

O'SHEA: Yes, so would I. The trouble is there
isn't anything to do—now.

[*He goes.*

KATIE (*after a long pause*): He's going through
with it, and so am I. To get even a part of the
truth known, I'd burn at the stake.

AUNT CAROLINE: This will be worse than the
stake, if I know anything about English divorce
courts. You might as well be stripped naked for
the crowd to spit on.

KATIE: Aunt Caroline, there is only one thing
that matters to me at all. Everything else—just
isn't there.

AUNT CAROLINE: Very well, my dear.

KATIE (*kneeling beside* AUNT CAROLINE): But it
will be dreadful for you. Oh, Aunt Caroline—
don't—don't stay in England.

AUNT CAROLINE: Katie—we have travelled a
long road together, since you used to bring me
wilted daisies and wet kisses. We won't part now.

[*The door opens and* PARNELL *comes in.*

PARNELL: What was O'Shea doing here ? I
passed him on the drive.

[KATIE *and* AUNT CAROLINE *rise.*

AUNT CAROLINE : I wanted to speak to him.

PARNELL : Was he disagreeable ?

AUNT CAROLINE : Oh, no. I'll claim that prize. I tried to force him to withdraw his suit.

PARNELL : And—is he going to ?

AUNT CAROLINE (*crossing to the door*) : No. But I think I have convinced him that Katie's defence——

PARNELL : Katie's defence ?

AUNT CAROLINE : Yes, it will be something more than he bargained for. (*She exits.*)

PARNELL (*crossing to* KATIE, *who turns into his arms*) : You're not going to defend the suit, Katie.

KATIE : I didn't tell you till I was sure that Willie meant to go on. I have engaged Counsel.

PARNELL : We are not going to defend the case, Katie.

KATIE : But we can prove that Willie and Bridget——

PARNELL : I know we can prove many things. So many that O'Shea will never get his divorce. What do you gain by that ?

KATIE : The truth. If people know the truth— oh, don't you see—you will not be blamed ?

PARNELL : And you will still be the wife of Willie O'Shea.

KATIE : You can't mean that you are going to stand by and do nothing while Willie ruins your life——

PARNELL : I have decided.

KATIE : This is political suicide, and you know it. You will be ruined.

PARNELL: There will be no defence.

KATIE: I won't consent. If you refuse to defend yourself—I shall——

PARNELL: I shall not even employ Counsel.

KATIE: I shall ! I shall have the best Counsel for the defence in London ! I shall tell the truth——

PARNELL: And be tied to Willie O'Shea for the rest of your life ?

KATIE: I have been for years—it will be no worse.

PARNELL: Won't it ? Willie coming to me for favours when we are friends is one thing. Willie —still your husband, after losing his divorce suit, is another. Do you think I'll leave you to him ? His physical property under the law ? (*Crosses to her. She cries on his shoulder. Tenderly*) Darling, isn't a divorce what we have always wanted ? Now it's come—and you weep.

KATIE: Not this way—not now.

PARNELL: Nothing comes the way you want it, or when you want it, but if you want it—enough —you take it. (KATIE *is sobbing.*) My sweet, don't—don't cry. Just because O'Shea wins his divorce doesn't mean that I am ruined. There will be some to stand by me.

KATIE: And will the Honourable William Ewart Gladstone be among them ?

PARNELL: When the Party sticks by me, he will. He'll have to. He knows that well enough.

KATIE: And will the Party stick ?

PARNELL: I think so.

KATIE: Oh, my darling—I am afraid.

PARNELL: Katie, look at me. Don't be afraid. We have no regrets, no fears, no remorse. We don't know the future—but in this instant, this present, I have you. It is enough.

KATIE: Is it? Is it enough? The work you've given your life for? Am I worth the bitterness of that?

PARNELL: Bitterness and sorrow are all no matter. Because there is no one else in the world that matters to me but you.

KATIE: The world? This brief moment—oh, my darling, so brief! And then, what? Shall I lose you?

PARNELL: No. Even in some other world—some other point in time—we two should be drawn together again by the sheer force of my longing for you.

CURTAIN

Scene: Mr. Gladstone's *study, 1 Carlton Gardens.*

(N.B.—Mr. Gladstone was at this time Leader of the Opposition.)

Large folding doors at the back which are closed. L., door leading to the hall. Long windows. R., Gladstone is seated at his desk writing. It is late afternoon in November, the lamps are already lighted. A young secretary, his name is Stanley, opens the door from the ante-room and comes in. He crosses and stands by Gladstone's side, waiting to be noticed.

Gladstone (*looking up after a moment*): Yes, Mr. Stanley?

Stanley: Mr. Timothy Healy is here, sir, by appointment.

Gladstone: Yes, yes. Quite so. (*He carefully lays down his pen, wipes it, then looks up.*) Mr. Stanley, will you be good enough to listen carefully. I have a few simple instructions which I wish you to understand before you show in Mr. Healy.

Stanley: Yes, Mr. Gladstone.

Gladstone: Thank you. Mr. Healy, I believe, has the appointment for four o'clock?

Stanley: Yes, sir. It is four minutes before four, sir, now, I think.

Gladstone (*looking at his watch*): Two and a half. I have an appointment with Mrs. Hamish and Mrs. O'Shea at a quarter past four?

Stanley: Yes, sir.

Gladstone: When they come they are to be shown into the library, not the ante-room, Mr. Stanley.

Stanley: Yes, sir.

GLADSTONE: And then, Mr. Stanley, as soon as they come, will you immediately let me know——

STANLEY: Interrupt you, sir?

GLADSTONE: Exactly. Interrupt me and then, contrary to our usual custom if other callers are present, will you announce their names?

STANLEY: Yes, sir.

GLADSTONE: And, Mr. Stanley, will you be good enough to announce their names in audible tones?

STANLEY: Yes, Mr. Gladstone.

GLADSTONE: This, too, is contrary to custom, your usual tones, even when spoken in my ear, being quite inaudible.

STANLEY: Yes, Mr. Gladstone.

GLADSTONE: You are sure you understand?

STANLEY: Yes, sir. When the ladies come I am to inform you of the fact in AUDIBLE tones.

GLADSTONE: Very good. You may ask Mr. Healy to come in now.

STANLEY: Yes, sir. (*He crosses, opens the door to the ante-room and we hear him say, just outside— softly*) Mr. Gladstone will see you, Mr. Healy.

[HEALY *enters followed by the* SECRETARY, *who closes the door behind him, crosses and goes out through the double doors to the library.*

GLADSTONE (*rises from his chair with hand out-stretched. He is beaming genially, though perhaps a trifle patronisingly*): My dear Mr. Healy (HEALY *crosses to* GLADSTONE, *who shakes hands with him*), how very good of you to come.

HEALY: Mr. Gladstone.

GLADSTONE: Will you smoke?

HEALY: Thank you, no, sir.

GLADSTONE: Do sit down, Mr. Healy. (HEALY *sits*.) One can so often arrive (GLADSTONE *sits*) at the solution of a problem if one can talk face to face.

HEALY: I can scarcely hope for such an outcome in the present instance, sir.

GLADSTONE: Why not, Mr. Healy?

HEALY: Mr. Gladstone, we want a direct answer to a direct question: whether the next election will be fought on Home Rule; and whether, in the event of a victory, Home Rule will be brought in—you promised the Irish Party——

GLADSTONE: Whatever I may have promised, I promised to Mr. Parnell.

HEALY: He *is* the Irish Party, Mr. Gladstone.

GLADSTONE: There, I am sorry, I cannot agree with you. How is he? I heard he had been ill.

HEALY: Very ill. He is recovered, however.

GLADSTONE: I cannot tell you how much he has been in my thoughts. Poor fellow, poor fellow. Have you seen him since the divorce suit?

HEALY: He was at a meeting yesterday.

GLADSTONE: And how did he look?

HEALY: Well—to be exact—he looked as though we were the ones who had committed the adultery.

GLADSTONE: Ah—a dominating personality—an unbending will. You will pardon me if I say that I have sometimes wondered how a man of your keen mind and strength of character could at all times submit yourself to the complete dominance of even a Parnell.

HEALY: I am proud to serve under him.

GLADSTONE: Ah—you are very modest, Mr.

Healy, exceedingly modest. Parnell *is* wonderful of course. What a tragedy ! Poor fellow, what a fall !

HEALY : I was not aware of any fall, sir. Parnell is still Leader of the Irish Party.

GLADSTONE : His continued leadership, Mr. Healy, would be fatal to the Irish cause.

HEALY : I do not agree with you, sir.

GLADSTONE : His usefulness is at an end.

HEALY : Why should a man's private life affect his public career ?

GLADSTONE : I cannot tell you why, Mr. Healy. I can only tell you that it does. Do not think me antagonistic—unsympathetic——

HEALY : I cannot reconcile your sympathetic thoughts with your actions, Mr. Gladstone. You have issued a public letter, printed in the newspapers, in which you say that unless Parnell resigns you will feel called upon to do so.

GLADSTONE (*smiling quietly*) : Did I say I would resign, Mr. Healy ?

HEALY : You said—well—everyone took it to mean that. What did you mean, Mr. Gladstone ?

GLADSTONE : I think I cannot usefully add to what I have already written. Consider for a moment my position in this matter.

HEALY : I have no doubt you have fully considered it, sir.

GLADSTONE : I am not only the Leader of the Liberal Party, but have come to be regarded as the unofficial Leader of the Nonconformist Church Party. Suddenly I find myself hand in glove with the chief figure in a hideous divorce scandal. What can I do ? I assure you these people view the matter entirely from the moral point of view. The pressure brought to bear on me has been enormous. I must heed their voice.

HEALY: Must you? Why, Mr. Gladstone?

GLADSTONE: Perhaps because it is the most shrill.

HEALY: You will pardon me if I suggest that it might be worth heeding the voice which once swept you to No. 10 Downing Street—and will again!

GLADSTONE (*raising a deprecating hand*): I am not unmindful of the Irish Vote, nor the Irish cause. But this question goes beyond the political. I beg you to consider it from the moral aspect.

HEALY: Mr. Gladstone, the Irish are fighting a political war. What would you think of soldiers who stopped in the midst of battle to enquire whether or not their general had broken one of the Ten Commandments?

GLADSTONE (*with a slight tightening of the lips—a repressed smile*): I should immediately surmise that they were of the Nonconformist Group.

HEALY: But we are not. If you have decided to break with us——

GLADSTONE: Mr. Healy, you wrong me. Such a thing was furthest from my thoughts. My manifesto was directed solely against Charles Parnell, not the Irish Party.

HEALY: He *is* the Irish Party.

GLADSTONE: Again I am impressed with your modesty, Mr. Healy.

HEALY: Because he has gone wrong in a private question is that a reason why he should fail in his duty to his people?

GLADSTONE (*in a ringing voice*): He would not fail. Others would fail him.

HEALY (*fighting back*): We shall not. I'm sure of that.

GLADSTONE: Are you—Mr. Healy—SURE? The Leader of the Irish Party is enveloped in the nauseous fumes of the divorce court. They rise to Heaven, and yet you persist in a policy which bids fair to wreck your Party. Is Mr. Parnell the only Irishman capable of leading you? Are the forceful, brilliant men of your Party a lot of weaklings? No, Mr. Healy, I am impressed with your modesty, but I find it deplorable.

HEALY (*less certainly, more pleadingly*): He has led us forth out of the wilderness. We are within sight of the Promised Land——

GLADSTONE: Call upon your knowledge of scripture further, Mr. Healy. Remember, Moses was allowed to see but not to enter the Promised Land.

[*The folding doors open and* STANLEY *enters and pauses.*

Yes, Mr. Stanley?

STANLEY: I beg your pardon, Mr. Gladstone. Mrs. Hamish and Mrs. O'Shea.

GLADSTONE (*watching* HEALY): Ask them to be seated. I shall be with them shortly.

STANLEY (*he goes, closing the double doors after him*): Yes, sir.

HEALY (*rises, as does* GLADSTONE): I will bid you good afternoon, Mr. Gladstone.

GLADSTONE: I have a following appointment. No doubt you heard the names of my callers.

HEALY: Yes, Mr. Gladstone.

GLADSTONE (*persuasively*): God knows how I regret being the instrument chosen for the downfall of such a man. But I cannot be entirely wrong in my estimate of the mettle of the Irish Party. I cannot but feel that the Irish cause is greater than the fall of one man. Do you not agree with me, Mr. Healy?

HEALY: I do not know, Mr. Gladstone.

GLADSTONE: Ah—you too wish only to do what is wisest and best. There is a hope in my heart that there shall arise some day a new and greater leader. One with whom I could join hands. Ah, what could we not do for Ireland. I shall pray to that end. (*Holding out his hand*) You were good to come to me, Mr. Healy. I thank you.

HEALY: I am most sensible of the honour, and most grateful. Good afternoon. (*He bows and goes through the ante-room.*)

[GLADSTONE *walks to his table desk and rings a bell. The* SECRETARY *opens the double doors and comes into the room.*

GLADSTONE (*with a beaming smile, a mellow, warming smile*): Ask Mrs. Hamish and Mrs. O'Shea to come in.

[STANLEY *goes into the library, and in a moment* AUNT CAROLINE *and* KATIE *come in.* STANLEY *enters.*

STANLEY: Mrs. Hamish and Mrs. O'Shea, sir.

GLADSTONE (*hand outstretched to* AUNT CAROLINE): My dear old friend.

AUNT CAROLINE: Mr. Gladstone.

GLADSTONE (*crosses to her*): And Mrs. O'Shea. I am glad to see you again after all these months. (*Shakes hands with* KATIE *too.*) I am indeed glad to see you. (*To R. chair.*) Will you sit here, Mrs. Hamish? And Mrs. O'Shea?

STANLEY: Shall you need me further, sir?

GLADSTONE: Anyone else waiting?

STANLEY: Only Morrison of the Foreign Office.

GLADSTONE: Ask him to leave a message with you, or if he prefers, I shall see him to-morrow.

STANLEY: Yes, sir. (*He goes into the ante-room.*)

AUNT CAROLINE: You are looking very well, Mr. Gladstone.

[KATIE *sits quietly, her eyes fixed on* GLADSTONE *most of the time.*

GLADSTONE (*sitting*): Thanks to a Fatherly Providence and my own simple habits of life, I am in most excellent condition.

AUNT CAROLINE: I congratulate you. Providence never seemed to take the least interest in my health, perhaps because I never practised the simple life.

GLADSTONE: Ah, you know where that leads.

AUNT CAROLINE: To gout.

GLADSTONE: And restlessness of soul.

AUNT CAROLINE: But I always did have a restless soul.

GLADSTONE: Yes, Caroline, you did.

AUNT CAROLINE: But, William, it doesn't junket about nearly as much as it used to. (GLADSTONE *smiles back.*) Well, enough of me—may I broach a more important subject?

GLADSTONE: There is nothing more important than consideration of the human soul.

AUNT CAROLINE: But it does take time—really to cover the subject?

KATIE: Mr. Gladstone—we have come to talk to you about Mr. Parnell.

GLADSTONE: Yes, Mrs. O'Shea.

KATIE: Why have you turned against him?

GLADSTONE: " Turned against him " ? Surely that is too strong a statement.

KATIE: Is it? I hope so.

GLADSTONE: I differ from Mr. Parnell on a question of political expedience.

KATIE: You insist that he resign. Why?

GLADSTONE: Because I think it best for the Irish Party.

KATIE: If you destroy him you destroy the Irish Party. Is that what you want to do?

GLADSTONE: Mrs. O'Shea, I can only repeat that I feel that Mr. Parnell's political usefulness is at an end.

KATIE: Why?

GLADSTONE: Need we go into that?

KATIE: Is he less able to lead his people?

GLADSTONE: He is not only less able—he is unable.

KATIE: Why?

GLADSTONE: Because he will be repudiated.

KATIE: No—no, he will not. They won't fail him. I know it.

GLADSTONE: Are you sure?

KATIE: Absolutely.

GLADSTONE: Then why do you come to me?

KATIE (*he has struck her*): You're right. I am not sure. I was until you turned against him. Oh, Mr. Gladstone, there was no question of his leadership until then. I have hurt him—but it is you who are hurting him now. Is he less skilful, less adroit, less devoted?

GLADSTONE: Mr. Parnell has deviated from the accepted code. This deviation has become public property.

KATIE: That's it, isn't it? The accepted code is " Thou shalt not be found out," because everyone knows that I'm his mistress.

GLADSTONE (*shocked*): Mrs. O'Shea!

KATIE: I am not yet his wife, Mr. Gladstone; what term shall I use?

GLADSTONE: My dear young lady—I entreat you——

KATIE: I beg your pardon. Because Mr. Parnell has figured in a divorce scandal——

GLADSTONE: Which has rocked London. Therefore he is disqualified from further public leadership.

KATIE: You are cruel.

GLADSTONE: In your sorrow, Mrs. O'Shea, you are unjust. But it is natural; I forgive you. My heart bleeds for you, but I must refuse to consider the fate of one man when weighed against the fate of a nation. My supreme duty is to Ireland.

KATIE: Is your heart really devoted to Ireland?

GLADSTONE: Have I not said so?

KATIE: And for the sake of Ireland you feel that Mr. Parnell must resign?

GLADSTONE (*feelingly*): For the sake of Ireland.

KATIE: He will resign, Mr. Gladstone.

GLADSTONE: He will—— Are you *assured* of this, Mrs. O'Shea?

KATIE: Quite. He will resign immediately if you will give him your word that you will continue to support Home Rule for Ireland, and keep it in the forefront of your programme in the coming Election.

[*There is a long pause, broken by* AUNT CAROLINE.

AUNT CAROLINE: Well, William. Two birds with one stone. Could you possibly miss a chance like this?

KATIE: We have come to your terms.

GLADSTONE: I made no terms.

AUNT CAROLINE: You demanded Parnell's resignation.

GLADSTONE: This is a very grave matter. I cannot possibly answer you now. I must take time to consider.

KATIE: The Irish Party meets to-night; there is no time.

GLADSTONE: It is my custom to give all questions my most serious consideration and prayerful thought.

AUNT CAROLINE: Mr. Gladstone, do you expect the Irish Party to wait till you finish praying ?

GLADSTONE (*sternly*): Caroline; I expect nothing of the Irish Party. They must act as they see fit.

KATIE: But if Mr. Parnell resigns, what further questions can there be ?

GLADSTONE: You seem to overlook one factor in this case and the most important.

KATIE: What is that ?

GLADSTONE: The moral issue.

KATIE: But what moral issue is involved in your continued support of Home Rule, Mr. Gladstone ?

GLADSTONE (*very specifically*): The question of how far one is justified, even for a great cause, in dealing with one who has defied the law of God and man. The evil of our time is the loss of the sense of sin. Shall I be condoning sin ?

AUNT CAROLINE: You condoned it as long as it was useful to you.

GLADSTONE (*indignantly*): You cannot mean that I was aware of the private life of Mr. Parnell.

KATIE: Were you not, Mr. Gladstone ? You are a man of the world as well as a Churchman. When you could not find Mr. Parnell in the House or at his rooms you called on me. You are not a priest or a monk. What did you think ? You must have known—the whole Government must have known.

AUNT CAROLINE: Not officially, my dear. Governments, especially Liberal Governments, are simple-minded and of child-like innocence.

KATIE: Once you asked me what my interest was in politics. I said, " Entirely a personal one." You smiled. For a moment I thought——

GLADSTONE: You surely did not think I knew.

KATIE: Only for a moment.

AUNT CAROLINE (*starts a temper, seething*): It was a matter of common gossip.

GLADSTONE: I do not listen to the gossip of the lobbies.

AUNT CAROLINE: Of course you don't ! But I have reason to believe that this situation was discussed by your Cabinet months ago. Parnell's help was indispensable. But should this scandal break, could you succeed in wriggling out with a whole tail left to your coat ? You decided you could and you were probably right.

[GLADSTONE *raps on table. He rises.*

KATIE (*alarmed*): Aunt Caroline, don't make unfounded accusations. (*Rises.*) We didn't come here for this, but to plead with you. Please. (GLADSTONE *half turns away.*) Surely if Mr. Parnell resigns, you will not be criticised. Oh, Mr. Gladstone, he could have saved himself politically if he had defended the divorce. But that would have left me tied to a man I loathed and feared. It was to save me——

GLADSTONE: Mrs. O'Shea, please—I do not doubt for an instant Parnell's personal honour or that he kept silent on many things——

AUNT CAROLINE: Yes—for instance that Captain O'Shea should bring his suit at this particular time.

GLADSTONE (*definite. Sharply to* KATIE): I think

we shall have something to regret if your aunt continues.

KATIE: Oh, Aunt Caroline, don't, don't—please—Mr. Gladstone, forgive anything unwise we may have said. Don't let it count against—— (*Her voice breaks.*)

AUNT CAROLINE (*rises and crosses to* KATIE): My dear, you are overwrought. (GLADSTONE *rises.*) We must go home. Come. We have done all we could.

GLADSTONE (*crosses to door*): Yes. Mrs. Hamish is right. You should go home and rest.

KATIE: And what of the offer I have brought you to-night from Mr. Parnell ?

GLADSTONE: I shall give it due consideration—but, of course, I should have to have such a proposal in writing. There is scarcely time for that before the meeting to-night.

KATIE (*rises*): I have brought you many important proposals before this—NOT in writing.

GLADSTONE: But never in so grave a crisis.

KATIE: Mr. Gladstone, Mr. Parnell has already arranged that a Committee from the Party bring you his proposals to-night.

GLADSTONE: I am very sorry, but—— (GLADSTONE *opens door.*)

AUNT CAROLINE (*after a look at* KATIE): Mr. Gladstone, good evening. (AUNT CAROLINE *exits.*)

KATIE: Mr. Gladstone—(*with a gasping little sob*) I beg you—I beg you.

GLADSTONE: My dear, good evening.

KATIE: No, please. Please you must listen to me. We are going away. We are going to be married as soon as they'll let us. We shall live out of England. We shall be forgotten.

GLADSTONE : Do you think so ? Good evening, Mrs. O'Shea.

KATIE (*hopelessly*) : Good evening, Mr. Gladstone.

[KATIE *exits.* GLADSTONE *closes door, crosses to desk and rings bell.* STANLEY *enters.*

STANLEY : I couldn't interrupt you—but Mr. Healy is back with Mr. Redmond.

GLADSTONE (*sternly and curtly*) : Their business ?

STANLEY : They said they were straight from Mr. Parnell. That you would understand.

GLADSTONE : I do quite. (*Turns to him.*) Mr. Stanley, will you give orders to have a supper tray brought to me here at once. Something light. I shall not dine.

STANLEY (*turns*) : Yes, sir. But—Mr. Healy and Mr. Redmond. What shall I tell them ?

GLADSTONE : To wait, Mr. Stanley—to WAIT. Offer them tea, whiskey, if they prefer. Ask the gentlemen to WAIT.

[*He sits.*

STANLEY : Yes, sir. (STANLEY *is moving to the ante-room door and* GLADSTONE *has seated himself at his desk and is making little drawings, quite absorbed in his thoughts, as the curtain falls.*)

CURTAIN

SCENE II

SCENE : *Committee Room Number 15, in the House of Commons. Evening. The room is lit by candles.*

MURPHY *is arranging chairs about a centre table.* MICHAEL DAVITT, *subdued and sad, comes in— anxious.*

Tension—MURPHY *feels all will be well as soon as* PARNELL *arrives.*

MURPHY (*pushing chair in—places it*): Evenin', Mr. Davitt.

DAVITT: Mr. Healy got back yet?

MURPHY (*putting in second chair*): No, sir. Neither Mr. Healy nor Mr. Redmond.

DAVITT (*sits*): They're a long time.

MURPHY: Well, I don't suppose a talk with Mr. Gladstone is easy come by. They likely had to wait. Mr. Parnell's here, sir.

DAVITT: Parnell? (*Rises.*) Where is he?

MURPHY: He and young Mr. Harrison are in the inner room.

DAVITT: Anyone else?

MURPHY: No, sir. They just came a few moments ago. I'm to let 'em know when the rest are come.

DAVITT: How did he look?

MURPHY: Haven't you seen him—since—the divorce?

DAVITT: No.

MURPHY: Bad. (*Sits.*) Like a fire burnin' him— inside.

DAVITT: Hell fire.

MURPHY: Look here, Mr. Davitt, he's not the first man to be led astray by a woman—nor yet the last.

DAVITT: Him! Of all men I'd a' said—not him.

MURPHY: If I had my way it would be that dirty, sneakin' little spy, with his monocle and his fine talk——

DAVITT: He had a right to sue for divorce. He was in his rights.

MURPHY: He wasn't weepin' about his rights when we ran him for Galway. Not O'Shea.

DAVITT (*obstinately*): Rights are rights.

MURPHY: An' feelin's are feelin's.

DAVITT (*savagely*): Whose feelin's?

MURPHY (*with a jerk of the head toward the inner room*): His feelin's—and hers. (*Pleasantly*) Ever see her?

DAVITT: I have. Hell take her.

MURPHY: Don't, Mr. Davitt.

DAVITT (*rises*): I'll not be the only one, Murphy, before this business is out. (*Knock on the door.*) I don't want to see 'em till I have to. (*Crosses to down L. door.*)

MURPHY: I'll call ye, Mr. Davitt.

[DAVITT *goes into the small clerk's room.* MURPHY *crosses and opens the door. It is* KATIE.

KATIE: Mr. Murphy——

MURPHY (*perturbed*): Good evenin'.

KATIE: Mr. Murphy, are Mr. Parnell and Mr. Harrison here?

MURPHY: Yes. They're both here. Shall I tell Mr. Parnell?

KATIE: No—I want to see Monty Harrison. You needn't say who it is. As quickly as possible, please.

MURPHY (KATIE *steps into the room and* MURPHY *closes the door*): I'll call him.

KATIE: Don't mention my name, please.

[MURPHY *walks to the door of the inner room and knocks.* MONTY *opens it.*

MURPHY: Mr. Harrison, will you step here a moment, please.

MONTY (*glances back to assure himself that he is not wanted by* PARNELL, *comes into the room, closing the door behind him. He is much surprised to see* KATIE): Mrs. O'Shea.

KATIE: Monty—I'm mad to come here—I know——

MONTY: Shall I tell Mr. Parnell?

KATIE: No. Is Mr. Healy back?

MONTY: Not yet. We'd better talk somewhere else—the Party's meeting.

KATIE: Yes—they didn't want to let me up. But there are ways of managing these things— you know.

MURPHY: Shall I leave you alone?

KATIE: No—please. I'll only be a moment. I saw Mr. Gladstone. I begged him—almost on my knees, but I think it's hopeless. Oh, Monty, even if Gladstone refuses—surely the Party will stand by him—— (*He shakes his head.*) You don't think the Party—— (*He nods. She looks into* MONTY's *face and reads doubt and sorrow.*) Then —there is only one thing now—they must know why he would not defend himself.

MONTY (*alarmed*): You know Mr. Parnell would not allow it.

KATIE: Oh, Monty, we are long past obeying and disobeying.

MONTY (*definite*): I couldn't—against his orders —and besides—it wouldn't do any good.

KATIE (*turns to* MURPHY): Mr. Murphy, Mr. Parnell refused to save himself by defending my husband's suit against him. If he had let the truth come out there would have been no divorce. I would still be married to Captain O'Shea. Can't they understand? He wouldn't save himself at that price. Can't they be made to understand ? Mr. Murphy—don't let them turn against him.

MURPHY: Mrs. O'Shea—there's nothin' I wouldn't do for him.

KATIE: Thank you. (*She sits down, unable to speak.*)

MONTY (*crosses to her*): You must go. I'll take you down.

KATIE: No. You will be needed here. I'll go.

MONTY (*follows her to door*): Please let me.

KATIE: No—I'll take the little stair. I won't be seen. That wouldn't help things much, would it ? (*She is at the door and smiles up at MONTY a heart-breaking smile.*) Monty, what are they going to do to him ?

MONTY: Don't. Everything will come out all right—I believe——

KATIE: I shall be waiting—at Eltham.

MONTY: It may be terribly late.

KATIE: I shall be waiting. (*She goes out.*)

MONTY (*turning his head to avoid letting MURPHY see the tears in his eyes*): Mr. Murphy, I must ask you never to repeat what Mrs. O'Shea has just told you.

MURPHY: Very well, Mr. Harrison.

[*There is a loud knock on the door. MURPHY crosses to it. MONTY goes into the inner room again and closes the door.*

O'GORMAN (*coming in as MURPHY opens the door*): Good evenin' to ye.

[*DAVITT comes in from the clerk's room.*

MURPHY: Good evenin', sir. Were ye expected ?

O'GORMAN: That I can't answer, me lad—but I'm here.

MURPHY (*dubiously to DAVITT*): Is it all right ?

DAVITT: Let him stay.

O'GORMAN: And why not? There's to be a meetin' of Irish leaders. Where Ireland is—there am I.

MURPHY: Or where Captain O'Shea is—I'm thinkin' ye're there, too.

O'GORMAN: Captain O'Shea is my very dear and much injured friend.

MURPHY: A much injured friend——

DAVITT: Let be, I tell ye, Murphy. (MURPHY *turns his back and walks to the window. There is another knock.*) Come in.

[*Four or five men come in. We will call them* 1ST, 2ND, 3RD, *etc.*, " LEADERS." *They say,* " Good evening," " How d'you do," " Good evening, Davitt," *etc.* DAVITT *bows, but says nothing. The atmosphere is funereal and no one knows how to lighten it.*

1ST LEADER: Good evening. Good evening. It's a bad night.

DAVITT: High wind.

O'GORMAN (*reminiscently*): Aye—once—when I was a lad—about the year——

3RD LEADER (*interrupting*): Mr. Parnell come yet?

O'GORMAN (*peevish at the interruption*): Mr. Parnell? Are ye really expectin' him this evenin'? I'm thinkin' ye'll have a long wait.

MURPHY: An' what makes ye think that?

O'GORMAN: A man who would stoop——

DAVITT: That'll do!

O'GORMAN: Very well, Mr. Davitt—but I'm saying nothin' but what the world's ringin' with. Defend him if ye like—but when he turns tail——

MURPHY: He's never turned his back yet—on friend or foe.

4TH LEADER: He will be here to-night?

MURPHY: He *is* here.

[*The door opens and* HEALY *and* JOHN REDMOND *come in.* HEALY *is flushed and excited.* JOHN REDMOND *quiet and set.*

HEALY: Well—boys—— (*He looks around.*) Where's Mr. Parnell?

MURPHY: In there. I'm to tell him when you're come.

HEALY: Thank you.

[*Silence falls on the room. They look at each other anxiously and then at the door to the inner room.* DAVITT *is staring at the floor.* MURPHY *crosses and knocks at the door.* MONTY *opens it.*

MURPHY: Will ye tell Mr. Parnell we're waitin' for him?

MONTY (*looks around and sees that* HEALY *and* REDMOND *are come*): Very well.

[*He turns back into the room,* PARNELL *comes to the door deadly white, only his dark eyes burning curiously. He comes in with that quiet, aloof and quite unconscious dignity which was his to so singular a degree.*

PARNELL: Good evening, gentlemen. (*He looks at* HEALY *and* REDMOND, *then his glance pauses for a moment on* MICHAEL DAVITT. DAVITT *drops his eyes.*) Will you be seated? (PARNELL *takes the large chair at the back of the table.*) Mr. Healy, did you and Mr. Redmond succeed in getting an interview with Mr. Gladstone?

HEALY: We did.

PARNELL: In that case we are ready for discussion.

O'GORMAN: Discussion of what?

H

PARNELL (*as though there had been no remark*) : This is in no sense a formal meeting. but a gathering of leaders to talk over our future policy.

2ND LEADER : In regard to what ?

PARNELL : In regard to the steps we must take to ensure that Home Rule is kept in the forefront of the Liberal programme.

O'GORMAN : I'm of the opinion there's other matters to come up before that.

PARNELL : The remark is out of order.

O'GORMAN : I protest. (*He looks around for encouragement but gets none. There are remarks of " Right of chair," " Out of order."*)

PARNELL : Sixteen year ago, I conceived the idea of an Irish Party welded into one complete whole. All the different factions of Ireland fighting together for one purpose, the freedom of Ireland. Our Party oath, " Sit together, act together, vote together." (*Cries of "Aye," " That we have," etc.*) I knew that only by presenting a common front to the enemy, could we hope for victory. Ten years ago I was elected Leader of that Party. (*There is dead silence.*) You have given me absolute loyalty, absolute obedience, and we have at last forced on the English the necessity of granting Home Rule to Ireland. (" *Hear, hear.*") By our votes the Liberals have twice been swept to power—and only by our votes can they hope to win the next election. The defeat of the first Home Rule Bill, four years ago, means little or nothing to us now. What we have to do is to see that the new Government brings in a new and better Bill. Mr. Gladstone appeared to be with us. . . . Now, for personal reasons, which I shall not discuss here——

2ND LEADER : That's what we've come for.

O'GORMAN : What are Mr. Gladstone's objections ?

["Aye." "What's the matter with Gladstone?" "Personal reasons," etc.

PARNELL: Mr. Gladstone refuses to continue his support because he objects to me, personally, as Leader of the Irish Party.

REDMOND: Since when have we taken orders from an Englishman?

[The 4TH LEADER rises to his feet. He is friendly to PARNELL but sorely troubled as to the wisest course. PARNELL looks at them and quiets by the sheer force of his personality the remarks which have followed REDMOND's question.

4TH LEADER: Mr. Parnell, if you, as Leader of the Irish Party, are the stumbling-block to Home Rule, if because of you a Parliament for Ireland is endangered, then, for the sake of the Party, for the sake of Ireland—I think you should resign.

["Hear, hear." "That's what I say."

PARNELL *(very quietly)*: I am in entire agreement with you.

[DAVITT's head comes up. He looks at PARNELL.

4TH LEADER: Well—Mr. Parnell—all I can say is—if we are in agreement—there is no need for further discussion.

HEALY *(jumps to his feet and with much emotion)*: Mr. Parnell, I believe you have chosen the course of wisdom, for Ireland and for yourself. If at some future time you elect to return and again lead your people I shall be among the first to welcome you as Chief. *(He sits down.)*

PARNELL *(he rises slowly to his feet. He has that queer calmness of manner, that strange aloofness which made him so irresistible to the Irish people)*: In a public letter, Mr. Gladstone demands my resignation. Putting aside the question of what right he, or any other Englishman, has to dictate to us, I say, putting this aside, although I consider it fundamental, I have replied to Mr. Gladstone. Since I am no longer acceptable to him as Leader of the Irish Party, I have told him I will resign at once—(*there is a complete hush over the room*)—if he will give me his assurance——

DAVITT (*interrupting*): In writing.

MURPHY: Aye—an' then put it in a glass case.

PARNELL (*as though there had been no interruption*): I said I would resign if he would give me his word that he would continue to support the cause of Home Rule for Ireland and to fight the next election upon that issue. (LEADERS: "*Aye*.") Gentlemen, Mr. Healy and Mr. Redmond have just left Mr. Gladstone. I have not yet talked to them. Mr. Healy, will you tell us the result of your visit.

[*The hush still holds.* HEALY *rises to his feet. He is somewhat ill at ease and prepared to be combative.*

HEALY: Yes. Mr. Gladstone assured us of his heartfelt desire that Ireland should have Home Rule——

MURPHY: Will he fight for it ?

HEALY: He received us with the greatest courtesy and politeness.

DAVITT: An' what did he promise ye ?

HEALY (*stung*): Am I to be interrupted in this manner ?

PARNELL: Come to the point, Mr. Healy. Did he, or did he not, promise to support Home Rule ?

REDMOND (*quietly, but in a very clear voice*): He did not.

[*Reaction.*

HEALY (*to all—not* PARNELL): He did not promise—and I don't think he could be expected at this juncture. He told us—and I agree with him—that our first business was to choose a Leader. Then he would discuss the question of Home Rule.

MURPHY: He ran all around ye—that's the size of it.

HEALY: As long as the world can point a finger of shame at the man who represents Ireland, what favours can ye expect ?

DAVITT: Favours—since when has Ireland asked favours ? It's rights we're askin' an' it's rights we are going to get !

REDMOND: Who'll get them for you ? Who forced the English to consider Home Rule ? Who is the one man among us who can force them ? Do you expect them to hand it to you on a platter ? Who'll get you your rights ?

HEALY: Is Mr. Parnell the only man who can face Gladstone ?

MURPHY: That was a foine fight ye put up to-night, Tim Healy.

REDMOND: Why is Mr. Gladstone so anxious to rid us of our Leader ? Why does he wrap around him the mantle of righteousness and demand a sacrifice ? Because the one man who can give him orders, the one man who can give orders to the House of Commons—to England— is Charles Stewart Parnell. Will you sell him to keep the favour of the English ? Then I ask, what will you get in return ?

HEALY (*shouting*): *Home Rule !* That's what we'll get.

PARNELL: Gentlemen. (*They sit.* PARNELL *rises.*) You really think that Mr. Gladstone is burning with a desire to free Ireland ? Very well, I accept that for purposes of argument. Nay, I even accept it as a fact. But not even Mr. Gladstone himself can fight an election or, when he becomes Prime Minister, introduce a Home

Rule Bill into the House of Commons without
the support of a united Irish Party.

[*Cries of* "*Aye.*"

Two courses are open to me. Either I may
retire or I may force you to a decision on my
retention or rejection. In either case the Irish
Party will be *irretrievably split*. As long as I
live, and am capable of leading the Party,
there will, in fact, be many now in this room
who will accept no other leadership. Is not that
true ?

[*Cries of* "*Aye.*"

I say to you therefore that if you wish to pre-
serve the unity of the Party, two courses only
are open to you. Either you must unanimously
accept my continued leadership, or—you must
assassinate me.

[*Sensation.*

HEALY : You don't face the facts. Mr. Gladstone
does. Your continued leadership makes an
alliance with the Liberals impossible.

REDMOND : What alliance ? It's broken already.

HEALY : Who broke it ?

REDMOND : Mr. Gladstone.

HEALY : No—it perished in the stench of a
divorce court.

[*Bedlam. Cries of* " *Shame,*" " *Hear,*" "*Away
with him,*" *etc.* REDMOND *and* MONTY *spring to*
PARNELL'S *side. He stands staring at* HEALY,
deadly pale and very quiet.

O'GORMAN (*above the din*) : And not a word in
his own defence.

MURPHY : It's not the first time in history a
man has opened not his mouth.

PARNELL (*raises his hand. There is almost instant
silence*) : I do not intend to plead to you excuses
or reasons. I am—as I am. But I do claim that

never in thought, word, or deed have I been false to Ireland. I ask you to-night, not to be swayed by Mr. Gladstone's scruples, nor by any personal feelings of hate or loyalty you may have for me. Your duty is clear—— ("*Aye*," " *That it is*," *etc.*) Ireland's welfare should be your sole consideration.

DAVITT : Aye—it is.

PARNELL : If you think you can fight Gladstone without me, that is for you to decide, but—don't sell me for nothing. If you surrender me—if you throw me to him—it is your bounden duty to secure value for the sacrifice. (*He pauses and looks at them.*) I have a parliament in the hollow of my hand. I give you my word I will get it for you—if you will let me.

REDMOND (*rises. Patriotic fervour*) : Gentlemen— Charles Parnell is not only the Leader—he is the MASTER of the Irish Party.

HEALY : And who is the MISTRESS ?

[PARNELL *hurls himself at* HEALY, *but* MONTY *and* DAVITT *hold him back.*

PARNELL : When a lying coward dares to insult a woman in the presence of Irishmen——

[*Cries of* " *Shame, shame, shame.*"

REDMOND : Gentlemen, the time has come to stop this discussion.

3RD LEADER : Put the motion.

O'GORMAN : VOTE.

LEADER : VOTE.

LEADER : VOTE.

HEALY (*rises; to the men*) : You'll have no vote from me this night. Do you think Parnell can get you Home Rule ? He'll get you nothing but insults. What can ye expect if ye are led by a man whose name is a stench in the nostrils of

decent people ? Will you besmirch Ireland by
such a leadership ? Then I'm done with you.
The Irish people shall know the issues in this
matter—and I'll not shirk the tellin'——

PARNELL: Go to the people, Tim Healy—as I
shall do. I appeal to the people of Ireland.
They've never failed me yet. On their answer
I stand or fall.

HEALY: I take the challenge. From to-night
there's a new Irish Party. Those who are with
me (O'GORMAN *rises*), those who have the
honour of Ireland at heart—who would have a
new Party—and a new leader—follow me.
I bid you good evening.

[HEALY *exits, followed by* O'GORMAN, *and all the*
LEADERS, *except* MURPHY, REDMOND, MONTY,
DAVITT.

DAVITT *is sitting staring at the floor. Suddenly he
realises that* HEALY *and his crowd are gone.*
REDMOND, MURPHY, *and* MONTY *are looking at*
PARNELL, *but* PARNELL *is looking at* DAVITT.
One of PARNELL'S *rare smiles comes to his lips.*
DAVITT *looks at him with eyes of utter woe. Then
slowly he raises himself and starts towards the door
without looking back.* PARNELL'S *face again
becomes the cold mask he usually shows his followers.
As* DAVITT *reaches the door,* PARNELL *sways and
puts his hand to his side.* REDMOND *and* MONTY
*catch him and lower him into the chair. At the sound
of feet* DAVITT *turns.*

DAVITT: What is it ? Are ye hurt ?

PARNELL: Monty ! (MONTY *gets from* PARNELL'S
*vest pocket a small capsule of amyl nitrate. He breaks
it on a handkerchief and holds it to* PARNELL. *In a
few moments the pain is lessened.*) That's better.
I'm quite all right.

REDMOND: We will help you to your hotel.

PARNELL (*still not breathing with ease*): No—I'm

going home. (DAVITT *and* MURPHY *look at each other.*) Monty——

MONTY : Yes, sir.

PARNELL : Take a cab—drive ahead—— Tell her—it's nothing—I'm quite all right.

MONTY : Mr. Parnell—oughtn't you to rest first ? It's a long drive to Eltham.

[PARNELL *raises his head and makes an effort to speak, but no words come.*

DAVITT (*fiercely*) : Ye'll take him where he wants to be. (*He looks at* MONTY *who goes on out.*) Murphy—see that Mr. Parnell's carriage is waitin'.

[MURPHY *follows* MONTY *out of the door.* REDMOND *starts to help* PARNELL.

PARNELL (*rising slowly from the chair*) : I shall be quite all right now. (REDMOND *takes his arm and together they start for the door.* DAVITT *crosses ahead and opens it. As* PARNELL *reaches the door, he looks at* DAVITT *standing waiting for him to pass through.*) Thank you, Michael.

[*The curtain falls as they go out,* DAVITT *following.*

CURTAIN

SCENE III

SCENE : *The drawing-room at Eltham. Late evening.*

The fire has burned low. One lamp sheds a pool of light near the fireplace. A moaning wind hurls itself against the windows.

KATIE *enters from study—looks out of L. window— turns up lamp. Blows out candle. Puts slippers to warm before the fire.*

The door opens and PHYLLIS *comes in with a small tray of tea.*

PHYLLIS (*crosses to a table and puts down the tray*) : Won't ye be afther havin' a bit of hot tea, ma'am ?

KATIE (*without turning*) : Phyllis—that wind.

PHYLLIS (*crosses down with tea*) : Sure a bit of tea is what ye need.

KATIE : No, thank you.

PHYLLIS : Excuse me speakin', ma'am—but ye look so white—sure a bit of tea.

KATIE : I'm sorry, Phyllis. I couldn't possibly. (PHYLLIS *returns tea to table.*) You must have made it for me yourself, too.

PHYLLIS : Cook's been in bed these two hours.

KATIE : Thank you, Phyllis. Listen—did you hear wheels ?

PHYLLIS (*at upper R. window*) : Sure ye could hear nothin' over this wind.

KATIE : Look.

PHYLLIS (*crosses to the window*) : It's so dark ye can't see anything but your own face in the window pane.

[MONTY *appears at the door.*

MONTY : Mrs. O'Shea.

KATIE : Monty, where is he ?

MONTY : I took a cab ahead. Mr. Parnell told me to tell you that he is quite all right.

KATIE : Quite all right. He's ill.

MONTY : A little. Not a bad attack.

KATIE : Was it because of the meeting ? What did they do ? Listen, he's here. Monty, you go. (MONTY *crosses to door.*) Phyllis, go and get the decanter of brandy from the study, quickly. (*She exits.*)

[MONTY *has opened the front door and voices are heard.* PARNELL *appears at the door, leaning on* MURPHY's *arm.* DAVITT *is just behind him. They pause for a second and* PARNELL *looks at* KATIE. *She goes to him. He leaves* MURPHY *and put his arm about her. It is an embrace as well as a confession of his need for support.* KATIE *looks into his eyes and he smiles.*

KATIE: Oh, you're frozen. Come to the fire. (*They move to the fire.* MONTY *springs forward to help lower* PARNELL *into the chair.* KATIE *removes cloak, hands it to* MONTY—*he gives it to* PHYLLIS. KATIE *crosses to slippers—returns—takes off boots.* DAVITT *and* MURPHY *watching, ill at ease and miserably anxious.*) There, that's better.

PARNELL: Yes, that's better.

MONTY: You'll be all right now.

MURPHY: Sure—he'll be fine.

PARNELL: Yes. I'm very grateful to you for coming down with me. Thank you. Monty—take them into the study and see that they have something to drink.

[*The men cross to the door.* PHYLLIS *goes out with* PARNELL's *cloak and boots.*

DAVITT: I'll not be drinkin', thank you.

PARNELL: Yes, Michael. (*With a smile*) On me.

DAVITT: Thank you.

MONTY: If you'll come with me—gentlemen——

MURPHY (*going towards the door*): A drop or two will not come amiss this night.

[*The three men go into the library, closing the door after them.* KATIE *is on her knees beside* PARNELL's *chair, putting on his slippers.* PARNELL's *words are said with some difficulty.*

KATIE: There—that's better. Now, will you have some brandy, dear?

PARNELL: No, thank you.

KATIE: Are you sure, dear?

PARNELL (*shakes his head*): Well—Katie—who would have thought we should come to this? They have nearly all gone. Healy——

KATIE: No.

PARNELL: And Michael——

KATIE: Michael! Michael Davitt!

PARNELL: Michael's gone too.

KATIE: Fools!

PARNELL: Children! We shall have to fight, Katie. Can you bear it?

KATIE: If you can. Oh, I tried—I begged him——

PARNELL: My darling—I never really thought for an instant that the Old Spider——

KATIE: He is not an Old Spider. He is a politician, and a devout Churchman.

PARNELL: But he's not done with me—not yet. I'll fight——

KATIE: Yes, my darling, but not now. You must rest now.

PARNELL: I shall go to the people.

KATIE: Yes, dear, yes—later on——

PARNELL: I shall write a letter to the people of Ireland.

KATIE: Yes, dear, but you are ill now. You must let—some of the others write it for you.

PARNELL (*with a smile*): No. I refuse to go down to posterity speaking bad English. I shall fight —if he thinks I am beaten——

KATIE: Of course you're not, darling. But first of all, you're going to come away with me, now.

PARNELL (*dreamily*): Where there is sunshine.

KATIE: Algiers——

PARNELL: Or Carcassonne. Yes, Katie—when this fight is over.

KATIE: No, dear, now. You're going to come away with me now. We are going to forget, darling—forget everything.

PARNELL: Forget—that I ran away?

KATIE: After a while you will come back—and then——

PARNELL: Katie—don't make me less than the man you loved—I'll fight—— (*He has a sudden spasm of pain.* KATIE, *alarmed, starts to get up to go for help.*) Don't go. Don't leave me.

KATIE: I was only going to get help, darling.

PARNELL: There is nothing to do. You know that. Don't leave me. Give me your hand. (KATIE *puts her hand in his.*) Don't ever leave me. (*After a pause : his mind is wandering*) I have a Parliament for you. Kill me and you kill Ireland.

KATIE: Yes, dear. Listen. Won't you try to rest a little now?

PARNELL: Yes. (*He leans back and closes his eyes.*) Michael—Michael.

KATIE: Yes, dear. Yes. You must try to rest a little now. (*He becomes quiet.* KATIE *moves towards the door, to get help.*)

PARNELL: Where is your hand? Don't leave me. (KATIE *comes back to him, and takes his hand.*)

KATIE: I'm here, darling. I won't leave you.

[*There is a long pause.*

PARNELL (*in his normal voice*): Kiss me.

[KATIE *leans forward and kisses him on the mouth. He dies in her arms.*

KATIE (*looking at him closely*) : Darling—darling,
speak to me. Darling, I'm here, I won't leave
you. Speak to me. . . . No, no, no, no ! Oh,
God, oh, God, oh, God—oh, God—oh, God——!
(*There is only silence. She gathers his head to her
shoulder almost as though she had a child in her
arms, swaying a little. Then*) Monty !—Monty !
(*The three men come into the room,* MONTY *first. He
looks at* KATIE, *then at the figure in the chair.*
DAVITT *picks up the lifeless hand, and then lays it
quietly down. He looks at the other two. They cross
themselves, and* DAVITT *drops on his knees by the
chair.*) Oh—he will miss me so.

MONTY (*loyal, but ever literal*) : You mean, you
will miss him.

KATIE (*with agony in her voice*) : Is that all I
mean ?

MONTY : You had better come away.

KATIE (*unemotionally*) : I killed him.

DAVITT : No. No more than all of us.

CURTAIN

THE TWO BOUQUETS

Eleanor and Herbert Farjeon

THE TWO BOUQUETS

A Victorian Comedy
with music

All applications for permission to perform this play should be made to the London Play Company Ltd., 51 Piccadilly, W.1, the authorised agents of the authors

CHARACTERS

MR. GILL

MRS. GILL His wife.

EDWARD GILL Their son.

KATE GILL Their daughter.

LAURA RIVERS Their niece.

JULIAN BROMLEY In love with Kate.

ALBERT PORTER In love with Laura.

PATTY MOSS An actress secretly
married to Edward.

GEORGE An actor.

BELLA MANCHESTER A fast girl.

FLORA GRANTLEY A silly girl.

AMELIA A servant.

CHORUS OF GUESTS, THESPIANS, AND
REGATTEERS.

SCENES

ACT I

Conservatory at Mr. Gill's house in
Twickenham.

ACT II

The Gardens of Mr. Gill's house.

ACT III

The River-bank at Twickenham.

PERIOD: *Circa 1875.*

This play was first produced at the Ambassadors Theatre, London, W.C.2, on the 13th August, 1936, with the following cast:

Mr. Gill	FREDERICK RANALOW
Mrs. Gill, his wife	JOYCE BARBOUR
Edward Gill, their son	GEORGE BENSON
Kate Gill, their daughter	ADELAIDE STANLEY
Laura Rivers, their niece	EDITH LEE
Julian Bromley, in love with Kate	BRUCE CARFAX
Albert Porter, in love with Laura	WARREN JENKINS
Patty Moss, an actress secretly married to Edward	GERTRUDE MUSGROVE
George, an actor	JAMES PAGE
Bella Manchester, a fast girl	HEATHER BOYS
Amelia, a maid	ELEANOR HALLAM

Chorus Ladies: *Brenda Clether, Laura Gorton, Eleanor Hallam, Betty Pugh, Sonia Weston, Phyllis Zemin*

Chorus Gentlemen: *Gerald Aintree, Webster Miller, Peter Mosley, Barry Sherwood, James Thurgood, Evan Williams*

Production by MAXWELL WRAY

ACT I

SCENE: *Conservatory, and ballroom beyond; double
doors, glass, centre; rather circular effect to back,
with glass above and wainscot below; inset against
wainscot, red plush seats, to accommodate sitters-out,
well up stage. The scene comes round with a circular
movement, with two particularly bosky groups of
palms and flowers in tubs and majolica pots, about
halfway down, allowing plenty of space in the
middle, forming a sort of narrow passage R. and L.,
between the plants and the sides of the conservatory,
so that couples can pass up and down the stage behind
the plants, and leave the centre for free play. The
walls of the conservatory come right round to the
front, but on the right, facing the audience, is a
painted panelled door, with painted finger-plates,
leading to EDWARD'S snuggery; on the opposite side,
L. front, in full view of the audience, is an open
archway, hung with red portières, looped up, through
which an ascending staircase is visible; and presumably there is a passage beyond it, leading to other
rooms in the house. Lustre chandeliers and branched
candlesticks. The central lustre in the conservatory is
lit; there is a light behind the portière L. (gas-in-
the-passage atmosphere); at back, the ballroom
atmosphere, dimly visible. Under the left group of
plants, mid-centre, is a sort of ottoman, one of those
three-seated clover-leaf affairs, with the wooden
frame showing, and the upholstery set plumply with
buttons.*

*Under the right-hand group of plants, LAURA sits
at her harp, while KATE stands, music in hand,
singing. Both aged about twenty, and dressed for the
ball.*

SOLO: KATE

(*Air: " Fly Forth, O Gentle Dove "*)

I sent a letter to my love
  Made bright with loving words and sweet;
I gave it to a tender dove
  To carry to my darling's feet.

" Fly forth, O gentle dove," I cried,
  " Spread westward, spread thy pinions fleet,
  O'er hills and woods and meadows wide,
    And bear my letter to my sweet !
  Fly forth, O gentle dove," I cried,
    " And bear my letter to my sweet ! "

LAURA : Charming, my dear Kate ! If you sing it as well to our guests this evening, you will enchant them all.

KATE : Pooh ! guests are obliged to praise the daughter of the house, whether she sings like Patti or yelps like a puppy.

LAURA : You can be certain of the sincerity of at least *one* young gentleman.

KATE : And who's that, pray ?

LAURA : Mr. Julian Bromley.

KATE (*tossing her head*) : Oh, him !

LAURA : What ! Have you had another tiff ?

KATE : A tiff ? An earthquake ! I have sent him three letters, telling him I'll never, never speak to him again. And, oh, Laura ! he hasn't answered one of them.

LAURA : Take care, my dear ! There is a point beyond which it is imprudent for a girl to trifle with her choice. Mr. Bromley is so high-spirited. If you really love him——

KATE : Love him ! Oh, Laura ! He is so hand-some, so dashing, so intense !

LAURA : Then make the most of to-night. There's no peacemaker like a dance.

KATE : You are right. You are always right. I will begin by forgiving him—that will be delightful. Then, I will sit by him at supper—that will be heavenly. And after, as I come to the end of my song, I will cast him a meaning glance. That will be—Oh, do let's practise it ! (*She sings again.*)

" My love shall love thee for my sake
  And give thee happy welcome, dove;
Then westward swift thy journey take,
  And bear my letter to my love !
Then westward swift thy journey take,
  And bear my letter to my love ! "

LAURA: That will be irresistible !

[*Enter* MRS. GILL *from ballroom, waving a list, in a state of great agitation.*

MRS. GILL: Girls ! girls ! The Maids of Honour are ruined !

KATE: Good gracious, mamma ! *All* of them ?

MRS. GILL: At least two dozen. Amelia dropped the tray !

LAURA: Dear aunt, how distressing !

MRS. GILL: Everything is at sixes and sevens. Cook is upset, Edward not home yet, and your uncle fussing all over the place. You know how he insists on helping ! As a consequence, the cloak-rooms are now unfit for use.

KATE: Heavens, mamma ! How ?

MRS. GILL: He suddenly took it into his head there weren't enough pegs, started knocking in others, damaged the panelling, and now he's touching it up with paint. As though it could possibly dry in time !

KATE: It will ruin the wraps !

MRS. GILL: And make everybody sick ! (*Sinks on to ottoman.*)

LAURA: Aunt, you must not agitate yourself. Remember, darling ! Let me take things in hand.

MRS. GILL: Look at this supper-table list ! Perhaps you will take *that* in hand, too.

LAURA: What is wrong with it ?

MRS. GILL: Everything ! This comes of leaving it to Kate. Have I not told you, Kate, that *you* must sit by Sir Willoughby Fox, M.P. ? Yet here I find you thrown away on Julian Bromley.

KATE (*turning aside with a toss of the head*) : It was extremely hard to arrange.

MRS. GILL: Nonsense, child. It is extremely simple to arrange. (*Using her pencil.*) *You* will sit by Sir Willoughby—so—and Laura, who has somehow got next to Albert Porter, will sit by Julian Bromley. You might do worse, Laura, than improve the occasion. Mr. Bromley is very well off. So much for that. But the fatal mistake is *here* ! By what oversight, Kate, has your brother Edward been seated next to Bella Manchester ?

KATE: They get on so well together, mamma.

MRS. GILL: Precisely ! Bella Manchester shall sit by Albert Porter. He is quite a safe young man. In any case, this is the last time we shall invite Miss Manchester to *our* house. In future we shall not recognise her.

LAURA: Why, what has she done ?

MRS. GILL: She was seen yesterday riding in a hansom cab, all by herself. In Gower Street.

GIRLS: No !

MRS. GILL: Had it occurred sooner, I should not have asked Bella here to-night.

SOLO: MRS. GILL

(*Air: " Just Look at all These "*)

The miss who rides alone in cabs, girls,
And goes the pace that's known as fast,
                                Loses caste !
If she impairs her moral tone, girls,
She's sure to find herself at last
                                With a past.

No girl is respected
Who isn't really circumspect,
She won't be selected
Unless she's select.
                    Oh !
Our strictures fall on Bella Manchester,
We will not bow, we will not dine,
Or call at all on Bella Manchester——
We must know where to draw the line.

On those who will not come to heel, girls,
Our doors must not be open, but
                              Must be shut !
The miss who cuts a dash will feel, girls.
Extremely dashed when she is cut——
                    Tut, tut, tut !

We must be defensive
And always look before we leap—
It comes so expensive
To make oneself cheap.
                    Oh !
Just you wait, Miss Bella Manchester !
While British matrons all combine
To spiflicate Miss Bella Manchester—
We must know where to draw the line !

[MR. GILL *fusses in, a petunia in one hand, a
hydrangea in the other : no flower-pots to them, but
they are still in the shape of their earth.*

MR. GILL : Amelia ! Where's Amelia ? (*Calls*)
A-*me*-lia !

MRS. GILL : Why do you want Amelia ?

MR. GILL : My dear, to sweep up the litter.

MRS. GILL : What litter ?

MR. GILL (*defensively fretful*) : Well, my dear, you
can't shift two dozen flower-pots without a
certain amount of litter.

MRS. GILL : Why shift two dozen flower-pots at
all ?

MR. GILL : The florist has sent petunias instead of azaleas. So I have been putting the petunias where we had the hydrangeas, and the hydrangeas where we meant to have the azaleas. A couple of flower-pots fell through the aquarium, that's all. (*Calls*) A-me-lia ! (*Plumps down plants on ottoman.*)

MRS. GILL (*wrings her hands*) : This is the last straw !

MR. GILL : Now, now, darling, don't upset yourself. Remember ! remember !

MRS. GILL : It is too much ! Flower-pots broken—Maids of Honour ruined—supper-table upside down—cloak-room *hors de combat*——

LAURA (*picking up plants from ottoman*) : Come, come, aunt, you must be careful ! Remember ! If you will only rest upstairs until the guests arrive——

MRS. GILL : And where, pray, with the cloak-room all over paint, will they take off their things ?

LAURA : The ladies shall have the little ante-room through there (*points through portière L.*) ; the gentlemen can use Edward's snuggery on *this* side. It can be arranged quite easily.

MR. GILL : Easily, easily. Things might be ever so much worse. Think of all the people dying in China ! Every other second ! Chinaman dead ! Chinaman dead ! Things might be *ever* so much worse.

[LAURA *accompanies* MRS. GILL *towards the door.*

MRS. GILL (*making a last protest*) : But the Maids of Honour——

LAURA : Can be dispensed with. (*As they go off, mounting the staircase*) Why, what with the jellies, and the lemon cheese-cakes, and the Charlotte Russe, *and* the trifle—— (*They disappear.*)

MR. GILL (*going R.*) : Now I will go and fix up the snuggery for the gentlemen.

KATE: Papa !

MR. GILL: My pet ?

KATE: What *is* the matter with mamma ?

MR. GILL: Matter, my pet ?

KATE: Why do you all keep telling her to *remember* ?

MR. GILL: Well, well—for the best of reasons. Because she *must* remember. (*Going.*)

KATE: Has anything happened ?

MR. GILL: No, no. Certainly not. At least— well—after all, you are quite grown up now——

KATE: Yes, papa ?

MR. GILL: The fact is, Kate, your mamma— your poor dear mamma——

SOLO : MR. GILL

(*Air: " Voices of the Past "*)

The course of Nature none can stem,
    Upon the oak the acorn grows,
The rose-bush for a diadem
    In sunny June puts forth the rose,
And even as the buds appear
    Each season on their spray,
Your sweet mamma once more, my dear,
    Is in the family way.

The bird that builds each year anew
    Supplies its nest with little ones,
The cow, the cat, the kangaroo,
    Are blessed with daughters and with sons.
It is in vain, yes, all in vain,
    Dame Nature's course to stay—
And so your dear mamma again
    Is in the family way.

KATE: Well, papa, I *am* surprised !

MR. GILL: So were we, my pet, so were we. Of course, we are overjoyed. But what with the income tax at twopence in the pound, and your cousin Laura to support, and Edward's debts, and the two boys at Harrow—I suppose you don't happen to be in love, my pet ?

KATE: Papa ! How *can* you !

MR. GILL: Well, it would be a great relief to your mamma. And to my banker, too. You understand why we give these balls. A kind of speculation, my pet—I hope not a rash one.

KATE: I hope not, papa. In fact—since you wish to know—I shouldn't be surprised if to-morrow morning——

MR. GILL: Capital ! A handsome match would ease things all round. And if you *could* drop a hint to Laura to follow your example . . . There ! (*Kisses her.*) This is good news, indeed. I will go and tell your mamma at once. (*Exit.*)

KATE: Poor dear papa ! For his sake, I must. And, after all, why not ?

[*Enter* LAURA.

How is mamma ?

LAURA: It is by no means certain that she can come down to-night. Meanwhile, she has left me in control of everything.

KATE (*clapping her hands*) : Including the supper-list ?

LAURA: What do you mean ?

KATE: That you shall *not* sit by Mr. Julian Bromley at supper. If anybody is to improve the occasion with that very well-off young man, it will be your obedient cousin Kate.

LAURA: Obedient—you !

KATE: More so than you think. Papa has told me everything. Mamma is going to have a—you know.

LAURA: I know.

KATE: While, as for me—I am to have a——

LAURA: Kate !

KATE: Laura, how *can* you ! I am to have—a husband.

LAURA: Then to-night you have every reason to encourage Mr. Bromley to pop the question.

KATE: I shall feel quite justified. And if he won't—well, then, I suppose, in duty to papa I shall be obliged to encourage somebody else. And which of the young gentlemen of Twickenham will *you* encourage ?

LAURA: Oh, Kate, there is no hope for me !

KATE: Laura ! You are in love ! Confess !

LAURA: I have hardly dared admit it to myself. Even if he does respond, he is too shy to speak. He is so good—but, oh, dear ! he is so bashful.

SOLO: LAURA

(*Air : " Bobby Shafto "*)

Albert Porter's good as gold,
But he is not very bold ;
I must keep my love untold
    For my Albert Porter.
If he were not quite so shy
To his arms I'd gladly fly,
And for ever live and die
    Mrs. Albert Porter.

KATE: Bashful, I dare say, but that you must overcome.

LAURA: Kate—how can I ?

KATE: It is your duty. Papa dropped me a strong hint that we are both upsetting his banker. *You* must make Albert speak. *I* will make Julian speak. And to-morrow, when they win the Double Sculls at the Regatta, our engagements will be the envy of all Twickenham. Quick, Laura, the supper-list !

LAURA: Here it is.

[*They sit on the ottoman with their heads together, as* KATE *scribbles the alterations.*

KATE: Kate—Mr. Bromley. Laura—Mr. Porter. Now to restore the bold bad Bella to Edward.

LAURA: Where *is* Edward ?

[EDWARD, *in outdoor clothes, comes through the doors at the back, and, kneeling on the third seat of the ottoman, bends over the top, with an arm round each of the girls' shoulders, trying to see the paper.*

EDWARD: *Me voici !* What's up, *mes enfants ?*

LAURA: That's what we'd like to know. Where *have* you been all day ?

EDWARD: Little girls mustn't ask questions.

KATE: Oh, yes, they must ! Edward—who is *your* preference for a supper-partner ?

EDWARD: *Pourquoi ?* Why do you ask ? (*Strikes an attitude.*) Is this an attempt to invade the sacred privacy of my heart ?

LAURA: That would be far too risky. There's no telling whom we might meet there.

EDWARD (*carelessly*): Then shall we say—oh, anyone—Miss Bella Manchester ?

KATE: How curious ! You had already been allotted to Miss Bella Manchester. But mamma wouldn't hear of it.

EDWARD: Ah ?

KATE: She insisted on shuffling the cards.

EDWARD: Oh !

LAURA: But now she is indisposed—she may not come down to-night——

KATE: So we are *re*-shuffling the cards.

EDWARD (*gaily*) : Then *shall* we say—Miss Bella
Manchester ?

LAURA : There is still your papa to reckon with.

EDWARD : Oh, we can manage the old boy.
After all, he's a block of the young chip. We
have only to put him in an acquiescent humour
—and then, if mamma comes to hear of it——

KATE : Papa must sink or swim with us !

LAURA : But how will you make him acquiesce ?

EDWARD : Simplicity itself. He shall imbibe
acquiescence ! *In vino, libertas !* A glass or two
of fizz before the guests arrive, and we'll have
the old boy in such a state of acquiescence he'll
be nodding for the rest of the evening !

TRIO : EDWARD, KATE, LAURA

(*Air :* " *The Bells they are Ringing for Sarah* ")

EDWARD : When the head of the household is
fretful,
Let children remember with tact,
The bottle that makes him forgetful
Will substitute fiction for fact.
One glass of the beautiful bubbles,
Will settle the family jar—
There's nothing for drowning our
troubles
Like a little champagne for papa !
OH !

ALL : A little champagne for dear father,
father,
father,
And when his condition is rather,
We'll know just where we are !

KATE : Then I'll go to supper with Julian—

LAURA : And Albert my partner will be,

EDWARD : And I will find matters cerulean
As Bella canoodles with me.

KATE : And no one will know what we're
doing—

LAURA : Or tell us we're going too far—

EDWARD : The key to our billing and cooing
Is a little champagne for papa !
OH !

ALL : A little champagne for dear father ! (*etc.*)

[*Exit* EDWARD.

Enter MR. GILL.

MR. GILL : Now, now, now, this is no time to be practising steps. We don't want our guests to take us for Eskimos, you know.

LAURA : Everything, dear uncle, has been attended to.

MR. GILL : Well, heaven knows what would happen if *I* didn't keep an eye on things. Who is looking after mamma ?

KATE : Mamma is resting.

[*Enter* EDWARD *at back, with tray.*

EDWARD : Mamma is too poorly to come down this evening.

MR. GILL : Poor mamma ! I won't have her vexed. She was vexed about the seating at supper. Where is the supper-list ?

KATE (*waving list*) : We have settled everything.

MR. GILL : I dare say, I dare say. Let me see.

EDWARD (*interposing*) : Come, sir, the girls have done admirably. You know how safe things are in Laura's hands. (*Winks at the girls.*) Now, sir, we are all a trifle *distrait, dérangé, un peu* what-you-may-call-it ! Let us put our worries behind us, and get into a happy frame of mind for the party. (*Draws a cork with a pop.*)

MR. GILL : Eh ? You extravagant young scoundrel——

EDWARD : One glass before they come !

MR. GILL : Really, I must say——

EDWARD: Come, sir, a toast! " Health to Mamma ! "

MR. GILL: Ah, well, there you are ! " Health to Mamma ! " I can't resist that.

EDWARD (*hilariously mounts ottoman, assuming the airs of a toast-master*): Mamma.

ENSEMBLE: MR. GILL AND OTHERS

(*Air: " Schneider, how you was ? "*)

MR. GILL:
Ladies and gents ! I now propose the pattern wife and mother,
    One who is our bright domestic star.
From Hammersmith Bridge to Twickenham there isn't such another—
    Need I say I mean our dear mamma ?

Mamma !

KATE: Mamma !

LAURA: Mamma !

EDWARD: Mamma !

MR. GILL: Mamma !

KATE: Mamma !

LAURA: Mamma !

EDWARD: Mamma !

MR. GILL: HIP, HIP,

ALL:
        Hurrah, hurrah, hurrah !
    A Health to dear Mamma !

MR. GILL:
Ladies and gents ! I've known her all my life and wouldn't change her
    Not for Queen Vic-tor-i-or-i-ar !
Long may she live to bless our home with many a little stranger—
    Cheers for Baby ! Here's to dear Mamma !

[CHORUS *as before.*

I

[*The song ends with the ringing of bells, on which everybody exclaims:* " The guests ! The guests ! Good heavens, the guests ! " MR. GILL *gives an arm to* KATE *and goes up centre to receive them.*

LAURA (*shaking a finger at him*) : Edward ! You'll never be ready in time !

EDWARD : *Oui, oui, je serai, je serai !*

[EDWARD *runs his fingers through his hair wildly, and hurries off* L. LAURA *rings bell-pull by portière.*

LAURA : Jane ! Jane ! the door ! Amelia ! the lights !

[AMELIA *hurries on and off again, by another exit. Lights go up in the ballroom. The* GUESTS *are seen arriving behind the conservatory windows. They begin to pass on to the stage, in coats and mantles.*

Dumb-show scene, to the music of a varsovienne.

MR. GILL, KATE, *and* LAURA *take up positions to receive the* GUESTS *with different degrees of effusion, familiarity, and politeness, indicating that the* LADIES *are to pass down to the left, while* AMELIA *shows the* GENTLEMEN *that their way is down to the right. The two files of* GUESTS *pass down on either side behind the flowers, enter their respective doors in their outer garments, and, as the last of the cloaked and coated disappear, the first-comers begin to reappear in their evening dress. They pass up as before, music playing all through this dumb show, meeting their respective partners at the glass doors C. and pairing off into the ballroom. End of music.*

AMELIA *is about to close the doors, when* ALBERT PORTER *enters, in hat and coat, carrying a bouquet of white roses pinned up in paper.*

AMELIA (*pointing* R. *to* EDWARD'S *snuggery*) : Cloak-room that way, sir.

ALBERT : Thank you.   (*He goes in.*)

[AMELIA *closes doors, suddenly spies champagne tray, snatches it up, and hurries off* L. *as* ALBERT

*re-enters with his bouquet removed from its wrappings.
He seems ill at ease. The dancing has begun and the
figures of the dancers are seen passing across windows
at back. ALBERT cautiously tiptoes to glass doors,
opens them a crack, and peers through. Then he
retreats, pulls himself together, squares his shoulders,
and marches boldly up to the doors, but fails to go
through them. He returns, crestfallen.*

SOLO: ALBERT

(*Air:* " *Little Bo-Peep* ")

When she is near
I faint with fear,
Lest she my thoughts discover.
Pity his plight
Whose love burns bright,
Yet is a bashful lover !

Could I let fly
One tender sigh
Within her ear to hover !
Yet is my suit
For ever mute—
Alas, the bashful lover !

[*As the song ends,* ALBERT *sits down dejectedly on
the ottoman.* JULIAN *enters through doors at back
with a bouquet of pink roses.*

JULIAN: Albert !

ALBERT: My dear Julian !

JULIAN: Was it wise of you to come to-night ?
Have you forgotten that we are rowing for the
Twickenham Cup at the Regatta to-morrow.

ALBERT: Have *you* forgotten ?

JULIAN: Not a bit. But I am accustomed to
society, whereas you——

ALBERT: I know. I dread these festivities.

JULIAN: Well, if you want to be fit for to-morrow,
take no wine and don't dance too much.

ALBERT: Dance ! the bare thought of it terrifies me. Do you know, Julian, going into that room—— I haven't the courage.

JULIAN: You've courage enough to turn up flaunting a bouquet, you dog !

ALBERT: There ! I knew I looked conspicuous ! If there's one thing I hate, it's looking conspicuous.

JULIAN: Then the sooner you get rid of those flowers, the better. Come along ! (*Pushing* ALBERT *towards door*) In you go, Don Juan !

ALBERT: No, no ! I can't give it to her. I shall die of confusion. How do you propose to present yours ?

JULIAN: Hanged if I know. Even though these roses are for the belle of the ball——

ALBERT: Oh, Julian ! *not* Laura Rivers ?

JULIAN: So ! that lets *your* cat out of the bag !

ALBERT: Don't laugh at me. I love Miss Rivers with the only devotion of my life—but how can I hope to win one who must be loved by everybody ?

JULIAN: Except me. Admire Miss Rivers, esteem Miss Rivers—yes; but my love, curse it, is reserved for that maddening, frivolous little flirt—her cousin Kate.

SOLO : JULIAN

(*Air : " Ah, Gentle Maiden "*)

Ah, how capricious,
Yet how delicious,
The teasing maiden who claims my breast !
I love her madly,
She treats me badly,
I'd fain forget her, yet cannot rest.

> One moment kind,
> The very next I find
> She tries to drive me out of my mind !
> I long to grieve her,
> I swear to leave her,
> My pride is wounded, yet all I bear—
> Ah, how capricious,
> Yet how delicious,
> The teasing maid, the teasing maid,
>   who holds me in her snare !

ALBERT: What an uncomfortable affair.

JULIAN: Uncomfortable ?   Agonising !   For months she has dangled me on a string. The last time we parted, I vowed I would never speak to her again. Then came her mother's card for this evening. I hesitated. I fell. I accepted. I bought these roses. But how can I present her with this symbol of my love, and see her stamp on it, as she laughs in my face ? I will not do it ! Look. I have inscribed a card. (*Reads*) " You drive me to distraction ! You give me no sign that I mean anything to you ! Withhold that sign to-night and I withdraw for ever. To you I leave the movement that will unite you with your Julian."

ALBERT: There's a card in mine, too.

JULIAN: Oh ?

ALBERT: Would you care to hear it ?

JULIAN: Go on, then.

ALBERT (*reads*):

> " To make your happiness complete
>   I'd go through fire and water,
> Oh, speak the word I dare not speak,
>   And bless your Albert Porter."

JULIAN: Yes, yes, Albert, but what's to be done ?

[*Enter* EDWARD, *with empty champagne bottle, and half-filled glass.*

If we can't bring ourselves to present our
bouquets——

ALBERT: If only someone would present them
for us !

JULIAN: But who ?

EDWARD (*distinctly tipsy*): *Me voici !* Cupid's
messenger ! (*Drains glass and puts down bottle.*)

JULIAN: Where did *you* spring from ?

EDWARD (*clapping* JULIAN *on shoulder*): Evening,
Julian ! (*Clapping* ALBERT *on shoulder*) Albert,
bon soir ! So you two have been buying bouquets
for your diddle-darlings, eh ? Confide them to
me.

JULIAN: No, thanks ! You're far too irresponsible !

EDWARD: What ? Irresponsive ? A newly
married man like me ?

ALBERT: You married ?

JULIAN: Fiddlesticks !

EDWARD: 'Snot fiddlesticks ! I am married—
secretly married. Not a word to papa ! Not a
word to mamma ! But I'll tell *you* (*takes an arm
of each confidentially*) because you are my very,
very, very dearest friends. Yes, dear chaps, I am
married to the sweetest, sauciest diddle-darling
that ever wore tights behind footlights.

JULIAN: An actress ?

ALBERT: Good heavens !

EDWARD: *And* I'll tell you her name. Ready !
steady ! Patty Moss !

ALBERT: Never heard of her.

EDWARD: Never heard of Patty Moss of the
Travesty Theatre ! My dear—innocent—boy !

JULIAN: But your parents—your sister—your
cousin——

EDWARD: Don't know a thing. *Pas un mot*, dear

chaps, *pas un mot!* Discretion *omnia vincit.*
Promise ?

ALBERT : Promise.

JULIAN : I promise. But how do you manage ?

EDWARD : Easy enough. Got the lil puss half
mile up the river, in the most Arcadian lil
houseboat that ever blushed pink geraniums.
And while the Thames glides gently by . . .
(*Gesture.*) *L'amour, l'amour !* She's giving a lil
party herself to-night. Nearly pulled my hair
out when I said I couldn't turn up.

ALBERT : But what will your people say when
you tell them ?

EDWARD : Never tell to-day what you can put
off telling till to-morrow.

ALBERT : It all sounds very risky.

EDWARD : Love *is risqué.* You know that.
(*Seizing their bouquets, and flourishing them*) Are
you not both in love ? And am I not your
ambassador ?

JULIAN : Well, if you *would* undertake to present
my bouquet to your sister——

ALBERT : And mine to your cousin——

EDWARD : It shall be done. And Hymen's
blessings light upon you both. Shakespeare.

ALBERT : Remember—the white roses for Laura.

JULIAN : The pink roses for Kate.

EDWARD (*gaily*): White for Laura, pink for
Kate ! Pink for Kate, white for Laura !

JULIAN : Where do I leave my hat and coat ?

EDWARD (*points R. to snuggery*): *Le voilà !*

ALBERT : Julian ! You're not going to leave me !

JULIAN : I will join you in the ballroom.

EDWARD : *Courage, Albert !*

[*Exeunt* ALBERT, *through door C., and* JULIAN
into snuggery R.

SOLO: EDWARD

(*Air:* " *Heave Ho !* ")

The white bouquet for Laura,
The pink bouquet for Kate !
  How charming 'twill be
  The darlings to see
As the roses seal their fate !

[*Tosses bouquets, and catches them in different hands.*

The white for cousin Laura,
For sister Kate the pink—
  No, Kate has the white,
  I think that is right,
And Laura the pink ones—*je pense.*

The white ones for Kate,
The white ones for Kate,
The pink ones for Laura,
The white ones for Kate !
For Laura—I think—
The white—no, the pink !
The white ones, the white ones for Kate !
The pink ones for Laura,
The white ones, the white ones for Kate !

[LAURA *and* KATE *come in rather hurriedly from the ballroom.*

KATE : Edward, what *are* you doing here ?

LAURA : There's a whole row of wallflowers waiting for you to dance with them.

EDWARD : I fly to make the little angels happy ! But first—*me voici* ! Cupid's messenger !

KATE : What do you mean, silly ?

EDWARD : Ladies, I have been entrusted with a most agreeable task by two who shall be nameless. (*Produces flowers from behind his back.*)

GIRLS : Oh, what beautiful bouquets ! (*With an eager movement.*)

EDWARD: One at a time ! One at a time ! (*Presenting the wrong bouquets.*) The pink ones for Laura. The white ones for Kate.

LAURA: Who *can* have sent them ?

EDWARD: Ask me no questions ! (*Confidentially as he goes*) The senders' names are attached.

KATE: Their names ! Quick, quick !

LAURA: I can guess *yours*.

KATE: And *yours* !

[*The two* GIRLS *go apart, one to each corner of the stage, and examine their cards privately;* EDWARD *is up stage by double doors.*

(*Dismayed*) From Albert !

LAURA (*dismayed*): From Julian !

KATE: Can it be possible ?

EDWARD (*turning*): They're drunk with joy ! They can't believe their senses.

KATE (*beckoning to him so that* LAURA *shan't hear*): Edward !

EDWARD (*returning*): Sister mine ?

KATE: Did Albert Porter send me these flowers ?

EDWARD (*nodding*): Albert Porter.

KATE: Are you certain ?

EDWARD: Positive. He's simply swooning for you.

KATE: Oh, poor Laura !

LAURA (*beckoning to him so that* KATE *shan't hear*): Edward !

EDWARD (*sliding over to her*): *Ma cousine ?*

LAURA: Did Julian Bromley send me this ? (EDWARD *nods.*) Are you positive ?

EDWARD: Certain. He's raging mad for you.

LAURA: My poor Kate !

EDWARD (*goes up to double doors and turns*): Ladies, I wish you joy ! (*Kisses hands to each. Exit.*)

LAURA: My darling, you must be brave. I have bad news for you.

KATE: For me ? But I have worse for you. Listen to this.

(*Reads.*)

> " To make your happiness complete
> I'd go through fire and water !
> Oh, speak the word I dare not speak
> And bless your Albert Porter ! "

LAURA: Albert Porter ! In love with you ! Oh, Kate, how awful ! And Julian——

KATE: What about Julian ?

LAURA (*reads*): " You drive me to distraction ! You give me no sign that I mean anything to you ! Withhold that sign to-night and I withdraw for ever. To you I leave the movement that will unite you with your Julian."

KATE (*overcome*): Julian ! (*Recovering herself*) The wretch ! Then all these months he has been trifling with me, while his heart was secretly given to *you*. Intolerable !

LAURA: Oh, Kate, what shall we do ?

KATE: Send them about their business.

LAURA: Would that be right ?

KATE: Why not ?

LAURA: Consider uncle. Since you *must* marry, and Julian doesn't love you, and since *I* must marry, and Albert doesn't love me——

KATE: Why not accept them ? Oh, Laura !

LAURA: Oh, Kate !

KATE: *Could* you ?

LAURA: Could *you* ?

KATE: If we don't, they'll only go and marry somebody else.

LAURA: And we, perhaps, shall never be married at all.

KATE: After all, it will keep them in the family. You will often see Albert at my house. I shall often see Julian at yours. It will be something.

LAURA: Yes, it will be something.

DUET: LAURA AND KATE

(Air: "Dans la Prairie")

LAURA: Dearest cousin,
You shall come and stay with me,
When I am married
To the man you love.

KATE: Dearest cousin,
You shall spend the day with me,
When I am married
To the man you love.

LAURA: You'll both be able
At my house to meet, dear,
When I am married
To the man you love.

KATE: Next him at table
You shall have your seat, dear,
When I have married
The man you love.

TOGETHER: The man,
The man
You love.

You shall often
Lean upon his arm, dear,
Sometimes he'll carry
Your cloak and glove;
Time will soften
Sorrow with a charm, dear,
When I am married
To the man you love.

[*They embrace.* LAURA *goes upstairs* L. *to* MRS. GILL. KATE *sinks on seat, lays down* ALBERT'S *bouquet, picks up* JULIAN'S, *which* LAURA *has left behind her, presses it to her lips, and sits with it in her lap, as* JULIAN *appears at the door of the snuggery.*

JULIAN: She is alone. How lucky. I'll make my peace with her. (*As* KATE *rises*) Kate !

KATE (*turning*): Mr. Bromley ! How dare you call me by that name ?

JULIAN (*swiftly nettled*): It is not for the first time, Miss Gill !

KATE: But it is for the last.

JULIAN: I thought as much ! You have only regarded me as a pastime.

KATE: Well, and haven't you been amusing yourself with me ?

JULIAN (*bitterly*): Yes, yes, of course ! How could *you* suppose me serious ?

KATE: All Twickenham knows you for a trifler !

JULIAN: And all Twickenham knows you for a flirt !

KATE: Very well, then, we are quits !

JULIAN: Quits !

KATE: Quits ! And *that* (*flinging bouquet down at his feet*) is the end of it !

[*As* JULIAN *stands speechless with rage,* KATE *pulls the door open to go into the ballroom, and in waltzes* EDWARD *with* MISS FLORA GRANTLEY. JULIAN *being by the snuggery, and* KATE *partly screened by the door, they are unperceived.*

SOLO : EDWARD

(*Air*: " *All Round the Ring* ")

EDWARD (*as he dances*) :

> Dearest Miss Flo,
> I nevah tell lies,
> And I confess
> Without disguise,
> I nevah saw
> Such beautiful eyes
> As yours when they gaze in mine !

FLORA : Oh, Edward ! I do like your moustache !

EDWARD : Come into the pantry !

[FLORA *runs off L.*, EDWARD *after her.*

KATE : You must excuse me, Mr. Bromley. I am neglecting my guests. I regret I cannot reserve you a dance. My card is full. But Miss *Rivers*, I believe, has a dance or two to spare. I hate you !

[*She flounces out.* JULIAN *makes a furious gesture, and kicks the pink bouquet as* LAURA *appears through the portière L.*

LAURA : Oh, the poor flowers ! Pray, don't hurt them.

JULIAN : Pardon me, Miss Rivers. They lie there scorned.

LAURA (*concerned*) : Oh, I am so sorry. (*Picks up the flowers and touches them gently.*)

JULIAN : Ah, *you* have a tenderness for flowers, Miss Rivers.

LAURA : So much depends on the giver.

JULIAN (*aside*) : What can she mean ?

LAURA (*aside*) : He hesitates. Haven't I gone

far enough ? (*Takes a rose from the bouquet, and places it in her dress.*)

JULIAN: You honour that rose, Miss Rivers.

LAURA: Because of him—who—brought it here.

JULIAN (*aside*): By Jove ! I declare she loves me ! Very well, Miss Kate ! (*Aloud*) Have you a dance free ?

LAURA (*showing her programme*): Seven, or nine, or ten ?

JULIAN (*taking card and writing as he speaks*): Seven, *and* nine, *and* ten, and——

LAURA: Oh, stop, stop, stop ! What will everybody think ?

JULIAN: Let them think what they please ! Let them think the truth ! Miss Rivers— Laura !

LAURA (*faltering*): Mr. Bromley.

JULIAN: Why not Julian ?

LAURA (*whispering*): Julian.

JULIAN: Do not mistake me. I am no *trifler*. (*He kisses her hand.*) I will speak to your uncle to-morrow. Shall we dance ?

LAURA: Give me a few moments—oh, leave me to myself, I beg.

JULIAN: I respect your feelings. (*Bows and turns.*) (*Aside*) Good Lord ! I've done it ! (*Exit into ballroom.*)

LAURA: Oh, Albert, Albert, if you had only loved me !

[LAURA *sinks on ottoman, back to audience, as* EDWARD *waltzes in as before, but this time with* BELLA MANCHESTER.

SOLO: EDWARD

EDWARD (*dancing*):
>   Dearest Miss Bell,
>   I nevah tell lies,
>   And I confess
>   Without disguise,
>   I nevah saw
>   Such beautiful eyes
>   As yours when they gaze in mine !

[*He kisses her.*

BELLA: Oh, Mr. Gill, how *dreadful* of you !

EDWARD: Nonsense, you liked it.

BELLA: Oh, I *didn't* !

EDWARD: Are you positive ?

BELLA: Well, almost. (*Giggles.* EDWARD *kisses her again.*) Oh, Mr. Gill ! I'm still not perfectly positive.

EDWARD: Come into the snuggery !

[EDWARD *goes into the snuggery, pulling* BELLA *after him. Enter* ALBERT *timidly from ballroom. Dance music.*

ALBERT: She's there ! Shall I go or stay ? If she loves me, she will show it now. I must be bold.

LAURA (*aside*): Albert ! Courage, Laura !

ALBERT (*aside*): I *must* be bold.

LAURA: Good evening, Mr. Porter.

ALBERT: Miss Rivers—oh, Miss Rivers——

LAURA (*aside*): How he trembles ! He'll never screw up courage to speak to Kate.

ALBERT: I—I ventured—I mean, I was looking for——

LAURA (*encouragingly*): I think I can guess for whom.

ALBERT: I sent a message to—to——

LAURA: I know, Mr. Porter. It made her very happy. May I speak openly?

ALBERT: Oh, please!

LAURA (*earnestly*): Mr. Porter, your affection is returned.

ALBERT: Miss Rivers! Can it be true?

LAURA: Do not be deceived by appearances. Outwardly, I know, a girl may seem gay, capricious, even frivolous——

ALBERT: No, no!

LAURA: But below that lively surface, believe me, none has a sincerer, a more tender heart.

ALBERT: I have never doubted it. But how dared I hope?

LAURA: Hope on, Mr. Porter! My cousin Kate worships the ground you walk on.

ALBERT (*falling back, open-mouthed*): Your cousin Kate!

SOLO: LAURA
(*Air:* " *Regret thee!* ")

She loves thee! couldst thou only know
    What wealth of girlish faith is thine,
What tender thoughts around thee flow,
    What stars for thee in heaven shine,
Thou wouldst not hesitate to grasp
    The gift outpoured so lavishly,
But to thy breast the maid would clasp
    Who trusts, adores, and honours thee.
Be brave! be bold! accept thy luck!
    Dare all, and make thy love thy wife!
Stretch forth thy hand the rose to pluck—
    And thou wilt thank me all thy life.

[*Enter* KATE. LAURA *goes up, and leads her to the overwhelmed* ALBERT.

LAURA: Kate, my darling. Mr. Porter loves you. He has told me so.

[*She joins their hands as* JULIAN *comes in.*

ALBERT (*in a fluster of agony*) : Miss Rivers—Miss Gill——

JULIAN : Pardon me. I see I am *de trop*.

KATE : No, Mr. Bromley, stay. Mr. Porter, I accept your suit.

JULIAN : The devil !

KATE : Your congratulations, Mr. Bromley ?

JULIAN : I see. Albert—Miss Gill—I congratulate you. And now, perhaps you will congratulate *me*.

KATE : On your escape ?

JULIAN : On the contrary—on my captivity. (*Takes* LAURA's *hand*.)

KATE (*snappishly*) : I wish you joy, Mr. Bromley.

JULIAN (*snappishly*) : I wish you joy, Miss Gill.

LAURA (*mournfully*) : I wish you joy, Mr. Porter.

ALBERT (*mournfully*) : I wish you joy, Miss Rivers.

JULIAN (*masterfully*) : Come, Laura, our dance I think. You will honour me ?

LAURA (*sadly*) : I shall be delighted.

KATE (*pointedly*) : Do you reverse, Albert ?

ALBERT (*sadly*) : I never quite know.

[*Finale*.

The four lovers begin to dance a polka, which is soon joined by the GUESTS *from the ballroom, and by* EDWARD, *who prances out of the snuggery with* BELLA. *Polka comes to an end*.

EDWARD : Bella, you've given me an appetite ! Supper ! Supper ! Supper ! Supper ! Ladies and Gentlemen ! take your partners for the supper-dance !

[*A gallop is played. The* GUESTS *and principals dance round the room.* MR. GILL, *unpartnered, stands in the middle, prancing hilariously all by himself, and when the revels are at their height,* MRS. GILL *suddenly appears by the portière in full fig, red velvet, cameo jewellery, etc. She starts, and holds up her hands in disapproval.*

MRS. GILL (*as* EDWARD *sweeps by*): Edward !

EDWARD: Mamma !

MRS. GILL (*as* LAURA *ditto*): Laura !

LAURA: Oh, aunt !

MRS. GILL (*as* KATE *ditto*): Kate !

KATE: Heavens, mamma !

MRS. GILL (*as she spies* MR. GILL): Mr. Gill !

MR. GILL : Mrs. G. ?

MRS. GILL : Come here at once ! My salts ! My salts !

[*The piano stops. The dance is suspended. The orchestra strikes chords for the ensuing " Excuse me's." These, and the rest of the scene to the end, are sung.*

LAURA (*to* ALBERT): Excuse me ! (*Hastens to* MRS. GILL.)

KATE (*ditto*): Excuse me ! (*Ditto.*)

EDWARD (*to* BELLA): Excuse me ! (*Ditto.*)

MR. GILL (*on a hiccough*): Excuse me ! (*Ditto.*)

MRS. GILL : I trusted—you wholly—
            How could you—abuse me !

KATE :   Hush, hush, dear !

MRS. GILL :   The ruin—

MR. GILL :   There, there, dear !

MRS. GILL :   —of all I'd worked for—

LAURA :   Be calm, dear !

MRS. GILL :   —in planning—this ball !
(*to* KATE):   Tell me why your brother prances
                With a minx beneath my ban ?
(*to* EDWARD):   Why your sister spoils her chances
                With that negligible man

(*to* LAURA):   Tell me how your uncle *can*
Make himself an exhibition,
Demonstrating, while he dances,
His unspeakable condition ?

LAURA: Now, now, dear !

MRS. GILL: Such romping !

EDWARD: Come, come, dear !

MRS. GILL: Such orgies !
(*At* MR. GILL) Resembling—the days of—

MR. GILL: Hush, hush, dear !

MRS. GILL: —the Georges !

THE FAMILY ⎧ Sit down, dear ! take care, dear !
FOUR: ⎩ The salts, dear ! more air, dear !

MR. GILL: Remember ! remember !
What's to happen in December !

THE GUESTS:
How painful—How awkward—How very
dismaying !
Don't listen—don't notice—the things she—
is saying !
What ought we—to do ?—We must not—
seem depressed.
To dance and—pretend we—see nothing—
is best !

[*The* GUESTS *go on dancing,* MRS. GILL, *seated
centre, rejects the salts offered by* MR. GILL, *the fan
offered by* EDWARD, *and the supplications of* KATE
and LAURA, *as the*

CURTAIN FALLS

ACT II

SCENE: *The garden, at about three o'clock in the morning. L., the portico of the house, with three or four steps. Window above. R., a gazebo, backed by a shrubbery which admits of various exits and entrances. Back, the river, with some means of approach from the garden on the bank. Moonlight. Very tender atmosphere.*

Before the curtain rises, JULIAN *is heard singing the first lines of the old song " Juanita "; he continues this after the rise of the curtain, singing very smoothly and melodiously from the house, unseen by the audience.*

The GUESTS *are departing.* KATE *and* LAURA *stand under the portico at the top of the steps, saying good-bye to them. Their remarks and those of the* GUESTS *are sung in snatches which fit in with the melody of " Juanita."*

A LADY: Good night ! such a delightful party !

LAURA: How nice of you !

KATE: So glad you came !

LAURA: Good night !

A GENTLEMAN: Good night !

A LADY: Thanks for a charming party.

A GENTLEMAN: How calm the night is.

A LADY: Isn't the moon bright !

A GENTLEMAN: Good night, Miss Gill.

A LADY: Good night to you, Miss Rivers.

A LADY: Such a sweet frock, love !

BELLA: Do come and see us soon.

A LADY: Good night.

A GENTLEMAN: What a delightful party ! Take care how you go, dear.

A LADY: What a moon !

KATE: Good night !

LAURA: Good night !

A LADY: Such a delightful party.

A GENTLEMAN: You'd better put your shawl on.

A GIRL: Oh ! oh dear !
If only balls went on for ever and ever.

A GENTLEMAN: The cab has come, dear.

A LADY: Isn't the night clear !

A LADY: Just smell the jasmine !

A GENTLEMAN: Good night, dear Miss Rivers.

A LADY: Good night, Kate darling.

A LADY: Why, the moon is bright
Enough to read by !

A GENTLEMAN: *The* most delightful party
I've been to for an age !

ALL: Good night ! Good night !

[*When the last* GUEST *has disappeared,* JULIAN
*strolls out of the house, singing the last lines of
" Juanita " on the stage; he bows cuttingly to*
KATE—*who, upset, runs into the house—then
courteously to* LAURA, *and departs.*

BELLA *has loitered expectantly beside the gazebo.*

ALBERT *appears from the house, while the " Juanita " refrain is still being played by the orchestra,
and takes a silent, melancholy farewell of* LAURA,
who gazes sadly after him as he goes; meanwhile
EDWARD *pops from behind a bush and whispers
audibly to* BELLA, *following rapidly the tune of the
refrain.*

EDWARD (*singing*):

Bella !
Beautiful black-eyed Bella !
Though I know it's getting late,
Grant me
One little assignation——
Go in there, and wait !

[BELLA *slips into the gazebo.* ALBERT *has departed.* EDWARD *goes into the house, carelessly, to await his opportunity.* LAURA *is left alone, in a pensive attitude.*

Enter KATE *from house.*

KATE: Aren't you coming to bed, Laura?

LAURA: I suppose so.

KATE: It's very late.

LAURA: I shan't sleep.

KATE: Nor I. Oh dear! and I meant to have such delicious dreams of my future husband.

LAURA: So did I. If only we could exchange dreams!

KATE: Very well. You have full permission to dream of *my* future husband if I may dream of yours.

LAURA: Would that be quite proper?

KATE: We need never tell. Dreams are the one place where a girl's family can't interfere.

LAURA: Ah, but her conscience may!

KATE: Here is a charm that will lay conscience to rest. (*She takes both bouquets.*) These flowers have made us wretched. Now let them make us happy. Take mine; I will take yours; and with these by our pillows we will dream of the men we love, instead of the men we're going to marry.

LAURA (*pressing* ALBERT'S *bouquet to her bosom*): It sounds rather wicked.

KATE (*doing the same with* JULIAN'S): Very, very wicked.

LAURA: But rather nice.

KATE: Very, very nice.

DUET: LAURA AND KATE

(*Air:* " *Petits Enfants* ")

Sweet blossoms, born for so brief an hour,
Upon your petals tremble dreams
As bright as dew that falls at even.
Within each flower
Like starlight gleams
A glimpse of Heaven.
So swiftly born, so swiftly blown,
A dream that dies as soon as known,
A scent that lingers in our bosoms,
A memory that is our own,
Sweet blossoms.

[MRS. GILL *appears at door.*

MRS. GILL: Girls ! what are you doing ! Why aren't you in bed ? Where is papa ?

KATE: Isn't he in the house ?

MRS. GILL: I can find him nowhere. For all I know, he's at the bottom of the river. Anything might happen to a man in that state.

KATE: He's sure to be all right, mamma. We'll find him.

MRS. GILL: You, Laura, search the shrubbery ; you, Kate, the rosery—and don't fall over the croquet hoops.

LAURA: We won't. Do go back to bed, aunt. The night dews aren't good for you.

[MRS. GILL *turns to go.*

KATE: I hope you are no longer displeased with us, mamma.

MRS. GILL (*non-committally*): I shall see how I feel in the morning. It's as well I came down when I did. My presence made all the difference. It was a successful ball, I think.

KATE (*suppressing a sigh*): Most successful, mamma.

MRS. GILL: Everybody enjoyed themselves.

LAURA (*suppressing a sigh*): Everybody, aunt.

MRS. GILL: One of the pigeon pies was left intact. It will come in nicely for to-morrow.

LAURA: Yes, aunt. Good night.

MRS. GILL: Was all the trifle eaten?

KATE: Not quite, mamma. Good night.

MRS. GILL: See that the shutters are bolted. Put the cat out. And send your uncle in.

LAURA: Yes, yes, aunt.

KATE: Yes, yes, mamma. (*They disperse, each girl with the right bouquet.*)

MRS. GILL (*left alone after the girls have gone out—communing, so to speak, for a moment before turning in*):

SOLO: MRS. GILL

(*Air: " The Two Cousins "*)

Oh it was, after all,
A success as a ball,
In spite of a slight *contretemps* now and then;
I think I can say
That in my own way
I *do* know what pleases young girls and young men,
I *do* know what pleases young girls and young men.

Two tablespoons are missing,
I must have the silver checked,
There was rather too much kissing,
And my potted palm was wrecked!
I heard some language spoken
That would not pass at Court,
A claret-glass was broken,
And the Charlotte Russe ran short!

Still, it was, after all,
A success as a ball,
I fancy our girls will not need one again.
Though I don't wish to boast,
I know better than most
Exactly what pleases young girls and
young men,
Exactly what pleases young girls and
young men ! (*Exit.*)

[ALBERT *prowls on, a cloaked figure. He looks
up at the house.*

ALBERT (*in a whisper*): Edward ! Edward !
(*He throws a stone at* EDWARD'S *window.*)

EDWARD (*popping his head out*): Coming, poppet !

[EDWARD'S *head disappears again. The door
of the gazebo opens slightly, and* BELLA *peeps out,
expecting* EDWARD; *seeing* ALBERT, *she gives a
little shriek and closes the door rapidly.* ALBERT
turns in bewilderment.

ALBERT: God bless my soul !

[*He tries to see where the sound came from.* EDWARD
*comes out of the house in frogged and padded
crimson smoking-jacket and black Turkish smoking-
cap with red tassel. He glides up to the dark figure
of* ALBERT *in the shadow of the gazebo and clasps it.*

EDWARD: You little rogue !

ALBERT (*extricating himself*): Good gracious !

EDWARD (*roaring with laughter*): Ho, ho ! I took
you for somebody else.

ALBERT: Not so loud ! For whom ?

EDWARD (*leaning against gazebo door as it begins
to open again*): Who for ? Dash it all, now ! Let
me think. Ah, I know ! I took you for Patty.

ALBERT: Your wife ?

EDWARD: That's the ticket. As a matter of fact,
dear chap, she's having a spree with some of

her own jolly friends to-night, and threatened for two pins to turn up here and fetch me. So, when your stone hit my window, I naturally supposed—— (*The door of the gazebo begins to open again;* EDWARD *closes it with his weight.*)

ALBERT: Yes, naturally.

EDWARD: *Naturellement!* (*Airy and confidential*) There's nothing more useful in life than a perfectly natural explanation—always keep one handy, my dear fellah. Now let's have yours.

ALBERT: My what?

EDWARD: Your perfectly natural explanation. Why haven't you gone home to bed, you naughty boy?

ALBERT: Because I am distracted. There's been some horrible mistake. I want you to tell me what happened when you presented my bouquet? What was her attitude?

EDWARD: One of the purest ecstasy—as far as I recall. But to tell you the truth, I don't recall very much, dear boy. I was just a bit——

ALBERT: You were very much!

EDWARD (*gaily*): And still am, my dear fellah, and still am! (*Singing*) "Good night! such a delightful party! Dearest friends, go-o-ood night!" (*Goes towards house.*)

ALBERT: Wait! Listen to me. Miss Rivers has not only made it plain that she loves another— she seems strangely in error as to *my* feelings. I want to make sure my message did not miscarry. You *did* give my bouquet to her?

EDWARD (*indignant*): Of course I did! (*Confident*) I know I did! (*Considerative*) I think I did. (*Dubious*) Well, to be perfectly honest, I'm dashed if I can remember. But I gave your message to *some*body. (*Confident again, slapping*

ALBERT *on the shoulder*) Yes, cheer up ! *Some*body
knows you love her. So that's all right.

ALBERT : All right ? It could hardly be worse !
Rack your brains—think—think—to whom
did you give my bouquet ?

EDWARD : Ask me again to-morrow. *Demain
matin !* You really must excuse me. I've a
pressing engagement. Bed-time, Albert. Go
home and sleep.

DUET : ALBERT AND EDWARD
(*Air : " Stars of the Summer Night "*)

ALBERT : Hist ! I will watch and stay
　　　　 Here where the willow weeps,
　　　　 Under her bower till day—
　　　　　　 She sleeps ! she sleeps !
　　　　　　 My lady sleeps !
　　　　　　 My lady sleeps !
　　　　　　　 Sleeps !

EDWARD : Hist ! lest the prudish eye
　　　　　 See me undo the gates
　　　　　 Where, full of roguery,
　　　　　　　 She waits ! she waits !
　　　　　　　 My lady waits !
　　　　　　　 My lady waits !
　　　　　　　　 Waits !

ALBERT : Hist ! I will haunt this spot
　　　　 Till the grey morning creeps,
　　　　 Yes, though she knows it not—
　　　　　　 She sleeps ! she sleeps !
　　　　　　 My lady sleeps,
　　　　　　 My lady sleeps !
　　　　　　　 Sleeps !

EDWARD : Hist ! let me seize my chance !
　　　　　 Sweetest of tête-à-têtes !
　　　　　 Hid from censorious glance
　　　　　　 She waits, waits, waits !
　　　　　　 My lady waits !

ALBERT: My lady sleeps !

EDWARD: My lady waits !

ALBERT: She sleeps !

BOND {   My lady waits !
                          sleeps !
                My lady waits !
                          sleeps !

[At the close of the duet, ALBERT wanders off into the shrubbery.

EDWARD: And now for my little bird in the cage !

[EDWARD is about to enter the gazebo, when MR. GILL meanders across the stage in a zig-zag towards the house, singing unaccompanied.

MR. GILL:
          Oh, I know a maid
          In the Lowther Arcade,
     And upon my word you couldn't better her.
          She's my pretty, pretty Poll
          With a fol-de-rol-de-rol,
     And a fol-de-rol-etcetera-etcetera.

MRS. GILL (*calling*): Girls, girls, where *is* papa ?

[MR. GILL, at doorstep, swerves aside on hearing her voice.

MR. GILL: I think perhaps a single bed to-night. Hic ! Who *wants* to discover the North Pole ?

[Exit, up stage.

EDWARD: *Encore la gazebo !*

[The gazebo door opens: EDWARD is about to enter, when LAURA appears through the shrubbery. He shuts the door quickly and stands before it.

LAURA: Edward !

EDWARD: Adorable cousin !

LAURA: What are you doing?

EDWARD: Nothing!

LAURA: Where were you going?

EDWARD: Nowhere!

LAURA: Who is in the gazebo?

EDWARD: Nobody!

[*A chair is knocked over inside, followed by a little shriek.*

The deuce!

LAURA: A woman! You *were* going into the gazebo! What for?

EDWARD: To oil the lawn-mower. Didn't you hear it squeak?

LAURA: Who is she? I believe it's that Miss Manchester.

EDWARD: Nonsense! She doesn't squeak.

LAURA: Then who *is* she?

EDWARD: Look here, Laura, my sweet, hold your breath and I'll tell you a secret. I'm married.

LAURA: It's not true.

EDWARD: My darling little Laura, it *is* true. I *am* married. I've been married exactly five weeks and three days. To the sweetest, sauciest diddle-darling——

LAURA: In there?

EDWARD: In there. But mum's the word.

LAURA (*agitated*): Edward, how could you! Think of your parents.

EDWARD: I do! I do! *tout le temps!* That's why I keep her secret.

LAURA: Wouldn't they approve? Edward! Isn't she a lady?

EDWARD: Well, she isn't the Duchess of Teck.

LAURA: How shocking ! They'll never, never receive her.

EDWARD: But you, Laura, you'll stand by me, won't you ? After all, it was my diddle-darling who induced me to give up wild oats for the porridge of family life. If my parents won't let me settle down into family life, what hope is there for me ?

DUET: EDWARD AND LAURA

(*Air: " My Heart is like a Silent Lute "*)

EDWARD:
The youth who sows the wildest oats
    May yearn to reap the purest wheat;
Beneath the coats of giddy goats
    What steadfast hearts may often beat !
When on the altar raised to virtue
    You make a sacrifice in vain,
You're forced by those who love and hurt you
    To go and sow wild oats again.

BOTH:
You're forced by those (*etc.*)

LAURA:
If you will swear that you have made
    An honest woman of your love,
I'll take her hand and, unafraid,
    Your friend in this dilemma prove.
Tell her who waits in yon interior,
    And saved you from the Primrose Path,
That she, although of birth inferior,
    Has earned her pure domestic hearth.

BOTH:
That she, although (*etc.*).

[LAURA *has led* EDWARD *to the gazebo. She makes a gesture for him to enter. Enter* ALBERT *at back.*

EDWARD: You darling ! I am your eternal debtor. Kiss me ! (*He kisses her.*) Kiss me again !

(*He kisses her again.*) You know, you're *almost* a poppet ! (*He kisses her again.*) You *are* a poppet !

LAURA : Edward !

EDWARD : *Maintenant la gazebo !*

[*She runs off.* ALBERT *half follows her, then pauses. Meanwhile,* EDWARD *has slipped into the gazebo.*

RECITATIVE : ALBERT

Kissing ! Kissing !
Can I believe my eyes ?
Can Laura, whom I love so tenderly,
Laura, who is betrothed to Julian,
Be but a fickle poppet ?
Alas !
That she loves me not is manifest,
For in her hands she bore the white bouquet
I sent to her.
Then there was *no* mistake !
She *did* receive my message,
And yet she spurned me for my fellow
    oarsman !

[JULIAN *enters through the shrubbery, and strides up to* ALBERT.

JULIAN : Traitor !

ALBERT : What ?

JULIAN : *And* poltroon !

ALBERT : Why ?

JULIAN : Traitor for going behind my back with Kate. Poltroon for skulking here rather than risk meeting me !—you whom I thought my friend—you to whom I confided the secret of my love—you who row bow to my stroke—*you* engaged to Kate !

ALBERT : Really, Julian ! What about *your* engagement ?

JULIAN: It was inevitable. Kate had refused me. There was no hope for me. Laura was pining for me. There was no hope for you. I couldn't repel the poor creature.

ALBERT: Your excuse is mine. What we have done, we have done as men of honour to make those sweet girls happy. Julian !

JULIAN: Albert ! (*They grip hands.*)

ALBERT: I swear to guard your pretty Kate as the very apple of your eye.

JULIAN: And I your constant Laura.

ALBERT: Constant ? I always thought so—I think so still—but——

JULIAN: What are you hinting ?

ALBERT: I have just seen her in the arms of another.

JULIAN (*delighted*): Who ?

ALBERT: Edward.

JULIAN (*dejected*): Her cousin.

ALBERT: Yes—but he called her poppet.

JULIAN: Poppet ?

ALBERT: Poppet. And he kissed her. And he kissed her again. He kissed her three times. Out in the garden—all alone—at *this* time of night.

JULIAN: It's fishy.

ALBERT: It's very fishy. She should be warned.

JULIAN: Of what ?

ALBERT: Edward's marriage.

JULIAN: We promised Edward not to tell.

ALBERT: But where a lady's honour is concerned——

JULIAN: A lady's honour ? She shall be warned. Leave it to me.

ALBERT: Look ! She's coming ! I'll wait in the shrubbery. (*Exit.*)

[*Enter* LAURA.

LAURA: He's not in the boat-house ! Surely not the gazebo—— (*Sees* JULIAN.) Oh, Mr. Bromley—— (*Hesitatingly*) Julian.

JULIAN (*courteously*): My love. (*Suspiciously*) You are out very late.

LAURA: I am looking for my uncle.

JULIAN (*aside*): Uncle !

LAURA: Why have you come back ?

JULIAN: I have something on my mind.

[KATE *enters behind.*

KATE: He's not in the hothouse. Perhaps the gazebo—— (*Going towards gazebo, she sees* LAURA *and* JULIAN.) Oh !

[*She stands listening in the shadow of the gazebo.* JULIAN *leads* LAURA *to a seat and poses over her.*

JULIAN: Let me be frank. My happiness in the honour you have done me to-night is not un-clouded.

LAURA: I am sorry. Why ?

JULIAN: Have I not observed in you a partiality —no doubt a passing partiality—but a partiality—for another ?

LAURA (*aside*): Albert ! He suspects !

KATE (*aside*): Albert ! Poor Laura !

JULIAN (*aside*): She is confused. Albert was right. She *is* carrying on with Edward. (*Aloud*) If I am wrong, pardon the sensitiveness of a lover. *Am* I wrong ?

LAURA: Believe me, I will fulfil my engagement. You shall not have a moment's cause for jealousy.

K

JULIAN (*politely*) : You ease my mind. The more so, as the gentleman in question is already tied to another.

LAURA (*aside*) : To Kate, alas !

KATE (*aside*) : Alas, to me !

JULIAN : I had it this evening from his own lips that he is married.

LAURA (*with a cry*) : Married !

KATE (*aside*) : Albert Porter married !

JULIAN : You are surprised. You will be still more so to learn that his wife is an actress.

LAURA (*springing up*) : Impossible !

JULIAN : Miss Patty Moss, of the Travesty Theatre.

LAURA (*faintly*) : Mr. Bromley—is this true ?

JULIAN : Unquestionably. When it comes out, the fat will be in the fire—but that need not trouble you or me. He is nothing to us.

LAURA : No—nothing.

JULIAN : I thank you for that assurance. Pardon me for disturbing you at this hour. Attribute it to a lover's zeal. Good night.

[*He places an unzealous kiss on her brow, and exit into shrubbery.* LAURA *sits stunned.* KATE *runs forward and clasps her.*

KATE : Laura !

LAURA : Kate ! You heard——

KATE : Everything !

LAURA : Albert married——

KATE : And to an actress. I didn't think he had it in him !

LAURA : Kate—please !

KATE : But, really ! The effrontery of the fellow ! To propose to *me* when he was married already !

LAURA: You must have nothing more to do with him.

KATE: He must never be admitted to the house again.

LAURA: We must tell your papa.

KATE: And my mamma !

DUET: KATE AND LAURA

(*Air : " The Lover and the Bird "*)

KATE: I'll tell papa,
                         I'll tell mamma,
               They must never receive him more !

LAURA: I must be stern,
                         Yes, I must learn
               Not to welcome where I adore !

KATE: Think of my shame,
                         Hearing his name,
               To which another has prior claim !

BOTH: I'll tell papa,
                         Tell your papa,
                         I'll tell mamma,
                         Tell your mamma,
               They must never receive him more !

LAURA: No more !

KATE: No more !

LAURA: Ah !

KATE: Ah !

BOTH: Ah !

LAURA: Cousin, pity me !
                How cruel life can be !

BOTH: We must never receive him more !

[They run into the house. The sound of approaching banjoes and guitars from the river mingles with the end of their duet, and carries on as EDWARD *cautiously opens the door of the gazebo.*

EDWARD: *Doucement, mon enfant !* I'll see if the coast is clear. (*Banjoes nearer.*) Now, Bella, now's your chance ! No—wait ! What the deuce is that ? Patty and her party ! The little devil has kept her threat, after all.

PATTY'S PARTY

(*Heard singing a Plantation Song, off*)

Git on de boat, chillun,
Git on de boat, chillun,
Git on de boat, chillun,
An' we will sail away.

[EDWARD *disappears into the gazebo.*

I tho't I saw ol' Massa,
An' dis am wat he say,
Git on de boat, chillun,
An' we will sail away.

[*The song approaches, and the punt full of people appears during the last four lines.*

Git on de boat, chillun,
Git on de boat, chillun,
Git on de boat, chillun,
An' we will sail away.

[*The punt comes to a standstill. In it are* PATTY MOSS *and her party of* THESPIAN REVELLERS, *grouped in a picture—one with a banjo, one with a guitar, one with a rosetted punt-pole, others affectionately disposed, and* PATTY *in the centre of the piece. The man with the punt-pole is in full fancy dress, while some of the others, but not* PATTY, *have obviously " got themselves up impromptu "—an antimacassar over the shoulders, a patchwork quilt :* GEORGE *sports a tea-cosy instead of a hat.*

The PARTY *disembarks rowdily.*

PATTY: So this is where my hubby sows his tame oats, is it ? Behold the Haunt of Respectability !

GEORGE (*a large, blustering type of comic actor*): Where is the caitiff who stole thee from me ?

Speak ! that I may summon him, and run him through the gizzard ! Which is the villain's window ?

PATTY: Ask me another ! This is the first time I've so much as set foot on my darling's door-step.

GEORGE (*rolling his eyes*): *Thy* darling ! Ha, ha ! (*Seizes her wrist.*) Dost flaunt thy passion in my very teeth, thou shameless gy-url ?

PATTY: Here, not so much of the " shameless " ! Have I not me marriage-lines here in me buzzum ?

GEORGE (*dissolving into tears*): My che-ild ! My innocent, stainless, brainless che-ild, come to your father's arms ! (*They embrace. He sobs over her, and looks round at their friends.*) A little applause from a kind and indulgent audience !

[*The others boo. The banjoes strike up again, this time with the refrain of :* " *She does the Fandango.*"

In answer to your generous applause, Miss Patty Moss will now oblige.

[GEORGE *has taken* PATTY'S *hand, and they have bowed with flourishing acknowledgments of the booing. He kisses her hand as the refrain reaches its end, rolls his eyes at her, and bursts into the opening verse of the song, which he and she perform extravagantly as they sing.*

DUET : GEORGE, PATTY AND CHORUS

(*Air :* " *She does the Fandango* "[1])

GEORGE :

I've seen many beauties, whilst travelling around

The world, but in Spain, there my fancy I found ;

PATTY :

She'd hair black as coal, eyes bright as a star,

[1] Copyright. Reprinted by permission of Ascherberg, Hopwood & Crew Ltd. Two verses only are reprinted here. Messrs. Ascherberg, Hopwood & Crew's version has four verses.

GEORGE:
    And I felt fairly gone, as she twanged her
      guitar !

[GEORGE *sings refrain alone while* PATTY *does the
pantomime.*

    She sang like a nightingale, twanged the
      guitar,
    Danced the Cachuca, and smoked a cigar,
    O ! what a form, O ! what a face !
    And she did the Fandango, all over the place.

(*Patter*) On being introduced to her father, a
villainous-looking personage, he said something
like this :

PATTY (*breaking in*) : " Hah ! Stiletto ! Cigaretto !
You bet-o ! "

GEORGE: I said, " My dear sir, you are quite
right in your observation ! " There was something wrong somewhere, for he flourished a
dagger, and said :

PATTY (*as before*) : " Ho ! Desperado ! Intimi-
dado ! Lar-di-dar-do ! "

GEORGE : And so, to soothe him, (*sings*)

    To England I brought her, to make her my
      bride,
    And when my friends saw her, they laughed
      till they cried ;
    And the buttons flew off from a dozen white
      vests,

PATTY :
    When at breakfast she somewhat astonished
      the guests.
    She sang like a nightingale, twanged the
      guitar !

GEORGE : Danced the Cachuca,

PATTY :   And smoked a cigar,

GEORGE: O ! what a form,

PATTY: O ! what a face !

EVERYBODY:
  And she did the Fandango, all over the place !

  [*Repeat refrain, during which* PATTY *and* GEORGE
  *do the Fandango all over the place. At the end of the
  Fandango,* MR. GILL'S *voice is heard, singing off,
  one of his irresponsible little songs as he wanders
  in the garden. The* ACTORS *are arrested.*

GEORGE: What have we here ?

PATTY: Hark, hark, the lark ! Into the bushes,
boys !

  [*They take cover, as* MR. GILL *wanders in during
  his first stanza.*

SOLO: MR. GILL

(*Air: "Mandolinata"*)

I wish I was in Texas,
I'd travel to Indiana,
    I'd marry a squaw
    According to law,
Oh, that would be Nirvana !
I wish I was in Cuba,
I'd marry a gay gitana,
    Beholden to none
    I'd sit in the sun
And smoke a big Havana !

  [*The* ACTORS *begin to steal round him from behind,
  beckoned mischievously by* PATTY, *as* MR. GILL *sits
  on seat, singing " Tra-la-la ! "*

I wish I was in Turkey,
    I'd marry a small Sultana,
    With sherbet and scent,
    A moon, and a tent,
And such Arabiana !

  [GEORGE *leaps up behind the seat like the Demon
  King in the pantomime.*

GEORGE: Pinch him, fairies, black and blue !

[MR. GILL *staggers startled to his feet, while the* ACTORS *tease him.*

PATTY: Shut up, you fools ! I do believe it's my pa-in-law !

GEORGE: Varlet ! thy name !

MR. GILL: Ladies and gentlemen—(*trying to rise*)—this intrusion——

GEORGE (*grandly*): Is pardoned. Say no more. (*Putting tea-cosy on* MR. GILL'S *head*) Arise, Pomponius !

MR. GILL (*spluttering*): What the dickens——

PATTY: Oh, language, language ! Ladies present !

MR. GILL: Ladies ! ladies ! Who *are* you ? (*Pointing at* PATTY) Who are *you* ?

SOLO: PATTY

(*Air: " Mozzer bought a Baby "*)

I'm pretty, pretty Patty,
 Pretty Patty Moss !
I trip behind the footlights,
 And sometimes trip across !
Come to the theayter
 When you're at a loss,
And tip the wink to Patty,
 Pretty Patty Moss !

When I'm in my spangles and my rosy tights,
How the johnnies ogle me across the lights !
Necklaces and bracelets come by every post,
Pearls are very welcome—I like diamonds most.

I'm pretty, pretty Patty,
 Pretty Patty Moss ! (*etc.*)

Baronets in boxes, guardsmen in the stalls,
Scuttle to the stage door when the curtain falls;
They appear to take me for a goddess—pooh!
What d'ye think I'm made of? Flesh and blood
  like you!

All together boys!

CHORUS: She's pretty, pretty Patty,
              Pretty Patty Moss! (*etc.*)

[KATE *and* LAURA *enter from house as* JULIAN
and ALBERT *reappear in the garden.*

LAURA (*advancing with a cry*): Patty Moss!

KATE (*ditto*): Patty Moss!

JULIAN AND ALBERT: Patty Moss!

LAURA: *His* wife!

PATTY: Oh, law! the cat's out now!

MR. GILL: What's all this? *Whose* wife?

LAURA: Albert Porter's!

PATTY: *What's* that?

ALBERT: Mine!

JULIAN: No, no, a misunderstanding——

KATE (*vixenish*): Yes, shield him, do! You men
all hang together!

MR. GILL (*at his wits' ends*): What's going on?
What's happening? Kate—Laura—Albert—
Julian—and those Dancing Dervishes! Is
everybody mad? We might as well be in
Timbuctoo!

PATTY (*to* LAURA): Excuse me, young woman,
I don't know who the deuce you are, but are you
insinuating——

LAURA: That you are Mrs. Albert Porter? I
am!

PATTY (*indicating* ALBERT): And is *this* the lucky
man?

LAURA: You know he is.

ALBERT: Miss Rivers, how can you believe it? An actress—*me*!

PATTY: What's wrong with an actress, young man?

ALBERT: I swear before heaven I am *not* her husband. As if I could!

PATTY (*tossing her head*): Oh, you couldn't, couldn't you?

MR. GILL: Is he, or isn't he?

PATTY (*at* LAURA): Ask Miss Paul Pry.

LAURA: He *is*.

KATE: He *is*!

JULIAN: He's *not*!

ALBERT: I—am—*not*!

ENSEMBLE

(*Air:* "*I and You*")

Recitative

ALBERT AND JULIAN:
   What can be the meaning of this strange plot?
   Why should $\left\{\begin{array}{l} I \\ he \end{array}\right.$ be the sport of fate?

PAPA AND GIRLS:
      Are you Albert's wife, or are you not?
      Madam, to hear the truth we wait!

PAPA   } Are you his wife?
GIRLS   } She is his wife!

PAPA   } Or are you not?
ALBERT AND JULIAN } No, she is not!

Air

ENSEMBLE: Yes or no? Yes or no?
      Are you single? Are you plighted?
      And if so, let us know
      To what man you are united.

PATTY :   Go away ! Go away !
    I refuse to ! I refuse to !
    I shan't say, I shan't say,
    I shan't say until I choose to !

ALBERT :   Madam, please ! Madam, please !
    Tell the truth at once and clear me !
    On my knees, on my knees,
    I implore you, madam, hear me !

ALL :   Yes or no ?

PATTY :   I shan't tell !

ALL :   Is it so ?

PATTY :   I shan't tell !

ALL :   No or yes ?
    Come, confess !

PATTY :   Very well . . .
    I shan't tell !

ENSEMBLE : Yes or no ? Yes or no ?
    Are you single ? Are you plighted ?
    And, if so, let us know
    To what man you are united.
    Madam, pray, madam, pray
    See ⎰me   See ⎰me
    ⎨him righted ! ⎨him righted !
    ⎱us   ⎱us
    Go away ! Go away !
    She won't say ! No, she won't say !

PATTY (*singing with above eight lines*) :

    Yes, yes, yes ! No, no, no !
    I am single ! I am plighted !
    Wouldn't *you* like to know
    To what man I am united ?
    Why should I bother, pray,
    If you're wronged or if you're
       righted ?
    Go away ! Go away !
    I shan't say ! No, I shan't say !

(*Speaks*) Oh, very well ! If you *insist* on the name

of my husband, here goes ! And if you don't like it, lump it ! I am married——

MR. GILL : Yes ?

LAURA :   Yes ?

KATE :   Yes ?

PATTY : To——

MR. GILL : Out with it, madam !

PATTY : Your son Edward !

    [*Consternation.*

MR. GILL (*horrified*) : Edward !

LAURA (*in a ringing voice*) : It is false !

PATTY : Hoity-toity ! she's at it again !

LAURA : Don't believe a word she says, uncle ! Edward is *not* this person's husband——

PATTY : Person ! A precious lot you know about it, young woman !

LAURA : I will *not* allow you to use my cousin as a blind, even (*faltering*) even to protect Mr. Porter.

ALBERT (*in agony*) : Oh, Miss Rivers !

JULIAN : Laura, there is some confounded mistake. Your cousin Edward *is* married——

LAURA : I know it ! He has told me all. Uncle— (*seizes his hand*) be lenient with him ! Forgive him ! He is in there (*points to gazebo*) at this very moment—with his wife.

PATTY (*screams*) : WHAT ! !

EDWARD (*singing in gazebo*) :
    Dearest Miss Bell,
    I nevah tell lies,
    And I declare
    Without disguise,
    I nevah saw
    Such beautiful eyes
    As yours when they gaze in mine !

[ALL *stand listening, forming picture, till the end of the song; then* PATTY *marches over briskly, pulls open the door, and discovers* BELLA *in* EDWARD'S *embrace.* PATTY *shrieks;* BELLA *squeaks;* EDWARD *releases her and he and* PATTY *stare at each other.* BELLA *seizes the opportunity, covers herself hurriedly with her shawl, and flees through the shrubbery.* EDWARD *brazens it out with laughter.*

EDWARD: Ha-ha ! Ha-ha ! (*Peters out*) *Pour passer le temps*, Patty, *pour passer le temps !*

PATTY: You wretch !

MR. GILL: Edward ! Is Bella Manchester your wife ?

EDWARD: *Pas ce soir*, papa !

PATTY (*under her breath*): My word, my boy, if I find that's true !

EDWARD (*in a whisper, reaching for her hand*): But, Patty, my pet——

PATTY: Hands off, please ! What'll my husband think ?

EDWARD: Your husband ?

PATTY: What, didn't you know ? Everybody else seems to ! Ask Miss Paul Pry. *She* knows everything. (*Takes* ALBERT'S *arm.*) Cue for the "Wedding March," George.

GEORGE: Pom ! pom ! pom-*pom*-pom-pom-pom——

ALBERT (*protesting*): No, no !

LAURA: I knew it.

ALBERT (*breaking away and kneeling at* LAURA'S *feet*): Laura !

PATTY (*sternly*): Now, Albert darling ! I've told you about this before. Come along home !

ALBERT (*rounding*): I won't !

PATTY (*to* GEORGE): Hercules, forward ! (*She nods toward* ALBERT *and jerks a thumb toward punt.*) Just give my lord and master a helping hand, will you ?

GEORGE (*seizing* ALBERT *and tucking him under his arm*): Come along, my little *jeune premier* !

[*He begins to bear* ALBERT *towards the punt; the drama of the situation seizes the* THESPIANS, *who surround* PATTY *and* ALBERT *and, with appropriate business, break rowdily into song.*

REPEAT OFF: " *She does the Fandango* "
(*tune of Refrain*)

CHORUS:
　To Twickenham he brought me, to make me
　　his bride,
　And when my friends saw him, they laughed
　　till they cried !
　O ! what a form, O ! what a face !
　And we do the Fandango, all over the place !

[*Dawn is breaking. The Fandago music continues, livelier and noisier, to the end of the scene.* ALBERT *is hoisted up.*

ALBERT (*calling*): Julian !

JULIAN (*taking a step forward*): Albert !

LAURA (*running to her*): Kate !

KATE (*clasping her*): Laura !

EDWARD: Patty !

PATTY (*dropping a mocking curtsey*): Edward !

MRS. GILL (*within*): Papa-a-a !

[*She appears at window, with a candle, in her peignoir and nightcap. The stage grows a little brighter, as birds begin to twitter. A cock crows.*

CURTAIN

ACT III

SCENE: *The bank of the river during the Regatta. The river flows unseen at the back of the stage. PATTY's house-boat, L. In the foreground, R. and L., two small striped tents: one is a ginger-pop booth, the other displays a notice saying, " CONSULT MADAME ZENOBIA." At R., back, there is rising ground.*

TIME: *Late afternoon.*

The scene presents a fête-champêtre appearance, very gay and rather disordered, with groups of REGATTEERS *in boating costumes of the period— a crowded convivial effect, with a couple of competitors, in vests and shorts and whiskers, making merry with their parties. The mound is occupied by* MRS. GILL, *surrounded by her family. They have a hamper with them, and are drinking tea sedately. A certain air of constraint is evident in the family relationships,* EDWARD *being in disgrace and not quite at ease, while* KATE *and* LAURA *are a little forlorn.*

On the house-boat, PATTY *and her party are in festive contrast to the group on the mound. Bottles are much in evidence, and they are playing a rackety game of cards. Other lively groups are strewn over the scene. A whiskered gentleman is playing a concertina.*

OPENING CHORUS

(*Air: " Far from his Mountains "*)

Oh, the Regatta
At Twickenham, at Twickenham,
Oh, the Regatta
Upon a summer day.
Sweet flows the river
At Twickenham, at Twickenham,
Sweet flows the river
Upon a summer day.

Ah ! . . .
So runs the time away.
With eyes alight we watch the bright
Aquatical display.
At Twickenham, at Twickenham,
With blades agleam upon the stream,
I dote on the Regatta
Upon a summer day.

PATTY'S PARTY

(*Air: " Paddy's the boy for me ! "*)

Oh, a bottle of gin,
Or a bottle of whiskey,
They're both to my mind,
For they both make you frisky !
But there's nought to compare
With toddy all hot,
For toddy's the tipple that touches the spot !
    Hurrah, me boy !
        HIP !
Toddy's the drink for me !
With my rum, rum, rum-ti-addidy,
        rum, rum, rum-ti-addidy,
        rum, rum, rum-ti-addidy,
Toddy's the drink for me !

Oh, claret is fine,
And a bottle of porter
Is equal to wine
And much better than water,
But toddy's the brew
That ecstasy brings,
Hot toddy's a tipple for tinkers and kings !
    Hurrah, me boy !
        HIP !
Toddy's the drink for me !
With my rum, rum, rum-ti-addidy,
        rum, rum, rum-ti-addidy,
        rum, rum, rum-ti-addidy,
Toddy's the drink for me !

(*Return to First Chorus*)

Ah ! . . .
So runs the time away.
With eyes alight we watch the bright
Acquatical display.
At Twickenham, at Twickenham,
With blades agleam upon the stream,
I dote on the Regatta
Upon a summer day !

MRS. GILL: If you ask my opinion, this regatta has been shockingly mismanaged. We have been expecting the next event for half an hour. And when it does come, it is sure to be something else.

MR. GILL: It couldn't be run worse by Hottentots !

MRS. GILL: They announce the Third Heat of the Canoes, and we get the Second Heat of the Skiffs. They announce the Semi-finals of the Double-Punting, and along comes one miserable man in a dinghy. And how late we're getting !—an hour and a half behind time.

EDWARD (*consulting watch*): To be *ab-so-lu-ment* accurate, one hour and twenty-nine minutes.

MRS. GILL: Kindly spare us your flippancies, Edward. I should have thought, after last night——

MR. GILL: Yes, yes, my boy, under the circumstances you might have the grace to hold your tongue.

EDWARD: Good Lord ! I didn't mean anything.

MRS. GILL: Invective won't help matters.

[*Laughter from* PATTY'S *party, and* PATTY'S *voice* : " Oh, him ! I've quite done with him, thank you ! "

EDWARD: Curse it ! she knows I'm here, and she won't give me a glance !

[*More laughter from* PATTY's *party. Two sporting* GENTLEMEN *stroll to the ginger-pop booth.*

FIRST GENTLEMAN: What about a bun, old boy?

SECOND GENTLEMAN: Capital! What about a ginger-pop?

ATTENDANT: Two buns, two pops.

KATE (*aside*): Oh, Laura, isn't it awful!

LAURA (*aside*): Awful!

KATE: Not a sign of Julian all day!

LAURA: Or of Albert.

MRS. GILL: Do try and look a little brighter, girls! You seem quite washed out. What are all those boats doing over there? They line up for the start, they fuss around changing places, and then they all go away again.

MR. GILL: If I were a steward, I'd be ashamed to wear my rosette.

MRS. GILL: At this rate we shall never get through before the fireworks. Already they talk of abandoning the Greasy Pole. That would be a great pity. I *am* so fond of the Greasy Pole. I *must* see that!

MR. GILL: Would it be wise? Remember, darling, you mustn't excite yourself.

MRS. GILL: The Greasy Pole I *must* see. I'd rather they abandoned the Twickenham Cup.

LAURA (*impulsively*) ⎱ Oh, I hope not!
KATE ⎰ I hope not!

LAURA: At least we shall see them from a distance in the race.

[TWO GIRLS *nudge each other in front of* MADAME ZENOBIA's *tent.*

FIRST GIRL: I wouldn't! I wouldn't! I wouldn't go in for worlds!

SECOND GIRL: Oh, come *on*, Lottie !

FIRST GIRL: Well, you *made* me ! (*They go into the tent.*)

MRS. GILL: *What* is that man doing in the bathing dress ? Is it the Fancy Diving, or the Obstacle Swimming Race ?

KATE: Where, mamma ?

MRS. GILL: Never mind, never mind, I'll tell you when he gets into the water. There now ! he has gone back into the tent. That's the fourth time he's disappointed us. How very provoking !

[*Commotion in* PATTY's *party.*

GEORGE (*slapping down cards in rotation*): Jack— Queen—King—out ! Hands off, Patty. I collar the pool.

PATTY: Hi ! you seem to collar everything. He's cheating, boys !

A MAN: Examine the cards ! (*Small scuffle.*)

GEORGE: Patty, my darling, you've been swilling too much whiskey. Pay up, now !

PATTY: I'll pay up all right. (*Shies a peach at him.*) Take that ! (*Screams of laughter as* GEORGE *wipes his cheek.*)

GEORGE: No fruit, by request. (*More laughter.* MRS. GILL *bridles.*)

MRS. GILL: That is a very rowdy party over there. Cards in broad daylight ! They'll be cycling on Sunday next. Where are my spectacles ?

KATE (*looking across*): Oh, mamma ! it's that horrid woman !

MRS. GILL: What horrid woman ?

KATE: The actress who turned up in our garden last night.

MRS. GILL: Ah ! Mrs. Albert Porter. I wonder she has the face to show herself. Don't look at her, my dears. Where *are* my spectacles ? (ALBERT *appears at back, in rowing costume;* MRS. GILL *catches sight of him.*) And there's that horrid man !

LAURA: What horrid man ?

MRS. GILL: Her husband—the deceiver. Look the other way, girls. Remember. We do not speak to Miss Moss. We do not speak to Miss Manchester. We do not speak to Mr. Porter. And we do not speak to his fellow-conspirator, Mr. Bromley.

EDWARD: How awfully jolly !

MRS. GILL: And what, pray, do you find so awfully jolly, Edward ?

EDWARD (*sulkily*): The Regatta, of course, the Regatta !

MR. GILL: Ah, my boy, regattas aren't what they used to be !

SOLO: MR. GILL

(*Air:* " *When I was young* ")

When I was a bounding boy
Regattas were my only joy,
But soon I left the madcap whirl
For a very steady punt with a rather giddy girl.

I was young,
And so were you,
The sun was high,
The skies were blue,
The skies were blue,
The sun was high,
You were young,
So was I !

As I poled my angel's punt
I dripped the Thames all down her front,
She cried " Oh ! " in great distress,
So with my pocket-handkerchief I dried her
    pretty dress.

                I said Yes ?
                You said No !
                Soon your tears
                Began to flow.
                What I whispered
                None can guess—
                You said No !
                I said Yes !

    The sun went down, the moon came up,
    Joy and bliss o'erflowed our cup,
    Regattas were my only joy,
When I was a very happy, rather naughty boy !

    [*A gun goes off.*

MRS. GILL : Thank Heaven ! another race at last !

    [*She sweeps off, followed by her family; they pass* ALBERT *en route, and each cuts him in his or her own way—*EDWARD *last of all, in humorous imitation of the others. There is a general movement of everybody to leave the stage, including the gingerpop* ATTENDANT *and* MADAME ZENOBIA.

PATTY : Hip ! hip ! a race ! Come on !

GEORGE : I back the fat man !

ACTRESS : Yes, you *would* !

PATTY : Who's got the binoculars ?

ALL (*on boat*) : Where's my programme ?

PATTY : Where's that bottle of fizz ?

GEORGE : Drunk, pretty creature, drunk.

ACTOR : They're starting !

ACTRESS : They're starting !

PATTY: Oh, come on everybody, do !

[PATTY *and her party disappear from top of house-boat.* ALBERT *sees and calls after her.*

ALBERT: Miss Moss ! Miss Moss !

[*He is left alone on the stage, dejected. Enter* JULIAN, *clad like* ALBERT *in the rowing-costume of the times.*

JULIAN: So ! there you are ! I've been looking for you. What on earth have you been doing ?

ALBERT: Hiding.

JULIAN: From me ?

ALBERT: From everybody. Until Miss Moss clears my character, how can I show my face ?

JULIAN: What happened after we saw you last ?

ALBERT: What didn't happen ! Oh, what a night ! They carried me off to that infernal house-boat, and there they kept it up, singing, drinking, and shouting the roof down. I've got a head like a steam-engine.

JULIAN: Why did you stay ?

ALBERT: I couldn't help myself. They locked me up. Besides, I wanted to make her promise to tell the Gills she wasn't married to me.

JULIAN: Wouldn't she ?

ALBERT: My dear man, by six o'clock she seemed to think she was married to the whole party. By eight o'clock they were all asleep and snoring. So I forced the door, made my escape, mooned about all day—and here I am, feeling about as fit for the Twickenham Cup as for a trip to the moon.

JULIAN: I'd begun to think you meant to let me down.

ALBERT: No, Julian, I should never do that. You'll find me there when the gun goes off. But how can I hope to do myself justice with this cloud hanging over me ? I shall be thinking of Laura all the time.

JULIAN: And I shall be thinking of Kate. Suppose we lose? But we must *not* lose! Albert, you mustn't fail me.

ALBERT: I'll do my best. But I shall pull with a heavy heart.

DUET: ALBERT AND JULIAN

(*Air:* " My Pretty Jane ")

I'll pull, I'll pull with heavy heart
   Against, against the stream,
I'll strive to play the sculler's part
   In spite of love's lost dream.
But though I win the victor's crown,
   'Twill be an empty gawd
If one among th' assembly frown
   While all the rest applaud.
With heavy heart, with heavy heart
   I'll pull against the stream,
With heavy, heavy, heavy heart
   I'll pull against the stream.

[*Enter* PATTY.

PATTY: Hullo, you two ! You do look a couple of dismal Jimmies !

ALBERT: Miss Moss !

PATTY: Well ?

ALBERT: Miss Moss !

PATTY: Out with it !

ALBERT: Miss Moss ! . . . Oh, Miss Moss !

PATTY: Poor dear ! is that his only line ?

JULIAN: My friend, Miss Moss, is not unnaturally distressed. Last night, in the presence of witnesses, you brought against him a cruel and unfounded accusation. You declared him to be your husband.

PATTY: Well I never ! Unfounded, if you like. But cruel !

JULIAN: Yes, cruel ! When you made that false statement, the girl he loves was standing at his side—and his hopes of connubial bliss are now blighted for ever. Do you realise what that means ?

PATTY: I like that ! Aren't I in the same boat ?

ALBERT: You ?

PATTY: Yes, me ! Didn't I, with half the dukes in town at my heels, give 'em all the push for Edward Gill—yes, and get married to him, too ! And don't I find him now with a wife already, and making love to her in the small hours, for all the world as though I were some manager's mistake in the back row of the chorus ? (*Stamping her foot*) Don't come to *me* for pity. If I'd known Edward was married to *that* little hussy——

ALBERT: But he's not.

PATTY: What ! don't tell me there's a *third* !

ALBERT: Edward Gill told us himself he was married to *you*.

PATTY: When ?

JULIAN: Only last night. He confessed to us both, in the strictest confidence, that he was married to " the sweetest, sauciest diddle-darling that ever wore tights behind footlights." Those were his very words.

PATTY: That's me all right.

JULIAN: Of course it's you.

PATTY: H'm. That does rather alter the complexion.

[*Enter* EDWARD *at back.*

ALBERT: I know it was very wrong of Edward to philander with Miss Manchester——

PATTY: Oh, that's *her* look-out. As long as he's not been philandering with *me* ! As long as *I'm* the injured wife, and *she's* the peccadillo !

EDWARD (*coming forward*): Patty ! my angel ! (*Tries to embrace her.*)

PATTY: Here—hands off, please ! (*Pushes him away.*) Don't you know an injured wife when you see one ?

EDWARD: Don't you know a repentant husband when you see one ?

PATTY: No, I don't.

EDWARD: Then you'd better take a good look at me now and get used to it. I'm going to be *ever* such a repentant hubby, you know. You *do* forgive me ?

PATTY: No.

EDWARD: Not if I go down on one knee ? (*Does so.*)

PATTY: No.

EDWARD: Not if I go down on two knees ? (*Does so.*)

PATTY: I never forgive anyone in company.

EDWARD: Then *tête-à-tête* ? (*Beginning to recover his French with his spirits.*)

ALBERT: Mr. Bromley, ought we to retire ?

JULIAN: No, Mr. Porter, not until the slur on your name is cleared——

EDWARD: But Patty will own up and tell the old folk Albert's *not* her husband—won't you, my pet ?

PATTY: If you'll own up and tell the old folk I *am* your wife—will you, my precious ?

EDWARD: There'll be the deuce of a rumpus. How are we going to bring the old folk round ? *Voilà la question !* You don't know my mamma.

PATTY: And your mamma doesn't know me. Give me half a chance, and if I don't talk her round in two two's, I'll kiss my understudy !

QUARTET : PATTY, JULIAN, ALBERT, EDWARD

(*Air:* " *One Joy Alone* ")

How can we bring the old folk round ?
They never think youth's reason sound,
And when we seek our own delight
They say we tread on dangerous ground.
In prudent counsel they abound,
They hold their wisdom most profound—
But we are certain we are right—
How can we bring,
How can we bring,
How can we bring the old folk round ?

[*Exeunt.*

Towards the close of the Quartet, the stage has become a shade darker. When it is over, the sunlight has disappeared and the sky is overclouded. The music changes to the next number, and continues during the preliminary business.

A LADY *hurries on* R., *pauses, looks up, wipes her cheek with her handkerchief, puts up her parasol, and hurries off* L. *She is followed by a* CHORUS OF REGATTEERS *flitting across the stage.*

CHORUS

(*Air: " Kis ! Kis ! "*)

ENSEMBLE : Yes ! yes ! yes ! yes !
I felt a spot ! I felt a spot !
Yes ! yes ! yes ! yes !
I'm sure it's raining, is it not? (*bis*)

Oh, how upsetting !
We'll get a wetting !
Where can we fly ?
We must keep dry ! (*bis*)

SOME :   'Twill put the races back an hour.

OTHERS :   Perhaps it's nothing but a shower.

Perhaps it's nothing but a shower.

ENSEMBLE : Yes ! yes ! yes ! yes !
A most unfortunate reverse !
Yes ! yes ! yes ! yes !
It's getting worse ! It's getting
            worse ! (*bis*)

My feet are slipping,
I'm simply dripping !
Pray hurry, do !
I'm soaked right through ! (*bis*)

[*The stage empties. The rain continues. There is a clap of thunder and a flash of lightning.*

LAURA *runs on, looks about for shelter, and darts into tent* L. KATE *follows a moment later, and does the same* R. JULIAN *hurries on and makes for* KATE'S *tent : then* ALBERT, *making for* LAURA'S. *The* GIRLS *rise, startled. The* MEN, *taken aback, pause in their respective entrances.*

KATE : Good gracious !

LAURA : Oh, heavens !

JULIAN : I beg your pardon !

ALBERT : I'd no idea !

JULIAN: If I had known——

ALBERT: If I had dreamt——

LAURA: No, no, of course !

KATE: I understand !

ALBERT: I won't intrude.

JULIAN: I will withdraw.

KATE: Oh, but the rain !

LAURA: You'll get so wet !

JULIAN: It's quite all right.

ALBERT: I'll stay outside.

QUARTET: KATE, LAURA, ALBERT, JULIAN

(*Air:* " *What will you do, Love ?* ")

MEN: What can I do ?
Though the heavens are falling
In floods appalling
   That chill me through,
Since she condemns me
Like any stranger
To death and danger,
   What can I do ?
If I should die
While the thunder's rolling,
This thought consoling
   Will help me through :
Because I love her,
I'll not take cover !
That is the least
   That I can do !

GIRLS: What shall I do
When the heavens are falling
In clouds appalling
   That chill him through ?
Can I condemn him
Like any stranger
To death and danger——

What shall I do ?
If he should die
While the thunder's rolling,
Beyond consoling
   His fate I'd rue !
I'll ask my lover
To please take cover—
That is the least
   That I can do !

LAURA : Mr. Porter ! you'll get sopping wet.
There's plenty of room.

ALBERT : You are sure you don't mind ? If I
might have just a corner. . . . (*He enters her tent.*)

KATE : Mr. Bromley, you will catch your death
of cold. You had better come in.

JULIAN : I wouldn't think of it.

KATE : Why not ? Do you hate me so much ?
(*She suddenly bursts into tears.*)

JULIAN : Hate you ? Oh, Kate !

[*He goes in and stands watching her, tormented
by her tears. She keeps her head averted.*

ALBERT : Miss Rivers—I so long to explain.

LAURA (*sadly*) : Is there anything to explain ?

ALBERT : Everything ! Believe me, I never set
eyes on Miss Moss till last night.

JULIAN (*unable to contain himself*) : Don't cry, I
beg of you ! I love you !

KATE : If you did, how could you treat me
so ?

JULIAN : Wretch that I am ? What have I done ?

ALBERT : Only say that you believe me !

KATE : But you proposed to Laura.

LAURA: I do believe you, Mr. Porter.

JULIAN: In pique, I swear it!

KATE: But your bouquet to Laura!

LAURA: Your bouquet to Kate!

ALBERT: My bouquet to Kate!

JULIAN: My bouquet to Laura!

MEN: But my bouquet was sent to *you*!

GIRLS: To *me*?

MEN: To you!

ALL FOUR: My darling!

QUARTET: KATE, LAURA, ALBERT, JULIAN
(*Air: " What shall I do, Love ? "*)

I thought you scorned me
And loved another!
I sought to smother
    My feelings true.
I thought I never
Should rest so near you,
Or ever hear you
    Say " I love you!"
But now I know
That you are my true love,
What can I do, love,
    But say to you:
" Forgive, my own love,
The pain you've known, love "—
That is the least
    That I can do!

[*The lovers are in each other's arms in the tents.
Enter* MRS. GILL *at back.*

MRS. GILL: Kate! Laura! Laura! Kate!
Where can they be? Ah, thank Heaven! A
tent! (*She advances to tent R., from behind.*)

ALBERT: Are you really, truly fond of me?

LAURA: For ever! for ever!

MRS. GILL: Lovers! (*She approaches tent L. from behind.*)

JULIAN: My darling! have you quite forgiven me?

KATE: Everything! Everything!

MRS. GILL: A married couple! What *has* become of the girls? And how *wet* I'm getting!

[*Enter* PATTY *under a big family umbrella. She passes in front of the tents, peeping into each; as she does so, the men in turn draw the flaps, concealing the inmates.* PATTY *passes behind tent L. and comes on* MRS. GILL.

PATTY: Criminy! my ma-in-law! Lucky she don't know me!

MRS. GILL: Excuse me, but *have* you seen a young lady in pink-and-white taffeta—checks? —I mean, *two* young ladies?

PATTY: Both in pink-and-white taffeta—checks?

MRS. GILL: No, the other is in white-and-yellow—stripes!

PATTY: There are so many young ladies here to-day in checks and stripes. And *look* how wet your beautiful new sailor-suit is getting—it will be ruined.

MRS. GILL: Yes, yes, I know. The trees do drip so.

PATTY: Come under my umbrella. And if we turn this hamper upside-down—dry as a bone! (*Both seated.*) You know, you ought to take more care of yourself.

MRS. GILL: Why, did you know? How thoughtful you are!

PATTY: A shawl over the knees—and a cushion for the tootsies—— There!

[*They are now comfortably ensconced under the umbrella.*]

MRS. GILL: Such kindness!

PATTY: Ah, we could all do with a bit of kindness (*with a change of voice*) when we're in trouble.

MRS. GILL: My poor child! are *you* in trouble? (PATTY *turns away her head.*) What a shame! A pretty young thing like you!

PATTY: Ah, if only I hadn't been so pretty——

MRS. GILL (*on guard*): I see. Some man!

PATTY: Yes, yes. My husband!

MRS. GILL (*reassured*): Oh, your husband! (*Takes* PATTY's *left hand, and pats it, after a rapid glance at the third finger.*) There, there, my dear. Marriage is never all it should be. Let us be grateful that we *are* married.

PATTY: I am, I am! But if you only knew——

[*The rain has been easing off; it now stops.*]

MRS. GILL: Tell me, my dear.

PATTY: There's little enough to tell. You see, I lost my mother early—when she died I was faced with two great problems, to earn my living and to keep my self-respect. One must keep one's self-respect.

MRS. GILL: At all costs!

PATTY: One day, when I was at work, I saw a young gentleman watching me during the performance.

MRS. GILL: Performance ? What performance ?

PATTY: The performance of my duties, ma'am. One must perform one's duties. The next day he was in front again.

MRS. GILL: In front ? In front of what ?

PATTY: In front of me, ma'am. And the next day he came round behind——

MRS. GILL: Really ! Behind ?

PATTY: In a manner of speaking, ma'am. He had followed me home.

MRS. GILL: The wretch !

PATTY: Wait before you judge him. The acquaintance ripened. We had soon lost our hearts. He offered me marriage.

MRS. GILL (*drawing a deep breath*): Ah !

PATTY: I had no one to consult. I consented. Everything seemed perfect. I had a sweetheart, I had a new engagement, I was ready to play my part——

MRS. GILL: I am sure you were !

PATTY: He promised to be there on the first night——

MRS. GILL: I should hope so indeed !

PATTY: But in one thing he had deceived me. I found that he was not, like myself, an orphan.

MRS. GILL: So much the better for you. You would regain a mother.

PATTY: I thought so too. And his mother, from all he told me, was an angel upon earth ! But his father—— !

MRS. GILL (*nodding*): I can guess. A tyrant !

PATTY: A tyrant ! *He* would never admit me to the house.

L

MRS. GILL: The brute! Why not?

PATTY: He disapproved of the stage.

MRS. GILL: The stage?

PATTY: The stage we'd reached, madam.

MRS. GILL: *Had* you?

PATTY: After we married. Oh, madam, if you could advise me what to do!

MRS. GILL: You've come to the right shop, my dear. I was a young wife once.

PATTY: I'm sure you were.

MRS. GILL: *I* had my troubles too. My mother-in-law—a tartar! And no one to stand up for me—no one at all.

PATTY: Oh, you poor dear! What a pair we are!

MRS. GILL: Yes, yes—but *you* have a friend at court. Make the most of her, my dear. Go to this angel upon earth, your husband's mother, and tell her all.

PATTY: Then if you were in *her* place——

MRS. GILL: I would support you against the tyrant. We women must stand together.

PATTY: But do you think she will really mother me? (*Wipes her eyes.*)

MRS. GILL: How could she help it? She has only to see you, my dear sweet child. (*Wipes hers.*)

[*As they embrace, the umbrella tips forward, concealing them. A gun goes off. The tent-flaps are drawn simultaneously, revealing to the audience the conscience-stricken figures of* ALBERT *and* JULIAN.

ALBERT: The Twickenham Cup! I have let Julian down!

JULIAN: The gun for the race ! Albert will say I have failed him !

[EDWARD *hurries on.*

EDWARD: Albert ! Julian ! The race has begun !

[ALBERT *and* JULIAN *step forward, meeting in dismay;* KATE *and* LAURA *fly to each other.*

KATE: Laura, he loves me !

LAURA: Kate, Kate, he has spoken !

EDWARD: Aha ! the truant sportsmen !

[*Enter* MR. GILL.

MR. GILL: So ! there you are ! What a downpour ! Quite a Niagara ! Where is your mamma ?

[*He stumbles over the umbrella and kicks it aside. Picture:* PATTY *in* MRS. GILL's *arms, whispering confidentially together.*

EDWARD: Patty !

PATTY (*to* MRS. GILL): My husband !

MRS. GILL: Your husband—my son ?

PATTY: Your son—my *husband* ?—Mother !

[*She renews her embrace.* MRS. GILL *is momentarily staggered.*

MR. GILL (*advancing, bewildered and irritable*): Explain this, explain this !

PATTY (*to* MRS. GILL): His father ! Protect me !

MRS. GILL: Protect you ? Ah, yes ! The tyrant !

PATTY: Don't let him scold me.

MR. GILL: Scold you, young lady ! I should like to give you a good smacking !

MRS. GILL (*rising majestically*): Be silent ! This sweet child is Edward's legal wife. Edward,

come here ! (EDWARD *approaches cautiously*. MRS.
GILL *places* PATTY *in his arms*.) There, my dear !
did I not tell you that you might trust your
mother ?

MR. GILL: But——

MRS. GILL: Not another word ! If you turn
them out of the house, I go with them.

MR. GILL: My dear, I had no intention. . . .

MRS. GILL: So much the better.

KATE: Don't be cross with him, mamma—when
we are all so happy !

MRS. GILL: And why, pray, should *you* be
happy ?

JULIAN (*taking* KATE *by the hand*): If you will
allow me, Mrs. Gill——

ALBERT (*taking* LAURA *by the hand*): And if you
will allow me, Mrs. Gill——

MRS. GILL: Really ! Mr. Bromley ! Mr.
Porter !

EDWARD: Regattas will be regattas, mamma !
Vive l'amour !

MRS. GILL: Well, young gentlemen, if you will
first speak to Mr. Gill in the customary way—
Kate ! Laura !

[MRS. GILL *conducts the young ladies up stage,
out of earshot.*

MR. GILL: Well, gentlemen ?

TRIO : JULIAN, ALBERT, MR. GILL
(*Air : from " Le Pré aux Clercs "*)

JULIAN ⎱ I beg to have the honour
ALBERT ⎰ Of Laura's (Katie's) lilywhite hand.

MR. GILL: What can you settle on her ?
How much can you command ?

JULIAN ⎱
ALBERT ⎰ A lifetime of devotion——

MR. GILL: Which counts precisely nil;
A lover's fond emotion
Won't pay the butcher's bill.

ALL: Ah,
The butcher's bill,
Ah,
The butcher's bill.

[JULIAN *whispers*.

MR. GILL: A handsome increment!

[ALBERT *whispers*.

MR. GILL: What, seven per cent!
I gladly grant the honour,
Of this lady's lilywhite hand.

JULIAN ⎱
ALBERT ⎰ We thank you for the honour,

ALL: Of her lilywhite hand.

[*Just before last four lines*, MRS. GILL *brings
back the two young ladies, to be bestowed on their
respective suitors. The* CROWD *begins to pass across
the back of the stage, chattering excitedly.*

MRS. GILL: What is all this? What is happening?

MR. GILL: Another event, my dear.

MRS. GILL: The Greasy Pole! I distinctly
heard them say the Greasy Pole! Where?
Which way? We must *not* miss the Greasy Pole!

MR. GILL: Bless my soul! It's not the Greasy
Pole—it's the fireworks!

ALL: The fireworks! the fireworks! Oo—oo!

[*The first fireworks appear in the sky. The* LOVERS
regard them with rapture.

SEXTET:

(*Air : End of Serenade from " Paul Jones "*)

KATE: Oh !
                Look there !

ALL: Oh !

GIRLS: Darling !

MEN: Darling !

ALL: Look at the stars up there,
              Falling through the air !
They fill the sky with their sparkling flowers !
                   Oh !
                   Oh !

GIRLS: Darling !

MEN: Darling !

ALL: Look at the golden showers !
              Oh what a lovely sight !
The stars, the stars are in flight—
                   Oh lovely sight !
The stars, the stars are all in flight !
                Oh ! Oh ! . . . .

[CHORUS *repeats Sextet as picture forms.*

CURTAIN

BURY THE DEAD

BURY THE DEAD

Irwin Shaw

BURY THE DEAD

" . . . what is this world that you cling to it ? "

TO

MY MOTHER

CHARACTERS

PRIVATE DRISCOLL

PRIVATE MORGAN

PRIVATE LEVY

PRIVATE WEBSTER

PRIVATE SCHELLING

PRIVATE DEAN

JOAN BURKE

BESS SCHELLING

MARTHA WEBSTER

JULIA BLAKE

KATHERINE DRISCOLL

ELIZABETH DEAN

Generals One, Two and Three.

A Captain, a Sergeant, and four infantrymen, employed as a burial detail.

A Priest, a Rabbi, a Doctor.

A Reporter and an Editor.

Two Whores.

TIME

The second year of the war that is to begin to-morrow night.

SCENE

*The stage is in two planes—in the foreground, the
bare stage; in the rear, not too far back, going the
entire length of the stage, a platform about seven feet
above the level of the stage proper. No properties are
used to adorn the stage save for some sandbags, whole
and split, lying along the edge of the raised platform
and some loose dirt also on the platform. The entire
platform is painted dull black. It is lighted by a
strong spotlight thrown along it at hip-height from
the right wing. It is the only light on the stage. The
platform is to represent a torn-over battlefield, now
quiet, some miles behind the present lines, where a
burial detail, standing in a shallow trench dug in the
platform, so that the audience sees them only from
the hip up, are digging a common grave to accommodate six bodies, piled on the right of the platform,
wrapped in canvas. A* SERGEANT *stands on the right,
on the edge of the grave, smoking. . . . The* SOLDIER
*nearest him, in the shallow trench, stops his
digging. . . .*

FIRST SOLDIER: Say, Sergeant, they stink. . . .
(*Waving his shovel at the corpses*) Let's bury them
in a hurry. . . .

SERGEANT: What the hell do you think you'd
smell like, after you'd been lyin' out for two
days—a god-damn lily of the valley? They'll
be buried soon enough. Keep digging.

SECOND SOLDIER (*scratching himself*): Dig and
scratch! Dig and scratch! What a war! When
you're not diggin' trenches you're diggin'
graves. . . .

THIRD SOLDIER: Who's got a cigarette? I'll take
opium if nobody's got a cigarette.

SECOND SOLDIER: When you're not diggin'
graves you're scratchin' at fleas. By God, there're
more fleas in this army than . . .

FIRST SOLDIER: That's what the war's made for
—the fleas. Somebody's got to feed 'em. . . .

FOURTH SOLDIER: I used to take a shower every
day. Can you imagine?

SERGEANT: All right, Mr. Lifebuoy, we'll put
your picture in the *Saturday Evening Post*—in
colour!

SECOND SOLDIER: When you're not scratchin' at
fleas, you're bein' killed. That's a helluva life
for a grown man.

THIRD SOLDIER: Who's got a cigarette? I'll
trade my rifle—if I can find it—for a cigarette.
For Christ's sake, don't they make cigarettes no
more? (*Leaning, melancholy, on his shovel*) This
country's goin' to the dogs for real now. . . .

SERGEANT: Lift dirt, soldier. Come on! This
ain't no vacation.

THIRD SOLDIER (*disregarding him*): I heard of
guys packin' weeds and cowflop into cigarettes
in this man's army. They say it has a tang.
(*Reflectively*) Got to try it some day. . . .

SERGEANT: Hurry up! (*Blowing on his hands*)
I'm freezin' here. I don't want to hang around
all night. I can't feel my feet no more. . . .

FOURTH SOLDIER: I ain't felt my feet for two
weeks. I ain't had my shoes off in two weeks.
(*Leaning on his shovel*) I wonder if the toes're still
connected. I wear a 8A shoe. Aristocratic foot,
the salesman always said. Funny—going around
not even knowin' whether you still got toes or
not. . . . It's not hygienic really. . . .

SERGEANT: All right, friend, we'll make sure the
next war you're in is run hygienic.

FOURTH SOLDIER: In the Spanish-American
War more men died of fever than . . .

FIRST SOLDIER (*beating viciously at something in the
grave*): Get him! Get him! Kill the bastard!

FOURTH SOLDIER (*savagely*): He's coming this way ! We got him cornered !

FIRST SOLDIER: Bash his brains out !

SECOND SOLDIER: You got him with that one ! (*All the soldiers in the grave beat at it, yelling demoniacally, triumphantly.*)

SERGEANT (*remonstrating*): Come on now, you're wasting time. . . .

FIRST SOLDIER (*swinging savagely*): There. That fixed him. The god-damn . . .

FOURTH SOLDIER (*sadly*): You'd think the rats'd at least wait until the stiffs were underground.

FIRST SOLDIER: Did you ever see such a fat rat in your whole life ? I bet he ate like a horse— this one.

SERGEANT: All right, all right. You're not fightin' the war against rats. Get back to your business.

FIRST SOLDIER: I get a lot more pleasure killin' rats than killin' them. (*Gesture toward the front lines.*)

SERGEANT: Rats got to live, too. They don't know no better.

FIRST SOLDIER (*suddenly scooping up rat on his shovel and presenting it to* SERGEANT): Here you are, Sergeant. A little token of our regard from Company A.

SERGEANT: Stop the smart stuff ! I don't like it.

FIRST SOLDIER (*still with rat upheld on shovel*): Ah, Sergeant, I'm disappointed. This rat's a fine pedigreed animal—fed only on the choicest young men the United States's turned out in the last twenty years.

SERGEANT: Come on, wise guy. (FIRST SOLDIER *goes right on.*)

FIRST SOLDIER: Notice the heavy, powerful shoulders to this rat, notice the well-covered flanks, notice the round belly—bank clerks, mechanics, society-leaders, farmers—good feeding. (*Suddenly he throws the rat away.*) Ah—I'm gettin' awful tired of this. I didn't enlist in this bloody war to be no bloody grave-digger!

SERGEANT: Tell that to the President. Keep diggin'.

SECOND SOLDIER: Say, this is deep enough. What're we supposed to do—dig right down to hell and deliver them over first-hand?

SERGEANT: A man's entitled to six feet a' dirt over his face. We gotta show respect to the dead. Keep diggin'. . . .

FOURTH SOLDIER: I hope they don't put me too far under when my turn comes. I want to be able to come up and get a smell of air every once in so often.

SERGEANT: Stow the gab, you guys! Keep diggin'. . . .

FIRST SOLDIER: They stink! Bury them!

SERGEANT: All right, Fanny. From now on we'll perfume 'em before we ask you to put them away. Will that please you?

FIRST SOLDIER: I don't like the way they smell, that's all. I don't have to like the way they smell, do I? That ain't in the regulations, is it? A man's got a right to use his nose, ain't he, even though he's in this god-damn army. . . .

SERGEANT: Talk respectful when you talk about the army, you!

FIRST SOLDIER: Oh, the lovely army. . . . (*He heaves up clod of dirt.*)

SECOND SOLDIER: Oh, the dear army. . . . (*He heaves up clod of dirt.*)

THIRD SOLDIER: Oh, the sweet army. . . . (*He heaves up clod of dirt.*)

FIRST SOLDIER: Oh, the scummy, stinking, god-damn army. . . . (*He heaves up three shovelfuls in rapid succession.*)

SERGEANT: That's a fine way to talk in the presence of death. . . .

FIRST SOLDIER: We'd talk in blank verse for you, Sergeant, only we ran out of it our third day in the front line. What do you expect, Sergeant, we're just common soldiers. . . .

SECOND SOLDIER: Come on. Let's put 'em away. I'm getting blisters big enough to use for balloons here. What's the difference? They'll just be turned up anyway, the next time the artillery wakes up. . . .

SERGEANT: All right! All right! If you're in such a hurry—put 'em in. . . . (*The soldiers nearest the right-hand edge of the grave jump out and start carrying the bodies over, one at each corner of the canvas. The other soldiers, still in the trench, take the bodies from them and carry them over to the other side of the trench, where they lay them down, out of sight of the audience.*)

SERGEANT: Put 'em in neat, there. . . .

FIRST SOLDIER: File 'em away alphabetically, boys. We may want to refer to them, later. The General might want to look up some past cases.

FOURTH SOLDIER: This one's just a kid. I knew him a little. Nice kid. He used to write dirty poems. Funny as hell. He don't even look dead. . . .

FIRST SOLDIER: Bury him! He stinks!

SERGEANT: If you think *you* smell so sweet, yourself, Baby, you oughta wake up. You ain't exactly a perfume-ad, soldier. (*Laughter.*)

THIRD SOLDIER: Chalk one up for the Sergeant.

FIRST SOLDIER: You ain't a combination of roses and wistaria, either, Sergeant, but I can stand you, especially when you don't talk. At least you're alive. There's something about the smell of dead ones that gives me the willies. . . . Come on, let's pile the dirt in on them. . . . (*The* SOLDIERS *scramble out of the grave.*)

SERGEANT: Hold it.

THIRD SOLDIER: What's the matter now? Do we have to do a dance around them?

SERGEANT: We have to wait for chaplains. . . . They gotta say some prayers over them.

FIRST SOLDIER: Oh, for Christ's sake, ain't I ever going to get any sleep to-night?

SERGEANT: Don't begrudge a man his prayers, soldier. You'd want 'em, wouldn't you?

FIRST SOLDIER: God, no. I want to sleep peaceful when I go. . . . Well, where are they? Why don't they come? Do we have to stand here all night waiting for those guys to come and talk to God about these fellers?

THIRD SOLDIER: Who's got a cigarette? (*Plaintively.*)

SERGEANT: Attention! Here they are! (*A Roman Catholic* PRIEST *and a* RABBI *come in.*)

PRIEST: Is everything ready?

SERGEANT: Yes, Father. . . .

FIRST SOLDIER: Make it snappy! I'm awful tired.

PRIEST: God must be served slowly, my son. . . .

FIRST SOLDIER: He's gettin' plenty of service these days—and not so slow, either. He can stand a little rushin'. . . .

SERGEANT: Shut up, soldier.

RABBI: Do you want to hold your services first, Father?

SERGEANT: There ain't no Jewish boys in there. (*Gesture to grave.*) Reverend, I don't think we'll need you.

RABBI: I understand one of them is named Levy.

SERGEANT: Yes. But he's no Jew.

RABBI: With that name we won't take any chances. Father, will you be first?

PRIEST: Perhaps we had better wait. There is an Episcopal bishop in this sector. He expressed the desire to conduct a burial service here. He's doing that in all the sectors he is visiting. I think we had better wait for him. Episcopal bishops are rather sensitive about order. . . .

RABBI: He's not coming. He's having his supper.

FIRST SOLDIER: What does God do while the bishop has his supper?

SERGEANT: If you don't keep quiet, I'll bring you up on charges.

FIRST SOLDIER: I want to get it over with! Bury them! They stink!

PRIEST: Young man, that is not the way to talk about one of God's creatures. . . .

FIRST SOLDIER: If *that's* (*Gesture to grave*) one of God's creatures, all I can say is, He's slippin'. . . .

PRIEST: Ah, my son, you seem so bitter. . . .

FIRST SOLDIER: For God's sake, stop talking and get this over with. I want to throw dirt over them! I can't stand the smell of them! Sergeant, get 'em to do it fast. They ain't got no right to keep us up all night. We got work to do to-morrow. . . . Let 'em say their prayers together! God'll be able to understand. . . .

PRIEST: Yes. There is really no need to prolong it. We must think of the living as well as the dead. As he says, Reverend, God will be able to understand. . . . (*He stands at the head of the grave, chants the Latin prayer for the dead. The* RABBI *goes around to the other end and recites the Hebrew prayer. In the middle of it, a groan is heard, low, but clear. The chants keep on. Another groan is heard.*)

FIRST SOLDIER (*while the Hebrew and Latin go on*): I heard a groan. (*The* RABBI *and* PRIEST *continue.*) I heard a groan!

SERGEANT: Shut up, soldier! (*The Latin and Hebrew go on.*)

FIRST SOLDIER (*gets down on one knee by side of grave and listens. Another groan*): Stop it! I heard a groan. . . .

SERGEANT: What about it? Can you have war without groans? Keep quiet. (*The prayers go on undisturbed. Another groan. The* FIRST SOLDIER *jumps into the grave.*)

FIRST SOLDIER: It's from here! Hold it! (*Screaming*) Hold it! Stop those god-damned parrots! (*Throws a clod of dirt at end of trench.*) Hold it! Somebody down here groaned. . . . (*A head appears slowly above the trench rim at the left end, a man stands up, slowly facing the rear. All the men sigh—the service goes on.*)

SERGEANT: Oh, my God. . . .

FIRST SOLDIER: He's alive. . . .

SERGEANT: Why the hell don't they get these things straight? Pull him out!

FIRST SOLDIER: Stop them! (*As the services go on*) Get them out of here! Live men don't need them. . . .

SERGEANT: Please, Father, this has nothing to do with you. . . . There's been some mistake. . . .

PRIEST: I see. All right, Sergeant. (*He and* RABBI *join, hand in hand, and leave. Nobody notices them. All the men are hypnotically watching the man in the trench, arisen from the dead. The* CORPSE *passes his hand over his eyes. The men sigh—horrible, dry sighs. . . . Another groan is heard from the left side of trench.*)

FIRST SOLDIER (*in trench*): There! (*Pointing*) It came from there! I heard it! (*A head, then shoulders appear over the rim of trench at left side. The* SECOND CORPSE *stands up, passes his hands over eyes in same gesture which drew sighs from the men before. There is absolute silence as the men watch the arisen* CORPSES. *Then, silently, a* CORPSE *rises in the middle of the trench, next to the* FIRST SOLDIER. *The* FIRST SOLDIER *screams, scrambles out of the trench in rear, and stands, bent over, watching the trench, middle-rear. There is no sound save the very light rumble of the guns. One by one the* CORPSES *arise and stand silently in their places, facing the rear, their backs to the audience. The* SOLDIERS *don't move, scarcely breathe, as, one by one, the* CORPSES *appear. They stand there, a frozen tableau. Suddenly, the* SERGEANT *talks.*)

SERGEANT: What do you want?

FIRST CORPSE: Don't bury us.

THIRD SOLDIER: Let's get the hell out of here!

SERGEANT (*drawing pistol*): Stay where you are! I'll shoot the first man that moves.

FIRST CORPSE: Don't bury us. We don't want to be buried.

SERGEANT: Christ! (*To men*) Carry on! (*The men stand still.*) Christ! (*The* SERGEANT *rushes off, calling*) Captain! Captain! Where the hell is the Captain? (*His voice fades, terror-stricken. The* SOLDIERS *watch the* CORPSES, *then slowly, all together, start to back off.*)

SIXTH CORPSE: Don't go away.

SECOND CORPSE: Stay with us.

THIRD CORPSE: We want to hear the sound of men talking.

SIXTH CORPSE: Don't be afraid of us.

FIRST CORPSE: We're not really different from you. We're dead.

SECOND CORPSE: That's all . . . ?

FOURTH CORPSE: All—all . . .

FIRST SOLDIER: That's all . . . ?

THIRD CORPSE: Are you afraid of six dead men? You, who've lived with the dead, the so-many dead, and eaten your bread by their side when there was no time to bury them and you were hungry?

SECOND CORPSE: Are we different from you? An ounce or so of lead in our hearts, and none in yours. A small difference between us.

THIRD CORPSE: To-morrow or the next day, the lead will be yours, too. Talk as our equals.

FOURTH SOLDIER: It's the kid—the one who wrote the dirty poems.

FIRST CORPSE: Say something to us. Forget the grave, as we would forget it. . . .

THIRD SOLDIER: Do you—do you want a cigarette? (SERGEANT *re-enters with* CAPTAIN.)

SERGEANT: I'm not drunk! I'm not crazy, either! They just—got up, all together—and looked at us. . . . Look—look for yourself, Captain! (*The* CAPTAIN *stands off to one side, looking. The men stand at attention.*)

SERGEANT: See?

CAPTAIN: I see. (*He laughs sadly.*) I was expecting it to happen—some day. So many men each day.

It's too bad it had to happen in my company.
Gentlemen ! At ease ! (*The men stand at ease.
The* CAPTAIN *leaves. The guns roar suddenly. Fade-
out.*)

[*The spotlight is turned on to the lower stage, right,
below the platform on which the action, until now,
has taken place. Discovered in its glare are three*
GENERALS, *around a table. The* CAPTAIN *is
standing before them, talking.*

CAPTAIN : I'm only telling the Generals what I
saw.

FIRST GENERAL : You're not making this up,
Captain ?

CAPTAIN : No, General.

SECOND GENERAL : Have you any proof,
Captain ?

CAPTAIN : The four men in the burial detail and
the Sergeant, sir.

THIRD GENERAL : In time of war, Captain, men
see strange things.

CAPTAIN : Yes, General.

SECOND GENERAL : You've been drinking,
Captain.

CAPTAIN : Yes, General.

SECOND GENERAL : When a man has been
drinking, he is not responsible for what he sees.

CAPTAIN : Yes, General, I am not responsible
for what I saw. I am glad of that. I would not
like to carry that burden, along with all the
others. . . .

FIRST GENERAL : Come, come, Captain, confess
now. You were drinking and you walked out
into the cold air over a field just lately won and
what with the liquor and the air and the flush of
victory . . .

CAPTAIN: I told the General what I saw.

SECOND GENERAL: Yes, we heard. We forgive you for it. We don't think any the worse of you for taking a nip. It's only natural. We understand. So take another drink with us now and forget your ghosts. . . .

CAPTAIN: They weren't ghosts. They were men killed two days, standing in their graves and looking at me.

FIRST GENERAL: Captain, you're becoming trying. . . .

CAPTAIN: I'm sorry, sir. It was a trying sight. I saw them and what are the Generals going to do about it?

SECOND GENERAL: Forget it! A man is taken for dead and put in a grave. He wakes from his coma and stands up. It happens every day— you've got to expect such things in a war. Take him out and send him to a hospital!

CAPTAIN: Hospitals aren't for dead men. What are the Generals going to do about them?

THIRD GENERAL: Don't stand there croaking, " What are the Generals going to do about them? " Have 'em examined by a doctor. If they're alive send them to a hospital. If they're dead, bury them! It's very simple.

CAPTAIN: But . . .

THIRD GENERAL: No buts, sir!

CAPTAIN: Yes, sir.

THIRD GENERAL: Take a doctor down with you, sir, and a stenographer. Have the doctor dictate official reports. Have them witnessed. And let's hear no more of it.

CAPTAIN: Yes, sir. Very good, sir. (*Wheels to go out.*)

SECOND GENERAL: Oh, and Captain . . .

CAPTAIN (*stopping*): Yes, sir.

SECOND GENERAL: Stay away from the bottle.

CAPTAIN: Yes, sir. Is that all, sir?

SECOND GENERAL: That's all.

CAPTAIN: Yes, sir. (*The light fades from the* GENERALS. *It follows the* CAPTAIN *as he walks across stage. The* CAPTAIN *stops, takes out a bottle. Takes two long swigs. Blackout.*)

[*The guns rumble, growing louder. They have been almost mute during* GENERALS' *scene. The light is thrown on the burial scene again, where the* DOCTOR *is seen examining the* CORPSES *in their graves. The* DOCTOR *is armed with a stethoscope and is followed by a soldier* STENOGRAPHER, *two of the* SOLDIERS, *impressed as witnesses, and the* CAPTAIN. *The* DOCTOR *is talking, as he passes from the first man.*

DOCTOR: Number one. Evisceration of the lower intestine. Dead forty-eight hours.

STENOGRAPHER (*repeating*): Number one. Evisceration of the lower intestine. Dead forty-eight hours. (*To witnesses*) Sign here. (*They sign.*)

DOCTOR (*on the next man*): Number two. Bullet penetrated the left ventricle. Dead forty-eight hours.

STENOGRAPHER: Number two. Bullet penetrated the left ventricle. Dead forty-eight hours. (*To witnesses*) Sign here. (*They sign.*)

DOCTOR (*on the next* CORPSE): Number three. Bullets penetrated both lungs. Severe hemorrhages. Dead forty-eight hours.

STENOGRAPHER (*chanting*): Number three. Bullets penetrated both lungs. Severe hemorrhages. Dead forty-eight hours. Sign here. (*The witnesses sign.*)

DOCTOR (*on next* CORPSE): Number four. Fracture of the skull and avulsion of the cerebellum. Dead forty-eight hours.

STENOGRAPHER: Number four. Fracture of the skull and avulsion of the cerebellum. Dead forty-eight hours. Sign here. (*The witnesses sign.*)

DOCTOR (*moving on to next* CORPSE): Number five. Destruction of the genito-urinary system by shell-splinters. Death from hemorrhages. Dead forty-eight hours. Ummm. (*Looks curiously at* CORPSE's *face.*) Hum . . . (*Moves on.*)

STENOGRAPHER: Number five. Destruction of the genito-urinary system by shell-splinters. Death from hemorrhages. Dead forty-eight hours. Sign here. (*The witnesses sign.*)

DOCTOR (*on the next* CORPSE): Number six. Destruction of right side of head from supra-orbital ridges through jaw-bone. Hum. You'd be a pretty sight for your mother, you would. Dead forty-eight hours. . . .

STENOGRAPHER: Number six. Destruction of right side of head from supra-orbital ridges through jaw-bone. You'd be a pretty sight for your mother, you would. Dead forty-eight hours. Sign here.

DOCTOR: What are you doing there?

STENOGRAPHER: That's what you said, sir. . . .

DOCTOR: I know. Leave out—" You'd be a pretty sight for your mother, you would." . . . The Generals wouldn't be interested in that.

STENOGRAPHER: Yes, sir. Sign here. (*The witnesses sign.*)

DOCTOR: Six, is that all?

CAPTAIN: Yes, Doctor. They're all dead? (*The* FOURTH CORPSE *offers the* THIRD SOLDIER *a cigarette. The* THIRD SOLDIER *hesitates a second before taking it, then accepts it with a half-grin.*)

THIRD SOLDIER: Thanks, Buddy. I—I'm awful sorry—I—thanks . . . (*He saves cigarette.*)

DOCTOR (*eyes on* FOURTH CORPSE *and* THIRD SOLDIER): All dead.

CAPTAIN: A drink, Doctor?

DOCTOR: Yes, thank you. (*He takes the proffered bottle. Drinks long from it. Holds it, puts stethoscope in pocket with other hand. Stands looking at the* CORPSES, *lined up, facing the rear, nods, then takes another long drink. Silently hands bottle to* CAPTAIN, *who looks around him from one* CORPSE *to another, then takes a long drink. Blackout.*)

[*Spotlight on the* GENERALS, *facing the* CAPTAIN *and the* DOCTOR. *The* FIRST GENERAL *has the* DOCTOR's *reports in his hands.*

FIRST GENERAL: Doctor!

DOCTOR: Yes, sir.

FIRST GENERAL: In your reports here you say that each of these six men is dead.

DOCTOR: Yes, sir.

FIRST GENERAL: Then I don't see what all the fuss is about, Captain. They're dead—bury them. . . .

CAPTAIN: I am afraid, sir, that that can't be done. . . . They are standing in their graves. They refuse to be buried.

THIRD GENERAL: Do we have to go into that again? We have the Doctor's report. They're dead. Aren't they, Doctor?

DOCTOR: Yes, sir.

THIRD GENERAL: Then they aren't standing in their graves, refusing to be buried, are they?

DOCTOR: Yes, sir.

SECOND GENERAL: Doctor, would you know a dead man if you saw one?

DOCTOR: The symptoms are easily recognised.

FIRST GENERAL: You've been drinking, too. . . .

DOCTOR: Yes, sir.

FIRST GENERAL: The whole damned army is drunk! I want a regulation announced to-morrow morning in all regiments. No more liquor is to be allowed within twenty miles of the front line upon pain of death. Got it?

SECOND GENERAL: Yes, General. But then how'll we get the men to fight?

FIRST GENERAL: Damn the fighting! We can't have stories like this springing up. It's bad for the morale! Did you hear me, Doctor, it's bad for the morale and you ought to be ashamed of yourself!

DOCTOR: Yes, sir.

THIRD GENERAL: This has gone far enough. If it goes any farther, the men will get wind of it. We have witnessed certificates from a registered surgeon that these men are dead. Bury them! Waste no more time on it. Did you hear me, Captain?

CAPTAIN: Yes, sir. I'm afraid, sir, that I must refuse to bury these men.

THIRD GENERAL: That's insubordination, sir. . . .

CAPTAIN: I'm sorry, sir. It is not within the line of my military duties to bury men against their will. If the General will only think for a moment he will see that this is impossible. . . .

FIRST GENERAL: The Captain's right. It might

get back to Congress. God only knows what *they'd* make of it !

THIRD GENERAL: What are we going to do then ?

FIRST GENERAL: Captain, what do you suggest ?

CAPTAIN: Stop the war.

CHORUS OF GENERALS: Captain !

FIRST GENERAL (*with great dignity*): Captain, we beg of you to remember the gravity of the situation. It admits of no levity. Is that the best suggestion you can make, Captain ?

CAPTAIN: Yes. But I have another— If the Generals would come down to the grave themselves and attempt to influence these—ah—corpses—to lie down, perhaps that would prove effective. We're seven miles behind the line now and we could screen the roads to protect your arrival. . . .

FIRST GENERAL (*coughing*): Umm—uh—usually, of course, that would be—uh . . . We'll see. In the meantime it must be kept quiet ! Remember that ! Not a word ! Nobody must know ! God only knows what would happen if people began to suspect we couldn't even get our dead to lie down and be buried ! This is the god-damndest war ! They never said anything about this sort of thing at West Point. Remember, not a word, nobody must know, quiet as the grave, *mum !* *ssssh !* (*All the* GENERALS *repeat the ssssh after him.*)

[*The light fades—but the hiss of the* GENERALS *hushing each other is still heard as the light falls on another part of the stage proper, where two soldiers are on post in the front lines, behind a barricade of sandbags. The sound of guns is very strong. There are flashes of gun-fire.*

BEVINS (*a soldier past forty, fat, with a pot-belly,*

and greying hair showing under his helmet) : Did you hear about those guys that won't let themselves be buried, Charley ?

CHARLEY : I heard. You never know what's gonna happen next in this lousy war.

BEVINS : What do you think about it, Charley ?

CHARLEY : What're they gettin' out of it, that's what I'd like to know. They're just makin' things harder. I heard all about 'em. They stink ! Bury 'em. That's what I say.

BEVINS : I don't know, Charley. I kinda can see what they're aimin' at. Christ, I wouldn't like to be put six foot under now, I wouldn't. What the hell for ?

CHARLEY : What's the difference ?

BEVINS : There's a difference, all right. It's kinda good, bein' alive. It's kinda nice, bein' on top of the earth and seein' things and hearin' things and smellin' things. . . .

CHARLEY : Yeah, smellin' stiffs that ain't had time to be buried. That sure is sweet.

BEVINS : Yeah, but it's better than havin' the dirt packed on to your face. I guess those guys felt sorta gypped when they started throwin' the dirt in on 'em and they just couldn't stand it, dead or no dead.

CHARLEY : They're dead, ain't they ? Nobody's puttin' them under while they're alive.

BEVINS : It amounts to the same thing, Charley. They should be alive now. What are they—a parcel of kids ? Kids shouldn't be dead, Charley. That's what they musta figured when the dirt started fallin' in on 'em. What the hell are they doin' dead ? Did they get anything out of it ? Did anybody ask them ? Did they want to be standin' there when the lead poured in ?

They're just kids, or guys with wives and young kids of their own. They wanted to be home readin' a book or teaching' their kid c-a-t spells cat or takin' a woman out into the country in a open car with the wind blowin'. . . . That's the way it musta come to them, when the dirt smacked on their faces, dead or no dead. . . .

CHARLEY: Bury them. That's what I say. . . . (*There is the chatter of a machine-gun off in the night.* BEVINS *is hit. He staggers.*)

BEVINS (*clutching his throat*): Charley—Charley . . . (*His fingers bring down the top sandbag as he falls. The machine-gun chatters again and* CHARLEY *is hit. He staggers.*)

CHARLEY: Oh, my God . . . (*The machine-gun chatters again. He falls over* BEVINS. *There is quiet for a moment. Then the eternal artillery again. Blackout.*)

[*A baby spotlight, white, pickes out the* FIRST GENERAL, *standing over the prone forms of the two soldiers. He has his fingers to his lips.*

FIRST GENERAL (*in a hoarse whisper*): Sssh ! Keep it quiet ! Nobody must know ! Not a word ! Sssh ! (*Blackout.*)

[*A spotlight picks out another part of the stage—a newspaper office.* EDITOR *at his desk,* REPORTER *before him, hat on head.*

REPORTER: That's the story ! It's as straight as a rifle-barrel, so help me God.

EDITOR (*looking down at manuscript in hand*): This is a freak, all right. I never came across anything like it in all the years I've been putting out a newspaper.

REPORTER: There never was anything like it before. It's somethin' new. Somethin's happening. Somebody's waking up. . . .

EDITOR: It didn't happen.

REPORTER: So help me God, I got it straight. Those guys just stood up in the grave and said, " The hell with it, you can't bury us ! " God's honest truth.

EDITOR (*picks up the telephone*): Get me Macready at the War Department. . . . It's an awfully funny story. . . .

REPORTER: What about it ? It's the story of the year—the story of the century—the biggest story of all time—men gettin' up with bullets in their hearts and refusin' to be buried. . . .

EDITOR: Who do they think they are—Jesus Christ ?

REPORTER: What's the difference ? That's the story ! You can't miss it ! You goin' to put it in ? Lissen—are you goin' to put it in ?

EDITOR: Hold it ! (*Into telephone*) Macready !

REPORTER: What's he got to do with it ?

EDITOR: I'll find out. What are *you* so hot about ? . . . Hello ! Macready ? Hansen from the *New York* . . . Yeah. . . . Listen, Macready, I got this story about the six guys who refuse to be . . . Yeah. . . .

REPORTER: What does he say ?

EDITOR: Okay, Macready. Yeah, if that's the way the Government feels about it. . . . Yeah. . . .

REPORTER: Well ?

EDITOR (*putting down telephone*): No.

REPORTER: Holy god-damn, you got to. People got a right to know.

EDITOR: In time of war, people have a right to know nothing. If we put it in, it'd be censored anyway.

REPORTER: Ah, this is a lousy business. . . .

EDITOR: Write another human interest story about the boys at the front. That'll keep you busy. You know . . . that one about how the boys in the front-line sing " I Can't Give You Anything but Love," before they go over the top. . . .

REPORTER: But I wrote that last week.

EDITOR: It made a great hit. Write it again.

REPORTER: But these guys in the grave, Boss. Lloyds are giving three to one they won't go down. That's a story !

EDITOR: Save it. You can write a book of memoirs twenty years from now. Make that " I Can't Give You Anything but Love " story a thousand words, and make it snappy. The casualty lists run into two pages to-day and we got to balance them with something. . . . (*Blackout*.)

[*Rumble of guns. The spotlight illuminates the grave on the platform, where the* CORPSES *are still standing, hip-deep, facing the rear. The burial squad is there, and the* CAPTAIN, *and the* GENERALS.

CAPTAIN: There they are. What are the Generals going to do about them ?

FIRST GENERAL (*pettishly*): I see them. Stop saying " What are the Generals going to do about them ? "

SECOND GENERAL: Who do they think they are ?

THIRD GENERAL: It's against all regulations.

FIRST GENERAL: Quiet, please, quiet. Let's not have any scenes. . . . This must be handled with authority—but tactfully. I'll talk to them ! (*He goes over to brink of grave.*) Men ! Listen to me ! This is a strange situation in which we find ourselves. I have no doubt but that it is giving you as much embarrassment as it is us. . . .

M

SECOND GENERAL (*confidentially to* THIRD GENERAL): The wrong note. He's good on artillery, but when it comes to using his head, he's lost. . . . He's been that way ever since I knew him.

FIRST GENERAL: We're all anxious to get this thing over with just as quickly and quietly as possible. I know that you men are with me on this. There's no reason why we can't get together and settle this in jig time. I grant, my friends, that it's unfortunate that you're dead. I'm sure that you'll all listen to reason. Listen, too, to the voice of duty, the voice that sent you here to die bravely for your country. Gentlemen, your country demands of you that you lie down and allow yourselves to be buried. Must our flag fly at half-mast and droop in the wind while you so far forget your duty to the lovely land that bore and nurtured you? I love America, gentlemen, its hills and valleys. If you loved America as I do, you would not . . . (*He breaks down, overcome.*) I find it difficult to go on. (*He pauses.*) I have studied this matter and come to the conclusion that the best thing for all concerned would be for you men to lie down peaceably in your graves and allow yourselves to be buried. (*He waits. The* CORPSES *do not move.*)

THIRD GENERAL: It didn't work. He's not firm enough. You've got to be firm right from the beginning or you're lost.

FIRST GENERAL: Men, perhaps you don't understand. (*To* CORPSES) I advise you to allow yourselves to be buried. (*They stand, motionless.*) You're dead, men, don't you realise that? You can't be dead and stand there like that. Here . . . here . . . I'll prove it to you! (*He gets out* DOCTOR's *reports.*) Look! A doctor's reports. Witnessed! Witnessed by Privates McGurk and Butler. (*He reads the names.*) This ought to show you! (*He waves the reports. He stands on the brink*

of the grave, middle-rear, glaring at the CORPSES.
He shouts at them.) You're dead, officially, all of
you ! I won't mince words ! You heard ! We're
a civilised race, we bury our dead. Lie down !
(*The* CORPSES *stand.*) Private Driscoll ! Private
Schelling ! Private Morgan ! Private Levy !
Private Webster ! Private Dean ! Lie down ! As
Commander-in-Chief of the Army as appointed
by the President of the United States in accordance with the Constitution of the United States,
and as your superior officer, I command you to
lie down and allow yourselves to be buried.
(*They stand, silent and motionless.*) Tell me—What
is it going to get you, staying above the earth ?
(*Not a sound from the* CORPSES.) I asked you a
question, men. Answer me ! What is it going
to get you ? If I were dead I wouldn't hesitate
to be buried. Answer me . . . what do you want ?
What is it going to get you . . . ? (*As they remain
silent*) Tell me ! Answer me ! Why don't you
talk ? Explain it to me, make me understand. . . .

SECOND GENERAL (*in whisper to* THIRD GENERAL,
as FIRST GENERAL *glares hopelessly at the* CORPSES) :
He's licked. It was a mistake—moving him off
the artillery.

THIRD GENERAL : They ought to let me handle
them. I'd show 'em. You've got to use force.

FIRST GENERAL (*bursting out—after walking along
entire row of* CORPSES *and back*) : Lie down ! (*The*
CORPSES *stand, immobile. The* GENERAL *rushes out,
moaning.*) Oh, God, oh, my God. . . . (*Blackout.*)

[*Spotlight, red, picks out two* WHORES, *dressed in
the uniform of their trade, on a street corner.*

FIRST WHORE : I'd lay 'em, all right. They
oughta call me in. I'd lay 'em. There wouldn't
be any doubt in anybody's mind after I got
through with 'em. Why don't they call me in
instead of those Generals ? What do Generals

know about such things? (*Both* WHORES *go off into fits of wild laughter.*) Call the War Department, Mabel, tell 'em we'll come to their rescue at the prevailing rates. (*Laugh wildly again.*) We're willing to do our part, like the papers say—share the burden! Oh, my Gawd, I ain't laughed so much . . . (*Laugh again. A* MAN *crosses their path. Still laughing, but professional*) Say, Johnny, Johnny, what'cha doin' to-night? How'd ya like . . .? (*The* MAN *passes on. The women laugh.*) Share the burden—oh, my Gawd. . . . (*They laugh and laugh and laugh, clinging to each other. . . . Blackout. But the laughter goes on.*)

[*The spotlight illuminates the grave*—SOLDIERS *of burial detail are sitting around a covered fire,* SECOND SOLDIER *is singing " Swing Low, Sweet Chariot."*

THIRD SOLDIER: This is a funny war. It's rollin' downhill. Everybody's waitin'. Personally, I think it's those guys there that . . . (*He gestures to grave.*)

SERGEANT: Nobody asked you. You're not supposed to talk about it.

FIRST SOLDIER: Regulation 2035A . . .

SERGEANT: Well, I just told ya. (SECOND SOLDIER *starts to sing again.* SERGEANT *breaks in on him*) Say, lissen, think about those guys there. How do you think they feel with you howlin' like this? They got more important things to think about.

SECOND SOLDIER: I won't distract 'em. I got an easy-flowin' voice.

SERGEANT: They don't like it. I can tell.

FIRST SOLDIER: Well, *I* like to hear him sing. And I'll bet they do, too. I'm gonna to ask 'em. . . . (*He jumps up.*)

SERGEANT: Now, lissen ! (FIRST SOLDIER *slowly approaches the grave. He is embarrassed, a little frightened.*)

FIRST SOLDIER: Say, men, I . . . (CAPTAIN *comes on.* FIRST SOLDIER *stands at attention.*)

CAPTAIN: Sergeant . . .

SERGEANT: Yes, sir !

CAPTAIN: You know that none of the men is to talk to *them*. . . .

SERGEANT: Yes, sir. Only, sir . . .

CAPTAIN: All right. (*To* FIRST SOLDIER) Get back there, please.

FIRST SOLDIER: Yes, sir ! (*He salutes and goes back.*)

SERGEANT (*under his breath to* FIRST SOLDIER): I warned ya.

FIRST SOLDIER: Shut up ! I wanna lissen to what's goin' on there ! (CAPTAIN *has meanwhile seated himself on the edge of the grave and has brought out a pair of eyeglasses with which he plays as he talks.*)

CAPTAIN: Gentlemen, I have been asked by the Generals to talk to you. My work is not this. . . . (*He indicates his uniform.*) I am a philosopher, a scientist, my uniform is a pair of eyeglasses, my usual weapons test-tubes and books. At a time like this perhaps we need philosophy, need science. First I must say that your General has ordered you to lie down.

FIRST CORPSE: We used to have a General.

THIRD CORPSE: No more.

FOURTH CORPSE: They sold us.

CAPTAIN: What do you mean—sold you !

FIFTH CORPSE: Sold us for twenty-five yards of bloody mud.

SIXTH CORPSE: A life for four yards of bloody mud.

CAPTAIN: We had to take that hill. General's orders. You're soldiers. You understand.

FIRST CORPSE: We understand now. The real estate operations of Generals are always carried on at boom prices.

SIXTH CORPSE: A life for four yards of bloody mud. Gold is cheaper, and rare jewels, pearls and rubies. . . .

THIRD CORPSE: I fell in the first yard. . . .

SECOND CORPSE: I caught on the wire and hung there while the machine-gun stitched me through the middle to it. . . .

FOURTH CORPSE: I was there at the end and thought I had life in my hands for another day, but a shell came and my life dripped into the mud.

SIXTH CORPSE: Ask the General how he'd like to be dead at twenty. (*Calling, as though to the* GENERALS) Twenty, General, twenty. . . .

CAPTAIN: Other men are dead.

FIRST CORPSE: Too many.

CAPTAIN: Men must die for their country's sake —if not you, then others. This has always been. Men died for Pharaoh and Cæsar and Rome two thousand years ago and more, and went into the earth with their wounds. Why not you . . . ?

FIRST CORPSE: Men, even the men who die for Pharaoh and Cæsar and Rome, must, in the end, before all hope is gone, discover that a man can die happy and be contentedly buried only when he dies for himself or for a cause that is his own and not Pharaoh's or Cæsar's or Rome's. . . .

CAPTAIN: Still—what is this world, that you cling to it? A speck of dust, a flaw in the skies, a thumb-print on the margin of a page printed in an incomprehensible language. . . .

SECOND CORPSE: It is our home.

THIRD CORPSE: We have been dispossessed by force, but we are reclaiming our home. It is time that mankind claimed its home—this earth —its home. . . .

CAPTAIN: We have no home. We are strangers in the universe and cling, desperate and grimy, to the crust of our world, and if there is a God and this His earth, we must be a terrible sight in His eyes.

FOURTH CORPSE: We are not disturbed by the notion of our appearance in the eyes of God. . . .

CAPTAIN: The earth is an unpleasant place and when you are rid of it you are well rid of it. Man cheats man here and the only sure things are death and despair. Of what use, then, to remain on it once you have the permission to leave?

FIFTH CORPSE: It is the one thing we know.

SIXTH CORPSE: We did not ask permission to leave. Nobody asked us whether we wanted it or not. The Generals pushed us out and closed the door on us. Who are the Generals that they are to close doors on us?

CAPTAIN: The earth, I assure you, is a mean place, insignificantly miserable. . . .

FIRST CORPSE: We must find out for ourselves. That is our right.

CAPTAIN: Man has no rights. . . .

FIRST CORPSE: Man can make rights for himself. It requires only determination and the goodwill of ordinary men. We have made ourselves the right to walk this earth, seeing it and judging it for ourselves.

CAPTAIN: There is peace in the grave. . . .

THIRD CORPSE: Peace and the worms and the roots of grass. There is a deeper peace than that which comes with feeding the roots of the grass.

CAPTAIN (*looks slowly at them, in turn*): Yes, gentlemen . . . (*Turns away and walks off.* FIRST SOLDIER *moves slowly up to the grave.*)

FIRST SOLDIER (*to the* CORPSES): I . . . I'm glad you . . . you didn't . . . I'm glad. Say, is there anything we can do for you?

SERGEANT: Lissen, soldier!

FIRST SOLDIER (*passionately, harshly*): Shut up, Sergeant! (*Then very softly and warmly to* FIRST CORPSE) Is there anything we can do for you, Friend?

FIRST CORPSE: Yeah. You can sing. . . . (*There is a pause in which the* FIRST SOLDIER *turns around and looks at the* SECOND SOLDIER, *then back to the* FIRST CORPSE. *Then the silence is broken by the* SECOND SOLDIER'S *voice, raised in song. It goes on for a few moments, then fades as the light dims.*)

[*Coloured spotlights pick out three* BUSINESS MEN *on different parts of the stage.*

FIRST BUSINESS MAN: Ssh! Keep it quiet!

THIRD BUSINESS MAN: Sink 'em with lead. . . .

SECOND BUSINESS MAN: Bury them! Bury them six feet under!

FIRST BUSINESS MAN: What are we going to do?

SECOND BUSINESS MAN: We must keep up the morale.

THIRD BUSINESS MAN: Lead! Lead! A lot of lead!

SECOND BUSINESS MAN: What do we pay our Generals for?

CHORUS OF BUSINESS MEN: Ssssh! (*Blackout.*)

[*Spotlight on the congregation of a church, kneeling, with a* PRIEST *praying over them.*

PRIEST: O Jesus, our God and our Christ, Who has redeemed us with Thy blood on the Cross at Calvary, give us Thy blessing on this holy day, and cause it that our soldiers allow themselves to be buried in peace, and bring victory to our arms, enlisted in Thy Cause and the cause of all righteousness on the field of battle. . . . Amen. . . . (*Blackout.*)

FIRST GENERAL (*in purple baby spotlight*): Please, God, keep it quiet. . . .

[*Spotlight on newspaper office.*

REPORTER: Well? What are you going to do?

EDITOR: Do I have to do anything?

REPORTER: God-damn right you do. . . . They're still standing up. They're going to stand up from now till Doomsday. They're not going to be able to bury soldiers any more. It's in the stars. . . . You got to say something about it. . . .

EDITOR: All right. Put this in. " It is alleged that certain members of an infantry regiment refuse to allow themselves to be buried. . . ."

REPORTER: Well?

EDITOR: That's all.

REPORTER (*incredulous*): That's all?

EDITOR: Yes. Christ, isn't that *enough*? (*Black-out.*)

[*Spotlight on a radio-loudspeaker. A* VOICE, *mellow and beautiful, comes out of it.*

THE VOICE: It has been reported that certain American soldiers, killed on the field of battle, have refused to allow themselves to be buried. Whether this is true or not, the Coast-to-Coast Broadcasting System feels that this must give the American public an idea of the indomitable spirit of the American doughboy in this war. We cannot rest until this war is won—not even our brave dead boys. . . . (*Blackout.*)

[*Guns. Spotlight on* FIRST GENERAL *and* CAPTAIN.

FIRST GENERAL: Have you got any suggestions . . . ?

CAPTAIN: I think so. Get their women. . . .

FIRST GENERAL: What good'll their women do?

CAPTAIN: Women are always conservative. It's a conservative notion—this one of lying down and allowing yourself to be buried when you're dead. The women'll fight the Generals' battle for them—in the best possible way—through their emotions. . . . It's the General's best bet. . . .

FIRST GENERAL: Women—Of course! You've got it there, Captain! Get out their women! Get them in a hurry! We'll have these boys underground in a jiffy. Women! By God, I never thought of it. . . . Send out the call. . . . Women! (*Fadeout.*)

[*A baby spotlight on the loudspeaker. The* VOICE *again, just as mellow, just as persuasive.*

VOICE: We have been asked by the War Department to broadcast an appeal to the women of Privates Driscoll, Schelling, Morgan, Webster, Levy, and Dean, reported dead. The War Department requests that the women of these men present themselves at the War Department office immediately. It is within their power to do a great service to their country. . . . (*Blackout.*)

[*The spotlight illuminates the* FIRST GENERAL, *where he stands, addressing six women.*

FIRST GENERAL : Go to your men . . . talk to them . . . make them see the error of their ways, ladies. You women represent what is dearest in our civilisation—the sacred foundations of the home. We are fighting this war to protect the foundations of the homes of America ! Those foundations will crumble utterly if these men of yours come back from the dead. I shudder to think of the consequences of such an act. Our entire system will be mortally struck. Our banks will close, our buildings collapse . . . our army will desert the field and leave our fair land open to be overrun by the enemy. Ladies, you are all Gold Star mothers and wives and sweethearts. You want to win this war. I know it. I know the high fire of patriotism that burns in women's breasts. That is why I have called upon you. Ladies, let me make this clear to you. If you do not get your men to lie down and allow themselves to be buried, I fear that our cause is lost. the burden of the war is upon your shoulders now. Wars are not fought with guns and powder alone, ladies. Here is your chance to do your part, a glorious part. . . . You are fighting for your homes, your children, your sisters' lives, your country's honour. You are fighting for religion, for love, for all decent human life. Wars can be fought and won only when the dead are buried and forgotten. How can we forget the dead who refuse to be buried ? And we *must* forget them ! There is no room in this world for dead men. They will lead only to the bitterest unhappiness—for you, for them, for everybody. Go, ladies, do your duty. Your country waits upon you. . . . (*Blackout.*)

[*Spotlight immediately illuminates the place where* PRIVATE SCHELLING, CORPSE TWO, *is talking to his wife.* MRS. SCHELLING *is a spare, taciturn woman, a farmer's wife, who might be twenty or forty or anything in between.*

BESS SCHELLING: Did it hurt much, John?

SCHELLING: How's the kid, Bess?

BESS: He's fine. He talks now. He weighs twenty-eight pounds. He'll be a big boy. Did it hurt much, John?

SCHELLING: How is the farm? Is it going all right, Bess?

BESS: It's going. The rye was heavy this year. Did it hurt much, John?

SCHELLING: Who did the reapin' for you, Bess?

BESS: Schmidt took care of it—and his boys. Schmidt's too old for the war and his boys are too young. Took 'em nearly two weeks. The wheat's not bad this year. Schmidt's oldest boy expects to be called in a month or two. He practises behind the barn with that old shotgun Schmidt uses for duck.

SCHELLING: The Schmidts were always fools. When the kid grows up, Bess, you make sure you pump some sense into his head. What colour's his hair?

BESS: Blond. Like you. . . . What are you going to do, John?

SCHELLING: I would like to see the kid—and the farm—and . . .

BESS: They say you're dead, John. . . .

SCHELLING: I'm dead, all right.

BESS: Then how is it . . . ?

SCHELLING: I don't know. Maybe there's too many of us under the ground now. Maybe the earth can't stand it no more. You got to change crops sometime. What are you doing here, Bess?

BESS: They asked me to get you to let yourself be buried.

SCHELLING: What do you think?

BESS: You're dead, John. . . .

SCHELLING: Well . . . ?

BESS: What's the good . . . ?

SCHELLING: I don't know. Only there's something in me, dead or no dead, that won't let me be buried.

BESS: You were a queer man, John. I never did understand what you were about. But what's the good . . . ?

SCHELLING: Bess, I never talked so that I could get you to understand what I wanted while I—while I—before . . . Maybe now . . . There're a couple of things, Bess, that I ain't had enough of. Easy things, the things you see when you look outa your window at night, after supper, or when you wake up in the mornin'. Things you smell when you step outside the door when summer's on and the sun starts to turn the grass brown. Things you hear when you're busy with the horses or pitchin' the hay and you don't really notice them and yet they come back to you. Things like the fuzz of green over a field in spring where you planted wheat and it's started to come out overnight. Things like lookin' at rows of corn scrapin' in the breeze, tall and green, with the silk flying off the ears in the wind. Things like seeing the sweat come out all over on your horse's fat flank and seein' it shine like silk in front of you, smelling horsey and strong. Things like seein' the loam turn back all fat and deep brown on both sides as the plough turns it over so that it gets to be awful hard walkin' behind it. Things like taking a cold drink of water outa the well after you've boiled in the sun all afternoon, and feelin' the water go down and down into you coolin' you off all through from the inside out. . . . Things like seein' a blond kid, all busy and serious, playin' with a dog on the shady side of a house. . . . There ain't nothin' like that down here, Bess. . . .

BESS: Everything has its place, John. Dead men have theirs.

SCHELLING: My place is on the earth, Bess. My business is with the top of the earth, not the under-side. It was a trap that yanked me down. I'm not smart, Bess, and I'm easy trapped—but I can tell now. . . . I got some stories to tell farmers before I'm through—I'm going to tell 'em. . . .

BESS: We could bury you home, John, near the creek—it's cool there and quiet and there's always a breeze in the trees. . . .

SCHELLINH: Later, Bess, when I've had my fill of lookin' and smellin' and talkin'. . . . A man should be able to walk into his grave, not be dragged into it. . . .

BESS: How'll I feel—and the kid—with you walkin' around—like—like that . . . ?

SCHELLING: I won't bother you. . . . I won't come near you. . . .

BESS: Even so. Just knowin' . . .

SCHELLING: I can't help it. This is somethin'

bigger'n you—bigger'n me. It's somethin' I ain't had nothin' to do with startin'. . . . It's somethin' that just grew up outa the earth—like—like a weed—a flower. Cut it down now and it'll jump up in a dozen new places. You can't stop it. The earth's ready for it. . . .

BESS: You were a good husband, John. For the kid—and me—won't you?

SCHELLING (*quietly*): Go home, Bess. *Go home!* (*Blackout.*)

[*The spotlight picks out* CORPSE NUMBER FIVE, PRIVATE LEVY, *where he stands in the grave, with his back to the audience. His woman, a pert, attractive young lady, is sitting next to him, above him, facing him, talking to him.*

JOAN: You loved me best, didn't you, Henry—of all of them—all those women—you loved me the best, didn't you?

LEVY (FIFTH CORPSE): What's the difference, now?

JOAN: I want to know it.

LEVY: It's not important.

JOAN: It's important to me. I knew about the others, about Doris and that shifty-eyed Janet. . . . Henry, you're not a live man, are you, Henry?

LEVY: No, I'm all shot away inside.

JOAN: Must wars always be fought in the mud like this? I never expected it to look like this. It . . . it looks like a dump heap.

LEVY: You've gotten your shoes muddy. They're pretty shoes, Joan.

JOAN: Do you think so, Henry? They're lizard. I like them too. It's so hard to get a good pair of shoes nowadays.

LEVY: Do you still dance, Joan?

JOAN: Oh, I'm really much better than I used to be. There are so many dances back home nowadays. Dances for orphan relief and convalescent hospitals and Victory Loans. I'm busy seven nights a week. I sold more Victory Loans than any other girl in the League. I got a helmet . . . one of *their* helmets . . . one with a bullet-hole in it, for selling eleven thousand dollars' worth.

LEVY: Out here we get them for nothing, by the million—bullet-holes and all.

JOAN: That sounds bitter. You shouldn't sound bitter.

LEVY: I'm sorry.

JOAN: I heard Colonel Elwell the other day. You know Colonel Elwell, old Anthony Elwell who owns the mill. He made a speech at the monthly Red Cross banquet and he said that that was the nice thing about this war, it wasn't being fought bitterly by our boys. He said it was just patriotism that kept us going. He's a wonderful speaker, Colonel Elwell; I cried and cried. . . .

LEVY: I remember him.

JOAN: Henry, do you think we're going to win the war?

LEVY: What's the difference?

JOAN: Henry! What a way to talk! I don't know what's come over you. Really, I don't. Why, the papers say that if *they* win the war, they'll burn our churches and tear down our museums and . . . and rape our women. (LEVY *laughs*.) Why are you laughing, Henry?

LEVY: I'm dead, Joan.

JOAN: Yes. Then why—why don't you let them bury you?

LEVY: There are a lot of reasons. There were a lot of things I loved on this earth. . . .

JOAN: A dead man can't touch a woman.

LEVY: The women, yes—but more than touching them. I got a great joy just from listening to women, hearing them laugh, watching their skirts blow in the wind, noticing the way their breasts bounced up and down inside their dresses when they walked. It had nothing to do with touching them. I liked to hear the sound of their high heels on pavements at night and the tenderness in their voices when they walked past me arm in arm with a young man. You were so lovely, Joan, with your pale hair and long hands.

JOAN: You always liked my hair. (*A pause.*) No woman will walk arm in arm with you, Henry Levy, while you cheat the grave.

LEVY: No. But there will be the eyes of women to look at and the bright colour of their hair and the soft way they swing their hips when they walk before young men. These are the things that mean life and the earth to me, the joy and the pain. These are the things the earth still owes me, now when I am only thirty. Joy and pain—to each man in his own way, a full seventy years, to be ended by an unhurried fate, not by a coloured pin on a General's map. What do I care for the coloured pins on a General's map?

JOAN: They are not only pins. They mean more. . . .

LEVY: More? To whom? To the Generals—not to me. To me they are coloured pins. It is not a fair bargain—this exchange of my life for a small part of a coloured pin. . . .

JOAN: Henry, how can you talk like that? You know why this war is being fought.

LEVY: No. Do you?

JOAN: Of course, everybody knows. We *must* win! We must be prepared to sacrifice our last drop of blood. Anyway, what can you do?

LEVY: Do you remember last summer, Joan? My last leave. We went to Maine. I would like to remember that—the sun and the beach and your soft hands—for a long time.

JOAN: What are you going to do?

LEVY: Walk the world looking at the fine, long-legged girls, seeing in them something deep and true and passionately vital, listening to the sound of their light voices with ears the Generals would have stopped with the grave's solid mud. . . .

JOAN: Henry! Henry! Once you said you loved me. For love of me, Henry, go into the grave. . . .

LEVY: Poor Joan. (*Stretches out his hand tenderly as if to touch her.*)

JOAN (*recoiling*): Don't touch me. (*Pause.*) For love of me.

LEVY: Go home, Joan! *Go home!* (*Blackout.*)

[*The spotlight picks out the* THIRD CORPSE, PRIVATE MORGAN, *and* JULIA BLAKE, *he with his back to the audience, standing in the grave, she above and to the right.* JULIA *sobs.*

MORGAN: Stop crying, Julia. What's the sense in crying?

JULIA: No sense. Only I can't stop crying.

MORGAN: You shouldn't have come.

JULIA: They asked me to come. They said you wouldn't let them bury you—dead and all. . . .

MORGAN: Yes.

JULIA (*crying*): Why don't they kill me too? I'd let them bury me. I'd be glad to be buried—to get away from all this.... I—I haven't stopped crying for two weeks now. I used to think I was tough. I never cried. Even when I was a kid. It's a wonder where all the tears can come from. Though I guess there's always room for more tears. I thought I was all cried out when I heard about the way they killed Fred. My kid brother. I used to comb his hair in the morning when he went to school.... I—I ... Then they killed you. They did, didn't they?

MORGAN: Yes.

JULIA: It's hard to know like this. I—I know, though. It—it makes it harder, this way, with you like this. I could forget easier if you ... But I wasn't going to say that. I was going to listen to you. Oh, my darling, it's been so rotten. I get drunk. I hate it and I get drunk. I sing out loud and everybody laughs. I was going through your things the other day—I'm crazy ... I go through all your things three times a week, touching your clothes and reading your books. . . . You have the nicest clothes. . . . There was that quatrain you wrote to me that time you were in Boston and . . . First I laughed, then I cried, then . . . It's a lovely poem—you would have been a fine writer. I think you would have been the greatest writer that ever . . . I . . . Did they shoot your hands away, darling?

MORGAN: No.

JULIA: That's good. I couldn't bear it if anything happened to your hands. Was it bad, darling?

MORGAN: Bad enough.

JULIA: But they didn't shoot your hands away.

That's something. You learn how to be grateful for the craziest things nowadays. People have to be grateful for something and it's so hard, with the war and all. . . . Oh, darling, I never could think of you dead. Somehow you didn't seem to be made to be dead. I would feel better if you were buried in a fine green field and there were funny little flowers jumping up around the stone that said, " Walter Morgan, Born 1913, Died 1937." I could stop getting drunk at night and singing out loud so that people laugh at me. The worst thing is looking at all the books you piled up home that you didn't read. They wait there, waiting for your hands to come and open them and . . . Oh, let them bury you, let them bury you. . . . There's nothing left, only crazy people and clothes that'll never be used hanging in the closets. . . . Why not ?

MORGAN : There are too many books I haven't read, too many places I haven't seen, too many memories I haven't kept long enough. . . . I won't be cheated of them. . . .

JULIA : And me ? Darling, me. . . . I hate getting drunk. Your name would look so well on a nice simple chunk of marble in a green field. " Walter Morgan, Beloved of Julia Blake . . ." With poppies and daises and those little purple flowers all around the bottom, and . . . (*She is bent over, almost wailing. There is the flash of a gun in her hand, and she totters, falls.*) Now they can put my name on the casualty lists, too. . . . What do they call those purple flowers, darling . . . ? (*Blackout.*)

[*The spotlight follows* KATHERINE DRISCOLL *as she makes her way from* CORPSE *to* CORPSE *in the grave, looking at their faces. She looks first at* CORPSE SIX, *shudders, covers her eyes and moves on. She stops at* CORPSE FIVE.

KATHERINE : I'm Katherine Driscoll. I—I'm

looking for my brother. He's dead. Are you my brother?

FIFTH CORPSE: No. (KATHERINE *goes on to* CORPSE FOUR, *stops, looks, moves on to* CORPSE THREE.)

KATHERINE: I'm looking for my brother. My name is Katherine Driscoll. His name——

THIRD CORPSE: No. (KATHERINE *goes on, stands irresolutely before* CORPSE TWO.)

KATHERINE: Are you . . . ? (*Realising it isn't her brother, goes on to* CORPSE ONE.) I'm looking for my brother. My name is Katherine Driscoll. His name——

DRISCOLL: I'm Tom Driscoll.

KATHERINE: Hel—Hello. I don't know you. After fifteen years—and . . .

DRISCOLL: What do you want, Katherine?

KATHERINE: You don't know me either, do you?

DRISCOLL: No.

KATHERINE: It's funny—my coming here to talk to a dead man—to try to get him to do something because once long ago he was my brother. They talked me into it. I don't know how to begin. . . .

DRISCOLL: You'll be wasting your words, Katherine. . . .

KATHERINE: They should have asked someone nearer to you—someone who loved you—only they couldn't find anybody. I was the nearest, they said. . . .

DRISCOLL: That's so. You were the nearest. . . .

KATHERINE: And I fifteen years away. Poor Tom. . . . It couldn't have been a sweet life you led these fifteen years.

DRISCOLL: It wasn't.

KATHERINE: You were poor, too?

DRISCOLL: Sometimes I begged for meals. I wasn't lucky. . . .

KATHERINE: And yet you want to go back. Is there no more sense in the dead, Tom, than in the living?

DRISCOLL: Maybe not. Maybe there's no sense in either living or dying, but we can't believe that. I travelled to a lot of places and I saw a lot of things, always from the black side of them, always workin' hard to keep from starvin', and turnin' my collar up to keep the wind out, and they were mean and rotten and sad, but always I saw that they could be better and some day they were going to be better, and that the guys like me who knew that they were rotten and knew that they could be better had to get out and fight to make it that way.

KATHERINE: You're dead. Your fight's over.

DRISCOLL: The fight's never over. I got things to say to people now—to the people who nurse big machines and the people who swing shovels and the people whose babies die with big bellies and rotten bones. I got things to say to the people who leave their lives behind them and pick up guns to fight in somebody else's war. Important things. Big things. Big enough to lift me out of the grave right back on to the earth into the middle of men just because I got the voice to say them. If God could lift Jesus . . .

KATHERINE: Tom! Have you lost religion, too?

DRISCOLL: I got another religion. I got a religion that wants to take heaven out of the clouds and plant it right here on the earth where most of us can get a slice of it. It isn't as pretty a heaven—there aren't any streets of gold

and there aren't any angels, and we'd have to
worry about sewerage, and railroad schedules
in it, and we don't guarantee everybody'd love
it, but it'd be right here, stuck in the mud of
this earth, and there wouldn't be any entrance
requirement, like dying, to get into it. . . . Dead
or alive, I see that, and it won't let me rest.
I was the first one to get up in this black grave
of ours, because that idea wouldn't let me rest.
I pulled the others with me—that's my job,
pulling the others. . . . They only know what
they want—I know how they can get it. . . .

KATHERINE: There's still the edge of arrogance
on you.

DRISCOLL: I got heaven in my two hands to
give to men. There's reason for arrogance. . . .

KATHERINE: I came to ask you to lie down and
let them bury you. It seems foolish now. But . . .

DRISCOLL: It's foolish, Katherine. I didn't get
up from the dead to go back to the dead. I'm
going to the living now. . . .

KATHERINE: Fifteen years. It's a good thing
your mother isn't alive. How can you say good-
bye to a dead brother, Tom?

DRISCOLL: Wish him an easy grave, Katherine. . . .

KATHERINE: A green and pleasant grave to
you, Tom, when, finally . . . finally . . . green
and pleasant. (*Blackout.*)

[*The spotlight illuminates* PRIVATE DEAN, *the*
SIXTH CORPSE, *where he stands with his back to
the audience, listening to his mother, a thin, shabby,
red-eyed woman of about forty-five, sitting above
and to the right, in the full glare of the spotlight.*
DEAN *is in shadow.*

MRS. DEAN: Let me see your face, son. .

DEAN: You don't want to see it, mom. . . .

MRS. DEAN: My baby's face. Once, before you . . .

DEAN: You don't want to see it, mom. I know. Didn't they tell you what happened to me?

MRS. DEAN: I asked the doctor. He said a piece of shell hit the side of your head—but even so . . .

DEAN: Don't ask to see it, mom.

MRS. DEAN: How are you, son? (DEAN *laughs a little—bitterly*.) Oh, I forgot. I asked you that question so many times while you were growing up, Jimmy. Let me see your face, Jimmy—just once. . . .

DEAN: How did Alice take it when she heard . . . ?

MRS. DEAN: She put a gold star in her window. She tells everybody you were going to be married. Is that so?

DEAN: May be. I liked Alice.

MRS. DEAN: She came over on your birthday. That was before this—this happened. She brought flowers. Big chrysanthemums. Yellow. A lot of them. We had to put them in two vases. I baked a cake. I don't know why. It's hard to get eggs and fine flour nowadays. My baby, twenty years old . . . Let me see your face, Jimmy, boy. . . .

DEAN: Go home, mom. . . . It's not doing you any good staying here. . . .

MRS. DEAN: I want you to let them bury you, Baby. It's done now and over. It would be better for you that way. . . .

DEAN: There's no better to it, mom—and no worse. It happened that way, that's all.

Mrs. Dean: Let me see your face, Jimmy. You had such a fine face. Like a good baby's. It hurt me when you started to shave. Somehow, I almost forget what you looked like, Baby. I remember what you looked like when you were five, when you were ten—you were chubby and fair and your cheeks felt like little silk cushions when I put my hand on them. But I don't remember how you looked when you went away with that uniform on you and that helmet over your face. . . . Baby, let me see your face, once. . . .

Dean: Don't ask me. . . . You don't want to see. You'll feel worse—for ever . . . if you see. . . .

Mrs. Dean: I'm not afraid. I can look at my baby's face. Do you think mothers can be frightened by their children's . . .

Dean: No, mom. . . .

Mrs. Dean: Baby, listen to me, I'm your mother. . . . Let them bury you. There's something peaceful and done about a grave. After a while you forget the death and you remember only the life before it. But this way—you never forget . . . it's a wound walking around for ever, without peace. For your sake and mine and your father's . . . Baby . . .

Dean: I was only twenty, mom. I hadn't done anything. I hadn't seen anything. I never even had a girl. I spent twenty years practising to be a man and then they killed me. Being a kid's no good, mom. You try to get over it as soon as you can. You don't really live while you're a kid. You mark time, waiting. I waited, mom— but then I got cheated. They made a speech and played a trumpet and dressed me in a uniform and then they killed me.

Mrs. Dean: Oh, Baby, Baby, there's no peace this way. Please, let them . . .

DEAN: No, mom. . . .

MRS. DEAN: Then once, now, so that I can remember—let me see your face, my baby's face. . . .

DEAN: Mom, the shell hit close to me. You don't want to look at a man when a shell hits close to him.

MRS. DEAN: Let me see your face, Jimmy. . . .

DEAN: All right, mom. . . . Look ! (*He turns his face to her. The audience can't see his face, but immediately a spotlight, white and sharp, shoots down from directly above and hits DEAN's head. MRS. DEAN leans forward, staring. Another spotlight shoots down immediately after from the extreme right, then one from the left, then two more, from above. They hit with the impact of blows and MRS. DEAN shudders a little as they come, as though she were watching her son being beaten. There is absolute silence for a moment. Then MRS. DEAN starts to moan, low, painfully. The lights remain fixed and MRS. DEAN's moans rise to a wail, then to a scream. She leans back, covering her eyes with her hands, screaming. Blackout. The scream persists, fading, like a siren fading in the distance, until it is finally stilled.*)

[*The spotlight on* CORPSE THREE, PRIVATE WEBSTER, *and his wife, a dumpy, sad little woman.*

MARTHA WEBSTER: Say something.

WEBSTER: What do you want me to say ?

MARTHA: Something—anything. Only talk. You give me the shivers standing there like that—looking like that. . . .

WEBSTER: Even now — after this — there's nothing that we can talk to each other about.

MARTHA: Don't talk like that. You talked like that enough when you were alive. It's not my fault that you're dead. . . .

WEBSTER: No.

MARTHA: It was bad enough when you were alive—and you didn't talk to me and you looked at me as though I was always in your way.

WEBSTER: Martha, Martha, what's the difference now?

MARTHA: I just wanted to let you know. Now I suppose you're going to come back and sit around and ruin my life altogether?

WEBSTER: No. I'm not going to come back.

MARTHA: Then what . . . ?

WEBSTER: I couldn't explain it to you, Martha. . . .

MARTHA: No! Oh, no—you couldn't explain it to your wife. But you could explain it to that dirty bunch of loafers down at that damned garage of yours and you could explain it to those bums in the saloon on F. Street. . . .

WEBSTER: I guess I could. (*Musing*) Things seemed to be clearer when I was talking to the boys while I worked over a job. And I managed to talk so people could get to understand what I meant down at the saloon on F. Street. It was nice, standing there of a Saturday night, with a beer in front of you and a man or two that understood your own language next to you, talking—oh, about Babe Ruth or the new oiling system Ford was putting out or the chances of us gettin' into the war. . . .

MARTHA: It's different if you were rich and had a fine beautiful life you wanted to go back to. Then I could understand. But you were poor . . . you always had dirt under your fingernails, you never ate enough, you hated me, your wife, you couldn't stand being in the same room with me. . . . Don't shake your head. I know.

Out of your whole life, all you could remember that's good is a beer on Saturday night that you drank in company with a couple of bums. . . .

WEBSTER: That's enough. I didn't think about it then . . . but I guess I was happy those times.

MARTHA: You were happy those times . . . but you weren't happy in your own home ! I know, even if you don't say it ! Well, I wasn't happy either ! Living in three damned rooms that the sun didn't hit five times a year ! Watching the roaches make picnics on the walls ! Happy !

WEBSTER: I did my best.

MARTHA: Eighteen-fifty a week ! Your best ! Eighteen-fifty, condensed milk, a two-dollar pair of shoes once a year, five hundred dollars' insurance, chopped meat. God, how I hate chopped meat ! Eighteen-fifty, being afraid of everything—of the landlord, the gas company, scared stiff every month that I was goin' to have a baby ! Why shouldn't I have a baby ? Who says I shouldn't have a baby ? Eighteen-fifty, no baby !

WEBSTER: I woulda liked a kid.

MARTHA: Would you ? You never said anything.

WEBSTER: It's good to have a kid. A kid's somebody to talk to.

MARTHA: At first . . . in the beginning . . . I thought we'd have a kid some day.

WEBSTER: Yeah, me too. I used to go out on Sundays and watch men wheel their kids through the park.

MARTHA: There were so many things you didn't tell me. Why did you keep quiet ?

WEBSTER: I was ashamed to talk to you. I couldn't give you anything.

MARTHA: I'm sorry.

WEBSTER: In the beginning it looked so fine. I used to smile to myself when I walked beside you in the street and other men looked at you.

MARTHA: That was a long time ago.

WEBSTER: A kid would've helped.

MARTHA: No, it wouldn't. Don't fool yourself, Webster. The Clarks downstairs have four and it doesn't help them. Old man Clark comes home drunk every Saturday night and beats 'em with his shaving strap and throws plates at the old lady. Kids don't help the poor. Nothing helps the poor! I'm too smart to have sick, dirty kids on eighteen-fifty. . . .

WEBSTER: That's it. . . .

MARTHA: A house should have a baby. But it should be a clean house with a full icebox. Why shouldn't I have a baby? Other people have babies. Even now, with the war, other people have babies. They don't have to feel their skin curl every time they tear a page off the calendar. They go off to beautiful hospitals in lovely ambulances and have babies between coloured sheets! What's there about them that God likes, that He makes it so easy for *them* to have babies?

WEBSTER: They're not married to mechanics.

MARTHA: No! It's not eighteen-fifty for them. And now . . . now it's worse. Your twenty dollars a month. You hire yourself out to be killed and I get twenty dollars a month. I wait on line all day to get a loaf of bread. I've forgotten what butter tastes like. I wait on line with the rain soaking through my shoes for a pound of rotten meat once a week. At night I go home. Nobody to talk to, just sitting, watching the bugs, with one little light because the Government's got to save electricity. You had to go off and leave me to that ! What's the war to me that I have to sit at night with nobody to talk to ? What's the war to you that you had to go off and . . . ?

WEBSTER : That's why I'm standing up now, Martha.

MARTHA : What took you so long, then ? Why now ? Why not a month ago, a year ago, ten years ago ? Why didn't you stand up then ? Why wait until you're dead ? You live on eighteen-fifty a week, with the roaches, not saying a word, and then when they kill you, you stand up ! You fool !

WEBSTER : I didn't see it before.

MARTHA : Just like you ! Wait until it's too late ! There's plenty for live men to stand up for ! All right, stand up ! It's about time you talked back. It's about time all you poor miserable eighteen-fifty bastards stood up for themselves and their wives and the children they can't have ! Tell 'em *all* to stand up ! Tell 'em ! *Tell 'em !* (*She shrieks. Blackout.*)

[*A spotlight picks out the* FIRST GENERAL. *He has his hands to his lips.*

FIRST GENERAL : It didn't work. But keep it quiet. For God's sake, keep it quiet. . . . (*Blackout.*)

[*A spotlight picks out the newspaper office, the* REPORTER *and the* EDITOR.

REPORTER (*in harsh triumph*) : It didn't work ! Now, you've got to put it in ! I knew it wouldn't work ! Smear it over the headlines ! It didn't work !

EDITOR : Put it in the headlines. . . . They won't be buried ! (*Blackout. Voices call.*)

VOICE (NEWSBOY *spotted*) : It didn't work ! Extra ! It didn't work !

VOICE (*in dark. Hoarse whisper*): It didn't work ! They're still standing. . . . Somebody do something. . . .

VOICE (*spotted, a* CLUBWOMAN *type*): Somebody do something. . . .

VOICE (NEWSBOY *spotted*): Extra ! They're still standing. . . .

VOICE (CLUBWOMAN): Don't let them back into the country. . . .

REPORTER (*spotted. Triumphantly*): They're standing. From now on they'll always stand ! You can't bury soldiers any more. . . .

[*Spotted, a group, owners of the next four voices.*

VOICE: They stink. Bury them !

VOICE: What are we going to do about them ?

VOICE: What'll happen to our war ? We can't let anything happen to our war. . . .

VOICE (*a* PRIEST, *facing the three men*): Pray ! Pray ! God must help us ! Down on your knees, all of you, and pray with your hearts and your guts and the marrow of your bones. . . .

VOICE (REPORTER *spotted, facing them all*): It will take more than prayers. What are prayers to a dead man ? They're standing ! Mankind is standing up and climbing out of its grave. . . . (*Blackout.*)

VOICE (*in dark*): Have you heard . . . ? It didn't work. . . .

VOICE (*in dark*): Extra ! Extra ! It didn't work ! They're still standing !

[*Spotted*, MRS. DEAN, MRS. SCHELLING, JULIA BLAKE.

MRS. DEAN: My baby . . .

MRS. SCHELLING: My husband . . .

JULIA BLAKE: My lover . . . (*Blackout.*)

VOICE (*in dark*): Bury them ! They stink !

[*The next set of characters walks through a stationary spotlight.*

VOICE (*a* FARMER): Plant a new crop ! The old crop has worn out the earth. Plant something besides lives in the old and weary earth. . . .

VOICE (*a* NEWSBOY, *running*): Extra ! It didn't work !

VOICE (*a* BANKER, *frantic*): Somebody do something ! Dupont's passed a dividend !

VOICE (*a* PRIEST): The Day of Judgment is at hand. . . .

VOICE (*the* FIRST WHORE): Where is Christ ? (*Blackout.*)

VOICE (*in dark*): File 'em away in alphabetical order. . . .

[*Spotlight on a man in academic robes, reading aloud from behind a table, after he adjusts his glasses.*

VOICE: We don't believe it. It is against the dictates of science. (*Blackout.*)

[*Spot on* SECOND GENERAL.

SECOND GENERAL: Keep it quiet !

[MRS. SCHELLING *walks in front of him. The others follow.*

BESS SCHELLING: My husband . . .

JULIA BLAKE: My lover . . .

MRS. DEAN: My baby . . . (*Blackout.*)

VOICE (*a* CHILD): What have they done with my father ?

[*Spot on* BANKER *at telephone.*

BANKER (*into phone*): Somebody do something.

Call the War Department ! Call up Congress !
Call up the Roman Catholic Church ! Somebody do something !

VOICE : We've got to put them down !

REPORTER (*spotted*) : Never ! Never ! Never !
You can't put them down. Put one down and
ten will spring up like weeds in an old garden.

[*Spots at various parts of the stage.*

VOICE (*the* THIRD GENERAL) : Use lead on them,
lead ! Lead put 'em down once, lead'll do it
again ! Lead !

VOICE : Put down the sword and hang the
armour on the wall to rust with the years. The
killed have arisen.

VOICE : Bury them ! Bury the dead !

VOICE : The old demons have come back to
possess the earth. We are lost. . . .

VOICE : The dead have arisen, now let the living
rise, singing. . . .

VOICE : Do something, for the love of God, do
something. . . .

VOICE : Extra ! They're still standing.

VOICE : Do something !

VOICE (*in dark*) : We will do something. . . .

VOICE : Who are you ?

VOICE (PRIEST *in spot*) : We are the Church and
the voice of God. The State has tried its ways,
now let the Church use the ways of God. These
corpses are possessed by the devil, who plagues
the lives of men. The Church will exorcise
the devil from these men, according to its
ancient rite, and they will lie down in their
graves like children to a pleasant sleep, rising
no more to trouble the world of living men.

N

The Church which is the Voice of God upon this earth. Amen. . . . (*Blackout*).

CHORUS OF VOICES: Alleluia, alleluia, sing. . . . (*The scream of the bereft mother fades in, reaches its height, then dies off as the holy procession of priests moves solemnly on with bell, book and candle. A* PRIEST *sprinkles the* CORPSES *with holy water, makes the sign of the cross over them and begins in the solemn Latin of the service. At the end he goes into English—his voice rising in ritualistic passion.*)

PRIEST: I exorcise thee, unclean spirit, in the name of Jesus Christ; tremble, O Satan, thou enemy of the faith, thou foe of mankind, who hast brought death into the world, who hast deprived men of life, and hast rebelled against justice, thou seducer of mankind, thou root of evil, thou source of avarice, discord, and envy. (*Silence. Then the* CORPSES *begin to laugh, lightly, horribly. There is a sign from the living men present, and the priestly procession goes off, its bell tinkling. The laughter goes on. Blackout. The* VOICES *call again.*)

VOICE: No. . . .

VOICE: NO !

VOICE: It didn't work. . . .

VOICE: We are deserted by God for our evil ways. It is the new flood, without rain. . . .

NEWSBOY: They're licked.

VOICE: This isn't 1918 ! This is to-day !

VOICE: See what happens to-morrow !

VOICE: Anything can happen now ! Anything !

VOICE: They're coming. We must stop them !

VOICE: We must find ways, find means !

VOICE (*the* REPORTER, *exulting*) : They're coming! There will be no ways, no means !

SEMI-CHORUS (*mocking*): What are you going to do?

CHORUS: *What are you going to do?* (*They laugh sardonically.*)

THIRD GENERAL: Let me have a machine-gun! Sergeant! A machine-gun! (*A bolt of light comes down to a machine-gun set to the left of the grave, mid-way between the edge of the grave and the wings. The* GENERALS *are clustered around it.*)

THIRD GENERAL: I'll show them! This is what they've needed!

FIRST GENERAL: All right, all right. Get it over with! Hurry! But keep it quiet!

THIRD GENERAL: I want a crew to man this gun. (*Pointing to* FIRST SOLDIER) You! Come over here! And you! You know what to do. I'll give the command to fire. . . .

FIRST SOLDIER: Not to me, you won't. . . . This is over me. I won't touch that gun. None of us will! We didn't hire out to be no butcher of dead men. Do your own chopping. . . .

THIRD GENERAL: You'll be court-martialled! You'll be dead by to-morrow morning. . . .

FIRST SOLDIER: Be careful, General! I may take a notion to come up like these guys. That's the smartest thing I've seen in this army. I like it. . . . (*To* DRISCOLL) What d'ye say, Buddy?

DRISCOLL: It's about time. . . . (*The* THIRD GENERAL *draws his gun, but the other* GENERALS *hold his arm.*)

FIRST GENERAL: Stop it! It's bad enough as it is! Let him alone! Do it yourself! Go ahead, do it!

THIRD GENERAL (*whispers*): Oh, my God. . . . (*He looks down at gun, then slowly gets down on one knee behind it. The other* GENERALS *slide out behind him. The* CORPSES *come together in the middle of the grave, all facing the gun.* THIRD GENERAL *fumbles with the gun.* VOICES *call.)*

REPORTER: Never, never, never !

JULIA: Walter Morgan, Beloved of Julia Blake, Born 1913, Died 1937.

MRS. DEAN: Let me see your face, Baby ?

MARTHA WEBSTER: All you remember is a glass of beer with a couple of bums on Saturday night.

KATHERINE DRISCOLL: A green and pleasant grave . . .

BESS SCHELLING: Did it hurt much, John ? His hair is blond and he weighs twenty-eight pounds.

JOAN: You loved me best, didn't you, Henry . . . best . . . ?

VOICE: Four yards of bloody mud . . .

VOICE: I understand how they feel, Charley. I wouldn't like to be underground . . . now . . .

REPORTER: Never, never !

VOICE: Never !

MARTHA WEBSTER: Tell 'em all to stand up ! Tell 'em ! *Tell 'em !*

[*The* CORPSES *begin to walk toward the left end of the grave, not marching, but walking together, silently. The* THIRD GENERAL *stiffens, then starts to laugh hysterically. As the* CORPSES *reach the edge of the grave and take their first step out, he starts firing, laughing wildly, the gun shaking his shoulders violently. Calmly, in the face of the chattering gun, the* CORPSES *gather on the brink of the grave, then walk soberly, in a little bunch, toward the* THIRD GENERAL. *For a moment they obscure him as they pass him. In that moment the gun stops. There is absolute silence. The* CORPSES *pass on, going off the stage, like men who have leisurely business that must be attended to in the not too pressing future. As they pass the gun, they reveal the* THIRD GENERAL *slumped forward, still, over the still gun. There is no movement on the stage for a fraction of a second. Then, slowly, the* FOUR SOLDIERS *of the burial detail break ranks. Slowly they walk, exactly as the* CORPSES *have walked, off toward the left, past the* THIRD GENERAL. *The last* SOLDIER, *as he passes the* THIRD GENERAL, *deliberately, but without malice, flicks a cigarette butt at him, then follows the other* SOLDIERS *off the stage. The* THIRD GENERAL *is the last thing we see, huddled over his quiet gun, pointed at the empty grave, as the light dims—in the silence.*

CURTAIN

BOY MEETS GIRL

Bella and Samuel Spewack

BOY MEETS GIRL

A Play
in Three Acts

To

Jo Davidson

WHOSE HOSPITALITY AND
ENCOURAGEMENT DELAYED THE COMPLETION
OF THIS PLAY THREE MONTHS

CHARACTERS

(in order of their appearance)

ROBERT LAW
LARRY TOMS
J. CARLYLE BENSON
ROSETTI
MR. FRIDAY (C.F.)
PEGGY
MISS CREWS
RODNEY BEVAN
GREEN
SLADE
SUSIE
A NURSE
DOCTOR
CHAUFFEUR
YOUNG MAN
STUDIO OFFICER
CUTTER
ANOTHER NURSE
MAJOR THOMPSON

SCENES

ACT I

Mr. Friday's Office, the Royal Studios in Hollywood.

ACT II

SCENE I: A Neighborhood Theatre. Seven months later.

SCENE II: Mr. Friday's office.

SCENE III: The same. Several hours later.

ACT III

SCENE I: A hospital corridor. Three weeks later.

SCENE II: In your home.

SCENE III: Mr. Friday's office.

Boy Meets Girl was produced by George Abbott at the Cort Theatre, New York City, Wednesday evening, November 27th, 1935. The production was directed by Mr. Abbott; the settings designed by Arne Lundborg.

THE CAST

Robert Law	ALLYN JOSLYN
Larry Toms	CHARLES MC CLELLAND
J. Carlyle Benson	JEROME COWAN
Rosetti	EVERETT H. SLOANE
Mr. Friday (C.F.)	ROYAL BEAL
Peggy	PEGGY HART
Miss Crews	LEA PENMAN
Rodney Bevan	JAMES MAC COLL
Green	GARSON KANIN
Slade	MAURICE SOMMERS
Susie	JOYCE ARLING
A Nurse	HELEN GARDNER
Doctor	PERRY IVINS
Chauffeur	EDISON RICE
Young Man	PHILIP FAVERSHAM
Studio Officer	GEORGE W. SMITH
Cutter	ROBERT FOULK
Another Nurse	MARJORIE LYTELL
Major Thompson	JOHN CLARKE

This play was first presented in London on May 27th, 1936, at the Shaftesbury Theatre, by Mr. Gilbert Miller in association with Mr. George Abbott, with the following cast:

Robert Law	CLINTON SUNDBERG
Larry Toms	DON DOUGLAS
J. Carlyle Benson	DONALD MACDONALD
Rosetti	DOUGLAS GERARD
Mr. Friday (C.F.)	FRANK FENTON
Peggy	QUEENA BILOTTI
Miss Crews	ETHEL REMEY
Rodney Bevan	BRAMWELL FLETCHER
Green	SYDNEY ANDREWS
Slade	BEN GUY ODLEY
Susie	HELEN CHANDLER
A Nurse	HELEN PETRI
A Doctor	SCOTT MOORE
Chauffeur	JOHN SYKES
Young Man	LAMAR KING
Studio Officer	RALPH MOORHOUSE
Cutter	SIMEON GREER
Another Nurse	ARDEN YOUNG
Major Thompson	EVAN THOMAS

Play produced by GEORGE ABBOTT

ACT I

The room we see is one of a suite of three, comprising the sanctum of MR. C. ELLIOT FRIDAY, *a supervisor, sometimes called a producer, who is engaged in manufacturing motion pictures in Hollywood, California.*

In its present state the room is a happy combination of the Regency and Russell Wright periods—given over to pale green, mauve and canary yellow, with Rodier cloth-covered easy chairs and couch. A magnificent, be-French-phoned desk is at one end of the room. On it rests the inner-office dictograph, over which in the course of the play we hear the voice of the great B.K., chief executive of the studio. Beside it, appropriately, stands an amiable photograph of Mrs. C. Elliot Friday, a cultured if fatuous lady; a copy of " Swann's Way " (leaves uncut), a bronze nude astride an ash tray, a bottle of Pyramidon and a copy of " Variety." In the trash basket is a copy of " Hollywood Reporter." (It was very unkind to MR. FRIDAY.) *On the wall back of the desk are bookshelves with pots of hanging ivy on the top shelf, the rest given over, curiously enough, to books— and occasional bric-a-brac. There are a few end tables with ash trays and boxes of cigarettes, for it is the unwritten law in Hollywood that supervisors must provide cigarettes for writers during conferences and other times of stress. The two windows, although of the old-fashioned, non-casement kind, are framed by tasteful, expensive drapes and are partially concealed by half-drawn Venetian blinds. (A supervisor would lose cast without Venetian blinds.) The door left leads to an anteroom where sits* MISS CREWS, *secretary to* MR. FRIDAY. *The door at right rear leads to a smaller office where* MR. FRIDAY *sometimes thinks in solitude. This room contains* MR. FRIDAY'S *Commencement Day photograph (Harvard '19), snapshots of B.K.'s wedding at which* MR. FRIDAY *served as an usher. There are other photographs with florid inscriptions upon faces once famous and since vanished in film dust. The room is also memorable for the fact that* MR. FRIDAY—*a bit of a diplomat in his way—sometimes keeps earnest writers here while he submits their scripts to other writers in his inner office. At times as many as fifteen bright minds are thus let loose upon a C. Elliott Friday production, with sometimes startling results.*

All this, however, is very much by the by. It is really more important to note that through those Venetian blinds you can feel the sweet sterility of the desert that is so essentially Southern California. The sun is bright, of course, and it pours endlessly through the windows. The time is two o'clock, and the boys have been at it since noon.

One of the boys is BENSON—J. CARLYLE BENSON, *whom we discover prone on a couch. He is in his thirties and in his flannels. Years ago, as he will tell you, he worked as a scene painter and a property boy. He became a writer because he learned how bricks were made and laid. He knows every cliché, every formula, and in his heart of hearts he really believes the fairy tale is a credo of life. And he's a damned nice guy; handicapped somewhat by the fact that he married a beautiful but extravagant young woman who obviously doesn't love him. They live in a gorgeous home, have four dogs, two cars and, as* MR. FRIDAY *would put it, "a menage."*

The other member of the writing team is ROBERT LAW *whom you will find listed in O'Brien's " Best Short Stories." He came to Hollywood to make a little money and run right back to Vermont where he could really write. He is rather handsome, a little round-shouldered; smokes incessantly. He's a damned nice guy, too.*

There is a deep and abiding affection between the two men, even though LAW'S *nostalgia for realism and sincerity and substance finds no echoing response in* MR. BENSON. *They have one great thing in common—their mutual love of a great gag, a practical joke to enliven the monotony of the writing factory.*

For we are dealing here with a factory that manufactures entertainment in approved sizes; that puts the seven arts right on the belt. And it is this very quality that makes MR. FRIDAY'S office as fascinating as a power house and a good deal more entertaining.

The other inmates of the room are LARRY TOMS— you know LARRY TOMS—a Western star, and one ROSETTI, an agent. It is MR. ROSETTI'S business to see to it that MR. TOMS is profitably employed, for MR. ROSETTI collects ten per cent of MR. TOM'S weekly salary which, despite the star's fading popularity, is still a respectable sum. MR. TOMS is handsome, of course. He is also parsimonious. He leads a completely righteous life, and if you don't like him it isn't our fault; in all respects he is an extremely admirable character.

As the curtain goes up we see that LAW is on his feet and obviously he has been telling a story to MR. TOMS—a story that MR. TOMS is expected to re-enact before the camera.

LAW: And this bozo comes up to you and you look him straight in the eye and you say, " Why, damn your soul, I loved her before you ever married her." And then in walks the bitch, and she cries, " Larry, I heard everything you said." And you just look at her, and there's a long pause—a *long* pause. And then finally you say, " Did you ? " That's all. Just a plain, quiet, simple " Did you ? " Boy, what a moment ! (*He lies down on the couch beside* BENSON.)

LARRY: But what's the story about ?

BENSON (*rolling over*): Love !

LAW (*singing*): " Love is the sweetest thing——"

LARRY: Now, come on, boys—get off the couch. This ain't fair. I got a lot at stake in this picture. It's the last one in my contract. If I get a poor story I'm out in the cold.

LAW: Shivering with a million dollar annuity.

ROSETTI: Now, gentlemen, don't let's get personal.

LARRY (*rises and crosses to couch*): When they told me I was getting the star team of writers on the lot, I was all for it. But you've done nothing but clown around, and the shooting date's only two weeks off. I've got to play this picture.

LAW: Why?

LARRY (*swallowing*): Tell me your story in a few simple words.

LAW: Mr. Benson, what's our story?

BENSON: How the hell do I know?

LAW (*sits up*): Didn't you listen?

BENSON: No. We ought to have a stenographer.

LAW: But they won't wear tights. And I can't dictate to a stenographer who won't wear tights.

LARRY: Now listen, boys——

LAW: Don't speak to me. You don't like our story.

LARRY: I didn't say I didn't like it. I couldn't follow it. (*He slumps in disgust.*)

BENSON (*indignantly*): You couldn't follow it? Listen, I've been writing stories for eleven years. Boy meets girl. Boy loses girl. Boy gets girl.

LAW: Or—girl meets boy. Girl loses boy. Girl gets boy. Love will find a way. Love never loses. Put your money on love. You can't lose. (*Rises and saunters to window.*) I'm getting hungry.

BENSON: It's a sorry state of affairs when an actor insists on following a story. Do you think this is a golf tournament?

ROSETTI (*earnestly*): If I may make a point, I don't think you're showing the proper respect to one of the biggest stars in this studio. A man who's not only captivated millions of people but is going to captivate millions more——

BENSON (*wearily*): With his little lasso——

LARRY: Just because I don't get Gable's fan mail don't mean I ain't got his following. A lot of those that want to write me ain't never learned how.

LAW: Benson, injustice has been done. We've been lacking in respect for the idol of illiteracy.

BENSON: Do we apologize?

LAW: No!

ROSETTI: Well, let me tell you something. Before I became an agent I taught diction for years, and Larry Toms is potentially the greatest actor I've ever met. And I can prove it with X-rays. I was just taking them up to show B.K. He's got the Barrymore larynx. I'll put his larynx against John Barrymore's and I defy you to tell me which is which. (*Takes X-rays from brief-case. Gives one to* BENSON, *one to* LAW.)

LARRY: I couldn't tell it myself and it's my own larynx.

BENSON (*drawling*): Say—are you sure this is his *larynx*?

ROSETTI (*the diplomat; retrieving X-rays*): Gentlemen, I wouldn't be surprised with the proper training if Larry couldn't sing. That opens up the whole field of musicals. (*Puts brief-case on chair.*)

BENSON (*to* LAW): What are we waiting for?

LAW: Lunch.

LARRY (*angrily rising*): I'm getting fed up with this. I got writers who are just plain crazy—a producer who can't concentrate—and ain't even here—and—— (*Throws hat on floor and starts for* BENSON *and* LAW. LAW *moves to back of couch and* BENSON *goes up to door.*)

ROSETTI (*crossing down on* LARRY's *left*) : Now . . . now . . . Larry . . . don't lose your temper.

LARRY (*righteously*) : The idea of writers getting fifteen hundred a week for acting like hoodlums.

LAW : I agree with you.

LARRY : Huh ?

LAW : We're not writers. We're hacks. If we weren't, would I be sitting here listening to your inarticulate grunts ?

LARRY : Huh ?

LAW : That's exactly what I mean. For two cents, Benson, I'd take the next train back to Vermont.

LARRY : That's all right with me.

BENSON : Will you forget Vermont ?

LAW : At least I wouldn't have to sit around with *that* in Vermont. I'd write—really write. My God, I wrote once. I wrote a book. A darn good book. I was a promising young novelist. O'Brien reprinted three of my stories, and wanted more. And in 1935 I'm writing dialogue for a horse !

LARRY (*enraged*) : Now, listen——

ROSETTI (*pleading*) : Larry—Larry, take a deep breath. The boys mean no harm. . . . Exhale !

LAW (*sniffing*) : I smell carbon monoxide.

LARRY : One more crack, that's all—just one more crack ! (*Phone rings.*)

ROSETTI (*at phone*) : Hello . . . oh, yes . . . just a minute. For you, Benson.

BENSON (*taking up phone*) : Yes, speaking. Who ? Of course, Mrs. Benson's check is good. How much is it for ? Thirty-five hundred ? Oh ! I hope it was real ermine. . . . Certainly it's all right. You put the check through tomorrow. (*Hangs up; dials phone.*)

ROSETTI (*with a feline purr*): Ermine is a nice fur. (MISS CREWS *enters regally; puts letters on desk.*)

LARRY (*grumbling*): Miss Crews, what's keeping C.F.?

MISS CREWS: He's still up with B.K. (*She exits regally.*)

BENSON (*into phone*): Jim? Benson. Listen, sell three of my Municipal Fives this afternoon, will you? And put it in my joint account in the Security. I've got a check to meet. Never mind about that. I'll talk to her. Right. (*Hangs up.*)

LAW: Pearl is certainly spreading prosperity.

BENSON: What the hell? She's only a kid. She's having a good time. What's money for? (C.F. *enters.* C.F. *is, of course,* C. ELLIOT FRIDAY.)

C.F. (*briskly*): Good morning.

ROSETTI (*rises*): Good morning, C.F.

LARRY (*rises and sits*): Hello, C.F. (BENSON *lies on sofa.* LAW *rises and salaams Hindu fashion, as popularized by Mr. De Mille.*)

C.F.: Boys, no antics, please. We've got a heavy day ahead of us. (*Sits at desk; picks up phone. Into phone*) I don't want to be disturbed by anybody —understand? And order some lunch. A plate of raw carrots, and a bottle of certified, raw milk. See that it's *raw*. Bring enough for everybody. (*About to hang up.*)

LAW (*rises*): Just a moment. (*Takes phone.*) Mr. Benson and Mr. Law want two cups of chicken broth—some ham hocks—cabbage—lemon meringue pie—and some bicarbonate of soda. (*Hangs up; returns to couch.*)

C.F.: You're slaughtering yourselves, boys. You won't be able to think with that poison in your stomachs, and we've got to think. I've just seen the front office. Boys, we're facing a crisis.

ROSETTI (*eagerly*) : Any truth in the report, C.F., that British Bulldog Pictures wants to buy the studio ?

C.F.: You know as much about it as I do, Rosetti.

LAW: Why sell ? I thought we were sitting pretty. We're in receivership.

ROSETTI: Well, I'm going up to see B.K. I hope you boys get a good story for Larry.

C.F (*ignoring him; C.F. can ignore beautifully*) : As a matter of fact, you may as well know it. There may be a reorganization.

BENSON: Again ?

C.F.: And you know my position. I'm the only college-bred man in the studio. They resent me.

LAW: The big snobs.

C.F.: Just because I've always tried to do something fine, something dignified, something worth while, I'm being hammered on all sides. Boys, if my next picture fails, I'm out. And you're out, Larry. And it won't do you boys any good either. Of course you can always write plays.

LAW: I don't see why not. We never wrote any.

C.F.: I have an idea for a play I want to discuss with you some time. You'll be wild about it. Just one set, too—simple to produce, and practically anybody can play it. Anyone would be marvelous for the girl. She dies in the first act.

LARRY: Listen here, C.F., I ain't in the theatre. What about my picture ?

C.F.: Boys, we need a big picture. Not just a good story. I want to do something fine—with sweep, with scope—stark, honest, gripping, adult, but with plenty of laughs and a little hokum.

LARRY (*bitterly*) : And no " Did you ? " scenes.

C.F. : Something we'll be proud of. Not just another picture, but the picture of the year. A sort of Mutiny on the *Bounty*, but as Conrad would have done it. Maybe we could wire Conrad and get him to write a few scenes. It would be darned good publicity. (PEGGY *enters; PEGGY is the manicurist on the lot.*) Oh, come in . . . come in, Peggy. (PEGGY *puts tray of manicurist's paraphernalia on desk; moves small chair at C.F.'s side; takes bowl and exits for water.*)

BENSON (*in astonishment*) : He doesn't think we're as good as Conrad.

C.F. (*quickly*) : Mind you, not that I think Conrad is a great writer. A story-teller, yes. But greatness ? Give me Proust any time. Now, boys, how about a story ?

LAW : Nestling on your desk for two weeks there's a script we wrote for Larry Toms.

BENSON : A beautiful script. That one with my fingerprints on the cover.

C.F. (*picking up script, holding it in his hands as if weighing it*) : This ? This won't do.

LAW : That's where you're wrong. I had it weighed at the grocer's and the manager went wild over it. (C.F. *puts script on top of dictograph.* MISS CREWS *enters.*)

MISS CREWS : Excuse me, Mr. Friday, but Casting wants to know how many midgets you'll need.

C.F. (*irritably*) : Midgets ? I don't need any midgets.

MISS CREWS : Casting says you ordered midgets and they've got them.

C.F. : They're crazy. I'm not doing a horror story. (*Phone rings; at phone*) Hello. . . . It's for you, Benson.

BENSON: For me?

C.F.: I think it's Mrs. Benson. Listen, Miss Crews, we're in conference. Please don't disturb us again.

MISS CREWS: Yes, Mr. Friday. (*She exits.*)

BENSON (*into telephone*): Oh, hello, darling. . . . Yes, I know you've been shopping. . . . Why don't you try Woolworths? . . . No, I'm not mad. . . . Oh, you're taking the dogs for a walk? That's good. . . . Oh, no, I can't take you to lunch. I'm in a story conference. . . . But look, darling, I'm in a story conference. . . . Hello . . . (*He mops his brow and tries to shake off his gloom.*)

C.F.: How is Mrs. Benson?

BENSON: Swell.

C.F.: I must get Mrs. Friday to invite her over to her French class. All the wives are taking it up very seriously. Gives them something to do, and as I said to Mrs. Friday: I'm a linguist— why shouldn't you be? That's the great thing in marriage—mutual interests. (BENSON *crosses to couch.*) Of course, Mrs. Benson isn't the studious type, is she? Beautiful girl, though. . . . Where were we? What was I saying?

BENSON (*crosses back to desk; sighs; indicates script*): You were saying that this is one of the greatest picture scripts ever written.

C.F. (*with a superior smile*): Now, just a minute——

LAW (*quickly*): And do you know why? Because it's the same story Larry Toms has been doing for years.

BENSON: We *know* it's good.

LAW: Griffith used it. Lubitsch used it. And Eisenstein's coming around to it.

BENSON: Boy meets girl. Boy loses girl. Boy gets girl.

LAW: The great American fairy tale. Sends the audience back on the dole in a happy frame of mind.

BENSON: And why not?

LAW: The greatest escape formula ever worked out in the history of civilization . . .

C.F.: Of course, if you put it that way . . . but, boys, it's hackneyed.

LAW: You mean classic.

C.F. (*triumphantly*): *Hamlet* is a classic—but it isn't hackneyed!

LAW: *Hamlet* isn't hackneyed? Why, I'd be ashamed to use that poison gag. He lifted that right out of the Italians. (PEGGY *enters and crosses to her chair and sits.*) Ask Peggy. (PEGGY *puts the bowl now half-filled with water down on the desk.*)

BENSON: Yes, let's ask Peggy . . . if she wants to see Larry Toms in a different story. She's your audience.

PEGGY: Don't ask me anything, Mr. Benson. I've got the damnedest toothache. (*She takes C.F.'s hand and looks up at him suddenly.*) Relax! (*She begins filing.*)

BENSON (*wheedling*): But, Peggy, you go to pictures, don't you?

PEGGY: No.

BENSON: But you've seen Larry's pictures and enjoyed them?

PEGGY: No.

BENSON: . . . As millions of others have. . . .

LAW: Why, one man sent him a rope all the way from Manila—with instructions.

C.F.: Boys, this isn't getting us anywhere.

BENSON (*assuming the manner of a district attorney; barking at* PEGGY): Peggy, do you mean to sit there and tell me you haven't seen *one* Larry Toms picture?

PEGGY: I saw one.

BENSON: Ah!

PEGGY: *Night in Death Valley.*

BENSON: This isn't getting us anywhere, eh? How would you like to see *Night in Death Valley* again—with a new title?

PEGGY: I wouldn't.

BENSON: That's all. Step down. (*Crosses to couch; slaps* LAW *on shoulder.*) May I point out to this court that the body was found only two feet away, in an open field, with every door and window shut? (*To* LAW) Your witness. (*He exits.*)

LAW (*rises*): I've got to see a man about a woman. (*He exits. Our writers have vanished. They love to vanish from story conferences.*)

C.F. (*rises*): Come back here! (*Picks up phone.*)

LARRY: That's what I mean—clowning.

C.F. (*at phone*): Miss Crews, leave word at the gate Benson and Law are not to be allowed off the lot. They're to come right back to my office. (*Hangs up.*)

LARRY: Why do you stand for it?

C.F.: Larry, those boys are crazy, but they've got something.

LARRY: They've been fired off every other lot.

C.F.: I'll fire them off this one, after they've produced a story. I've made up my mind to that. Meanwhile, patience.

LARRY: That's easy to say.

C.F.: You can't quibble with the artistic temperament when it produces.

LARRY (*grumbling*): They've been producing nothing but trouble around here. (YOUNG ACTOR *enters in the resplendent uniform of the Coldstream Guards. His name is* RODNEY. *Both uniform and actor explain themselves as the play proceeds.*)

MISS CREWS: Right in here.

RODNEY: How do you do.

C.F.: What do *you* want?

RODNEY: Why, Wardrobe sent me. Do you approve the uniform?

C.F.: Uniform for what?

RODNEY: *London Life.*

C.F.: You see, Larry—three pictures in production—all going on at the same time—I'm standing on my head—and then they wonder what's wrong with the industry. (*Rises; barks at* RODNEY.) Stand over there. (MISS CREWS *exits.* C.F. *surveys the actor judicially.*) I can't say I like the hat. (*He is referring, of course, to the awe-inspiring busby.*)

RODNEY (*mildly*): The hat is authentic, sir.

C.F.: I still don't like it. You can't photograph it. (*Phone rings.*) Yes?—What midgets? I didn't send out any call for midgets. Get rid of them. (*Hangs up. He jiggles the phone.*) Get me Wardrobe. (*Hubbub is heard outside window.*) Who's making all that noise? (PEGGY *goes to the window*) This is C.F.—I don't like the hat.—I don't care if it's authentic or not—— Who's making all that noise?

PEGGY (*at window*): Midgets.

C.F. (*into phone*): Change the hat. . . . You can't photograph it. . . . We want to see faces, not hats. (*Hangs up. Stone crashes through the window left.*) Good God! Somebody's thrown a rock through my window. (*To* RODNEY) Here, you—pull down those blinds.

RODNEY (*always the little gentleman*): Yes, sir.

C.F. (*in phone*): Get me Casting. . . . This is C.F. . . . Somebody's thrown a rock through my window. One of the midgets. Of course they're indignant ! Sour grapes ! I'm telling you to get rid of them. (*Hangs up.*)

RODNEY: What shall I tell Wardrobe, sir ?

C.F.: Tell them I don't like the hat.

RODNEY (*smiles diffidently*): Well, it's very peculiar that you should take umbrage at the hat as it happens to be the only correct item in the entire outfit.

C.F.: What's that ?

RODNEY: This coat doesn't hang properly— these buttons are far too large. These shoulder straps are absurd, of course. And the boots . . . if I may say so . . . are too utterly fantastic. Any Guardsman would swoon away at the sight of them.

C.F.: So !

RODNEY: The hat, however, *is* authentic.

C.F.: It is, eh ? What's your salary ?

RODNEY: As I understand it, I'm to receive seven dollars a day, Monday and Tuesday, when I speak no lines, and fifteen dollars a day Thursday, Friday and Saturday, when I propose a toast.

C.F.: And you're telling a fifty-thousand-dollar-a-year man how to run his picture. Look here—I spent two weeks in London, my man, at the Savoy, and I watched them change the Guards, personally.

RODNEY: At the Savoy ?

C.F.: Young man, we have a technical adviser on this picture. And it doesn't happen to be you.

RODNEY: Quite. He's a splendid fellow, but he's a third generation Canadian. He's never even been to London.

C.F.: So you don't like the uniform and you don't like the technical expert. (*Smoothly*) What's your name?

RODNEY: Rodney Bevan. Of course, it's a sort of nom de plume, or nom de guerre——

C.F.: Rodney Bevan. (*Picks up phone.*) Give me Casting. . . . This is C.F. . . . Extra here by the name of Rodney Bevan, doesn't like his uniform. Fire him.

RODNEY (*aghast*): Fire? Have you given me the sack?

C.F.: I've enough trouble without extras telling me how to make pictures. That's the trouble with this business. A man spends his life at it, and anybody can walk in and tell him how to run it.

RODNEY: But I merely suggested—— (MISS CREWS *enters.*)

MISS CREWS: Mr. Green and Mr. Slade are outside, Mr. Friday. They want you to hear the song.

RODNEY: I've waited a long time for this opening——

C.F.: Get out! (*To* MISS CREWS) I'm in no mood for *music.* (GREEN *and* SLADE *enter.*)

GREEN: We've got it, and you're going to listen. If you don't like it, Schulberg's nuts about it. (SLADE *crosses to piano and starts playing the song.*) We wrote it for *London Life,* but it's flexible —flexible as hell. (MISS CREWS *exits.* RODNEY *turns forlornly and fades out through the door. What else can he do?)*

C.F.: Boys, I'm in no mood for——

GREEN: It's a touching little thing, but, boy, what power! There's a " Pain in My Heart, and My Heart's on My Sleeve." Like the title? (SLADE *is one of those who glues himself to a piano. He's all pasted together now, and his fingers fly.* GREEN *sings with all the fervid sincerity of Georgie Jessel with a cold.*)

> You promised love undying,
> And begged me to believe;
> Then you left, and left me crying
> With a pain in my heart, and my heart
>   on my sleeve.

> It isn't right to show it,
> To flaunt the way I grieve;
> But the world will quickly know it,
> For the pain's in my heart and my
>   heart on my sleeve.

> I confess that I'm a mess—
> The way I lived my life,
> But what does it matter?
> Yes, I guess that happiness
> Is only for a wife;
> Sorrow isn't served on a silver platter.

> I really shouldn't blame you
> Because you chose to leave;
> But one thing forever will shame you—
> It's the pain in my heart, and my heart
>   on my sleeve.

[*During the song* MISS CREWS *enters with glass of orange juice. She crosses around desk, puts glass in front of* C.F., *gets book from lower drawer.*

C.F. (*as* GREEN *finishes song*): Miss Crews, get hold of Benson and Law! (MISS CREWS *exits.*)

LARRY (*as the din grows*): I've worked for Biograph. . . . I've worked for Monogram. . . . I've worked for Columbia. . . . I've worked for Warners. . . . I've worked for Metro . . . but this is the first screwy outfit I ever did see ! (BENSON and LAW *enter in costume of beefeaters. They, too, wear busbies.*)

C.F. (*whose nails are being buffed*): What do you want ? (*At the musicians*) Quiet ! (*At the busbies, for C.F. doesn't deign to look at actors' faces*) I told Wardrobe I don't like the hats.

BENSON: He doesn't like the hats.

LAW: Call Jock Whitney. We want to be in color.

C.F. (*exasperated*): For God's sake ! This is a fine time to be masquerading.

BENSON (*leaping into character; picking up stone*): Wait ! What a pretty stone ! I wonder where that came from.

LAW (*in his own big scene*): I wonder.

BENSON (*transporting himself to the desert*): I think we've found gold, partner.

LAW (*grabbing for it*): Gold !

BENSON: Stand back—you desert rat !

LAW: Gold—after all these years ! I'm going mad . . . mad . . . mad. . . .

C.F.: Oh, stop it, boys.

LARRY (*suddenly inspired. To* C.F.): I wouldn't be surprised if they threw that there rock through the window.

BENSON: What an innuendo !

C.F.: You didn't do that, did you, boys ? Smash my Vita-glass ?

LAW: To think—after all these years of loyal, faithful service—— Larry Toms, you ought to be ashamed !

O

BENSON: The man with the poison-pen mind. We're going to tell on you.

C.F. (*impatiently*): *Very* well . . . *very* well. . . . But I still have my suspicions. (*Snaps.*) Now what about our story?

BENSON: Right here. (*Indicating script on desk.*)

LAW (*takes a statuette from top of desk*): Mr. Benson, for the most brilliant script of the year, the Academy takes great pleasure in presenting to you this little gargoyle——

BENSON: Wrap it up, please. (LAW *drops it in* LARRY's *hat and stands back of couch. Music plays.*)

LARRY (*rising in a dither*): Now, listen—— (C.F. *crosses below desk, retrieves statue, places it back on desk.*)

GREEN (*to* SLADE *at piano*): What do you say to this, Otto, for the second chorus:

> Yes, I've been kissed,
> But like Oliver Twist,
> I'm still crying for more.

(*Without waiting for an answer; to* C.F.) How did you like the song, C.F.?

LAW: Darn good. Can you play *Over the Waves*?

C.F.: Boys, can't you be sensible for a moment? You're trying my patience. What about our story?

LAW: What about it? It's a rich, protean part for Larry.

LARRY: It just don't make sense.

LAW: I resent that as a gentleman and a grammarian.

C.F.: Now really, boys, I'm tolerant, but I've got to see results. I'm not one to put the creative

urge in a strait-jacket. But you've been fired off
every other lot in this industry for your pranks.
Perhaps you've forgotten, Benson, but when
I hired you for this job you promised me to
behave in no uncertain terms. And you promised
me Law would toe the line. Now, I'm warning
you, boys. Let's get to work. Let's concentrate.
(*Crosses above desk to chair back of desk.*) Do you
realize you boys are making more than the
President of the United States ?

LAW: But look at the fun he's having !

LARRY (*angrily*): Now looka here——

GREEN: How do you like the song, C.F. ?

C.F.: It lacks body.

LAW: No breasts.

C.F.: That's exactly it—— Pallid.

GREEN: Come on, Otto.

SLADE (*starts for door*): This isn't my idea of a
fair audition.

GREEN: Wait'll they hear it at the Cocoanut
Grove. They'll be sorry. (GREEN *and* SLADE *exit.*
PEGGY *enters and* LAW, *humming " Merry Widow,"
intercepts her, dances a few measures with her.*)

C.F.: Listen, boys—we've had enough of this.
(SUSIE *enters carrying a tray.* SUSIE *is a waitress.
We worship* SUSIE. *Why describe her ? We'll tell
you what she wears—the full-blown costume of a
Hollywood waitress. Of her blonde fragility, her
intricate but blameless sex life, and the ineffable
charm of her touching naïveté we won't say a word.*)

LAW: *Lunch !*

BENSON: Grub ! Susie, I love you. (PEGGY *exits.
She never comes back. Why should she ?*)

C.F.: Wait a minute—wait a minute—— (LAW
gets end table and places it in front of couch. BENSON
takes tray from SUSIE.)

SUSIE (*weakly*): Please, Mr. Benson, be careful.

LAW: Put that tray right down here.

SUSIE (*quavering*): Thanks. . . . It's not very heavy . . . (*She then collapses neatly on the floor.*)

C.F.: Good Lord!

LAW (*bending over her*): Susie—Susie——

BENSON (*grabbing phone*): Get the doctor over here—right away——

LAW: Somebody give me water. (BENSON *takes glass from tray on table.*)

C.F. (*disapprovingly*): This is a nice thing to happen in my office. . . . Who is this girl, anyway?

LAW (*putting water to her as he kneels beside her*): Come on Susie. (*Lifting her head up to glass.*)

LARRY (*whose father wrote letters to the papers*): That commissary shouldn't employ people with epilepsy.

C.F. (*bitter, still*): I had an actor who did that to me once. Held up my shooting schedule fourteen days.

LAW: She's all right. Here.

SUSIE: Did you all get napkins? (*Opens her eyes for the first time.*)

BENSON: Now, Susie—get into this chair.

SUSIE: Thanks. (*She sits.*)

C.F. (*sharply*): What's wrong with you, young woman?

SUSIE (*still quavering*): Nothing. . . . I'm much better now. . . . Thanks.

C.F.: Where's that doctor?

SUSIE: Did you call for a doctor? You didn't have to.

C.F.: Do you get these epileptic fits often?

SUSIE: I didn't have an epileptic fit.

C.F.: Then what's wrong with you?

SUSIE: There's nothing wrong . . . it's only natural.

C.F.: Only natural for you to come into my office and collapse on the floor.

SUSIE: Oh, no, sir . . . it's only natural for you to feel sick when you're going to have a baby.

LAW: A baby!

BENSON: Susie, you're not going to have a baby!

SUSIE: That's what they told me. . . .

BENSON: Susie's going to have a baby!

LAW: Let's get drunk!

C.F. (*into phone*): Tell that doctor not to come. You heard me. I don't want him. (*He hangs up.*) I won't have my office converted into a maternity ward! (*He turns on* SUSIE.) I don't think much of your husband—letting you work at a time like this!

SUSIE: Oh, but I haven't got a husband.

C.F.: Huh?

SUSIE (*rises*): You'd better eat your lunch before it gets cold. Have you all got napkins?

LAW (*humbly*): The new generation! Faces the facts of nature without squeamishness, without subterfuge. " I haven't got a husband," she says. " It's only natural," she says. " I'm going to have a baby." . . . Susie, you're magnificent.

SUSIE: I'm quitting at the end of the week so I thought I'd tell everybody why. I wouldn't want them to think I was discontented.

LAW: Our little mother!

SUSIE: Oh, don't make fun of me.

LAW (*rises*): Fun? I've never been so touched in my life. Susie, I feel purified.

BENSON: Susie—can we be godfather?

SUSIE: Do you mean it?

BENSON: Do we mean it? We haven't got a baby. And we've been collaborating for years.

SUSIE: Oh, I think that would be wonderful for Happy to have writers for a godfather.

BENSON: Happy?

SUSIE: I'm going to call him Happy—even if he's a girl. Because I want him to be happy— even if he's a girl.

BENSON: Beautiful! A beautiful thought! Where are you going to have this baby, Susie?

SUSIE: In the County Hospital. It's all fixed. I was very lucky because I've only lived in the county three months and I'm not eligible.

C.F.: Now, listen, boys—enough of this.

LAW (*into phone*): Give me the Cedars of Lebanon Hospital—and make it snappy.

BENSON (*jubilant*): We've got a baby!

C.F.: Just a minute. Hang up that phone. (BENSON *good-naturedly brushes his arm down.*)

LAW: Dr. Marx, please. . . . Willy, this is Law of Benson and Law. Reserve the best suite in the house for us. I'm serious. Dead serious. A little friend of ours is going to have a baby and we want the goddamnedest confinement you've got in stock. . . .

BENSON: Day and night nurse.

LAW (*to* BENSON): And not the one with the buck teeth either. She's dynamite. (*Into phone*) We want everything that Gloria Swanson had— only double. What's that? Bill? Bill the studio, of course. (*He hangs up.*)

C.F.: You'll do no such thing! What kind of a gag is this? (MISS CREWS *enters.*)

MISS CREWS: Do you want to hear the trumpet call? The men are here. Music Department wants your O.K.

C.F.: Trumpets?

MISS CREWS: For *London Life.*

C.F.: Look here—I haven't time to listen to them now. Come back here at two o'clock. And give it to me from out there. I don't want them blasting in my ear. (*Meanwhile* BENSON *and* LAW *have been in whispered conference.*)

MISS CREWS: Yes, Mr. Friday. (*Exits.*)

C.F.: Now, boys—let's get together on this. (*Turns on* SUSIE *from below desk.*) And you— what are you sitting here for? Get out! (SUSIE *tries to rise.*)

LAW: Sit right where you are. (*Crosses to front of desk.*) Don't you bark at our inspiration! We've got it!

C.F.: What?

LAW (*with mounting excitement*): A baby!

C.F.: Boys, I'm a patient man, but you're trying me.

BENSON (*awed*): *Larry Toms and a baby!*

LAW (*to* C.F.): Do you see it?

LARRY (*bellowing*): Wait a minute—wait a minute!

LAW (*quickly*): He finds a baby—in the Rockies——

BENSON (*inspired; quickly to* C.F.): Girl with a no good gambler—out of Los Vegas—has a baby . . . gambler is killed. Girl leaves baby on the ranger's doorstep. Larry is the ranger.

LAW (*dramatizing it all*): My God, he says— a baby !

BENSON (*awed*): A baby !

LAW: The most precious thing in life. The cutest, goddam little bastard you ever saw.

BENSON: Tugging at every mother's heart. And every potential mother.

LAW: And who isn't !

BENSON: A love story between Larry and the baby——

LAW: The two outcasts ! Get it ?

BENSON: And then he meets the mother !

LAW: She wants her baby back.

BENSON: She's been through the fires of hell.

LAW: The man she loved . . . let her down. . . .

BENSON: She hates men . . . all men. . . .

LAW: She won't look at Larry.

BENSON (*to* LARRY): No. There she sits . . . bitter, brooding, cynical, but underneath— a mother's heart.

LAW: Out on the Rockies——

BENSON: The hell with the Rockies—back to the Foreign Legion !

LAW: Right ! Larry's joined to forget. He's out on the march. We can use all that stock stuff— and he finds a baby !

BENSON: He's gone off to fight the Riffs.

LAW: The hell with the Riffs ! Ethiopians !

BENSON: Stick to the Riffs. We don't want any race problem.

LAW: Right ! She doesn't know if he's coming back.

BENSON: She's waiting—waiting !

LAW: We cut to the Riffs——

BENSON: Cut back——

LAW (*to* BENSON): Right into the battle.

BENSON (*really inspired now*): His father's the Colonel !

LAW: Talk about Conrad——

BENSON: Talk about scope—sweep—what a set-up !

LAW: A love story !

BENSON: A great love story !

LAW: Mary Magdalen of the Foreign Legion and the West Point man who wanted to forget !

BENSON (*rises*): The baby brings them together, splits them apart, brings them together——

LAW: Boy meets girl——

BENSON: Boy loses girl——

LAW: Boy gets girl !

C.F. (*rising in excitement*): Boys, I think you've got something ! Let's go up and try it on B.K. while it's hot.

LAW: Let's go ! (*They move forward.*)

LARRY (*crosses to behind couch*): Wait a minute —you can't act with a baby. They steal every scene——

LAW: Are you selling motherhood short ? (LAW, BENSON *and* C.F. *exit through next speech.*)

LARRY: They'll be looking at the baby when they should be looking at me. I tell you—I won't play it. (*Follows off.* SUSIE *tries to rise, now she is left alone. She sits down again.* RODNEY, *in the Coldstream Guards' uniform, enters.* SUSIE *turns.*)

RODNEY: Oh, I'm sorry. I hope I didn't startle you.

SUSIE: Oh, no. (*Then, as he looks at C.F.'s desk.*) They all stepped out—and they didn't even touch their lunch.

RODNEY (*licking his lips involuntarily*): Lunch?— You don't happen to know when Mr. Friday is coming back?

SUSIE: No, I don't.

RODNEY: I did want to see him. It's rather urgent. Do you mind if I wait here?

SUSIE: No, of course not. (*He seats himself on couch, near a tray. There is an awkward silence. SUSIE stares straight ahead. RODNEY plays with a cracker. Finally SUSIE breaks the silence.*) What are you supposed to be?

RODNEY: Eh? Oh! That's just it. . . . I'm supposed to be a Buckingham Palace Guard, sergeant-major—— (*He pops the cracker into his mouth and swallows it. SUSIE looks at him rather intently.*) Good Lord! What am I doing?

SUSIE: You're eating Mr. Friday's cracker.

RODNEY: I'm awfully sorry. I don't understand how I——

SUSIE: You must be very hungry.

RODNEY: Not a bit. Not at all.

SUSIE: You *look* hungry.

RODNEY: Do I?

SUSIE: Why don't you have something? They'll never eat it. They're always sending things back they order—never even touched.

RODNEY: Really?

SUSIE: You'll only be doing me a favor.

RODNEY: Oh?

SUSIE: I won't have so much to carry back to the commissary. Sometimes I think I carry back more than I bring.

RODNEY: You're pulling my leg, of course.

SUSIE: What did you say?

RODNEY: You're not really a waitress.

SUSIE: Sure I am.

RODNEY (*triumphantly*): Waitresses don't usually sit in producer's offices.

SUSIE: They do when they don't feel well.

RODNEY: You don't feel well? Oh, I'm sorry. Is there anything I can do?

SUSIE: No, thanks.

RODNEY: But what's wrong?

SUSIE: Oh, there's no use telling you. I told Mr. Friday and he made such a fuss about it I guess I better keep it to myself.

RODNEY: I'm afraid I don't quite understand.

SUSIE: Try the chicken soup. It's very good.

RODNEY: Are you seriously suggesting that I filch some of this broth?

SUSIE: We make it special for B.K. with nine chickens.

RODNEY: Well, dash it, I will eat it. Just to make the joke good! (*He laughs weakly and picks up the bowl and puts it to his lips, and sips it.*)

SUSIE (*warningly*): It's hot!

RODNEY (*now quite gay*): So I've learned.

SUSIE: When did you eat last?

RODNEY (*lying, of course*): I had my lunch an hour ago.

SUSIE: Have some crackers with it.

RODNEY: Thanks.

SUSIE: You're English, aren't you?

RODNEY: Yes, of course.

SUSIE: So is Ronald Colman.

RODNEY (*bolting his food*): So he is.

SUSIE: I like the way the English talk.

RODNEY: Do you?

SUSIE: It's very soothing.

RODNEY: What an idea!

SUSIE: Of course, that's only *my* idea. I'm very ignorant.

RODNEY: Oh, please, don't say that. I think you're very intelligent.

SUSIE: Oh, I'm intelligent. But I don't know anything.

RODNEY: You're an extraordinary girl.

SUSIE: I've never been to high school.

RODNEY (*gallantly*): May I say that's the high school's loss?

SUSIE: But some day I'll go to high school. That's my secret ambition. Try the ham hocks. The cook eats them himself. He comes from Czechoslovakia.

RODNEY: Does he really? Look here—I feel an awful swine guzzling by myself. Won't you join me?

SUSIE: Well, I'm not very hungry, but I can eat.

RODNEY: Good! (*He rises and adjusts a chair for her.*)

SUSIE: It's funny how I keep on eating.

RODNEY: Some ham hocks?

SUSIE: No. Happy doesn't like ham. He likes milk.

RODNEY (*mystified*): I beg your pardon? (*But he doesn't press the point.*) Did you say milk?

Susie: Yes. Milk.

Rodney (*as he pours*): There you are.

Susie: Thanks.

Rodney: Cozy, this—what?

Susie: It's good milk. Have some.

Rodney: Do you know, I think you're the most extraordinary girl I ever met.

Susie: Why?

Rodney: You're so kind. You're so direct, so sincere. Most girls one meets play about with words so. They're so infernally smart. They make one feel like a worm.

Susie: Of course, I'm different on account of my condition. Most girls aren't in my condition.

Rodney: Your condition?

Susie: The minute I found out about Happy I said to myself: I'm going to be very good and very sincere, because then Happy will be very good and very sincere.

Rodney: I'm afraid I don't quite follow.

Susie (*sighing*): Nobody does.

Rodney: Eh? Oh, yes. . . . As I was saying—— What was I saying?

Susie (*looking into his eyes and feeling strangely stirred*): Have some mustard.

Rodney: Do you know, I must confess. I was hungry. As a matter of fact, I was close to wiring home for funds today. But I didn't. (*Looks very determined, righteous.*)

Susie: You mean you need money, and you can get it—and you won't wire for it?

Rodney: I can't—and keep my pride. I told *them* I was on my own. You see, my family didn't want me to act. Not that they've any prejudices against the stage—or the films. Not

at all. In fact, one of my aunts was a Gaiety
girl. Quite all right. But they don't think I
can act. That's what hurts.

SUSIE: Can you act?

RODNEY: No.

SUSIE: Not at all?

RODNEY: Not at all. I'm awful!

SUSIE: Oh, that's too bad.

RODNEY: But I only realized it in the stock
company . . . out in Pasadena. I was the worst
member of the company. At first I thought it
was because they were always giving me
character parts—American gangsters—and that
sort of thing. And then one week I played a
Cambridge undergraduate. And, mind you, I've
been a Cambridge undergraduate. And do you
know that I was utterly unconvincing?

SUSIE: Then why don't you give it up?

RODNEY: Pride.

SUSIE: I can understand that—— Pride.

RODNEY: Can you really?

SUSIE: Sure I can.

RODNEY: That's why I simply must see Mr.
Friday. (*Suddenly*) Look here—— (*He takes a book
from couch and opens it.*) Look at this color plate.
Does this uniform remotely resemble the one I'm
wearing? (*He crosses down right.*)

SUSIE (*looks at book; then at* RODNEY): Yes, I
think so.

RODNEY (*crosses to her left*): But, my dear girl,
look at the coat and the buttons—and the boots
—note the heels—and look at mine. (*Steps back.*)

SUSIE: Well come to think of it, I guess it is
different.

RODNEY: Of course. And I've taken this book right out of their own research department. When I show this to Mr. Friday he's bound to be sporting enough to admit an error.

SUSIE: Oh, sure.

RODNEY (*leaning over her*): You see, all I want is to appear in *one* picture—and then I can tell the family: " I've done it." But it's not good enough. I'm chucking it. But I'll have my pride.

SUSIE (*gazing at him*): I see.

RODNEY: Oh . . . I say . . . I'm not boring you ?

SUSIE: Oh, no. Finish your ham.

RODNEY: Eh ? Oh ! Don't mind if I do. A bit of pie for you ? (*He extends plate with fork.*)

SUSIE (*brightly. Almost flirting*): Well, I'll try. (*She smiles at him and he at her, fork poised in mid-air.*)

RODNEY: Do you know, I've never enjoyed a lunch quite as much as this one—thanks to you. (*Suddenly*) Would it bore you if I tried out my lines—in *London Life*, you know.

SUSIE: Oh, no.

RODNEY: Very well. (*He rises, holding glass of milk.*) Gentlemen, the Queen—— (*He waits.*)

SUSIE: Is that all ?

RODNEY: That's all. But of course I could say: " Gentlemen, I give you the Queen." Fatten up the part a bit, what ? . . . Gentlemen, I give you the Queen ! . . . Sounds rather better, doesn't it ? (*Then with profound bass*) Gentlemen, I give you the Queen ! (LARRY *enters followed by* C.F. C.F. *stares.*)

LARRY: I don't cotton to the whole idea, and if B.K.'s got any sense, he won't listen to those maniacs.

C.F.: What's going on here ?

RODNEY: How'd you do. . . . I . . . I . . . (*Puts glass of milk back on tray.*)

C.F.: What is this ? A tête-à-tête in my office ! Good Gad ! You've been drinking my milk !

SUSIE: It's all right, Mr. Friday. I told him he could have it.

C.F.: *You* told him ?

RODNEY: I'm awfully sorry. I owe you an apology, and money, of course. Will you accept my I.O.U. ? And I have the book—from Research. I can show you the really authentic uniform. I'm sure if you study this—— (SUSIE *finds the page and hands book to* RODNEY.)

C.F.: I've a good mind to call the studio police.

SUSIE (*rises*): Oh, please don't do that, Mr. Friday.

LARRY: That's what you get for having foreign actors around. Take the food right out of your mouth !

RODNEY: I'm terrible sorry, of course.

C.F.: Get out !

RODNEY: I realize there's nothing I can say— (*he turns to* SUSIE) except—my eternal gratitude. (*He grabs her by the hand and shakes it. Exits.*)

SUSIE: Oh, you shouldn't have done that. He's been having a terrible time.

C.F. (*glaring at* SUSIE): Get these dishes out of here.

SUSIE (*meekly*) : Yes, sir. (*She begins piling up dishes on tray.*)

LARRY: The idea of a baby ! The more I think of it, the less I like it.

C.F. (*crosses to chair at desk*): Larry, you're driving me into a nervous breakdown. I had to take you out of B.K.'s office so you'd stop arguing before he could make a decision.

LARRY: There's nothing to decision. I won't play it.

C.F.: If B.K. likes the idea, you'll play it.

LARRY: Maybe—and maybe not. I'm willing to bet ten to one right now B.K. kicks the whole story in the ash can. He's no fool. (BENSON *and* LAW *enter in shirt-sleeves. They've obviously had a hot session with* B.K.)

BENSON: Sold ! Lock, stock and baby ! B.K. says it's the best mother-love story he's heard in years.

LARRY: What ? What's that ?

LAW (*magnificently*): Susie, put that tray down !

SUSIE: Please, Mr. Law, I've got to get back to the commissary.

LARRY: You sold him that story, huh ?

BENSON: Lie down, actor !

LARRY: I'll see about this. (*He exits.*)

BENSON: Now listen, Susie—and listen carefully.

LAW: Let me tell her, will you ? (*He faces her.*) Susie, nature meant you for a sucker. You were designed to get the short end of the stick. The girl who gets slapped.

BENSON (*quickly*): But we're changing all that.

LAW: Susie, in real life you'd have your baby in the County Hospital . . . get yourself a job, if lucky, with a philanthropic Iowa family of fourteen adults and twelve minors for twenty bucks a month. And when your grateful son grew up he'd squirt tobacco juice in your eye and join the Navy.

BENSON: There you go with your goddamn

realism. (*Turns to* SUSIE *with paper and pencil.*)
Sign, please——

SUSIE: Here? (*She signs; and then turns, brightly*)
What is it?

BENSON: Just a power of attorney authorizing
us to deal for you in all matters with this
studio.

C.F.: What power of attorney? What are you
boys up to?

LAW: We said to ourselves upstairs—why
shouldn't Susie have the good things of life?

BENSON: After all, we're godfathers.

SUSIE: I—I don't feel very good.

LAW: Get this, Susie. We've just sold a story
about a baby.

BENSON: Sweetest story ever told!

LAW: A new-born baby.

BENSON: Brand new.

LAW: We're going to watch that baby—the first
hair—the first tooth—the first smile——

BENSON: The same baby. No switching—first
time in the history of pictures. That baby's going
to grow before your eyes.

LAW: Open up like a flower. . . . Just like the
Dionne quintuplets.

BENSON: Minute he's born we set the cameras on
him. We stay with him——

LAW: That baby's going to gurgle and google
and drool his way to stardom!

SUSIE: But——

LAW: And that baby, Susie, is Happy. Upstairs
in B.K.'s office we put your unborn child into
pictures!

SUSIE (*transported*): Happy—in pictures! Oh—

that's wonderful—— (*Then, with a sudden gasp*) Oh !

LAW (*quickly*) : Susie ! What's the matter ?

SUSIE : I don't know . . . I . . . I . . . I don't feel so good . . . I think . . . I . . . (*In these broken words,* SUSIE *tells* all. BENSON *helps* SUSIE *to lie on couch.* LAW *looks over* SUSIE'S *shoulder; whistles; runs to phone.*)

LAW (*into phone*) : *Emergency ! Get the ambulance over to Mr. Friday's office right away—get the doctor—get the nurse. . . .*

C.F. (*staring*) : What is it ? In *my* office. Good Gad ! Miss Crews ! (*Door opens.*)

MISS CREWS (*at door*) : The trumpets are here ! (*Trumpets sound their triumphant clarion call.*)

LAW (*through the Wagnerian brass, to* BENSON, *awed*) : Happy's on his way !

CURTAIN

ACT II

SCENE I

We are in your neighborhood theatre, seven months later.

As the curtain rises we face a motion picture screen, and to the sound-track accompaniment of " Home on the Range," these glaring titles pop out at us:

IF YOU LIKED HAPPY

IN

" WANDERING HEARTS "

YOU'LL ADORE HIM

IN

" GOLDEN NUGGET "

This is what is known as a trailer, in technical terms. It is shown at neighborhood theatres prior to the release of the picture so that the customers will be teased into returning the following week.

There are, of course, beautifully composed shots of horses, men and open spaces, and finally we come upon a series of close-ups of HAPPY, *over which these titles dance:*

HAPPY !

HAPPY !

HAPPY !

The sound track blares forth " Ride of the Valkyries."

CROWN PRINCE OF COMEDY !

KING OF TRAGEDY !

EMPEROR OF EMOTION !

Just prior to these titles we have seen a Chinese, who has emerged from God knows where, but what is a ranch without a Chinese ? The general idea is that the Chinese finds HAPPY *on the doorstep and communi-*

cates his discovery to LARRY TOMS. *There follows a title which explains all:*

THE DESERT WAIF WHO MADE
A SOFTIE OF A BAD MAN

The picture is further described as:

THE BIG GOLD STRIKE
OF MOTHER LOVE

We see horses galloping, men falling, revolvers barking, and nice, big, wavy

THRILLS

CHILLS

The credit card is as follows:

FROM A STORY BY DICKENS
ADAPTED BY J. CARLYLE BENSON
AND ROBERT LAW
DIRECTED BY SERGE BORODOKOV

and, appropriately enough, in solitary grandeur:

PRODUCED BY C. ELLIOT FRIDAY

SCENE II

The screen lifts, and once more we are in MR. FRIDAY'S *office.*

C.F. *is at his desk,* MISS CREWS *is seated upstage and at desk;* BENSON *is on the couch beside* LARRY. ROSETTI *is seated on the piano bench.*

BENSON: Read those figures, Miss Crews.
MISS CREWS: Eighty-two thousand at the Music

Hall. Forty-eight thousand five hundred and thirty-eight in Des Moines.

BENSON: Without a stage show.

LARRY: I always went big in Des Moines.

MISS CREWS: Twenty-eight thousand in Newark.

LARRY: That's one of my big towns.

MISS CREWS: Forty-two thousand three hundred and eighty-four in San Francisco.

LARRY: I'm big there, too.

MISS CREWS: Twenty-six thousand eight hundred and seventy-five in Detroit.

BENSON (*to* C.F.): And you sit there and tell me Happy isn't worth thirty-five hundred a week?

C.F.: But, Benson, be reasonable. I can't go to B.K. with any such fantastic figure.

BENSON (*sighing*): Read that list again, Miss Crews.

C.F.: Never mind, Miss Crews.

LARRY: What about me? *Wandering Hearts* was my picture, wasn't it? Folks came to see me. They didn't come to see Happy.

BENSON (*taking " Variety " from his pocket*): Let me read " Variety " to the assembled multitude. *Wandering Hearts* socko in Minneapolis despite Larry Toms. . . .

LARRY: Huh?

BENSON: Mexico nuts about Happy but no like Larry Toms——

LARRY: Where? Where does it say that? (*He takes paper.* ROSETTI *rises and looks over* LARRY's *shoulder.*)

BENSON: This is an accidental business in an accidental world. Happy is going to get it while it's hot.

C.F.: Benson, you owe me something.

BENSON: What?

C.F.: Gratitude. . . . After all, the idea of a baby was mine—more or less.

BENSON: More or less.

C.F.: I made that baby act.

BENSON: All right, Svengali.

C.F.: Shall we say three hundred a week for Happy?

BENSON: Shall we say thirty-five hundred a week for Happy?

C.F.: I've a good mind to have you thrown out of this studio.

BENSON: All right. Happy goes with us. We've still got that power of attorney.

C.F.: Of course, I didn't mean that literally.

BENSON: I did. (*Telephone rings.*)

C.F.: Hello. . . . Yes, Miss Goodwin. . . . What? You can't write about Brussels because you've never been there? My dear girl, why do you think we have a research department? After all, Bernard Shaw wrote *Don Juan* and he never went to Bulgaria. Imagination, my dear girl— imagination. (*Hangs up.*) Look here, Benson, I knew I couldn't deal with Law. I thought I could with you. After all, you're in no position to antagonize this studio. Some day you may need my friendship.

BENSON: I'm supposed to be working with our Mr. Law on a story. To wit: *Tiger Tamer*. Do you mind if I join my partner in a little English composition?

C.F.: Some day you may be very sorry for this, Benson.

BENSON: What do you think, Miss Crews?

MISS CREWS: I think Happy ought to get it while it's hot.

C.F.: Get back to your desk.

MISS CREWS: Yes, Mr. Friday. (*She exits.*)

LARRY (*waving " Variety "*): I said that baby'd ruin me ! Well, he ain't going to steal no more pictures ! I won't play that new scene.

C.F. (*irritably*): What new scene ?

LARRY: I'm supposed to wash Happy.

C.F.: That's a cute scene. I read it.

LARRY: Am I the type that washes babies ?

C.F.: Why not ?

LARRY: 'Tain't manly !

BENSON: No. You want the baby to wash you !

LARRY: Listen !

BENSON: Any further business before the house ? (*Turns to* LARRY) By the way, I saw you with Susie at the Trocadero last night. We don't approve of you as an escort. Remind me to speak to her about that.

C.F.: Benson, I'm asking you once more. Be fair—be reasonable.

BENSON: I am. We're asking thirty-five hundred a week. We'll consider three thousand and settle for twenty-five hundred. But not a penny less. Incidentally, Fox'll pay twenty-five hundred for Happy. We promised to let them know by Saturday. No hurry, of course. (*Exits.*)

C.F.: Have you ever seen anything more damnably unfair ? Imagine *writers* holding up this studio at the point of a gun. It's nothing but blackmail.

ROSETTI (*rises*): I've got a hunch, C.F. When did you sign Happy ? Do you remember ?

C.F.: Of course I remember . . . July four-
teenth. . . . Fall of the Bastille. I remember my
wife pointing out the coincidence at the time.
Why?

ROSETTI (*crosses to desk*): I've got a hunch that
power of attorney expires pretty soon. I want to
be prepared.

C.F.: Rosetti, I'm not interested in the future.
I'm interested in signing Happy right now—
before we lose him to Fox. (*Phone rings.*)

ROSETTI: You've got to have vision in this
business, C.F. (*He reaches for other phone, changes
his mind, and then exits.*)

C.F. (*into phone*): Hello. . . . Yes, listen, Gregg.
. . . I ran the sound track on *London Life* last
night. I don't like the trumpets. They're sour.
They spoil the whole mood. . . . What? . . .
What's that? You can't walk out on a picture
like that. What kind of a director are you if you
can't take constructive criticism . . . hello . . .
hello . . . (*Hangs up.*) Gregg is walking out on
London Life, I can't sign Happy——

LARRY: What about me?

C.F.: Ten thousand feet of film sick—and he
walks out. I'll have to run the picture all the
afternoon and sit up all night cutting it. (MISS
CREWS *enters.*)

MISS CREWS: Happy's through for the day.

NURSE (*wheeling in a stream-lined baby carriage*):
Through for the day.

DOCTOR (*as he enters*): Through for the day. Is
his mother here?

MISS CREWS: No, Doctor, but she should be here
very soon.

NURSE (*backing carriage in front of desk*): Say da-da
to Mr. Friday.

C.F. (*waving obediently*) : Da-da, Happy.

DOCTOR : Nurse, take the little trouper out into the garden and keep him in the sunshine.

LARRY : He's through for the day and I'm working until eight. He's sure got it soft. (NURSE *exits with* HAPPY. ROSETTI *enters*.)

DOCTOR : They've been overworking you, have they ?

LARRY : I ain't feeling so hearty, doc. I wish you'd look me over.

C.F. (*rises and goes below desk*) : Just your imagination. I wish I had your constitution. I've got to see B.K. (*He exits*.)

DOCTOR : All you picture people are hypochondriacs. However, come up to my office and I'll look you over. (*He exits*.)

LARRY : I'm a star. I've been a star for ten years. I've worked hard to get where I'm at—— (*He rises. Phone rings*.)

ROSETTI (*at phone*) : Hello. . . . Yes . . . speaking——

LARRY : I don't drink. I don't smoke. I don't swear. I don't get into no scandal. And the girls I passed up !

ROSETTI (*into phone*) : Oh, you've got that, Mr. Williams ? Fine. When does it expire ? . . . It *did* expire ? Last week ? . . . No, don't do that. I'll tell the boys. . . . You see, I may be handling Happy's new contract. Right. (*He hangs up*.)

LARRY : They ain't making pictures here no more. They're shooting nothing but close-ups of babies. Happy laughing ! Happy crying ! Happy ! . . . Happy ! . . .

ROSETTI : Larry, I've just checked with the Legal Department. The boys' power of attorney expired last week. And they don't even know it.

LARRY: What's that got to do with me?

ROSETTI: Larry, there's been something developing in the back of my mind for some weeks. Why do you think I asked you to take Susie to the Trocadero?

LARRY: She talked me deaf, dumb, and blind about going to high school. Set me back fourteen bucks. Lucky she don't drink.

ROSETTI (*the dreamer*): I wanted you to get friendly with her because I visualized a way for you and me to get Happy—for life.

LARRY: Huh?

ROSETTI (*with Napoleonic intensity*): Larry, here's the tactical move. You marry Susie.

LARRY: Marry her?

ROSETTI: That's what I said.

LARRY: I won't do it.

ROSETTI (*who knows his client*): All right, suit yourself.

LARRY: We got community property in California. If there's a bust-up the woman gets half.

ROSETTI: Larry, I don't want to hurt your feelings, but I can't get you a new contract the way things are now. B.K. is dickering to borrow Clark Gable or Gary Cooper for Happy's next picture.

LARRY (*touched to the quick*): What?

ROSETTI: I'd marry her myself if I was free. Show me a girl with a better heart—with more culture——

LARRY: You don't expect me to believe what the studio hands out—her husband was a prominent portrait painter who went down on the *Morro Castle*?

ROSETTI (*indignantly*): Who are you to cast the first stone?

LARRY: I don't want to marry nobody. Anyways, there's no sense to it.

ROSETTI (*patiently*): If you marry her, you're Happy's legal guardian and we control the situation. A father and son team off the screen as well as on! Is that practical or am I just an idealist? Look at Guy Lathrop! He argued with me when I told him to marry Betty Bird. But he finally had the sense to play along with me and we've been drawing top money ever since.

LARRY: I don't want to marry nobody.

ROSETTI: Larry, you're at the crossroads right now. One road leads to stardom and big pictures, with Happy and me. The other leads to Poverty Row and cheap Westerns. Will you put your hand in mine and let me guide you? (MISS CREWS *enters.*)

MISS CREWS: Mr. Toms, you're wanted on the set.

LARRY (*growling*): All right.

MISS CREWS: Oh, hello, Mrs. Seabrook . . . how nice you look. (*For* SUSIE *enters. She wears a white middy-blouse and a navy blue, pleated skirt.*)

SUSIE: We had gym today. . . . Hello, Larry. . . . Hello, Mr. Rosetti. . . . I hope I didn't interrupt anything important.

ROSETTI: Not at all. . . . (*Significantly*) I'll be in the Legal Department, Larry. (*He exits.*)

SUSIE: Where's Happy?

MISS CREWS: Happy's in the garden with his nurse. He's all through for the day.

SUSIE: Oh, that's wonderful. I don't get to see

him very much. He's working and I'm going to high school. (CHAUFFEUR *enters*.)

CHAUFFEUR: Excuse me, Miss.

SUSIE: What is it, Simpson?

CHAUFFEUR: You forgot your algebra book, Miss.

SUSIE: Oh, thank you, Simpson. That was very thoughtful. (CHAUFFEUR *exits*.)

MISS CREWS: And I have a new batch of fan mail for you and Happy. (*Exits*.)

SUSIE: It's wonderful to get mail. Nobody used to write me before. Now I even get letters from Japan. (MISS CREWS *enters with letters*.) All those letters? Thank you, Miss Crews.

LARRY (*sighs*): Miss Crews, call the set and tell 'em I may be a little late.

MISS CREWS: Very well. (*She exits*.)

SUSIE (*sitting on desk, poring over her hand-written, moronic literature*): Here's one from North Carolina. Oh, the poor thing! There's so much sadness in this world. (LARRY *sighs; she looks up at him*.) You look sad, too, Larry. What's the matter?

LARRY: Well—(*He rises and crosses to* SUSIE)— uh—I been waiting a long time to talk to you, Susie. I couldn't go to the high school. All those girls would mob me for autographs, especially when I tell them who I am.

SUSIE: All the girls are crazy about Clark Gable.

LARRY (*clears his throat*): Susie—I can get two tickets for the opening at the Chinese—the De Mille picture.

SUSIE: Can you?

LARRY: I knew that'd knock you over.

SUSIE: Oh, it'll be wonderful!

LARRY: I'm always thinkin' of little things to make life wonderful—for you.

SUSIE (*nods*): Everybody is.

LARRY (*bridling*): What do you mean—everybody?

SUSIE: Only the other day Mr. Benson said something very true. He said: "Susie, you're Cinderella." And that's just what I feel like. And you know what else he said? He said: "All you need now is a Prince Charming."

LARRY: He did, huh? Who did he have in mind?

SUSIE: Oh, nobody.

LARRY: He didn't mention me, did he?

SUSIE: Oh, no. (LARRY *grunts*.) Of course, I've never met a Prince Charming. I wouldn't know what he looks like. Although, one day an awful nice boy came in here.

LARRY: Who?

SUSIE: I don't even know his name. He was in uniform and I was in my condition—I've never seen him since.

LARRY: You shouldn't be thinking of him. You should be thinking of Happy.

SUSIE: But I do . . . only sometimes it gets lonesome for me, especially at night. And of course, Mr. Benson and Mr. Law are busy all the time. Happy used to say good night to them every night on the telephone. Not really good night—just goo-n'—just like that. But they're so busy they won't come to the telephone any more.

LARRY: Happy needs a father.

SUSIE: Do you think so?

LARRY: Well, you want him to be able to look the whole world in the face, don't you?

SUSIE (*twinkling*): He does !

LARRY: I mean when he grows up. He's gonna be ashamed when he finds out he never had a father.

SUSIE: Of course he had a father.

LARRY: I mean—a married father.

SUSIE: He was married—but I didn't know it. (LARRY *winces*.)

LARRY: Uh—listen, Susie—I'm mighty fond of you and Happy. (*He tries playing the bashful Western hero*.) Mighty fond.

SUSIE: Are you really, Larry ?

LARRY: Mighty fond.

SUSIE: Who would have thought six months ago that I'd be sitting in the same room with Larry Toms and he'd be saying to me he was——

LARRY: Mighty fond.

SUSIE: Do you know something very odd ? When I first came to California, it was raining very hard—oh, it rained for three weeks—it was very unusual—and I was looking for a job, and I couldn't find one—and I had fifteen cents—and I just had to get out of the rain—and I went into a theatre and there you were—on the screen——

LARRY: Mighty fond——

SUSIE (*awed*): That's just what you were saying to Mary Brian—and now you're saying it to me.

LARRY: What was the picture ?

SUSIE: *Thunder over Arizona*. It was a beautiful picture. I don't remember what it was about, but I saw it four times. Until I got dry.

LARRY: Susie, soon's this picture's over, how'd you like to come up to my ranch ? You and Happy——

SUSIE (*rises*): Ranch? Oh, that would be lovely! Maybe Mr. Benson and Mr. Law could come, too?

LARRY: Maybe they could, but they won't.

SUSIE: But I couldn't go alone—without a chaperon.

LARRY: Susie—you and Happy'll love that ranch. I got a mighty nice house, big and rambling. I got plenty of barns and a corral and plenty of live stock. But no baby.

SUSIE: I know Happy'll just love it.

LARRY: Susie—I know you don't expect this, and I don't want you to get too excited—but, Susie, I been thinkin' about you and Happy— thinkin' a lot. Ever since the day you come into this office and fell on that there floor, I said to myself: Larry, there's your leadin' lady—for life.

SUSIE: Me?

LARRY: Nobody else.

SUSIE: But I don't—you won't get mad?—but I'm not in love with you.

LARRY: You shouldn't be thinking of yourself— I'm not thinking of myself—you should be thinking of Happy.

SUSIE: I guess you're right. I don't know what to say. (*Pauses.*) I'll ask Mr. Benson and Mr. Law——

LARRY: Huh?

SUSIE: They've been so good to me.

LARRY: I'm not proposing to them!

SUSIE: I know, but——

LARRY: You don't mean nothing to them. Before you came along they had a Spanish snake charmer until they got tired of her. And before that they had a broken-down pug who wiggled his ears. They was groomin' him for my place. There ain't nothin' holy to them !

SUSIE: But they've done everything for me.

LARRY (*crosses to* SUSIE): I'm offering you my ranch—my name—and a father Happy'll be proud of !

SUSIE: I know, but——

LARRY: Don't give me your answer now. Think it over. (*Pats her arm.*) Only don't think too long. I'll be waiting for your answer in the Legal Department. You know where that is ?

SUSIE: Oh, yes. (MISS CREWS *opens the door.*)

LARRY: I'll be there. (*He exits.* SUSIE *looks a little dazed.*)

MISS CREWS: Oh, Mrs. Seabrook—I've located that young man you were looking for. He's outside.

SUSIE: Oh, you have ? Really ?

MISS CREWS (*at door*): Come in. (SUSIE *tenses herself. A strange* YOUNG MAN *enters and stops.*)

SUSIE (*staring at him*): Oh ! Oh, no, that's not him—I mean—he.

YOUNG MAN (*earnestly*): Won't I do ? I've just finished a short for Hal Roach—I'm making a test for Metro tomorrow, and——

MISS CREWS (*firmly escorting him out*): Thank you for coming ! (YOUNG MAN *shrugs and exits, and* MISS CREWS *closes the door.*)

SUSIE: He's not English.

MISS CREWS: English ? We didn't have **any** English actors in *London Life*.

SUSIE: This boy was an extra.

MISS CREWS: Does he owe you a lot of money ?

SUSIE: Oh, no. It was nothing like that.

P

MISS CREWS (*as it dawns on her*): Oh, I see! A personal matter! Well, I'll try again. (*Brightly.*)

SUSIE: I guess it's no use, Miss Crews. (*Sighs.*) He probably swallowed his pride and went back to England. (BENSON *and* LAW *enter.* BENSON *carries paper and pencil.* BENSON *sits upstage end of desk.* LAW *crosses to front of couch.*)

LAW: Hi, Susie! How's the little mother? Clear out. We're trying to work and a hundred chorus boys are practising fencing underneath our windows. (*Turns to* MISS CREWS.) Miss Crews, leave a note for C.F. He's got to change our office. We can't work with fencing fairies! (*Sits on couch.*)

MISS CREWS: Yes, Mr. Law. (*She exits.*)

SUSIE: Are you very busy?

BENSON: We still need an opening.

LAW: Fade-in. . . . A zoo!

SUSIE (*crossing to* BENSON): I just wanted to thank you, Mr. Benson, for the beautiful white teddy bear.

BENSON: What teddy bear?

SUSIE: Mrs. Benson brought it herself.

BENSON (*looking up from typewriter*): Oh, she did?

SUSIE: She played with Happy, too. And even after he went for his nap, she stayed and looked at him.

BENSON (*to* LAW—*covering*): Where were we?

SUSIE: When she left, she was crying. I think she ought to have a baby of her own.

BENSON (*angered*): Come on, Law—come on—fade-in on the zoo.

LAW: I've got it! Larry's carrying a hunk of meat for his pet tiger. He's crossing the road.

Bang ! The dame comes tearing down ninety miles an hour.

BENSON: Give her a little character.

LAW: She's a high-handed rich bitch. Bang ! She almost runs the bastard down. . . . Where the hell do you think you're going ? . . . She burns. . . . Society girl. . . . She's never been talked to like that before. . . . Why, you lousy bum, she snarls. . . . Listen, here's a cute piece of business. She bawls the hell out of him and he throws the hunk of meat right in her puss !

BENSON (*enthusiastically*): That's charming !

LAW: Listen, Susie, what are you standing there for ? Go home and write in your diary.

SUSIE: Boys, I wanted to ask you something . . .

BENSON: Fade-out !

LAW: Fade-in !

SUSIE: . . . and then I'll go.

LAW (*wearily*): What is it ?

SUSIE: Do you think I should marry Larry Toms ?

LAW: Who ?

SUSIE: Larry Toms.

LAW (*rises, crosses below couch*): No. . . . Fade-in. . . .

BENSON: Better get a different background. We've been staying in the zoo too long.

LAW: Right ! Girl's home—a Pan shot—fifteen hundred butlers with white socks. . . . (*Turns to* SUSIE.) Did he ask you to marry him ?

SUSIE: Yes.

LAW: Did you spit in his face ?

SUSIE: He's taking me to the opening tonight. He says he's mighty fond of Happy and me.

LAW (*crosses to back of couch*) : Why shouldn't he be ? His contract depends on it. Nobody wants him and they're still calling for——

SUSIE : Don't you think he'd be good for Happy ? He's an outdoor man.

LAW : So is the fellow who collects my garbage.

BENSON : Listen, let's get on with this. Introducing the fiancé. A pale anemic louse. A business man !

LAW : Right ! The minute the audience sees him they yell : Don't marry that heel.

SUSIE : I know you're very busy. . . .

LAW : Go away, Susie.

SUSIE : You boys were so sweet to me. I felt I had somebody. But lately I've been awfully alone. . . .

LAW : Sure ! Everybody's alone. What do you think life is ? Why do you have crowds ? Because everybody's alone. (*Stops; crosses above couch to front.*) That's a thought. That's what I should be writing instead of this titivating drivel. Life as it is. People as they are.

SUSIE : But that would be terrible. You don't know, Mr. Law; you don't know how awful life can be.

BENSON : When you philosophers are through I'd like to get on with this story.

SUSIE (*eagerly, to* BENSON) : You wouldn't like to come out and say hello to Happy ? He's in the garden. (LAW *waves her away; crosses and sits on couch.* SUSIE *is quite defeated now.*)

BENSON (*ignoring her*) : I've got it. (*To* SUSIE) Don't bother me ! (SUSIE *crosses to desk, gets mail, and fades from the scene.*) I've got it ! Introducing Happy ! Back to the zoo—Larry gets up in the morning and there, curled up with his pet tiger cub, is a baby ! Happy !

LAW: Not bad !

BENSON: Larry looks at him. " How'd you get here ? " (*He mimics* LARRY'S *voice.*)

LAW: The baby can't answer. The tiger begins to growl. Happy cries. Larry takes the baby to his hut.

BENSON: We meet Larry's drunken pal, the comic. (*Rises and crosses to* LAW.) That's where we have swell business. Two clumsy men pinning up his diapers——

LAW (*his enthusiasm gone*): Formula 284 . . . Diapers gag.

BENSON (*exulting*): Ah, yes, but the tiger runs away with the diapers ! Fade-out ! Now we need excitement. The tigers are loose——

LAW: How did they get loose ?

BENSON (*crosses to* LAW): The comic's drunk. He opens the cages by accident. Christ ! I see it ! The city in uproar—the police—National Guard—the girl's come down to the zoo—she's trapped with Larry—and the baby. Fifty tigers snapping at Happy's throat.

LAW: And where does my priceless dialogue come in ? (*Rises and crosses to chair back of desk.*) That's the worst of hack writing. It's hard work.

BENSON: Suppose — Larry — thinks — it's — the girl's baby ?

LAW: Society girls go around leaving foundlings in the zoo ? (*Drinking*) Prostitution of a God-given talent ! (*Sits.*) Pasteboard pictures of pasteboard people.

BENSON: Will you shut up ? I've got to get this line-up today. Pearl expects me to take her to the opening.

LAW (*fiddling with the dictograph*): Eenie . . . Meenie . . . Mina . . . Mo . . . (*Dictograph buzzes.*) Music Department?

GREEN'S VOICE: Yes, this is the Music Department. This is Mr. Green.

LAW (*mimics C.F.'s voice*): Not Mr. Green! This is C.F. . . . Can you write me a roundelay with a symphonic undertone in about fifteen minutes? . . . Do it! (*Dictograph buzzes.*) Yes?

GREEN'S VOICE: Look, Mr. Friday, did you say a lullaby?

LAW: No, I didn't say a lullaby. I said a roundelay. The sort of thing Beethoven dashes off. (*He clicks the dictograph off.* ROSETTI *enters.*)

ROSETTI (*genially*): Hello, boys . . . have a cigar.

LAW: Hello, buzzard. What's the occasion?

BENSON: Fade-out, stooge, we're busy.

ROSETTI: Same old boys! Anything for a gag! Well, I'm feeling pretty good myself. I've just set Larry to a long-term contract. And he didn't have to take a cut, either. I got him a nice little set-up. A joint contract with Happy!

BENSON: With Happy?

LAW (*rises*): Huh? You're crazy!

ROSETTI: Well, the mother came to me just now and said you two were tired of her. And I happened to look up your power of attorney, and it seems you didn't even care to get a new one when it expired.

BENSON: Is this on the level?

LAW: Where's that power of attorney?

BENSON: I thought you had it.

LAW (*aghast*): What'd you get for Happy?

ROSETTI: Three hundred!

LAW: Why, we turned down fifteen hundred from Fox!

ROSETTI: You should have taken it. But three hundred's a lot of money. Anyway, what's the difference? It's all in the family—now.

LAW: Where's Susie?

ROSETTI: She went out with Larry. They're going to the opening tonight. They're celebrating.

LAW: Who thought this up—you?

ROSETTI: Sure.

LAW: Why, you scavenging son of a——

ROSETTI: You better be careful how you talk to me. And you'd better be careful how you talk to Larry from now on. He's fed up with your gags and insults. You got away with a lot of stuff around here because you had Happy. Well, Larry's got him now, and he's going to have plenty to say around here. I'm warning you. He'd like to see you boys off this lot. And he's in a position to do it—now. So be careful. If you want to keep your jobs. (*Turns away to door.*) And if I had a wife who was throwing my money away before I even made it, I'd be plenty careful.

BENSON: Why, you—— (ROSETTI *exits quickly.* BENSON *crosses to door, then turns to* LAW.) Why the hell didn't you keep track of that power of attorney?

LAW: Why didn't *I*?

BENSON: Why the hell didn't you talk to Susie? She was in here.

LAW: Yeah.

BENSON: I see it—I see it now. Larry—Rosetti—and we let her walk right into it. Do you realize what this means? We're on our way out. (*Crosses to piano.*)

LAW: That's fine.

BENSON: Fine?

LAW: Now I'll have to go back to Vermont. Now I'll have to write.

BENSON: Pearl doesn't like Vermont.

LAW: The whims of your wife don't interest me. I've got a book—all planned.

BENSON: Listen—I want to stay in pictures. I love pictures. I'm knee-deep in debts. We've got to bust this Larry thing wide open. We've got to get Happy back.

LAW: But it's closed.

BENSON: Well, what of it? We'll open it. We've got to get Happy back.

LAW: How?

BENSON: Suppose we get Larry Toms to break that joint contract.

LAW: All right—but how?

BENSON: He's scared green of scandal. Suppose we show up at the opening tonight with a drunken dame. *Larry's deserted wife!*

LAW: Has he got one?

BENSON: We'll get one of your tarts.

LAW: That's too damned obvious.

BENSON: Can you top it?

LAW: Let me think.

BENSON: How about a poor deserted mother? I'll bet he's got one.

LAW (*rises, carried away*): I know! *Happy's father!*

BENSON: Huh?

LAW: We're going to produce Happy's father on the air—tonight. (*Crosses to phone.*)

BENSON: Happy's father! That's swell! That's marvellous. . . . (*Pause.*) But where'll we get a father?

LAW (*into phone*): *Central Casting, please.* . . . Hello. I want a handsome young extra, a gentleman, a little down at the heel, not too well fed, neat business suit—shiny but well pressed; quiet manner . . . (*Door opens and* RODNEY *enters.*)

BENSON: What do you want?

RODNEY: I received a message from Miss Crews but apparently she's stepped out. Is Mr. Friday here? I assume I've been called for a part.

LAW (*into phone, as his eyes refuse to leave* RODNEY): Never mind—cancel it. (*Hangs up.*)

BENSON: Will you shut the door, please? (RODNEY *complies.*) So you're an actor, my boy? (*Paternally.*)

RODNEY: Of course, I haven't had much experience. As a matter of fact, I never appeared in a picture. I almost did. Since then I've been out of the profession, so to speak. Odd jobs—barbecue stand, and when that closed I offered to show tourists homes of the movie stars. Unfortunately I haven't a motor-car and they won't walk. . . . I don't mind saying this call was an extremely pleasant surprise.

LAW: He's perfect!

RODNEY: Do you really think I'll do?

LAW (*inspired*): Benson, take these lines. . . . (BENSON *goes to chair.*)

RODNEY: Oh, are there lines? Then the fee will be fifteen dollars, I assume?

LAW: Fifteen? One hundred for you.

RODNEY: I'm afraid I'm not worth that.

LAW: This is a trailer we're making tonight. We pay more for trailers.

RODNEY: Oh, I say !

BENSON (*at desk, with paper and pencil*): We're going to shoot this at Grauman's Chinese in the lobby. There'll be a girl at the microphone. Her name is Susie. You come running up . . . you say . . .

LAW (*at downstage end of desk*): Susie, why did you leave me ? . . . Say it.

RODNEY: Susie, why did you leave me ?

BENSON: With feeling.

RODNEY (*with feeling*): Susie, why did you leave me ?

LAW: I'm Happy's father.

RODNEY: I'm Happy's father.

BENSON: Louder.

RODNEY: *I'm Happy's father.*

LAW: I did not go down on the *Morro Castle*. . . . Susie, I've searched for you in the four corners of the earth. . . . *Susie, why did you leave me ?*

RODNEY (*who has been repeating the ends of the phrases in* LAW'S *speech*): Susie, why did you leave me ?

BENSON (*jubilant*): Right !

BLACKOUT AND CURTAIN

SCENE III

A radio voice is heard in the theatre before the rise of the curtain. We're right in Grauman's Chinese Theatre in Hollywood.

RADIO ANNOUNCER: Folks, this is the première of Cecil B. de Mille's super-spectacle of Egyptian life—*King Saul*—at Grauman's Chinese. Your favorite stars, folks, in person—and the *crowds.*

They're pushing and shoving and yelling for autographs, but it's all in good-natured fun. Only two hurt and they've refused medical treatment. There's Constance Bennett, folks, with her husband, the Marquis de la Falaise. No, I'm wrong. Sorry. It's not the Marquis . . . it's not Constance Bennett. It's Mary Pickford. By the way, I've been reading our Mary's book, folks. She's selling God, folks, and that's something we all ought to be in the market for. Give a thought to God and He'll give a thought to you. That's the big lesson in *King Saul*, folks. Oh, there's Leotta Marvin. . . .

[*As the curtain rises, the booming voice softens to the normal tone of a radio.*

Again we are in MR. FRIDAY's *office, later in the evening. At the rise of the curtain,* C.F. *is seated with a* CUTTER, *and* BENSON *sits a little apart from him, in chair back of couch, near the radio, which is on.*

RADIO ANNOUNCER: . . . And if you've seen her on the screen, I don't have to tell you she's blonde, beautiful and gorgeous. Folks, I want to tell you that this is the most thrilling première it's been my privilege to cover. *King Saul*, de Mille's super-spectacle of Egyptian life at Grauman's Chinese——

C.F.: Benson, turn down that radio. We've got to get three thousand feet out of *London Life*. It's a sick picture, Benson. Where's Law? I left word at his hotel.

BENSON: He'll be here. I'm inside man tonight. He's outside.

C.F. (*to* CUTTER): Cut the coronation scene—it drags. And give me an underlying something that means something. I want a stirring Britannic quality. (BENSON *turns up the radio.*)

RADIO ANNOUNCER: . . . And that, folks, was Mr. Stanley Oswald, veteran of old silent films. . . .

This is the première of *King Saul*, Cecil B. de Mille's super-spectacle at Grauman's Chinese....

C.F.: Benson, turn to page 94 and read that scene. I want to lap dissolve through Queen Victoria. Simmons, you're supposed to be a cutter. Give me some ideas.

RADIO ANNOUNCER: . . . And now, folks, I'm told that none other than Larry Toms is with us to-night. And he's not altogether by his lonesome for hanging on his manly arm is none other than Mrs. Susan Seabrook, mother of America's Crown Prince—Happy !

BENSON: Hooray !

CUTTER: I got a way of cutting all that Boer War stuff so you won't even miss it.

RADIO ANNOUNCER: . . . And now I have the honor to present Mrs. Seabrook, the mother of Happy . . .

C.F.: Will you turn that infernal thing off ? (*To* CUTTER) I can't cut the Boer War. It's historically valuable.

RADIO ANNOUNCER: . . . And now I have the honor to present Mrs. Seabrook, the mother of Happy——

SUSIE'S VOICE: But I don't know what to say !

BENSON: Susie's on the air.

RADIO ANNOUNCER: Is it true, Mrs. Seabrook, that you and Larry have been window shopping ?

SUSIE'S VOICE (*and it's very nervous indeed*): Well——

RADIO ANNOUNCER: The microphone is yours.

SUSIE'S VOICE: I would like to thank all of you for the thousands of letters and gifts that you've sent my baby Happy. I read all your letters and some of them make me cry—they're so pathetic. I would like to send all of you money only I haven't got that much and the studio won't let me. I'd like to say a few words about the letters asking about Happy's diet. You read a lot of advertisements of what he eats but if Happy ate everything they said he ate I guess he'd be a giant, and he's really got a very little stomach.

BENSON: Good for Susie! Truth in advertising!

C.F. (*struck by appalling thought*): Benson, was Queen Victoria alive during the Boer War?

BENSON: If she's alive in the picture, she was.

RADIO ANNOUNCER (*through this*): Folks, this is the première of Cecil B. de Mille's superspectacle of Egyptian life, *King Saul*, at Grauman's Chinese——

SUSIE'S VOICE: Can I say hello to all my girl friends at the Julia Marshall High School? . . . *Hello!*

C.F.: Benson——

BENSON: Ssssh . . . Susie's talking.

SUSIE'S VOICE: A lot of you wonder in your letters how a grown woman can go to high school. Well, it's not easy. I'm a mother, and the other girls aren't . . .

BENSON: Let's hope not.

SUSIE'S VOICE (*brightly*): . . . although some of the girls are very developed.

RADIO ANNOUNCER (*quickly*): Folks, this is the première of *King Saul*, Cecil B. de Mille's superspectacle of Egyptian life. . . .

C.F.: Shut that infernal thing off. (BENSON *lifts hand like traffic signal " Stop."*)

SUSIE'S VOICE: I didn't finish. I wanted to explain that I'm going to high school so I can keep up with Happy when he goes to college. Because I'm the only one Happy can go to. He hasn't got a father, and——

RADIO ANNOUNCER (*very, very firmly*): That was Happy's mother, folks. . . . She was wearing a white evening gown. And folks, meet Larry Toms, the lucky man.

C.F.: Benson, can we lap-dissolve through, do you think, on page 94?

LARRY'S VOICE: I know this is going to be a wonderful picture.

RADIO ANNOUNCER: A little bird has whispered to me that you and Mrs. Seabrook are contemplating marriage, Larry.

BENSON: Well, what do you know about that!

C.F.: Will you come here, Benson, with that script?

LARRY'S VOICE: Well, to tell you the truth——

BENSON: He's blushing.

LARRY'S VOICE: I kinda missed the little fella after the day's work was done. So I guess pretty soon I'll be Happy's father off the screen as well as on——

BENSON: Who wrote his speech? You or Rosetti?

RODNEY'S VOICE: Stop! I'm Happy's father!

C.F. (*rises*): What's that?

RODNEY'S VOICE: I did not go down on the *Morro Castle*. I've searched for you in the four corners of the earth. Susie, why did you leave me?

C.F. (*excitedly*): Did you hear that?

BENSON (*softly*): Yes. I wonder what that was . . . (*Cries are heard of " Here, Officer "—inarticulate shouts—a siren.*)

RADIO ANNOUNCER: Folks, there was a slight interruption. That voice you heard was a young man . . . he . . . well, he threw his arms about Mrs. Seabrook and kissed her. There's some confusion—a police officer is making his way through—they've got the young man . . . no, they haven't got him . . . Folks, this is the opening of Cecil B. de Mille's super-spectacle of Egyptian life, *King Saul*, at Grauman's Chinese. . . . (BENSON *turns it off.*)

C.F. (*stunned*): Good Gad! (*Phone rings. He moves to it.*)

BENSON (*shakes his head*): Strangest thing I ever heard.

C.F.: Oh, hello, B.K. . . . Yes, I've just heard it over the radio . . . (*Miserable.*) I'm sitting here trying to cut *London Life* . . . what? . . . But, B.K., . . . yes, of course, it's a serious situation . . . I agree with you . . . yes, . . . yes . . . of course . . . I'll get hold of the mother immediately. (*He rises; hangs up, still dazed. To* BENSON) B.K.'s coming down to the studio! (*Phone rings.*) Yes . . . Look here, I've nothing to say to the press. It's a canard. (*He hangs up.*) (*Phone rings again.*) I won't answer it. (MISS CREWS *enters.*)

MISS CREWS: Doctor Tompkins is calling you, Mr. Friday. He says it's important.

C.F.: What's he want? I'm not in. Call Mrs. Seabrook's house and have her ring me the minute she comes in.

MISS CREWS: Yes, Mr. Friday. (*She exits.*)

C.F.: Benson, do you think that young man was genuine?

BENSON (*rises, crosses around downstage end of couch*): Search me.

C.F.: Well, we'll soon find out. B.K.'s set the police after him.

BENSON (*a little disturbed*): Why do that? Best thing the studio can do is ignore it.

C.F.: We can't ignore it. This has brought up the whole paternity issue.

BENSON: What of it?

C.F.: Suppose Happy has a skeleton in his closet?

BENSON (*lies on couch*): I don't even know if he's got a closet.

C.F.: Save your gags for your pictures. They need them. I've never heard B.K. so excited. (*Crosses to window.*) What do you think the reaction will be in the sticks—in the provinces? An illegitimate baby!

BENSON: This is 1935.

C.F.: To me, yes. But how many intellectuals have we in America?

BENSON: One.

C.F.: You don't seem to realize——

BENSON: Why, this is going to send Happy's stock up one hundred per cent. From now on he's not only cute, he's romantic.

C.F.: He's illegitimate! I know America!

CUTTER (*studying the script*): What about Prince Albert? I can cut him out of the picture and you won't even miss him.

C.F. (*crossing below desk*): Yes, yes, Simmons. You go to the cutting room and do the best you know how. (SIMMONS *rises and puts chair up against wall.*) I've something more urgent right now. (*Crosses to* SIMMONS.) And, for God's sake, Simmons, get me some trumpets that sound like trumpets.

CUTTER (*not gruffly, but politely*): You sure you don't mean a trombone, C.F.?

C.F.: No. I mean trumpets. I'm not a musician but I know what I mean. Trumpets—that slide. (*He pantomimes a trombone, of course.*)

BENSON (*to* CUTTER): He wants a slide trumpet. (CUTTER *exits.*) (*Simultaneously through other door* GREEN *and* SLADE *appear.*)

GREEN: Well, we've got that roundelay.

C.F.: What do you want? What roundelay? (*Phone rings.*)

GREEN: Park it, Otto. (*Both go to piano.*)

C.F. (*at phone*): Yes—yes—no, Mr. Friday is not here. He has nothing to say to the press. (*He hangs up.*)

GREEN: You're going to be enthusiastic about this. We've been up all night working on it. (SLADE *starts playing Beethoven's "Turkish March."* As C.F. *starts toward the piano, the phone rings.*) Smooth, ain't it?

C.F. (*at phone*): Miss Crews? Where's Mrs. Seabrook? Why haven't you got her? (*To* GREEN) I will not listen to any more music.

GREEN: Get a load of this. It's the real McCoy.

C.F. (*at phone*): Yes—I'm holding the line—all right, never mind. Call me. (*Hangs up. To* SLADE *and* GREEN) I'll call the studio guards if you don't stop that infernal din. I'll report you to B.K. for insubordination. I'll have your contracts torn up!

GREEN: Are you kidding, or is this on the level?

C.F.: Get out!

GREEN: O.K. Don't get tough! Come on, Otto. (*Crosses back of couch to door.*) But it's a fine how-do-you-do when you call up a couple of artists late at night and put 'em to work going through

Beethoven's symphonies for a little inspiration and then give them the bum's rush just because you ain't in the mood. (GREEN *and* SLADE *exit*.) (LARRY *and* ROSETTI *enter, both in tails and toppers*.)

ROSETTI: Now calm down, Larry, calm down——

LARRY: I'm not saying a word.

C.F.: Where's Mrs. Seabrook? What did you do with her?

LARRY: I don't know, and I don't care.

BENSON (*mockingly*): " I kinda missed the little fella after the day's work was done——"

C.F. (*quickly*): Look here, Larry, I want to know what Susie said. Did she know the young man? What did she say?

LARRY: You listen to what *I* gotta say. I ain't goin' to go through with no contract to play with no unbaptized baby!

ROSETTI (*placatingly*): Just a moment, Larry——

LARRY: I'm through! (*Overwhelmed with the memory*.) On the air—with all my fans listening in! I'm serving you notice now. I ain't marrying her. I ain't doing no more pictures with Happy.

ROSETTI: Larry, will you listen to reason?

LARRY: There's only one thing you can do for me, Rosetti. Get me a doctor. I'm going up to my dressing room. I need a sedative. (LAW *enters quietly*.)

BENSON: Don't stand there. Get him a doctor——

LAW: Take me. I'm a qualified veterinary. (ROSETTI *exits with* LARRY.)

C.F.: LAW—— (BENSON *sits up*.)

LAW: Hello, C.F. I just got your message at the hotel. *London Life* in trouble? Well, the old salvaging crew will pitch in. (*Takes off his coat.*)

C.F.: Were you there?

LAW: Where? At the opening? Yes. Extraordinary, wasn't it?

BENSON (*significantly*): *We* heard it over the radio.

LAW (*casually*): How'd it come over?

BENSON (*admiringly*): Clear as a bell!

LAW: It certainly broke Larry up. You should have seen our chivalrous hero running from the rescue. Why, the wind whistled right past me!

C.F.: Law, do you think that fellow was a crank, or do you think he was really——

LAW (*judicially*): Hard to say. He had a sinister underlip.

C.F. (*into phone*): Miss Crews, did you get Mrs. Seabrook's house? No one answers? Someone *must* answer—she has a ménage! (*Hangs up. Dictograph buzzes.*) Hello?

B.K.'s VOICE: Look here, Friday . . .

C.F.: Yes, B.K.

B.K.'s VOICE: Did you get any dope on that young man?

C.F.: No. I can't get any information. No one seems to know.

B.K.'s VOICE: Why not? I ask you to do the simplest little thing and, as usual, you fall down on me.

C.F. (*piteously*): Why blame me? I was sitting here cutting *London Life*.

B.K.'s VOICE: Don't bother me with *London Life*. You come up here—I want to talk with you.

C.F.: Yes, B.K. I'll be right up. (*He moves to the door; sighs.*) Sometimes I wonder if this industry is worth the sacrifice. (*He exits.*)

BENSON (*smiles*): What'd you do with him?

LAW: Put him in an office across the hall.

BENSON (*aghast*): What? Why here?

LAW: They won't look for him here.

BENSON: Why didn't you dump him somewhere else?

LAW: And leave him free to roam—and blab? Listen, Benson, B.K.'s called the Chief personally and the whole damn police department is scouring the town for Rodney. (*Crosses to liquor cabinet; pours a drink.*) And you don't know what I've been up against with Rodney. (*He drinks.*) In his own peculiar English fashion, he's not entirely nitwitted. I had to shove him at the mike, and he's been demanding explanations ever since.

BENSON: One question: What'll we do with him?

LAW (*crossing back to couch; sits*): Frankly, I planned everything but Rodney's disposal. I don't know. But given a little time we'll work this problem out.

BENSON (*really aghast now*): Time?

LAW: Rodney's all right. He doesn't know it, but I've locked him in.

BENSON: Listen: I've got a wife to support! I've got a job to keep! I haven't got Vermont on my mind! I *like* writing pictures! I'm no goddamn realist!

LAW (*soothingly*): Easy, there, easy——

BENSON: If B.K. even dreamed we had anything to do with this we'd be blacklisted in the industry.

LAW (*rising*) : Give me a chance to think, will you ? Why the panic ? I'll admit I've over-looked a few details.

BENSON : Get that guy out of the studio. Put him on a plane to Mexico. Strangle him ! I don't care what you do.

LAW : No—no. Murder leads to theft and theft leads to deceit. Haven't you read De Quincey ?

BENSON : C.F. may breeze in here any minute. Will you get going !

LAW : Very well, my sweet—I go. (*He starts for door, remembers that he had a coat, looks around room and finally locates it on couch. Gets it and exits.*) (*Phone rings.*)

BENSON (*into phone*) : Hello . . . Yes. Right here. Oh, hello, darling. How are you feeling ? (*Tenderly.*) Of course I recognized your voice . . . Pearl, I'll be home in half an hour. . . . Less . . . Well, what are you crying about ? . . . But I told you I couldn't take you to the opening. Well, if Louise was going why didn't you go with them ? They'd be tickled to have you . . . Listen, darling . . . I know . . . I know . . . Yes, I'm listening. . . . (LAW *re-enters—a changed* LAW. *He goes right to the second telephone.*)

LAW (*picking up the second telephone*) : Give me the front gate !

BENSON (*into phone*) : Yes, darling . . . yes . . . (*Sincerely*) Darling, please—please don't say that.

LAW : Smitty, this is Mr. Law. Any stranger go through the gate in the last ten minutes ? . . . No ?

BENSON (*sighs*) : Yes, darling. . . .

LAW : Well, listen. The fellow that was on the air tonight—Happy's father—yes ! He's loose in the studio . . . Yeah. . . .

BENSON (*turns to* LAW, *still holding the phone*):
What ?

LAW: Grab him and hold him. Don't let anyone come near him. Report to me personally . . .
yeah . . .

BENSON: Darling, I'll call you back. (*Slams down
the phone.*)

LAW (*hangs up*): The damn cleaning woman
let him out !

BENSON (*apoplectic*): I told you, didn't I ? I
told you you shouldn't have brought him
here ! (SUSIE *enters. She has been magnificently
decked out for the opening, but despite her splendor
she seems extremely unhappy.*)

SUSIE: Oh, Mr. Benson . . . I tried to get you
at your house but Mrs. Benson said you were
here. I tried to get you, too, Mr. Law, at the
hotel.

LAW: Now, now, Susie—I know—I know.

SUSIE: Oh, I should never have gone to that
opening. I didn't want to go. When I was dressing I put my slip on the wrong side. I knew
something terrible was going to happen.
And then in the nursery when I went to say
good night to Happy, he wouldn't eat his
formula. And he wouldn't say good night to
me. He was so cross. I told Larry I didn't
want to leave Happy—but he insisted—and
then the way Larry ran out on me——

LAW (*consolingly*): Now, now——

SUSIE: Why should he do that ? Oh, I was so
ashamed . . . I didn't even see the picture. And
then when I got home—I knew I shouldn't
have gone—I should never have left Happy.
When I went to the hospital . . .

LAW: Hospital ?

BENSON: Hospital?

SUSIE: They won't let me in . . . not for two weeks.

BENSON (*crosses to* SUSIE): Happy's in the hospital?

SUSIE (*puzzled*): Happy's got the measles.

LAW: What?

SUSIE: And they won't let me come near him.

BENSON: Measles!

LAW: He certainly picked the right time for it!

SUSIE: That's why he wouldn't eat his formula.

C.F.'s VOICE (*off-stage; grimly*): Well, we'll see—— (*As he opens the door*) I brought you some visitors, boys. Come in. (RODNEY *enters with* STUDIO OFFICER.) (*To* RODNEY) Are these the men?

RODNEY: They most certainly are.

SUSIE (*crosses to* RODNEY): You know you're not Happy's father.

RODNEY: Of course not, but——

SUSIE: You couldn't be!

RODNEY: Of course not! My Dear, I'm very sorry. Look here, we always seem to meet under extraordinary circumstances . . . I never dreamt . . . I'd no idea . . . It was all so spectacular . . . And to do this to you—— You were so kind to me . . . They said it was a trailer . . . I didn't realize until I was in the midst of it . . . And then I found myself in a car . . . with him . . . (*Indicates* LAW.) I asked him to bring me to you at once. Instead, he locked me in a dusty office.

C.F.: So you boys put him up to it!

LAW: Before you say anything you'll be sorry for, C.F. . . . (*Turns to officer.*) Smitty, who called you tonight to tell you this unfortunate young man was loose in the studio ?

OFFICER : *You* did, Mr. Law.

LAW (*grandly*) : That's all.

BENSON : Take him away.

LAW : It's an obvious psychiatric case, C.F.

BENSON (*to* C.F.) : I wouldn't be surprised if he's the boy that's been springing out of bushes.

LAW : Certainly. Look at the way he kissed Susie !

RODNEY (*appalled*) : But you coached me for hours. Both of you. Wait—here are my lines. (*He fumbles in his pocket.*) I know I have them—unless I've lost them.

LAW : So you're an author, too ! And I thought it was extemporaneous.

RODNEY : Here—here they are ! My dear, will you please read these lines ? (*He hands the paper to* SUSIE.) They're the very words I spoke over the radio.

SUSIE (*reads and backs away from* RODNEY) : You never said *these* lines. You *must* be a crank. Maybe you do spring out of bushes.

RODNEY (*stares*) : Oh, I beg your pardon. My lines are on the other side.

LAW (*grabs for paper*) : I'll take that ! Susie——

C.F. (*taking paper out of* SUSIE'S *hand, brushes* LAW *aside*) : Just a minute. (*Reads.*) " She's a high-handed rich bitch."—*Tiger Tamer !*—There it is in the corner. *Tiger Tamer* by J. Carlyle Benson and Robert Law !

LAW (*hurt to the quick*) : It's a forgery. Benson, we've been framed !

C.F. (*grimly*) : This is the last prank you'll ever play. (*Clicks the dictograph.*)

Miss Crews (*enters*): The new trumpets are here. (*For once, C.F. is not interested. The trumpets blare out.*)

C.F. (*into dictograph*): B.K.? I just found out—Benson and Law put that young man on the radio.

B.K.'s Voice: Are you sure of that?

C.F.: I have the proof. The young man is in my office.

B.K.'s Voice: All right, fire them. I don't want them on this lot. If they think they can get away with that——

C.F.: Fire them? Of course I'll fire them. (Larry's Voice *is heard as he enters.*)

Larry: Don't tell me nothing—let go of me. (Doctor *and* Rosetti *enter, following* Larry *and struggling with him.*)

C.F.: Quiet there——

Larry: Let go of me!

C.F.: Larry, I have neither the time nor the patience to pander to actors!

Larry (*bellowing with the hurt roar of a wounded bull*): No? Babies, huh . . . (*Turns on* Susie) You—you——

Susie (*frightened; runs to* Benson): What do you want?

Larry: What do I want? That goddamn baby of yours has given me the measles!

CURTAIN

ACT III

A hospital corridor. Several weeks later. Facing us are several doors, punctuated by the little white cards identifying the patients within.

As the curtain rises, a white-clad NURSE *is walking down the corridor bearing a covered tray. Before she disappears,* BENSON *enters. He knocks on the door of the room where* HAPPY *is ensconced.* SUSIE *opens the door.*

SUSIE: Oh, hello, Mr. Benson. I'd ask you to come in but Happy's still sleeping. The doctor says he can be discharged tomorrow or the day after, he's getting along so fine. Where's Mr. Law?

BENSON: I don't know. We haven't been patronizing the same bar-rooms.

SUSIE: You look as if you didn't get much sleep.

BENSON (*slumping into a wheel chair*): I didn't.

SUSIE (*pityingly*): Why don't you go home?

BENSON: Home?

SUSIE: Is there anything wrong?

BENSON: Not a thing! Everything's fine.

SUSIE: How's Mrs. Benson?

BENSON: She's fine.

SUSIE: That's good. I called your house to thank her for the radio for Happy but they said you moved.

BENSON: We *were* moved.

SUSIE: You mean you were thrown out?

BENSON: If you want to be technical about it, yes.

SUSIE: Oh, I'm sorry.

BENSON (*broodingly*): What hurts is Aggrafino Jesus.

SUSIE: Who?

BENSON: My favorite Filipino butler. He slapped a lien on my brand-new Packard.

SUSIE: Oh!

BENSON: That's what the missionaries taught *him*!

SUSIE: You boys shouldn't have played that joke on me. You only hurt yourselves. Please don't drink any more, Mr. Benson.

BENSON: So it's come to that! You're going to reform me.

SUSIE: Well, I feel just like a sister to you boys. That's why I couldn't stay mad at you. Please, Mr. Benson, if you need money—I can give you some. I mean—when the studio sends Happy's checks. They haven't sent them yet.

BENSON (*looking up*): They haven't? How many do they owe you?

SUSIE: Two. I called Mr. Friday but he wouldn't talk to me. Do you think they're docking Happy?

BENSON: They can't do that. Measles are an act of God. (NURSE *enters with box of flowers.*)

NURSE: Some flowers for you, Mrs. Seabrook.

SUSIE (*extending her hand for it*): Oh, thank you.

NURSE: And he'd like to know if he can come up to see you. He's downstairs.

SUSIE (*embarrassed*): Oh . . .

BENSON: Who's downstairs? Who's sending you flowers?

SUSIE (*reluctantly*): It's Mr. Bevan. You know——

BENSON: You haven't been seeing our Nemesis?

SUSIE: Oh, no. But he's been writing me every day and sending me flowers. I didn't tell you. I didn't want to get you excited.

BENSON (*to* NURSE; *sweetly*): Tell him to come up, Nurse. And stand by.

SUSIE (*quickly*): Oh, no, Nurse. He's not to come up. I don't want to see him. Ever. And give him back his flowers. (*She hands box back to* NURSE.)

NURSE (*taking it*): Very well. (*She exits.*)

BENSON: Why deprive me of the pleasure of kicking an actor?

SUSIE: It wasn't his fault. After all, you put him up to it.

BENSON (*outraged*): Are you defending him!

SUSIE: Oh, no, I'm just as disappointed in him as you are. But I'm trying to be fair. (*She pauses.*) He writes very nice letters. (*A far-away look comes into her eyes.*)

BENSON (*suspiciously*): What kind of letters do you write him?

SUSIE (*hastily*): Oh, I don't write *any* letters.

BENSON: Good!

SUSIE: I'm afraid of my spelling. (LAW *enters. There's an air of on-my-way about him.*)

LAW: Hello, Susie. . . . And good-bye, Susie.

SUSIE: Hello, Mr. Law. Are you going away?

LAW: I am.

SUSIE: Where?

LAW: Where I belong. Vermont. Where you can touch life and feel life, and write it! (*Glares at* BENSON.)

BENSON: When does the great exodus begin?

LAW: In exactly thirty-five minutes. I'm flying back to my native hills, like a homing pigeon. No stopping in New York for me ! I've chartered a plane—right to Vermont.

BENSON: Chartered a plane ! Where'd you get the money ?

LAW (*grudgingly*): Well, there are twelve Rotarians coming along.

BENSON: You'll be back in a week.

SUSIE (*eagerly*): Will you, Mr. Law ?

LAW (*scornfully*): Back to what ? Sunshine and psyllium seed ? Listen, I've got me a little shack overlooking the valley . . . I'm going to cook my own food, chop my own wood, and *write*——

BENSON (*sardonically*): At twenty below ?

LAW (*rapturously*): Snow ! . . . God, how I love snow ! (*He raises his eyes to Heaven.*)

> And since to look at things in bloom
> Fifty springs are little room,
> About the woodlands, I will go
> To see the cherry—hung with snow !

SUSIE: That's poetry.

LAW: A. E. Housman ! *Shropshire Lad.* (*He pats the book in his pocket.*)

BENSON: There's plenty of snow in Arrowhead.

LAW: Yeah: they deliver it in trucks. And even when it's real you think it's cornflakes.

SUSIE: You won't drink too much in Vermont, will you, Mr. Law ?

LAW: Only the heady wine air that has no dregs !

SUSIE: Because you're crazy enough without drinking.

LAW (*defensively*) : I drank for escape . . . escape from myself . . . but now I'm free ! I've found peace !

SUSIE : You'll say good-bye to Happy before you go ? I want him to remember you.

LAW : Right now !

SUSIE : Wait ! I'll see if he's awake. (*She enters* HAPPY'S *room.*)

BENSON : Will you send me a copy of the book— autographed ?

LAW : You get copy number one—first edition.

BENSON : What's the book about ?

LAW : I'm going to bare my soul. . . . I'm going to write life in the raw. I've got the opening all planned—two rats in a sewer !

BENSON : Sounds delightful.

LAW (*scornfully*) : You wouldn't appreciate real writing. You've been poisoned. On second thought, I won't send you a book.

BENSON : Tell me more about the rats. What's your story ?

LAW (*slightly patronising*) : This isn't a picture that you paste together, Mr. Benson. I'm going to write Life. Life isn't a story . . . it's a discordant overture to death !

BENSON : Well, if you want people to read it, the boy had better meet the girl.

LAW : There is no girl. There is no boy. These are people—real, live people—listen ! I'm not even going to use a typewriter ! I'm going to weigh every word—with a pencil !

BENSON : Well, maybe you're on the right track. You've got something to say—and the talent to say it with.

LAW: It's finally penetrated !

BENSON: You're probably doing the right thing.

LAW: The only thing. It's different with you— you've got a wife.

BENSON: I had.

LAW: Huh ?

BENSON: Oh—uh—Pearl left last night.

LAW: No ! I'm sorry.

BENSON (*shrugs*): You can't blame her. She wasn't wild about marrying me in the first place. I coaxed her into it. I painted some pretty pictures for her. It just didn't pan out.

LAW: You still want her ?

BENSON (*almost to himself*): I guess I do.

LAW: Personally, I'd say the hell with her.

BENSON (*smiles bitterly*): The trouble is I don't mean it when I say it. (ROSETTI *enters.*)

ROSETTI: Hello, boys.

LAW (*cheerily*): Hello, louse. Get Benson a job, will you ? He wants to stay in this God-forsaken hole.

ROSETTI: Listen ! I'm not handling second-hand writers. Chicken feed ! Right now I'm immersed in a three million dollar deal.

LAW (*interested*): Yeah ?

ROSETTI: Yeah. With British Bulldog Pictures, and I'm underestimating when I say three million because B.K.'s turned down three million. Why should I bother with writers on the black-list ? So don't go calling me a louse ! (SUSIE *enters.*)

SUSIE (*gaily*): Happy has his eyes open. You want to come in now, Mr. Law ?

LAW: Coming, Susie. (*He follows* SUSIE *into* HAPPY'S *room.*)

BENSON: Rosetti—(*going to him, whispering*)— Law wants to leave. He's flying in half an hour. Can you call up the studios? Can you get us a one-picture contract? We'll make you our agent for life. *He's leaving!*

ROSETTI: Sure, he's leaving. Nobody wants him.

BENSON: How do you know? You haven't tried.

ROSETTI: I've tried. I don't let my personal feelings interfere with commissions.

BENSON: Listen, I've been a scene painter, prop boy, camera man, director, producer. . . . I even sold film in Australia . . . they can't throw me out of this business!

ROSETTI (*crosses to a door and throws it back*): They won't touch you with a ten-foot pole. You, Law, or Happy.

BENSON: Or Happy?

ROSETTI: I gave B.K. a swell angle. Listen in on KNX this afternoon.

BENSON: Huh?

ROSETTI: The world is full of babies. You can get them two for a nickel. (*He opens inner door and meets* LARRY *coming out.*) Hello, Larry. I was just coming in to see you. (NURSE *pushes* LARRY *in wheel chair into corridor.*)

LAW'S VOICE: Good-bye, Happy. (*He enters with* SUSIE.) Good-bye, Susie.

SUSIE: Good-bye, Mr. Law.

LAW: Hello, Larry. How's every little spot?

LARRY: What's the idea?

Law: What idea?

Larry: What's the idea of sending me a box of dead spiders?

Law: Didn't you like the box?

Larry: You wait until I'm through convalescing!

Nurse: Now, don't excite yourself. You heard what the doctor said. You're going for your sun bath now. (*She wheels him out.*)

Rosetti: I'll go along with you, Larry. I've got some great news for you. B.K.'s lending you out to Mascot! (*He exits.*)

Larry (*as he goes out*): What?

Law: Well, Susie, take good care of Happy.

Susie: Oh, I will.

Law: Continue your education.

Susie: I'm doing that.

Law (*quickly*): What's the capital of Nebraska?

Susie: Lincoln.

Law: Who hit Sir Isaac Newton on the bean with an apple?

Susie: The law of gravity.

Law: Who said, " Don't give up the ship?"

Susie: Captain James Lawrence in the battle of Lake Erie, 1813.

Law: Don't give up the ship, Susie. I'll write you. (*He kisses her on the forehead.*)

Susie: Good-bye, Mr. Law. I've got to go back to Happy. (*Her voice breaks.*) I feel awful funny— your going away. (*Exits.*)

Benson (*finally*): Well, you bastard—get out of here.

Q

LAW: I'm going, stinker. (*Crosses to* BENSON. *They look at each other. A pause. Then* LAW *extends hand. They shake.* LAW *moves to go.*)

BENSON (*without turning*): Say—— (LAW *stops.*) I don't suppose you'll be interested—Rosetti finally admitted Paramount wants us. Two thousand bucks a week. We can close the deal in three or four days.

LAW (*turns slowly*): My plane leaves in twenty-five minutes. And you're a liar !

BENSON: I'm not trying to hold you back. But I figured this time you might *save* your money and——

LAW: I can live on twelve dollars a week in Vermont—in luxury !

BENSON: It would kind of help *me* out. If I could lay my hands on some ready dough Pearl might listen to reason.

LAW (*casually*): Well, we loaned out a lot of money in our time. Collect it. And send me my share.

BENSON: I thought of that. The trouble is I don't remember just who it was—and how much. The only one I remember is Jascha Simkovitch.

LAW: Who ?

BENSON: Jascha Simkovitch. The fellow that came over last year. Don't you remember ? You made a wonderful crack about him. He said, " There's a price on my head in Russia." And you said, " Yeah—two roubles." (*Laughs. He is flattering* LAW *smoothly.*)

LAW (*laughs with him*): Sure, I remember him. Why, we gave that bed-bug three thousand bucks ! Get hold of him and collect it.

BENSON: He's in Paris. What's-his-name came over and said Jascha was living at the Ritz bar.

LAW: Then you can't collect it. Well, I'm off. (*He moves to exit once more.*)

BENSON (*as if struck with sudden thought*): Wait a minute ! I've got a great gag for you ! Let's call Jascha up in Paris—on Larry's phone ! (*Chuckles, throws arms around* LAW. *Both laugh.*) Can you imagine Larry's face when he gets the bill ? A farewell rib !

LAW (*hesitates*): Have I got time ?

BENSON (*reassuringly; looks at his watch*): You've got plenty of time.

LAW: I'll work fast. Stand guard, Benson. (*He enters* LARRY'S *room.* BENSON *follows and partly closes door.*)

LAW'S VOICE: I'm talking for Mr. Toms. I want to put a call through to Paris, France. . . . I want Jascha Simkovitch . . . Hotel Ritz, Paris. . . . Listen, don't worry about the charges . . . That's right—Jascha, as in Heifetz . . . S-i-m-k-o-v-i-t-c-h. (BENSON *closes door on* LAW. NURSE *enters with registered letter, knocks on* SUSIE'S *door.* BENSON *looks at his watch.* SUSIE *appears.*)

NURSE: Registered letter for you, Mrs. Seabrook.

SUSIE: For me ?

NURSE: You'll have to sign for it. There's a return receipt on it. (SUSIE *signs.*)

SUSIE: Now what do I do ?

NURSE: Now you give me the receipt back and I'll give it to the postman. He's waiting for it. Here's your letter. (NURSE *exits.* SUSIE *opens letter.*)

SUSIE (*cheerily*): Why—it's from Mr. Friday. (LAW *emerges, as she opens the letter.*)

LAW: The service had better be good or there'll be no farewell rib. I haven't got much time.

SUSIE : Oh, didn't you go yet, Mr. Law ?

LAW : I'm on my way !

SUSIE (*reading letter*) : What does Mr. Friday mean when he says they're taking advantage of Clause 5A ?

LAW : What ? Let me see that. (*He reads the letter.* BENSON *looks over his shoulder.*) Well, this is the god-damest . . .

SUSIE : You mustn't swear so much. I don't mind—I'm used to it—but Happy might hear you. What does it mean ?

LAW (*reading*) : Clause 5A—when an artist through illness—for a period of more than fourteen days——

BENSON : They're just using that for an excuse. It's the paternity issue !

SUSIE : What paternity issue ?

BENSON : They're crazy ! That kid's going to be as good as he ever was—better.

SUSIE : What does it mean ?

LAW : It means, Susie—Happy is out.

SUSIE : Out ?

BENSON : Yeah. Finished—done. At the age of eight months—in his prime !

SUSIE : Out of pictures ?

BENSON (*turning on* LAW) : And there's the man who did it. It was your brilliant idea !

SUSIE (*such a nice girl !*) : Oh, no. After all, it was just like a dream. I had to wake up some time.

LAW (*as phone rings*) : I guess that's Paris.

SUSIE : What's Paris ? (*Phone still rings.*)

BENSON : Go ahead and have your farewell rib, and get out, author ! (*Phone still rings.* LAW *enters room.*)

Susie: What's Paris?

Benson (*going to door of* Larry's *room*): A city in France.

Law (*in room*): Hello—right here.—Yes—yes— I'm ready. Hello! . . . Hello—Jascha? Jascha Simkovitch? This is Bobby Law. Is it raining in Paris? . . . well, it's not raining here!

Benson: Wonderful age we're living in!

Law (*in room*): Listen, Jascha, are you sober? . . . How come? . . . Oh, you just got there! . . . You're going to London? . . . Today? . . . Hold the wire. (Law *enters.*) I've got an idea! *Let's buy the studio!*

Benson: What?

Law: You heard Rosetti. British Bulldog Pictures is offering three million. Let's get Jascha to send a cable—sign it British Bulldog Pictures— offering four!

Benson: Why be petty? Offer five!

Law (*judicially*): Right! (*Exits into room.*

Susie: You boys are very peculiar.

Law (*in room*): Jascha—got a pencil and paper? Fine. Listen, Jascha, we want you to send a cable from London as follows: Quote. . . . (Larry *enters in his wheel chair.* Benson *closes the door hurriedly.*)

Larry: Hey, that's my room!

Benson (*firmly shutting the door*): A private conversation should be private.

Larry: What's the idea of using my phone?

Benson: Do you object?

Larry: Certainly I object. I ain't gonna pay for your calls.

Benson: All right, if that's the way you feel about it—here's your nickel!

BLACKOUT AND CURTAIN

SCENE II

In Your Own Home. That is, if you have one, and if you listen to the radio.

RADIO ANNOUNCER: Ladies and Gentlemen, this is Station KNX—the Voice of Hollywood. At this time we take great pleasure in announcing the winner of the Royal Studios' Baby Star Contest to find the successor to Happy who retired from the screen after his illness. Ladies and Gentlemen, the lucky baby is Baby Sylvester Burnett, infant son of Mr. and Mrs. Oliver Burnett of Glendale, California. Congratulations, Mr. and Mrs. Burnett. Contracts for your baby are waiting in Mr. C. Elliot Friday's office at the Royal Studios. Incidentally, Mr. Friday asks that you bring your baby's birth certificate and your marriage license. This is KNX, the Voice of Hollywood. (*Chimes are heard.*)

SCENE III

MR. FRIDAY's *office, the following day.* MR. FRIDAY *is sitting at his desk, dictating to* MISS CREWS.

C.F.: My dear Mr. Pirandello. . . . On second thought, you'd better make that Signor Pirandello. . . . I am writing to ascertain if possibly you have something in your trunk—every author has—which would be suitable as a vehicle for our new baby star, Baby Sylvester Burnett. It can be either a short story or sketch or a few lines which you can jot down at your leisure and which we can whip up into suitable material. I am writing of my own volition as both Mrs. Friday and I are great admirers of you. Very truly yours. . . . Now take a letter to Bernard Shaw. (*Dictograph buzzes.*) Yes ?

B.K.'s VOICE: Listen, Friday——

C.F.: What, B.K.?

B.K.'s VOICE: Come right up here. I want to see you. We've got a new cable from British Bulldog Pictures.

C.F.: British Bulldog Pictures? Yes, sir, I'll be right up. (*He rises.*) Miss Crews, have you the contracts for the Burnett baby?

MISS CREWS: Right on your desk, Mr. Friday. And the parents are in the commissary.

C.F.: Good. I've got to go up and see B.K. (*Exits.*)

GREEN (*who enters almost simultaneously, followed by* SLADE): Where is he? Where's C.F.?

MISS CREWS: You can't shoot him today.

GREEN: It's a wonder we don't. We're walking up and down in front of the projection room developing an idea when we hear a number— our number—— We go in, and it's in *London Life!* Our song! They don't even tell us about it—they murdered it! They run dialogue over it. You got to spot a song—we ask for Guy Lombardo and they give us a six-piece symphony orchestra!

MISS CREWS: If you buy me a handkerchief I promise to cry. Lace, if you don't mind.

GREEN: Lissen—play her the number the way it should be.

MISS CREWS: Must you?

SLADE: Oh, what's the use?

GREEN: Give her the chorus.

SLADE: I'm losing my pep.

GREEN: You might as well hear it. Nobody else will. (SLADE *plays.*) Will you listen to that? Ain't it a shame?

You promised love undying,
And begged me to believe;
Then you left, and left me crying
With pain in my heart, and my heart
    on my sleeve.

I really shouldn't blame you
Because you chose to leave;
But one thing forever will shame you——
It's the pain in my heart, and my heart
    on my sleeve.

(C.F. *has entered.*)

C.F.: Miss Crews !

MISS CREWS: Yes, Mr. Friday ?

C.F.: Miss Crews, get hold of Benson and Law right away !

MISS CREWS: Who ?

C.F.: Have Benson and Law come here—immediately.

MISS CREWS: Yes, Mr. Friday.

GREEN (*as* SLADE *pounds away*): That's the chorus ! That's the chorus that you murdered !

C.F.: Wait a minute, Miss Crews ! Get me the hospital. I want to talk to Happy's mother.

MISS CREWS: Yes, Mr. Friday. (*She exits.*)

C.F.: Miss Crews ! Call my florist and tell him to send Happy a bouquet of roses. And some orchids for his mother, right away. (*He turns to* GREEN.) Will you stop that noise ! (*He picks up telephone.*)

GREEN: Noise ? The song that you murdered ? We just wanna see if you got a conscience.

C.F. (*into phone*): Miss Crews, call up Magnin's and tell them to send a radio to the hospital for Happy. One of those slick, modernistic sets in white. And don't forget to have my card put in

with the flowers. Did you get Benson and Law ?
. . . Well, did you get Happy's mother ? . . .
Well, get them ! (*Hangs up.*)

GREEN: Is that a song that you run dialogue
over, C.F. ?

C.F.: What are you babbling about, Green ?
I haven't used any of your songs in *London
Life* !

GREEN (*outraged*): How about *Westminster Abbey
in the Moonlight* ? They wasn't our lyrics, but it
was our tune !

C.F.: I used an old Jerome Kern number we've
had for years, out of the library.

GREEN (*crestfallen*): You did ? (*To* SLADE) I
thought you said it came to you in the middle
of the night. Where ? In the library ?

C.F.: Will you get out of my office ?

GREEN (*with sudden enthusiasm*): We got a new
number you'll be crazy about.

C.F.: I've got too much on my mind to listen
to your tinny effusions. I told the studio to hire
Richard Strauss and no one else. One great
composer is worth twenty of your ilk ! (ROSETTI
enters with LARRY.)

LARRY: Looka here, C.F., I just got out of a sick
bed to see you.

C.F.: What do you want, Larry ? (SLADE *plays
on.*) What do you want ? I'm very busy. (*Turns
to* GREEN.) Will you please go ? I will not listen ?

GREEN (*as the worm turns*): . . . O.K., music
lover ! (GREEN *and* SLADE *exit.*)

LARRY: I shouldn't be here. I should be on my
ranch convalescing. I'm weak.

C.F.: Come to the point, Larry. Come to the
point.

LARRY (*bitterly*) : What's the idea of lending me out to Mascot ? I'm a star ! I ain't goin' to degrade myself by playing in no undignified thirty-thousand-dollar feature.

C.F. : Larry, face the facts—you're through.

LARRY : That's a nice thing to tell a sick man.

ROSETTI : Now, Larry, I told you. Your attitude is all wrong.

LARRY : Never mind about my attitude.

C.F. (*at the phone*) : Miss Crews, have you got Benson and Law ? . . . Who's gone to Vermont ? . . . What about Susie ? . . . What ? They left the hospital ? (*He hangs up.*)

ROSETTI (*eagerly*) : What's up, C.F.?

C.F. (*finally*) : This is confidential, Rosetti. (*Lowers his voice*) British Bulldog Pictures wants to buy the company intact.

LARRY : British Bulldog Pictures ?

C.F. : They want all our stars, including Happy. Naturally they want him. He's the sensation of London.

ROSETTI : But B.K. turned down three million. I've been handling that deal myself.

C.F. : They've raised it. They've just cabled an offer of five million.

ROSETTI : They did ? Say, that's marvellous. I'm in on that !

LARRY : Well, you better get me back from Mascot quick. British Bulldog Pictures wants *me*. Why, they made me an offer a year ago, only I was tied up.

C.F. : They make no mention of you.

LARRY : What ?

C.F. : Rosetti, we've got to sign Happy immediately. Get hold of Susie and let's close.

ROSETTI: You can sign the three of 'em for a hundred a week. They're broke. And they're low. I'm going right after it. (*He starts for door.*)

LARRY: Come back here. You're supposed to be *my* agent ! What are you going to do about *me* ?

ROSETTI: You're all right where you are—with Mascot. I'll call you later, C.F. (*Exits.*)

LARRY (*to* C.F.): My agent ! I been distrustin' that guy for years. (*Exits.*)

C.F. (*who can balance a budget, picks up phone*): Miss Crews, you didn't send those flowers off, did you ? . . . What ? . . . But they've left the hospital. What about the radio ? . . . Well, call them up right away and cancel it. . . . Who ? . . . She's here ? Send her right in ! (*He crosses to greet* SUSIE. *He is now cordial ; hearty, a thing of beauty and a joy forever.*) Well, Susie, I'm delighted to see you. You're looking well. I must say we've missed you. I hear the boys are in Vermont.

SUSIE (*stands in door*): Mr. Law was going but he missed the plane.

C.F. (*taken aback*): Well, where are they ?

SUSIE: They're in B.K.'s office, getting the contracts.

C.F.: Without consulting me ?

SUSIE: They said they don't trust you, Mr. Friday.

C.F.: Gad ! After all I've done for them !

SUSIE (*seating herself on the couch*): Do you mind if I sit here and do my homework ? I'm way behind and I don't want to be left back. I'm supposed to wait here until they get B.K.'s signature, and then I'm going to sign.

C.F.: I'm going right up to see B.K. (MISS CREWS *enters.*)

MISS CREWS: Mr. and Mrs. Burnett have had their coffee and now they want their contracts.

C.F.: What contracts?

MISS CREWS: The parents of the other infant.

C.F.: What other infant? What other infant is there except Happy?

MISS CREWS: But what'll I do with them?

C.F.: Send them away. (*Now he sees* RODNEY *looking in through door.* RODNEY *has a large box of flowers.*) What do you want?

RODNEY: Here's the check for the milk—and other odd items.

C.F.: Check.

RODNEY: I think you'll find it correct. I verified it at the commissary. And of course I included a service charge—and interest at six per cent. The total is two dollars and eighty-four cents. Thank you. (*Dictograph buzzes.*)

C.F. (*into dictograph*): Hello——

B.K.'s VOICE: Listen, Friday, you might as well be here. I'm settling the Happy contract with Benson and Law.

C.F.: Yes, B.K. I'm coming right up. (*Phone rings; into phone*) What? . . . I never asked for trumpets in the first place. I don't want any trumpets. I want a period of utter silence. See that I get it. (*Hangs up. To* RODNEY) *You* get out!

RODNEY (*firmly*): I've something to say to Mrs. Seabrook. (SUSIE *turns away. Softly*) I brought you some flowers.

C.F.: Give her her flowers, and get out. And don't let me find you here when I come back. Miss Crews, I'll be up in B.K.'s office. (*He exits.*)

RODNEY: I know you don't want to see me.

(*Extends flowers.*) Won't you take them ? (MISS CREW *exits.*) I wrote, you know. I explained everything.

SUSIE (*still not facing him*) : Happy's not allowed to have flowers.

RODNEY : Oh, but they're for Happy's mother—from Happy's father.

SUSIE (*turning; aghast*) : Are you joking about what you did ?

RODNEY : I'm not joking. Lord, no. I mean it. Look here—will you marry me ? (SUSIE *stares at him.*) I've thought it all out. I owe it to you. Shall we consider it settled ?

SUSIE : Did Mr. Law and Mr. Benson put you up to this, too ?

RODNEY : Good Lord, no. I haven't seen them and, what's more, I don't intend to.

SUSIE : Then why do you want to marry me ?

RODNEY : I owe it to you.

SUSIE (*angrily*) : That's no reason.

RODNEY : My visa's expired—I've two days' grace. I must get a train this afternoon. Are you coming with me ?

SUSIE : I don't think you'd make a very sensible father for Happy. I don't think so at all.

RODNEY : I'm not at all sensible. I'm frightfully stupid—impulsive—emotional—but I'm not really at my best these days. Most people aren't when they're infatuated.

SUSIE : You couldn't be infatuated with me !

RODNEY : But I am. Look here, it's no good debating. My mind's made up. I don't frequently make it up, but when I do, I stick to the end.

SUSIE: But you don't know about my past.

RODNEY: I've been through all that, in my mind. It doesn't matter.

SUSIE: But it does. I'm ashamed to tell you.

RODNEY: Please don't, then.

SUSIE: Happy's father was a bigamist.

RODNEY: Eh?

SUSIE: He married twice.

RODNEY: Is that it?

SUSIE: What did you think?

RODNEY: It doesn't really matter.

SUSIE: I didn't know he was married before.

RODNEY: But, good Lord, nobody can blame *you*.

SUSIE: His wife did.

RODNEY: Naturally.

SUSIE: How was I to know? And it wasn't his fault, either. He got a Mexican divorce and he didn't know it wasn't good.

RODNEY: Oh!

SUSIE (*drawing herself up à la Fairfax*): So I said to him, "Your duty is to your first wife." And I ran away. I didn't know I was going to have Happy, then.

RODNEY: Have you—heard from him?

SUSIE: Oh, no. Of course, he should have told me in the first place. But he was infatuated, too, and I didn't know any better.

RODNEY: Well, have you divorced him?

SUSIE: No.

RODNEY: You'll have to clear that matter up, I think—immediately.

SUSIE: I can't clear it up. He's dead.

RODNEY: Oh !

SUSIE: She shot him.

RODNEY: His wife ?

SUSIE: Yes.

RODNEY: Good Lord !

SUSIE: I hear from her sometimes. She's awfully sorry.

RODNEY (*brightly*): Well then, you're free to marry, aren't you ?

SUSIE: Oh, I'm free, but the point is—do I want to ? After all, I don't know you very well, and every time we meet something terrible happens. I didn't know Jack very well, either, and look what happened to him. I've got to be careful.

RODNEY: But I'm not a bigamist.

SUSIE: Maybe not. You may be something else.

RODNEY: But the British Consul'll vouch for me. He knows my family. I haven't had much of a life, but it's an open book.

SUSIE: Oh, I believe you. But I can't listen to my heart. I've got to listen to my head.

RODNEY: Of course, I haven't much to offer you. I've just come into a little money, and on my thirtieth birthday I come into a great deal more. We can have a flat in London and one of my aunts is going to leave me a place in the country.

SUSIE: That's in Europe, isn't it ?

RODNEY: Yes, of course.

SUSIE: Oh, I couldn't go to Europe.

RODNEY: But why not ?

SUSIE: The boys want to put Happy back in pictures.

RODNEY: I wouldn't hear of it. That's no life for a baby. Thoroughly abnormal. And, furthermore, I don't like the California climate. Now in England we have the four seasons.

SUSIE: You have?

RODNEY (*ardently*): Summer, winter, spring and fall.

SUSIE (*finally*): I want to ask you something.

RODNEY: Certainly.

SUSIE: When I come into a room—does something happen to you?

RODNEY: Eh? Of course—very much so.

SUSIE (*rises and turns away*): Well, I'll think it over.

RODNEY (*rises and take's* SUSIE'S *arm*): Look here, I couldn't possibly take no for an answer.

SUSIE: Of course, when you come into a room, something happens to me, too.

RODNEY: Does it really? (SUSIE *nods. He takes her in his arms. They kiss. Door opens and* LAW *enters with* BENSON.)

LAW: Susie, did my eyes deceive me? Were you kissing an actor?

BENSON: What's that?

LAW (*to* BENSON): An English actor!

BENSON: What? Didn't I tell you——?

SUSIE: Boys, I've been thinking it over——

BENSON (*wearily drops down to piano;* LAW *down to end of couch*): With what?·

SUSIE: I'm going to marry Rodney and I'm going to Europe. They've got the four seasons over there, and Happy'll be normal.

RODNEY: Well put, my dear. (C.F. *enters.*)

SUSIE: So I don't think I'd better sign the contract.

RODNEY: Most certainly not !

C.F.: You're not going to sign Happy ?

LAW: Susie, I've just given up Vermont for a whole year—for you. A whole year out of my life—because B.K. begged me to stay and handle Happy. I've sacrificed a great book—for what ? A paltry fifteen hundred dollars a week ? I didn't want it !

C.F.: If she doesn't sign, we'll break that contract with you, Law.

LAW: Try and do it.

SUSIE: I'm going to Europe with Rodney.

LAW: Do you want to tell Happy he's out of pictures ? Do you want to break his little heart ?

SUSIE: He'll understand !

BENSON (*suddenly*): Do you know who Rodney is ? English Jack ! Confidence man.

LAW (*quickly*): Yes ! Ship's gambler, petty racketeer and heart-breaker. (RODNEY *tries to speak.*)

BENSON: Served two terms for bigamy !

SUSIE: Bigamy ?

RODNEY: But that's absurd.

BENSON (*bitterly*): I've seen hundreds of your kind in Limehouse.

C.F.: So have I !

BENSON (*quietly*): Listen, C.F., stay off our side !

RODNEY (*to* SUSIE): You don't believe this, of course. They can't possibly believe it themselves.

LAW: Brazening it out, eh ? As sure as God made little green apples—and He did—you're not coming near Susie. We'll have you in the can and out of the country by morning.

BENSON: No sooner said—— (*Into phone*) Get me the Department of Justice.

SUSIE (*to* RODNEY): You see ? Something terrible always happens when you come.

LAW (*to* SUSIE): And you—sign that contract immediately.

RODNEY: She'll do nothing of the sort. You're not to intimidate her. Do you hear ? (*Door opens and* LARRY *enters, accompanied by middle-aged English gentleman.*)

LARRY: Come on in here, Major.

C.F.: What do you want, Larry ? I'm busy.

BENSON (*into telephone*): Department of Justice ? I want two of your best operatives to come down to the Royal Studios immediately. Report to Mr. Friday's office.

SUSIE: Oh, but you can't do that——

LARRY (*angrily*): Just a minute. Major Thompson is the representative here of British Bulldog Pictures.

C.F.: Oh ! I'm sorry. We've been rather upset. How do you do, Major. I'm Mr. Friday.

MAJOR: How do you do, sir. I won't be a moment. Mr. Toms suggested I come down here. He told me you'd received a cable from my home office.

C.F.: Yes—yes——

MAJOR: He was rather upset because his name wasn't mentioned.

C.F.: Yes, yes——

MAJOR: I called my home office, and they assure me they never sent such a cable.

C.F.: What ?

LARRY: That's what ! It was a phony.

RODNEY (*who has been trying to attract attention for some time*): Major !

MAJOR: Well ! Aren't you—— Why, how do you do. I thought I recognized you. Met you with your brother. By the way, I saw him a few weeks ago just before I sailed. Particularly asked me to look you up.

RODNEY: Is my name English Jack ? Am I a ship's gambler ? Have I served sentences for bigamy ?

MAJOR: Good Gad, no !

RODNEY: Will you vouch for me ?

MAJOR (*a bore of bores*): Vouch for Puffy Bevan ? Delighted ! His brother—splendid chap—— I met him first in India—he's a captain in the Coldstream Guards. His father is Lord Severingham. His sister is Lady Beasley—lectures, I believe. Now, let me see——

LAW (*interrupting*): Did you say—Lord Severingham ?

MAJOR: Yes.

BENSON: I beg your pardon, sir—*his* father ? (*He indicates* RODNEY.)

MAJOR: Yes. (BENSON *shakes his head in wonder*.)

SUSIE: Is your father a lord ?

RODNEY: It doesn't matter, does it ?

SUSIE: If you don't care, I don't care.

MAJOR: If I can be of any further service——

RODNEY: No. I think we'll sail along beautifully now. Thanks.

MAJOR: Good afternoon. (*Shakes hands with* RODNEY.)

C.F.: Who sent that cable ? That's all I want to

know ! Who sent that cable ! (MAJOR *and* LARRY *exit.*) Who perpetrated this hoax ? Who's responsible for this outrage ? By Gad, I'll find out ! (*Exits.*)

RODNEY (*turns to* SUSIE) : Shall we go ?

SUSIE : Good-bye, boys. Take care of yourselves.

LAW (*bows; bitterly*) : Thank you, milady.

SUSIE : Don't drink too much.

LAW : Thank you, milady.

SUSIE : You were awful good to me. Yes, they were, Rodney. They were awful good to me sometimes.

RODNEY : In that case, I don't mind shaking hands with you. (*Starts toward* LAW.)

LAW (*quickly*) : Don't shake hands. Just go. Dissolve—*slow fade-out !*

BENSON (*pantomiming*) : Shimmer away !

RODNEY : Eh ? (*Shrugs.*) Well—come, Susie.

SUSIE (*waving a delicate little hand*) : Good-bye, boys. (*Pause. They exit in silence.*)

LAW (*tense*) : I wonder what C.F.'s up to ?

BENSON (*struck all of a heap*) : The hell with that. Look at it—it checks ! Cinderella—Prince Charming—Boy meets girl. . . . Boy loses girl. . . . Boy gets girl ! Where's your damned realism now ? (*C.F. enters. He looks grimly at the boys.*)

C.F. (*finally*) : Well—it's a good thing you boys are not mixed up in this ! (*He goes to desk.*)

BENSON (*slowly*) : What ?

LAW (*slowly*) : What happened, C.F. ?

C.F. : I don't understand it at all. The cable was sent from London all right. But B.K. should have known it was a fake. It was sent collect. (*He picks up phone.*)

Law: Jascha always sends collect.

C.F.: Huh ? (*Into phone*) Miss Crews, get hold of the Burnett baby immediately. . . . Who ? . . . the *what* is here ? (*Puzzled. The answer comes in the clarion call of the trumpets, blaring their gay, lilting notes through the windows. Ta-ra-ta-ta-ta-ta-tata-tata-tata ! So much pleasanter than a factory whistle, don't you think ?*)

CURTAIN

TILL THE DAY I DIE

Clifford Odets

TILL THE DAY I DIE

This Play was first presented by the Group Theatre at the Longacre Theatre on the evening of March 26th, 1935, with the following members of the Group Theatre Acting Company:

	Played by
Karl Tausig	WALTER COY
Baum	ELIA KAZAN
Ernst Tausig	ALEXANDER KIRKLAND
Tilly	MARGARET BARKER
Zelda	EUNICE STODDARD
Detective Popper	LEE J. COBB
Martin, an orderly	BOB LEWIS
Another Orderly	HARRY STONE
Captain Schlegel	LEWIS LEVERETT
Adolph	HERBERT RATNER
Zeltner	DAVID KORTCHMAR
Schlupp	RUSSELL COLLINS
Edsel Peltz	WILLIAM CHALLEE
1st Storm Trooper	SAMUEL ROLAND
2nd Storm Trooper	HARRY STONE
3rd Storm Trooper	GERRIT KRABER
4th Storm Trooper	ABNER BIBERMAN
Boy	WENDELL KEITH PHILLIPS
Old Man	GEORGE HELLER
Other Prisoners	ELIA KAZAN, DAVID KORTCH-MAR, PAUL MORRISON
Major Duhring	ROMAN BOHNEN
Frau Duhring	DOROTHY PATTEN
1st Detective	GERRIT KRABER
2nd Detective	DAVID KORTCHMAR
Secretary	GEORGE HELLER
Arno	SAMUEL ROLAND
Stieglitz	LEE MARTIN
Julius	BERNARD ZANVILLE
Women	RUTH NELSON, PAULA MILLER

SCENES

SCENE I: An underground room.

SCENE II: Office room in the Columbia Brown House.

SCENE III: Barracks room, Brown House.

SCENE IV: Office room.

SCENE V: Tilly's room.

SCENE VI: An underground meeting room.

SCENE VII: Carl's room.

The action takes place in present-day Berlin.

The production was directed by CHERYL CRAWFORD.

The scenery was designed by ALEXANDER CHERTOFF *from suggestions by* PAUL MORRISON.

" TILL THE DAY I DIE " *was suggested by a letter from Germany printed in* " *The New Masses.*"

A small room underground in Berlin today.

A small man with a rueful face, named BAUM, *is silently operating a hectograph machine. Watching him are the two brothers* ERNST *and* CARL TAUSIG. *Downstage at a long littered table sits an alert girl who is concentrated on work before her. Her name is* TILLY WESTERMANN. *The two brothers watch the operating machine for quite some time.* CARL *finally picks up a leaflet which has just come from the machine. Scans it, replaces it finally.*

CARL : How long will this stencil hold out ?

BAUM (*singing out the answer*) : Another hundred.

ERNST : That's plenty. This particular leaflet's going to make some of our Nazi friends perspire once it gets into the workers' hands. Workers might like to know the American embargo on German goods has increased 50 per cent in the last six months. They might like to know wages are down one third and vital foods are up seventy-five per cent.

TILLY (*without looking up*) : Stop loafing, comrades.

ERNST (*humour ugly*) : She says that to a man who hasn't slept for thirty hours.

CARL : Listen, Dodo, you better take care. Just out of a sick bed, and——

ERNST : Good as new. I could swing you around my finger.

CARL (*laughing*) : Try it. (*They spar with good nature.*)

TILLY : Comrades ! Stop loafing !

CARL : That's right. (*Picks up leaflets.*) How many of these do I take ?

ERNST : Two hundred. Get them to Zeltner. He'll take care of distribution.

CARL: Listen, Ernst, I hate to say it, I don't trust Zeltner.

[TILLY *suddenly looks up*. BAUM *turns his head*.

ERNST: Why don't you trust Zeltner?

CARL: He is too damn brave, too damn willing to die for what he calls " The Cause," too damn downright curious.

ERNST: In the last analysis maybe just romantic.

CARL: He wanted to know this address. Is that romantic?

ERNST: He asked?

CARL: This morning. I told him Berlin's a big city.

TILLY: Did he press the point?

CARL: No, but his knuckles went white around the pencil.

ERNST: We are prepared to move on a moment's notice. Baum's removing the machine as soon as he is finished. In the meantime deliver this package to Zeltner.

CARL: Why take a chance?

ERNST: When we see what he does with this package we'll know where we stand.

CARL (*seriously*): I see.

BAUM: I used to be a peaceful man who planted tulips.

ERNST: Get going, Carl, the back streets.

TILLY (*not looking up*): All comrades to be referred to by the first names. Please remember to spread the word.

[BAUM *sings* " *Oh Tannenbaum*."

CARL: I don't suppose you and Tilly could come to Frieda's to hear some Bach to-night.

subway three years ago. Today is an anniversary for us.

ERNST: Really?

TILLY: Zelda took the wind out of my lungs. I wanted to propose . . .

ERNST: Something nice?

TILLY: A walk in the park—a small supper—then we would walk home slowly, quietly. You'd let me hold your hand. . . . Poor Zelda.

ERNST: My present dream of the world—I ask for happy laughing people everywhere. I ask for hope in eyes: for wonderful baby boys and girls I ask, growing up strong and prepared for a new world. I won't ever forget the first time we visited the nursery in Moscow. Such faces on those children! Future engineers, doctors; when I saw them I understood most deeply what the revolution meant.

TILLY: Maybe we could have one like that, a baby I mean.

ERNST: When the day comes that we don't have to live like rats in sewers—— Did I thank you for nursing me the past three weeks?

TILLY: Not a word came out of that stingy mouth. (*He kisses her in thanks.*) Did I thank you for the birthday card?

ERNST: Not a word came out of that stingy mouth. (*She kisses him in thanks.*) Did I thank you for the woollen socks?

TILLY: Ingratitude! (*Kisses her again.*) And you, Comrade Tausig, I never thanked you just for living!

ERNST: Ahhh . . . (*Kisses her fully this time. She finally breaks away.*)

TILLY: Stop loafing on my mouth, comrade. (*Looking at papers on table*) We have to finish this.

ERNST: Getting tough again?

TILLY: Seriously, I decoded the milk bill. There are nine names and addresses of party officials to be memorised by your most excellent brain.

ERNST: Berlin?

TILLY: Look it over. The rest of the room's as clean as a plucked chicken. Not a suspicious word.

ERNST: Who's Spitzer? (*Examines list.*)

TILLY: Rosenfeld, I think.

ERNST: And Strasser?

TILLY: My brother, Hans.

ERNST: Chris' sake, when did you see him last?

TILLY: Four months ago.

ERNST: I think we—— (*A low knock on the door stops him. Both freeze into position. From now on they whisper.*) Did someone knock?

TILLY (*listening*): Just a minute. (*Knock is louder.*)

ERNST: Don't answer. (*Tears name list in half.*) Memorise those. Quick!

VOICE (*outside*): Open the door!

ERNST: Sisst! (*Both stand there memorising.*)

VOICE (*as knocking increases*): Open the door—— Secret Police.

TILLY: The Gestapo!

ERNST: That bastard, Zeltner! (*Saying address aloud*): 783–783–783. . . . (*Finally the knocking stops.*) Don't stop. (*Her lips move rapidly and silently.*) All right?

TILLY: All right. (*But she goes on. Knocking comes again and " Secret Police." ERNST lights end of his paper. Watches her while paper burns. Finally she nods her head and he touches lighted paper to hers. Both burn down and are stamped to dust on the floor.*)

ERNST (*all in whispers*) : You and I were here on the couch. (*Puts coat and vest on back of chair.*)

TILLY: An affair ?

ERNST: You're in the business. Your room. (*Points to himself.*) Your customer. Push your hair around. (*She does so.*)

TILLY: All ready. (*Musses up couch.*)

VOICE (*outside*) : Open the door ! This is the Secret Police.

SLOW FADEOUT

In the dark between this scene and the next the shrill sounds of a half dozen whistles, variously pitched, slowing with hysterical intensity.

This device to be carried throughout.

Office in a Nazi Brown House. A fat detective in a trench coat and brown derby at telephone on desk which also holds typewriter. His name is POPPER. *Two* ORDERLIES *in Nazi uniform at the side sitting on a bench. They are counting from a list. To one side of the desk stands* ERNST TAUSIG, *a prisoner.*

POPPER (*excited and angry on phone*): I'm waiting for you. (*Waits, drums fingers, spits.*) I'm waiting for you, I said. Mommer God ! You think I've got all day.

ORDERLY (*begins to count aloud*): Thirty-seven, thirty-eight, thirty-nine——

POPPER (*yelling at them*): Dumbbells, can't you see I'm trying to work here. Mommer God, it's full of crazy people, the whole house. Hello ! The one I mean is the Communist Ernst Tausig. Find the rest of the report and bring it to me on the third floor immediately. Captain Schlegel is waiting for the report. What ? No, Schlegel. S as in Samuel. (*Hastily corrects himself.*) No, I mean S as in Storm Trooper. Also you made a mistake on the first part of the report. Don't give me back talk. Dumbbell, the report is in front of my eyes here. His girl friend was released. A plain out and out whore. What ? No, not war, whore. (*Turns to* ORDERLY—*in desperation*) You tell him.

ORDERLY 1 (*immediately at phone*): W-h-o-r-e. (*Retires primly.*)

POPPER (*back at phone*): We brought him in yesterday. So look in the top file right away. (*Hangs up.*) Imagine, that nobody tells me it's my fault, I'll poke my finger through his eye. Such confusion !

ORDERLY 1 (*sympathetically*): Terrible !

POPPER: The country is running over with those red ants. Such confusion.

ORDERLY 2: Terrible !

POPPER: Take the typewriter.

ORDERLY 2: Me?

POPPER: You.

ORDERLY 2: Yes, sir. (*Comes over to desk, a pleasant type.*) Where will I take it?

POPPER: What's the matter with you? To type, to type.

ORDERLY 2: I can't type.

POPPER: You can't type?

ORDERLY 2: No, sir.

POPPER: Dumbbell.

ORDERLY 1: Terrible!

POPPER (*to* ORDERLY 1): Can you type?

ORDERLY 1: No, sir.

POPPER: So shut up. Such disorder, such confusion. Every Brown House I was connected with in the past six months is like this. Mommer God, they'll say I'm inefficient, they'll kill me. (*Suddenly turning on* ERNST) You! You make trouble for Captain Schlegel and I'll—I don't know what I'll do to you. You know where you are?

ERNST: Yes.

POPPER: You know what happens in the Columbia Brown House to communists?

ERNST: Yes.

POPPER: Why did you say you never lived in Linden Street?

ERNST: I never did.

POPPER (*to* ORDERLIES): Did you hear that? He said he never lived there. (*To* ERNST) Never in possession of certain illegal materials in connection with the underground work?

ERNST: No.

POPPER (*shaking finger under* ERNST'S *nose*):
Listen, stinker, I—— (*Controls himself, goes back
to behind desk.*) Write down the liar's answer.
(*Writes it down himself.*) You were last employed
by the Musical Instrument Company, Eber-
hard ?

ERNST : Yes.

POPPER : Write down he was last employed by
that company. (*Writes it down himself. Trooper
passes through, whispers, " Courage " to* ERNST.)
You know we have here enough information to
burn you in hell. For three weeks we watched
you, you red fox. Do you—— (*Suddenly stops as*
CAPTAIN SCHLEGEL *enters, followed by an* OR-
DERLY *named* ADOLPH. POPPER *continues, fawn-
ingly.*) Good morning, Captain Schlegel.

SCHLEGEL (*a man like Goering*) : Is this him ?

POPPER : Yes, sir, this is the one, Captain
Schlegel.

SCHLEGEL : Any illegal papers found on him ?

POPPER : He got rid of them before the arrest,
Captain.

SCHLEGEL : Red fighter ?

POPPER : Without a doubt, Captain.

SCHLEGEL : Writer ?

POPPER : Former editor of a unit paper, Captain.

SCHLEGEL (*to* ERNST *as he examines report from
desk*) : That so ?

ERNST : Formerly so.

POPPER : Flat as the rug when you catch them.
Otherwise burning Reichstags twice a day.

SCHLEGEL : Never mind. Where's the rest of the
report ?

POPPER : Begging your pardon, Captain, they
can't find it downstairs.

SCHLEGEL: You'd better be careful, Popper. Such inefficiency will not be tolerated.

POPPER (*whining*): I do the best I can, Captain.

SCHLEGEL: Never mind, never mind. (*To* ERNST) How long have you belonged to the Communist Party?

ERNST: Since 1923.

SCHLEGEL: You deny belonging to the underground party at the present time?

ERNST: I do.

SCHLEGEL: You are on friendly terms with foreigners?

ERNST: No.

SCHLEGEL: You are not familiar with certain Bulgarian incendiaries?

ERNST: No.

SCHLEGEL: Married?

ERNST: No.

SCHLEGEL: Any children?

ERNST (*smiling*): No.

SCHLEGEL: What's funny?

ERNST: Nothing.

SCHLEGEL (*taking* ERNST *by his coat lapels*): Wipe off the smile. (*Releases* ERNST *and dusts off hands as if contaminated.*) What unit did you work with?

ERNST: Unit Number Twenty-fifteen.

SCHLEGEL: Who was the unit organizer?

ERNST: A man named Hess.

SCHLEGEL: Where is he now?

ERNST: I saw him last one year ago.

POPPER (*until now holding back his eagerness*): Where does he live, huh?

[CAPTAIN *gives* POPPER *a superior look.* POPPER *fades apologetically.*

SCHLEGEL: You had charge of a secret printing press on Hartsheim Street?

ERNST: No.

SCHLEGEL: You insist you did not help organize the underground press in Berlin.

ERNST: I did not.

SCHLEGEL: No illegal leaflets?

ERNST: No.

SCHLEGEL (*goes over and takes rifle from* ORDERLY. *Taps twice on floor with butt of rifle, hands it back to* ORDERLY *and returns to* ERNST *at the same time taking the report up from desk*): This report—all a tissue of lies you say?

ERNST: I cannot say.

[*A* MAN *enters—wears mask—limps.*

SCHLEGEL (*turning to the man*): What's his name?

MAN: Ernst Tausig.

SCHLEGEL: His work?

MAN: The underground press.

SCHLEGEL: You may go, Zerrago.

[MAN *goes.*

ERNST: We knew the rat as Zeltner.

[CAPTAIN *suddenly slaps him in the face.*

SCHLEGEL: Control your tongue. When you are asked you will speak, concerning three matters. A, identification of prisoners; B, names; C, addresses. Until then keep quiet. (*Turns from him, walks directly away, but suddenly turns and throws the whole sheaf of papers in* ERNST'S *face.*)

POPPER: He thinks he's in kindergarten.

SCHLEGEL: You'll be in kindergarten, if you don't keep your face shut. (*Approaches* ERNST, *examines him from all sides.*) I hear you're a musician of sorts.

ERNST: Yes.

SCHLEGEL: Play an instrument?

ERNST: Formerly the violin.

SCHLEGEL: Such sensitive hands. Hold them up. (ERNST *does so.*) So filthy. Put them on the desk. (ERNST *does so.*) So, a scraper of catgut. Now, what I have against the communists is (*holding and turning* ERNST'S *jaw in his hand*) the snout-like narrowness of their non-Nordic jaws. The nostrils display sensual and voluptuous self-indulgence, talking with the aid of hands and feet; non-Nordic characteristics. (*Walking away from* ERNST, *wipes his hands on a handkerchief.*)

ADOLPH: For every S.A. man killed in Berlin, Brandenburg, three communists will have to answer with their lives.

SCHLEGEL: A violin is an eloquent instrument. Perhaps you are familiar with Beethoven's Opus sixty-one, the violin concerto. Answer yes or no.

ERNST: Yes.

SCHLEGEL: In the key of D? (*Having taken rifle from* ORDERLY'S *hand, he suddenly brings down the butt of it on* ERNST'S *fingers, smashing them.*) (*Roars*) With the " Jochim Cadenza " ? (ERNST, *writhing with pain, puts his smashed right hand under his left armpit and almost faints.* CAPTAIN SCHLEGEL *now roars the rest.*) And if you think that's the end, let me tell you by tomorrow you'll find your neck half broken instead of three lousy fingers ! ! ! Stand up straight ! Do you hear me ? (ERNST *straightens up.*) Put your hand down. Put it down ! ! ! (ERNST *slowly does so.*) In ten minutes your old slut of a mother won't know you. (*Suddenly, softly*) Unless you answer my questions. (*Waits.*) You refuse . . . ?

ERNST (*finally, controlling his pain*): I have nothing to say.

SCHLEGEL: Take him to the barrack rooms. Take him out of my sight.

ORDERLY 2: Yes, sir.

SCHLEGEL (*to* ORDERLY 1): Get out.

ORDERLY 1: Yes, sir. (*Exits quickly.*)

SCHLEGEL: We've been too easy with that one.

POPPER: Yes, sir, he's a fresh guy.

SCHLEGEL: What the hell are they saving him for?

POPPER: I can't say. I seen the order myself signed by Major Duhring. Handle him with kid gloves, it says. He was in a position to know a big pile of names and addresses. Major Duhring is expected next week to personally question him.

SCHLEGEL (*bitterly*): Duhring? Duhring?

POPPER: He's soft as butter, but he knows how to make them talk.

SCHLEGEL: Oh, I see he can make them talk, but I can't.

POPPER: No, Captain, I only meant——

SCHLEGEL: Get out. You make me vomit.

POPPER: Yes, Captain. (*Bows his way out backwards and bunks into chair. Exits.*)

SCHLEGEL (*turning around the room in anger*): I think that Popper one must have Jewish blood. He hasn't the brains of a trained flea. What strikes you as being funny, Adolph?

ADOLPH: How that fat slob bowed his way out.

SCHLEGEL: I have seen you in a few peculiar positions at times. In fact, it might be much better for both of us if you weren't so graceful with those expressive hands of yours. Flitting around here like a soulful antelope. I'm lonely, I've got no one in the whole world.

ADOLPH: You've got me, Eric.

SCHLEGEL: Hitler is lonely too. So is God.

ADOLPH: I know.

SCHLEGEL: I lost my temper and smashed him against orders.

ADOLPH: You need a rest. You're nervous.

SCHLEGEL: Say it—nervous as a woman—say it ! Yes, that's the third one in a week I haven't been able to get a word out of. All I need is for them to find out about us and I am through for good. My God, you don't know who to trust.

ADOLPH: Trust me.

SCHLEGEL (*examining* ADOLPH's *face between his hands*): You ? You're as fickle as a girl. You know that song by Hugo Wolf, " I wish all your charm was painted." It's written for you and me. Last night I heard a lieder concert. There weren't fifty people in the audience. The country is gripped by fear. Houses are locked by day and night.

ADOLPH: Please . . . I'm very fond of you.

SCHLEGEL: Fond ? You probably carry tales. . . . I know, you love the captain's uniform, not the man.

ADOLPH: You're hurting me.

SCHLEGEL: What does a child like you know ?

ADOLPH: Please, I mean. . . . (*Suddenly begins to cry.*)

SCHLEGEL: Sisst ! You'll drive me crazy. Where

do you think you are? Go out and wash your
face. (*Looks at papers on desk.*) Who's crazy, they
or me? Saving a communist because they think
he'll spill the beans. I thought I told you to go.

ADOLPH: Please.

SCHLEGEL: Get out of here, don't you hear me?
Get out!

ADOLPH: Yes, sir. (*Hurries out.*)

SCHLEGEL (*looks at papers, scatters them around*):
My God! My God! What's the world coming
to? Where's it going? My God!

BLACKOUT

Whistles in the dark

SCENE III

The barracks room. TROOPERS *playing pinochle.
Drink beer. Guns and blackjacks on table. Five*
PRISONERS *lined up against wall, backs to audience.*
YOUNG TROOPER *marching back and forth behind
them.* PELTZ *and* WEINER, *two* TROOPERS, *having
hot argument downstage.*

PELTZ: I'm always for the practical side of the
thing.

WEINER: Was you ever in a school, if I'm not
getting too personal?

PELTZ: I went to school.

WEINER: Where, if I'm not getting too personal?

PELTZ: Right here in Berlin. We learned all
that stuff in school, Napoleon an' all that stuff
but it didn't help in business. Adages an' all
that. They're for the idlers. When I was in
business we didn't talk about Napoleon. We
talked about how much.

WEINER: You are absolutely without doubt the
most ignorant man I ever met.

PELTZ: I know, I know, we just don't agree.

WEINER: What made Von Hindenburg a great
general?

PELTZ: There was other great generals besides
him.

WEINER: There never was a greater one.

PELTZ: How about the few others who was
great? Don't you know every generation must
have its magnet? You don' see that!

WEINER: What's the use of arguing. It's like
religion. Some say——

PELTZ: You got that student stuff, artistic. Me,
I'm more for the practical side. But you are a
good scholar. Yes, I can see that, Weiner. Was
you always that way? More on the student side.

WEINER: What? What the hell are you talking about?

PELTZ: Now you know——

WEINER: You're so dumb! (*Walks away.* PELTZ *shrugs his shoulders, goes back to newspaper.*)

YOUNG TROOPER (*to* OLD MAN): Can't you stand still when you're told to stand still!! (*Kicks him strongly;* MAN *falls; trooper picks him up.*) You weren't too old to be a Social-Democrat, were you!! (*Shoves him back in line. Another brings in two more* PRISONERS—*One feebly attempts a Nazi salute, says,* "Heil Hitler," *but is shoved in line.*)

TROOPER 1 (*at table*): The bastards think they'll save their skin like that!

[TROOPER 2 *squirts beer from mouth at* PRISONER.

YOUNG TROOPER: The old one wanted a good day's rest on the floor.

TROOPER 2: Which one? (*Goes to him with bottle.*)

YOUNG TROOPER: This one. (TROOPER 2 *fills mouth with beer, squirts it in* OLD MAN's *face. All roar with laughter.*)

TROOPER 1 (*coming over*): Dammit! I know this one. You know where you are?

BOY: Yes, sir.

TROOPER 1 (*points to boy*): You was here before, wasn't you?

BOY: Yes, sir.

TROOPER 1: What was you arrested for that time?

BOY: I was accused of distributing pamphlets.

TROOPER 1: And what now?

TROOPER 5: Riding on a truckload of illegal literature.

TROOPER 1 : Jesus, Mary and Joseph !

BOY: He came up to me—the man. I was standing on the corner, and he offered me five marks to help drive the load.

TROOPER 2 : You didn't know what was in the boxes ?

BOY: No, he didn't tell me that and I didn't ask questions.

TROOPER 1 : This little one is telling fairy-tales.

BOY: I was glad to earn the five marks.

TROOPER 3 (*at the table*): What did you do it for ? They won't believe you now.

BOY: I didn't work since I left school. The labor camps won't accept me because I'm a communist. What can I do ?

TROOPER 1 : What you can do ? Eat floor wax ! (*Hits him; the* BOY *falls.*) Good appetite !

TROOPER 3 (*coming forward*): Leave the boy alone, Max !

TROOPER 5 : Look at these remarks. (*Reads from pamphlets.*) "The Brutal Slaughter of Red Front Comrades by Hitler's Brown Murder-Hordes——"

TROOPER 1 : Jesus, Mary and Joseph ! (*Kicks the fallen* BOY.)

TROOPER 3 : Leave the boy alone, Max. (*Sorry for him.*)

TROOPER 1 : I'll leave him alone !

TROOPER 4 (*still at the table with handful of cards*): If you're playing cards, play.

TROOPER 3 : Play cards, Max !

TROOPER 1 : All right, Professor. (*The game begins and presently* POPPER *walks in with* ERNST.)

POPPER: Over there. (ERNST *goes into line.*

POPPER *watches fallen* BOY *get up into line.*) What happened with him?

TROOPER 3: The Thunderbolt made a visit. (*Indicates* TROOPER 1.)

TROOPER 1 (*jumping up*): You are just too damn smart, Hassel!

POPPER: Silence! (POPPER *goes to them, whispers. They nod heads as they furtively look* ERNST *over.* POPPER *says, " Don't forget," and exits.* TROOPER 2 *marches around* OTTO *and examines him insolently. Goes back to seat and says to other*)

TROOPER 2: Not a blemish on the lily!

TROOPER 4: Are we playing cards or not?

TROOPER 1: I will say three fifty in spades.

TROOPER 2: You pay double if you lose.

TROOPER 1: Don't put no evil eye on me, Hassel!

TROOPER 2: Don't you act so mean, Herr Thunderbolt!

TROOPER 1: You wanna make something of it?

TROOPER 2: To me you can't talk like to your snotnose friends!

TROOPER 1: You must think——

TROOPER 3: Boys! Is this the trust the Leader puts in you—to start fights in the barracks with Jews and Bolsheviks watching you.

TROOPER 2: That's right!

TROOPER 4: Heil Hitler. (*All salute as if toasting and all sit. Card improvization.* TROOPER *scene.* WEINER *edges his way over to* PELTZ.)

WEINER: What kind of education can you get from the newspapers?

PELTZ: I see how it is. You like to lay around in those cafés with all the Bohemians. See them lying around with frocks on—dreamers. They can't come to the front—just dreamers.

WEINER: Did you read what Thyssen said?

PELTZ: A big man, a big man.

WEINER: Success is ninety per cent luck, five per cent work, he said.

PELTZ: Exactly, exactly, an' don't any intelligent man say the same? The same thing, he says, the same.

WEINER: What?

PELTZ: That means something, don't it? (*Improvization on pinochle game goes on in loud voices. The* OLD MAN, *who has been swaying, now falls again. The* YOUNG TROOPER *looking over a shoulder at the game finally turns and sees the fallen man.*)

YOUNG TROOPER: Look at him—can't stand no more. (*Examines him.*) He's bleeding from the mouth.

TROOPER 3: Take him to the hospital. My trick.

TROOPER 1: He's been standing seven hours.

OLD MAN: Don't hit me, please don't hit me.

YOUNG TROOPER: No, just dusting you off. (*Hits hard.*)

OLD MAN: Please don't hit me. I was in the war. I was decorated for bravery. Von Macksen decorated me for merit.

YOUNG TROOPER: *General* Von Macksen.

OLD MAN: I swear. Don't hit me again. I swear I—yes, I was—— (*Now laughs and goes very hysterical.*) . . . Please, please. . . . (*The* THUNDERBOLT *runs over—hits the* OLD MAN, *who crumples silently.*)

TROOPER 1: These Social-Democrats is a noisy bunch. (*Has retained hand of cards. Starts back to table and on way says*) The ace of diamonds. (*Puts it on table, says to* YOUNG TROOPER) Court-plaster on his head, Fritz ! (*The* YOUNG TROOPER *drags the* OLD MAN *out like a sack of sawdust.*)

TROOPER 4 (*as they play cards*) : Your muscle's better than his.

TROOPER 1 : Whose ?

TROOPER 4 : Tauchner in 120. He bets anything he can knock a man out in one blow—nine out of ten. Why, yesterday he won fifteen marks and a smoking pipe.

TROOPER 2 : That's scientific. Just how you hit them . . . like tearing telephone books.

TROOPER 1 : I guess you can do it too !

TROOPER 2 : If I want . . .

TROOPER 1 : Only you don't want ?

TROOPER 2 : Maybe I'll show you and maybe I won't.

TROOPER 1 : How about a bet—the pack of cards against my belt ?

TROOPER 2 : With the silver buckle ? (*A scream heard from below.*)

TROOPER 1 : Yeah.

TROOPER 2 : You go first.

TROOPER 1 : Then you go, and if I don't do it, you go again.

TROOPER 2 : That's right.

TROOPER 4 : Hand over the bets. (*They do so.*) Try the one Popper brought in. He's the biggest and freshest. (*Calls to* ERNST) Hey Blackhead ! Fall out of line ! (*Pulls him out by coat tail.*) Stand there, pig. (ERNST *stands in place.* TROOPER 3 *stays at table. The others approach.*)

TROOPER 2 : Who takes this one ?

TROOPER 1 : You're his size. I'll take that boy. Hey—— ! (*Pulls out* BOY.)

TROOPER 4: I count three. You both hit together. Ready.

TROOPER 2 (*preparing for blow with the other*): Yes, ready . . .

TROOPER 4: Gentlemen, one . . . (TROOPER 1 *spits on his fist.* TROOPER 2 *stands motionless. The* BOY *at the count of two will cover his face with his hands.*)

TROOPER 2: Remember, only in the head!

TROOPER 4: Gentlemen—two!

BOY (*covering face*): No.

TROOPER 1: Put your hands down, stinker! (BOY *refuses.*) Put them down, bastard!! (BOY *does so.*)

TROOPER 4: Gentlemen—two and a half. . . .

TROOPER 2: Just a minute.

TROOPER 1: What's the matter——

TROOPER 2: Yours is half fainting—a pushover——

TROOPER 1: Well, I'll take him. You! (*Pulls another out—pushes* BOY *who falls sitting and cries monotonously.*)

TROOPER 4: Now—1—2—3—— ! (*Both men let blows fly. The victim of* TROOPER 1 *goes down in a heap.* ERNST *stands stunned. In disgust* TROOPER 2 *goes back to seat.*)

TROOPER 1 (*delighted*): Well, who is the big scientist now?

TROOPER 2: That was a pushover.

TROOPER 4: Max won the bet. (*Hands over the prizes to* TROOPER 1.)

TROOPER 1: You wasn't so smart. (*Suddenly* TROOPER 2 *in a fury lets fly at* ERNST, *who slowly crumples to his knees.*)

TROOPER 2: Get back in the line, you louse!

(*Stalks back to table and sits moodily with chin on fist.* ERNST *slowly crawls back into line and rises painfully.*)

TROOPER 3 : Fritzie, get a bucket of water for the kid. (*He laughs triumphantly.*)

TROOPER 1 : Ha, ha, Professor ! (*Laughs.* TROOPER *scene.* PELTZ *and* WEINER *have been arguing throughout this last scene.*)

PELTZ : Oh, there's no question, no question. Then what's the use of cursing the world and blaming it on a handful of rich men ?

WEINER (*disgusted completely*) : I'm not cursing the world !

PELTZ : Now you was pretty strong there. Tell the truth, wasn't you, Weiner ?

WEINER : All I said was——

PELTZ : I don't care what this one or that one says about the rich men. It really don't interest me. Or taxes or socialism. I don't listen to them artists. But just because there's a depression I wouldn't say, " Oh, the goddamn rich men."

WEINER : I didn't say the goddamn rich men.

PELTZ : Absolutely, absolutely. . . .

WEINER : My God, you're dumb ! If I'm not getting too personal.

PELTZ : I know, Weiner, I know. Naturally people ain't of the same temper-a-ment. Naturally . . . the practical side—like Herr Doctor Goebbels says here in the paper. (*Reads*) " The head of a prominent Jew must be displayed on every telegraph pole from Munich to Berlin." No dreamy stuff, Weiner. That's practical. . . . (*A scream heard from below.*)

FADEOUT

SCENE IV

The same as III. Nazi swastika flag as background.
ORDERLIES 1 *and* 2 *rediscovered, respectively* EDSEL
and MARTIN.

EDSEL: " What's the world comin' to," he says
to poppa. Poppa began cryin'. My uncle said,
" Don't cry 'cause it won't help nothin'." After
all he didn't work for three years.

MARTIN: The Leader has promised a job to
every German.

EDSEL: Don't you think I said that ? " Read the
papers," I told him. " Plenty of work in
Munich." So he laughs and says that he just
came from Munich and not a job to be had
there. But their papers say plenty of jobs in
Berlin.

MARTIN: That sounds to me like red propaganda. Why didn't you arrest him ?

EDSEL: My own uncle ?

MARTIN: He told a lie, didn't he ?

EDSEL: I don't know.

MARTIN: The Leader says there's jobs for everyone.

EDSEL: I know. . . .

MARTIN: Government work on the roads.

EDSEL: Two and a half marks a week. Can a
mouse live on it ?

MARTIN: Is that a nice thing to say ?

EDSEL: Well, can a mouse live on it ?

MARTIN: I don't know. Dr. Goebbels spoke on
the radio last night. He says we must be prepared for a war with them any day.

EDSEL: Momma said some Jews were very nice
people.

MARTIN (*jumps up and goes away*): Say, you

better be careful—saying things like that. I don't wanna even know you.

EDSEL: Oh, she says it. Of course I don't agree.

MARTIN: You better be careful. They're hot as hornets around here today. This morning they found the zoological garden plastered with red propaganda. They can't find out who done it. They cleaned them all away on one side and when they turned around it was all plastered up on the other side.

EDSEL: They will lose their heads, all them communists.

MARTIN: Of course. . . .

EDSEL: If they catch them.

MARTIN: The Major brought in some of the leaflets for examination. Right there on the desk. (EDSEL *backs away from the desk as if stung*.)

EDSEL: Those things there?

MARTIN: The tissue paper—they print it on tissue papers so the wind blows them all over. A certain lady on Friedrichstrasse, one flew right on her face and when she seen what it was she fainted dead away.

EDSEL (*craning his neck for a look at the desk*): Can you see what they say? Read what it says.

MARTIN: Say, read it yourself.

EDSEL: You're closer to the desk than me.

MARTIN (*they are whispering now*): It don't prove nothing 'cause I'm closer to the desk. (*Slowly edges over. Looks around. Finally whispers*) " Workers of Germany ! " (*Springs away, amazed at his own audacity*.)

EDSEL (*whispering*): What?

MARTIN: That's what it says. . . .

EDSEL (*both whispering*): Read some more, Martin, Shh. (*Tiptoes to right side and watches out*.)

MARTIN (*looks around and tiptoes to desk. Picks up slip nervously, clears throat, reads*) "The Krupp armament works ran at a loss until Hitler came into power. Now it announces a 6 per cent dividend——" (*Breaks off nervously.*) Watch out, Edsel.

EDSEL: I'm watching. (*Looks off left.*)

MARTIN (*looks left, continues nervously in a whisper*): "While five and a half million workers are unemployed, which with their families, constitutes one third of the German working class, increased military forces are the basis of the Hitler economic . . ." (*Paper drops out of his nervous hands.*)

EDSEL: Pick it up.

MARTIN: I can't.

EDSEL (*comes over*): What are you so nervous for?

MARTIN (*chattering*): Who's nervous?

EDSEL (*himself shaking*): You're sweating.

MARTIN: It's a hot day.

EDSEL: Stand at the door. (MARTIN *does so.* EDSEL *looks around, then picks up paper, reads*) "In the meantime there is no bread, no milk. The Hitler-controlled newspapers print lies. The——"

MARTIN (*suddenly panic-struck*): The Major! (EDSEL *runs around not knowing where to put the slip. Tries to find a place. Suddenly puts it in his mouth and chews violently. As* MAJOR DUHRING *enters, ceases chewing and with* MARTIN *comes rigidly to attention.* MAJOR *walks in, notices* EDSEL.)

MAJOR: What's wrong?

MARTIN: Beg pardon, sir?

MAJOR (*pointing to* EDSEL *who has a mouthful*): You! (*Waits.*) Can't talk? (EDSEL *finally swallows strongly.*)

EDSEL: Yes, sir ?

MAJOR: Why are you men loafing around here ?

EDSEL: Beg pardon, sir, we were assigned to this room.

MAJOR: What room ?

EDSEL: To the examination room.

MAJOR: Now, boys, does this look like an examination room ? Clear out before I lose my temper. (*They scramble out with heels clicking and salutes.*) All right, all right, get out. (*Laughs when they exit, a tired, civilized man. Calls one back.*) You !

MARTIN (*badly scared*): Yes, sir, this is not the examination room.

MAJOR: Here, don't stand there like a whipped dog. I'm not calling you down. Inform them on the floor below to send up the Communist Ernst Tausig.

BOTH (*bowing and scraping*): Yes, sir. (*Try to get out of door together and comic mix-up, finally out.*)

MAJOR (*shakes head with pity*): Hmmm. . . . (*Picks up red leaflet.*) " Workers of Germany . . ." (*Puts down slip, shakes his head again. Goes up to Nazi insignia, examines it reflectively, with bitterness. ERNST is brought in. His back still turned, says to ORDERLY*) Leave us alone. (*ORDERLY clicks heels, salutes. MAJOR with back turned*) Sit down, Tausig. (*ERNST, wearied, mistrustful, does not move. MAJOR slowly turns, handkerchief at lower portion of face.*)

MAJOR: What ? Another whipped and frightened dog ? You may be seated. . . . (*ERNST looks at him a long time and finally sits.*) Cigarette ? . . . (*ERNST takes one, MAJOR putting it in his mouth and lighting it. Waits to see what MAJOR has up his sleeve.*) You look different, Tausig, than when I saw you last—a meeting—in Charlottenburg.

ERNST: I remember you—Duhring.

MAJOR: What happened to your hand?

ERNST: What happened to your "social ideals"?

MAJOR: Why I am in a Nazi uniform happens to be unimportant. A realistic necessity. I am married into one of the finest old German families, Nordic from the year one. The work I do for the National Socialists harms no foe of the Nazi State: in fact I am inclined to believe that if the truth were known, my work may often be interpreted as a positive hindrance. (*Laughs, and then adds soberly*) Not for publication. Perhaps I don't care. . . . That's nearer the truth. I will not deny the justness of the scorn in your eyes. This may cost me my head. . . . I'm not sure I care. (*Turns around room and comes back.*) I want to warn you. . . . They'll get what they want out of you. Trust me to——

ERNST (*bitterly*): A man tortured by his conscience?

MAJOR: Call it what you will. Here they use—— (*Voices heard without.* MAJOR *harshly, tearing cigarette from* ERNST'S *mouth*) Stand up! When these three questions are answered—— (*Breaks off to greet a blonde woman escorted by* CAPTAIN SCHLEGEL) Good afternoon, dear.

HEDVIG (*his wife, vacuous but energetic*): Ruppert, the handsome captain showed me the way. I had to ask your advice about an important matter.

MAJOR (*ironically to* CAPTAIN): Thank you, Captain.

SCHLEGEL (*with ironic courtesy himself*): You're welcome, Major. Your wife and I chatted pleasantly for ten minutes on the lower floor before I realized her identity.

HEDVIG: Yes, the place is full of nasty-mannered men. They kept me waiting ten minutes. (*Suddenly aware of* ERNST) Who is this?

MAJOR (*with ironic intent*): A communist, Hedvig. . . .

HEDVIG (*shrinking away to other side of desk, now protected by* CAPTAIN): Oh !

MAJOR (*smiling in spite of himself*): They don't bite.

SCHLEGEL: Only in the dark.

HEDVIG: Such dirty beasts. Don't they ever wash ?

MAJOR: When they have the facilities.

HEDVIG: And these were the ones who were supposed to be masters of the coming new world. (*Slaps him with glove.* ERNST *stands unflinchingly. She drops her glove.* CAPTAIN *picks it up and proffers it to her.*) Oh, no, I couldn't wear it again. (CAPTAIN *puts it on desk.* MAJOR *takes it up.*)

MAJOR (*ironic*): They're expensive gloves. What was on your mind, Hedvig ?

HEDVIG: About my broadcast speech. (*Takes it from purse.*)

MAJOR: Did you write it yourself, Hedvig ?

HEDVIG: No, Poppa's secretary wrote it, but of course I believe every word of it myself, so it's the same thing, isn't it ?

MAJOR: I should think so, Hedvig. (*With ironic seriousness.*)

HEDVIG: I wanted you to hear it before I broadcasted. I don't have to tell you that at least a half million German housewives——

MAJOR: Will put down their housework to listen to Hedvig von Barbossa explain their reason for existence.

HEDVIG: Oh, you ! Always anticipating my next word !

MAJOR: A perfect husband. Don't you think so, Captain Schlegel ?

CAPTAIN (*ironic. A constant fight goes on between the two men*) : By all means.

MAJOR : Hedvig, we are having a very heavy day here.

SCHLEGEL (*ironic*) : Oh, very heavy. (MAJOR *gives him a penetrating look—a slight duel goes on between their eyes.*)

MAJOR : So I must ask you to merely give me the gist of the speech, dear. Suppose we say, merely the summation.

HEDVIG : Oh, you ! You just aren't interested in my intellectual development.

SCHLEGEL (*ironic*) : Your husband is really the busiest officer in our section.

MAJOR : That answers you, my dear. So merely the gist.

HEDVIG : Well . . . I thought I would conclude as follows. (*Reads speech*) " Women must understand their part in this moral renaissance of the German people. Well has it been said by our great Leader, ' In eternal warfare mankind will become great. In eternal peace mankind would be ruined.' Yes, my dear friends, war alone puts the stamp of greatness on a people ! Let women tend the home ! Let women breed warriors ! Let women forget the pursuit of culture ! Germany must expand ! Germany must push her frontiers east and west ! Women of Germany, give your lives for this cause ! " Is that all right, Ruppert ?

MAJOR : Splendid—the whole theory of the Fascist State in a paragraph. You might be one of our leading theoreticians one of these days.

HEDVIG : I told Poppa's secretary what to write, I truly did.

MAJOR : Yes, now you must run along, Hedvig. Leave us to our work. Good-by.

HEDVIG: And remember dinner at the Hauptmanns' tonight.

MAJOR: I won't forget. Captain, please see my wife safely out.

SCHLEGEL: Yes, sir. (*Goes with her.*)

MAJOR (*to* ERNST): You see the sort of convenient marriages one can sometimes be forced to make.

ERNST: The Captain is not your friend.

MAJOR: Nor yours. (*Indicating wife's glove in his hand.*) The Captain suspects me of leniency to prisoners. My lineage. (*In a sudden emotional outburst*) I tell you a civilized human can't stand it ! A great sermon requiem is being played. It's a nightmare ! (*Gets himself in control.*) He holds his knowledge over my head like a sword—the Captain, I mean. In turn I have collected certain data concerning the Captain's private life and loves—enough to have him purged to a bloodstain on the wall ! We will duel ourselves to death, we two ! This amuses you ?

ERNST: Yes.

MAJOR: I can understand. Briefly, here is some information. (*Businesslike now*) You can take it or leave it, Tausig. Our side wants information from you. Addresses and names of party officials.

ERNST: Don't have them !

MAJOR: I'm not asking. They're sure you can identify prisoners. They mean to make you do it. You've been here three weeks. Until now they've been comparatively mild. They'll beat you to within an inch of death. You won't want to live. Then they'll nurse you back to health. This will happen several times.

ERNST: I will remember my proletarian task.

MAJOR: It's possible you may forget your proletarian task. Don't smile. A man's made of flesh

SCENE V

In the dark, under the whistles we pick up on radio music, full and classical. With the lights fading up we see TILLY's small room. A rough cot. One window looking out on a world of clear light. A small bureau, wash basin and pitcher of water on it. A door. TILLY in an old bathrobe. Music coming from her little radio. TILLY dips a corner of a towel in the water, slowly wipes her face clean with it. She finishes. Turns down cot covers. Goes to window, raises shade —blue night comes in. She turns down lamp. Turns off radio, but puts it on again. Sits on bed and just as she bends to remove slippers there is a tap on her door. She stays in her bent position for a second, finally when a second knock comes—she slithers to the door. Listens. The knock again.

TILLY (*in a faint whisper*): Who is it?

VOICE: Ernst. . . .

TILLY (*does not believe it. Comes to center of room. Listens, looks around, finally in a full impulse goes to door. Throws it open. ERNST is there. She is away from door. He slowly comes in, closes door, stands against it. For a long time they look at each other silently, finally*): Ernst!

ERNST (*and they are in each other's arms*): Tilly!

TILLY: Alive!

ERNST: Alive!

TILLY: Please, sit here on the bed. (*She escorts him to the bed. He sits. She lowers shade. Turns on lamp. Turns and looks at him: is shocked by his appearance.*) Dear. . . . (*She throws herself at his feet, on her knees, holds him as a mother might do with a child.*) You're hurt. . . .

ERNST: Not as much as I might be. Only my back is raw . . . the shirt is stuck to it.

TILLY: Here, I'll fix it. (*Goes to wet towel.*)

ERNST: No, darling, if you touch me there I'll faint.

TILLY: Are you hungry?

ERNST: No, dear, no. Here, someone gave me cigarettes. We'll smoke and talk. Don't be excited. I want news. Here—— (*They light cigarettes. She gets a little ashtray—they sit together on cot.*)

TILLY: News, what news? You've been released.

ERNST: They held me in the Columbia House since the arrest. I counted the days when I could remember—twenty-two. . . .

TILLY: Twenty-three, Ernst.

ERNST: You counted too.

TILLY: What then?

ERNST: You don't know what happens, you don't know. No one knows until he walks through that hell. . . .

TILLY: Why have they released you?

ERNST: I am being followed. I'm expected to make party contacts. Don't look out the window. Two of them in the grocery doorway. . . . I couldn't give them the slip. Maybe I shouldn't have come.

TILLY: A man must have some place.

ERNST: It won't harm. We fooled them about your identity. Where's Carl?

TILLY: Safe at work in the suburbs.

ERNST: Good.

TILLY: Were you afraid there?

ERNST: A man who knows that the world contains millions of brothers and sisters can't be afraid. Don't think I haven't screamed with pain—they have ways of arousing every corpuscle to pain—but you keep your mouth shut.

TILLY: Your hand . . .

ERNST (*wincing*): Don't touch it. (*Gets up. Walks away.*)

TILLY: Sit down again. Don't be afraid of softness, of sorrow. . . .

ERNST (*holds back his emotional impulse to cry on her shoulders. Finally*): What news of the others?

TILLY: Raff is dead.

ERNST (*deeply touched*): How?

TILLY: The report they gave out was that he jumped from a window. And Hans Mathieson. . . .

ERNST: The same?

TILLY: The same.

ERNST: Those brave fighters. . . .

TILLY: I'm glad you're living, Ernst.

ERNST (*suddenly crying out in protest*): Tilly, I must tell you. Tilly, for a week I have been chewing my heart to pieces. All the time I was in the Brown House they were offering me bribes, any inducements to turn informer. First a session of endearment. Then a session of torture. The human body is a tower of strength. After a while comes numbness, but the mind begins to wander. I'm afraid, Tilly—do you hear that, afraid! Something might happen. There is no rest, no possible contact with party members permitted. They will seize me again, return me to the same program. I'm afraid of what might happen. I ask for one hour of peace.

TILLY: Peace in this war?

ERNST: Yes, peace! In the cell there—I know I stayed alive because I knew my comrades were with me in the same pain and chaos. Yes, I
S*

know that till the day I die there is no peace for an honest worker in the whole world.

TILLY: Till the day we die there is steady work to do. Let us hope we will both live to see strange and wonderful things. Perhaps we will die before then. Our children will see it then. Ours!

ERNST (*bitterly*): Our children!

TILLY: I'm going to have a baby, Ernst. . . .

ERNST: Who is?

TILLY: I am.

ERNST: You mean it?

TILLY: Your baby. (*Dawn—where even the tea-kettle sings from happiness.*)

ERNST (*finally, after looking at her and not knowing what to say*): Please, allow me to change the subject. . . . Overgaard, I met him three streets away from here. I made signals with my eyes. He understood. Passed by like a stranger. (*Finally*) A baby?

TILLY: Yes.

ERNST (*walks to window*): It's almost morning. . . .

TILLY (*joining him*): Ernst, the tenderness I feel for you. . . . I don't know how to say. . . . Part of my deepest life came back to me when you walked in the door here. You keep coming up in my eyes like the sense of tears. . . .

ERNST: I understand.

TILLY: It is true our work comes before our personal happiness. But we must try to wrest some joy from life.

ERNST: How can that be when presently I shall be a decoy to trap other wild ducks?

TILLY: We'll manage. Escape is possible one way or another. Now I want you to undress and sleep.

ERNST: Sleep?

TILLY: Under the warm blankets.

ERNST: Sleep in your little bed? My sister, comrade . . . my wife. . . . (*Sits on bed. She takes off his shoes. His coat. He winces as he stretches out.*)

TILLY: It hurts?

ERNST: Yes.

TILLY: Tomorrow we'll fix all these things. Sleep, Ernst, sleep. Tomorrow you can read the full report on the united front. *L'Humanité* came through, several copies.

ERNST (*suddenly sitting up*): What united front?

TILLY: The united front in France.

ERNST: It has happened?

TILLY: I thought you knew?

ERNST: In France they have joined to make a solid front against the fascists?

TILLY: Please don't get so excited, Ernst. (*Tries to calm him.*)

ERNST: Our work is bearing fruit? In that beautiful classic country. The united front? Oh, Tilly, oh, Tilly ! ! (*And suddenly he is crying in the pillow for all his pains and for the joy of this news. TILLY soothes him with understanding.*)

TILLY: Yes, cry, cry. . . . (*She strokes him until the sobs become more quiet. Suddenly there is a knock on the door. TILLY whispers*) Quiet ! You're sleeping. Don't move. (*He lies still. She stealthily goes to the door.*) Who is it?

VOICE (*also whispering*): Open the door. . . .

TILLY: Who is it?

VOICE: Carl ! (*TILLY looks around at ERNST who raises himself on his hands. TILLY quickly opens the door, admits CARL, quickly closes door.*)

TILLY: You're spotted ! Get out quick !

CARL: Where?

TILLY: They must be right behind you. Watching the house. (CARL *quickly goes over to the cot, touches* ERNST. *Starts for door again where* TILLY *has been listening.*)

TILLY: They're coming! (*Suddenly in a loud voice which* CARL *immediately takes up*) I'm telling you to get out. What's the matter—can't a respectable girl entertain her boy friend.

CARL: You made a date with me. (*Simulates a drunkard.*)

TILLY: You're a liar. Now get out before I call the police.

CARL: Didn't you say it! In the park didn't you tell me to come tonight? Why, for two marks—— (*Door is pushed open: two detectives in trench coats stand there.*)

TILLY: My God! What's this, more customers?

DICK 1: Who's this?

TILLY: A fresh guy who pushed his way in. There's my boy friend, dead tired on the bed, fresh from the jug, and this garbage-can won't let him rest.

CARL: Never mind that stuff! When I met her in the Kunzterplatz, Tuesday, she tells me to come up tonight. " I love you," she tells me.

TILLY: Yah, yah, yah!

DICK (*comes in and looks around. Assistant blocks the door*): Is this your boy friend?

TILLY: Yeah. He's dead tired. He was——

DICK: All right, all right! (*To* CARL) What do you wanna start up with this alley-cat for. You know they do it for anyone.

CARL: Sure. . . . But the next time I meet you in that same place at lunch time——

TILLY: Yah, yah, yah, yah. . . . Thanks officer —a real man ! (DICK *pushes out protesting* CARL *and looks superciliously at* TILLY *as he closes door.* TILLY *stands in her place for a second, listens, then turns down to* ERNST.)

ERNST: Did he get away ?

TILLY: They believed every word. (*Suddenly door pushed open.* DICK *stands there again.*) What do you want ? . . .

DICK (*advancing into room. Finally*) : I forgot my glove, cutie. (*Picks it up from table, goes back to door.*) You wanna be careful. Better girls than you are in the jails.

TILLY: All right.

DICK: Lemme know if anyone makes trouble. . . .

TILLY: All right.

DICK: Or if you're lonely some night.

TILLY: All right.

DICK (*winking. Taps his chest*) : A real man, me. . . .

TILLY (*first locking door*) : Sleep, Ernst, sleep. . . . (*But he is already asleep. She sits herself in window light in profile as daylight comes fuller in the window.*)

BLACKOUT

Whistles

SCENE VI

Comrades' Scene.

   About a dozen party members seated in a small locked room. The SECRETARY *of the unit is finishing a report.* CARL *sits downstage with back to audience.* TILLY *is there. Also little* BAUM *of the first scene. Sitting with a woman holding his hand is a man with a fine looking head, a famous theoretician, a shawl over his shoulders, gray-haired—*STIEGLITZ. *Guard at door.*

SECRETARY (*reading*): Three new theater-of-action groups have been formed in the last week. They are now functioning regularly throughout the city. Three thousand cheap jazz records have been distributed since the 10th. These each end in one of our speeches. Since the 1st—— (*Stops to admonish a small man named* JULIUS, *who is wending his way through some seated comrades.*) Will the comrades kindly remain seated until the reports are concluded.

JULIUS (*who is revealed to be wearing only one shoe*): I left my shoe in the corner. My foot is cold.

SECRETARY (*continues*): Since the first we have spent on Hitler joke-books and leaflets the sum of two hundred and ten marks. (*Puts down report.*) I suggest that since we are all agreed on the accuracy of the report that we do not waste time but go ahead to other business. Will someone ask the question?

VARIOUS: The question, etc.

SECRETARY: All in favor will please assent in the usual manner.

ARNO: Just a minute. This seems to me to be in a way like a little steam rolling.

SECRETARY: Does the comrade have any suggestions in reference——

ARNO: No, but it seems——

OTHERS: Sit down, Arno.

ARNO: What about Comrade Tausig?

SECRETARY: Next.

ARNO: How was I supposed to know——

SECRETARY: All in favor. (*The suggestion is passed. There is a slight respite. Improvization.*) We will now read the roll of honor.

COMRADE (*gets up and reads*): "Unit 2026— "Killed in carrying out their proletarian duties, on the 3rd, Friedrich Meyers, Elsa Schorr. On the 12th, George Pfitzner." (*In the background a woman suddenly sobs. She is comforted by another and soon stops.*) "Imprisoned or captured during this month, Paul Schnitzler, Ernst Tausig." (*Sits.*)

SECRETARY: This is not time for sentiment, but it would not be wrong to stop for one minute to remark upon the fine qualities of those valiant fighters who are now lost to our cause, some for ever. In the case of our slain fighters their merits are known to all of us. In the case of Ernst Tausig we must pause for serious consideration. It has been proposed by the unit functionaries that his name be added to the blacklist. But in accordance with usual procedure we have brought this matter to your attention in the hope of arriving at a wider understanding of the case. Comrade Tilly Westermann.

TILLY (*rises, wipes hands with small handkerchief*): Since the reports on Ernst Tausig come from reliable sources we must give them strong credence. Briefly he was first arrested in March. Three weeks later he was released. (CARL *turns around and looks into the face of the audience.*) At that time he knew he was being followed. They were hoping he would contact party members. This he positively did not do. Four days later he was picked up again. I saw him once after that in the hospital with his brother. (*Lapsing for one line into a less official, less impersonal attitude*) I didn't recognize. him. He held my hand. . . . We wanted—— (*Breaks off, stops for a minutes, resumes the impersonal tone.*) It's no secret to most of you that I am bearing his child. This fact will seem to make for strong partiality on my part. But I protest that because Ernst Tausig was in a room when others identified prisoners is no reason to assume that he has turned informer. This is not the Tausig whom most of us have known and worked with in the last four years or more.

BAUM: Right !

ARNO: How about when Mickle saw him with the police in the Herfheim Street raid ? Maybe he was just knitting a muffler while he was sitting there next to the driver !

SECRETARY: The comrades will please ask permission for the floor. (ARNO *raises his hand.*) Comrade Arno ?

ARNO (*on his feet*): Personally, I'm sorry for Tausig. But who can take a chance nowadays ? Even if he is not guilty, who can take a chance when the secret police have any connection with him ?

SECRETARY: Please be more specific.

ARNO: I mean he must go on the blacklist. Every unit paper in the country must carry his name and description. For our purposes he is deadly, dangerous.

SECRETARY (*recognizing* TILLY): Comrade Westermann ?

TILLY: I can't disagree with what has just been said——

ARNO: I should say not !

TILLY: But will the chair permit me to read a small note I received from Ernst last week ?

SECRETARY: Please read the note.

TILLY (*reads*): " They are taking my life by the inch. Day and night they press me for an answer—identify prisoners or be killed. I cannot last much longer. The terrible truth is they do not kill me. I am enclosing money which they handed over to me yesterday after forcing me to sit beside their chauffeur when they made a street raid. You may be sure I have kept my mouth shut. Love to Carl and you." (*The man with one shoe comes over and looks at the note.*)

SECRETARY: Before we decide the action in this case would any other comrade care to say something ?

GIRL: Perhaps Comrade Stieglitz.

SECRETARY (*looking in his direction*): I don't think . . . (*Companion of* STIEGLITZ *whispers to him. He nods.*)

ZELDA: He says he will say a few words about the case.

SECRETARY: Comrade Stieglitz has just come back to us from three months in the Sonnenberg detention camp. (*Pointedly*) I will ask you to listen carefully—to these few remarks from one of our leading theoreticians. (*Small bandage on head. All wait. The imposing looking man gets up quietly and takes his place at the other side of the room, next to the* SECRETARY. *He looks around him gently, smiles softly at* TILLY.)

STIEGLITZ: Always in such rare cases where there is a doubt as to the accused one's guilt it is the custom to be careful in consideration of the known facts. But a different face is placed on the matter in times of stress and danger. Often . . . (*He stops, thinks, continues*) Often the class struggle . . . it seems to me . . . it seems to me . . . (*He stops, a little puzzled, plays with fringe of shawl.*) I was saying . . . (*Looks around helplessly. Walks over to his female companion.*) Where are we, Zelda ?

ZELDA : With friends, Benno.

STIEGLITZ : What was I saying ?

ZELDA : Please sit down, Benno.

STIEGLITZ : Take me home, Zelda. . . . (*Looks around helplessly.*) Zelda. . . .

SECRETARY (*into the breach*) : I think it would be best if he were home.

ZELDA : Yes. We're going, Benno. I have your hat.

STIEGLITZ : I'll hold your hand. Good-by, my friends, good-by. You must come to my house for breakfast. We have the sunniest breakfast room. . . . Yes. . . . (*She leads him out. The door is locked behind him. She has been admonished first to be careful. BAUM blows his nose vigorously.*)

BAUM : So have the devils broken that noble mind ! !

SECRETARY : Comrades, now is no time for sentiment. This is the hour of steel, when—— No sentiment ! (*But he himself has to hide his tear-filled eyes. Presently controls himself.*)

JULIUS : It's a pretty kettle of fish, I must say.

CARL (*suddenly up*) : I would like to say something in reference to my brother.

SECRETARY : Take the floor. (*Piano and violin duo begin downstairs.*)

CARL : Comrades, you are wondering where the music comes from. This is the very same house in which my brother and myself were born and raised. My uncle and his old friend, Seligmann are playing. The war, the revolution, the banishing of Jews from Germany have turned their poor old hearts to water. These days you will find them forever—the two of them—playing their Mozart and Beethoven sonatas. The music they are playing now is Mozart, the *andante* of the C major Sonata—C major, my dear comrades, is a very wholesome, beautiful key. You must excuse what may seem an irrelevant excursion into sentiment. But this is the first piece of Mozart my brother and I ever played together. When we came from school—I am surprised how fresh this dead life is in my memory—nineteen years back—but that's another story. (*Now suddenly turning hard*) But Mozart—is there time for music to-day? What are we fighting for? I need not answer the question. Yes, it is brother against brother. Many a comrade has found with deep realization that he has no home, no brother—even no mothers or fathers! What must we do here? Is this what you asked me? We must expose this one brother wherever he is met. Whosoever looks in his face is to point the finger. Children will jeer him in the darkest streets of his life! Yes, the brother, the erstwhile comrade cast out! There is no brother, no family, no deeper mother than the working class. Long live the struggle for true democracy! (*He sits now.*)

[*The music finishes before anyone speaks.*

The vote is called for. All raise their hands in assent except TILLY. *She looks around at the others. One of the men is eating small nuts loudly. Her hand slowly comes up.*

FADEOUT

CARL's *room. Small. Only a door set up in center. In darkness we hear two typewriters. When lights fade up we see* CARL *and* TILLY *each at a typewriter, typing.* TILLY *finally stops.*

TILLY: A few mistakes.

CARL (*older*): No matter.

TILLY: My heart hurts. Hurt me all day.

CARL: Take care. Lie down before we go.

TILLY: I can't rest. (*Comes down to him.*)

TILLY: Carl, I want to ask you—are you ever afraid?

CARL: Sometimes.

TILLY: Now? Tell the truth.

CARL: Yes, if you want it. The place we're going to is swarming with S.S. men. We might never come out alive. I'm not so masculine that I won't admit I'm scared.

TILLY: All day I had this pain under the heart.

CARL: When will the baby be coming?

TILLY: A long time yet.

CARL (*in a low voice*): What will you call him?

TILLY: If it's a girl, I don't know. If it's a boy . . .

CARL: Not *his* name.

TILLY (*suddenly clutching him*): Tell me, how do you know? What makes you so sure?

CARL: There's proof—plenty!

TILLY: You believe it?

CARL: In the beginning I didn't. Maybe the brown shirts spread the tales themselves.

TILLY: They've done it before.

CARL: I don't say no. That's why I didn't believe a word I heard at first.

TILLY: Now you believe it.

CARL: Yes. Too many reliable comrades have checked on his activity.

TILLY: Maybe he's drugged. Maybe he walks in his sleep. You know—yes, you know—he would have found some way to do away with himself before he was forced to act as a spy. You know that ! You know you do !

CARL: Don't tear my shirt. (*Trying to jest.*)

TILLY (*persistently*): Answer the question !

CARL (*finally, in a burst*): Goddamit, I say he's guilty !

TILLY: If he came here, broken in mind and body, would you refuse to see him ? Can you stand there and tell me you wouldn't even listen to what he had to say ?

CARL: To me he has nothing to say !

TILLY: He's your brother.

CARL: That won't sell a postage stamp !

TILLY: Suppose he knocks on the door this minute !

CARL: You're in love.

TILLY: Answer what I ask !

CARL: What makes you think you're the only one ? Maybe I slept better at night the last two months. Maybe I cried myself to sleep some nights. This big blustering idiot wept like a girl. (*Walks around.*) Yes, yes, the whole thing funnels up in me like fever. My head'll bust a vein !

TILLY (*catching herself*): We're talking too loud.

CARL (*whispering, but with same intense flow*): Seeing him together at the hospital the last time—the picture follows me like a dog. I'm sick, I tell you I'm sick of the whole damn affair ! (*Sitting*) Perhaps we ought to change— do our work apart. This way, this is a secret, eating thing between us. Each reminds the other.

TILLY: We'll talk about it to-morrow. I want to find a glass of milk before we start to work.

CARL: We'll get some on the corner.

TILLY: The baby has to eat. . . . (*He gets her coat. Smiles at its shabbiness.*)

CARL: Nothing is too good for the proletariat.

TILLY: I had a nice coat once. I had a mother. I had a father. I was a little girl with pigtails and her face scrubbed every morning. I was a good child. I believed in God. In summer I ate mulberries from our own tree. In late summer the ground was rotten where they fell. (*Knock at the door.*) Open the door. Don't ask who it is. It's Ernst, I know it is.

CARL (*looks at her, puzzled.* TILLY *goes to open door. He stops her, whispering*): Are you crazy ?

TILLY: I know it's him.

CARL: Let the door alone.

VOICE (*outside*): Carl. . . ,

CARL (*covers door*): You can't let him in.

TILLY: You can't keep him out. (*Waits.*) He's waiting. . . .

CARL: He'll go away.

TILLY: Maybe he's sick.

CARL: And the others in detention camps, they're not sick ?

TILLY: You might be wrong.

CARL: Then better one mistake like this than a thousand arrests and murders.

VOICE (*knocks without*): Carl. . . .

TILLY: He won't leave. (*After another knock*) Give me the key, Carl. (CARL *looks at her. Puts key on table. Walks away. She opens door with it. Opens wide the door. There stands* ERNST. *Looks terrible. Wears a large velour hat, black, making his face look small. This man, sick, broken, alone, desperate, humble, something of amusement in him too. Has a handful of coins he plays with. Clothes are too big on him. Looks like a ghost.*)

ERNST: Tilly. . . .

TILLY: Come in, Ernst.

ERNST: May I . . . ?

TILLY: Come in. . . . (*He does so.* CARL *on side, back turned.* TILLY *locks door. Retains key. She takes off his overcoat. He is revealed in a soiled shirt, tails out on one side. Takes off his hat while he plays with coins and looks at floor. His hair is streaked with white. He seems abstracted. Finally, becomes aware of room when coins drop out of his hand. He doesn't notice the coins.*)

ERNST: Tilly. . . . Let me. . . . (*He slowly walks over to her, falls on his knees, kisses her hand. She draws her hand away.*)

CARL (*turning*): Stand up. (ERNST *does so.*) What do you want?

ERNST: I came——

CARL: To tell us lies.

TILLY: Let him talk. There are enough executioners in Germany without——

CARL: For the present I'm not used to one in my own room. For the present I——

ERNST (*in a violent burst*): No. Stop it. No!

CARL: What is " no " ? Mickle saw you with the police. Arno saw you in the court. You give the secret police information!

TILLY: They'll hear you in the street!

ERNST: Listen to me—— (CARL *makes move for door.* ERNST *blocks it.*) I came to have a talk.

CARL: Get out of my way.

ERNST: No !

CARL (*pushes him away, throws him to floor. Finds door locked. Turns to* TILLY. *She puts the table between them*): Give me the key.

TILLY: No. (CARL *looks at* ERNST. *Picks him up from floor. Sits aside.*)

ERNST: It's all right—I understand—you don't want to listen. It's all right—I'll talk to myself. It's a habit now, I talk to myself on the street, frighten children—frighten myself. Don't listen to me. I'll talk to the chair. Here—— (*Turns chair around, addresses it as to a person.*) Mr. Chair ! First, we understand the situation. Second, the charges are listed in our minds. (TILLY, *out of pity and terror, removes the chair which he has been addressing very earnestly. Finally* ERNST *continues in a low, intense voice*) Now we must examine the living witness: what do you know of what happened ? Who told you ?

CARL (*jumping up fiercely*): I won't listen to you.

ERNST (*jumping up the same*): What am I asking of you ? Pity ? No ! You must *know*, Tilly must know the accusations against me are untrue. I want you both to stand clear and proud in the world—not to think your brother and husband turned . . .

CARL: I don't care for the personal issues.

ERNST: Then I care ! For my son I care. He need never be ashamed to bear my name.

CARL: Every unit paper in the country screams out you're a rat.

ERNST: And they know ?

CARL: You're damn right they know.

ERNST: When I was released from the barracks in General Pape Street—did they know then?

CARL: That's four months back.

ERNST: They left me free that time.

CARL: Because you were supposed to lead them to the comrades.

ERNST: But I didn't.

CARL: Because you couldn't walk.

ERNST: So far so good, no?

TILLY: Yes. . . .

ERNST: Then they picked me up again. The whole thing started fresh—questioned day and night. No let-up. Swollen, bleeding, the hospital again. What good was I to them dead? Suddenly you fall—a bucket of water—they stand you up—the lash—dig your nails into the wall to remain standing.

CARL: When did you make up your mind to tell?

ERNST: Not yet!

TILLY: Not yet?

ERNST: They tie your feet, seat you with the driver on the round-ups. This makes you seem a guide for them.

CARL: But you never sent a message, not a warning.

ERNST: Two dozen. Intercepted. You don't believe it?

CARL: No.

ERNST: You're made to stand outside the courtroom door where comrades pass.

CARL: We know all about it.

ERNST: Inside they say, " Don't make denials. Your former comrade told us everything." Some comrades believed that.

CARL: That explains the new clothes, money in your pocket?

ERNST: They dressed me up. That was the plan, to look like a paid stool pigeon. Then the first leaflet appears: " Ernst Tausig is a paid stool pigeon." Who printed them? Comrades? No, the Nazis. The comrades keep away. Out of the crowd some one hits me—it happens often. I turn around. Children hoot me on the street. All day and night the rank injustice freezes my heart to ice.

CARL: Why tell us, why—— ?

ERNST: They have a detective taking me home at nights. I live in his house. I can't understand. They did something to me. Sulphur is running in my veins. At night I wake up perspiring. My tongue is thick, my eyes won't open.

TILLY: Ernst, what can we do?

ERNST: Nothing, nothing. Only I want you to believe me. I must have someone believing me. I'm not a traitor. I'm not so far gone I don't understand the position I'm in. I see what you must do to me. Warn all party members against me. You can't know the truth. Yes, what is one person like me against the whole enslaved German working class? I know I must be cast away. But you two can believe me. Yes, officially you need not believe—but yourselves. Carl don't look at me that way!

CARL: What is that?

ERNST: What?

CARL: Perfume? You're using perfume? Lady-fingers and whipped cream for breakfast.

ERNST: No, you see how it was. They gave me money. It falls out of my hands. My mind wanders like smoke. I passed the store the other day and it was in the window. Perfumed soap. I bought some. A man must have something. It smells like flowers. (*Sits with abstracted quality. Finally says, after* CARL *removes leaflets on table from his sight*) Five weeks ago—I think it was the 8th of last month—I don't remember—the day we had the thunder shower—the hand was badly infected—it seems I knocked it against the wall or something—the 9th or 10th—they amputated it. We had that fine surgeon, D. B. Kellner. (*There is a luminous full pause. Yes, his hand has been removed and all this time he kept the stump in a pocket. Does not take it out now either.* TILLY, *unbearably moved, comes to him. He refuses her touch. Jumps up.*) Don't touch me. No, it isn't so easy. Three months—it's not so easy. That's why I'm telling you. *You must know everything!* Last night I sat in my room and it came to me. I was thinking that when I went there the next day I would tell them everything. (*Laughs and changes voice to a whisper.*) Do you know what you must do? I brought the whole thing with me. A gun, cleaned, oiled. This morning I did it. With one hand it isn't easy. Kill me!

CARL: What?

ERNST: Take the gun. Carl, you loved me once. Kill me. One day more and I'll stand there like an idiot identifying prisoners for them. I know so many. In all honor and courage you must pull the little trigger. I brought the money. Put it in the fighting fund. Maybe tell a few comrades the truth.

CARL: It is the truth?

ERNST: Yes.

TILLY: There must be no talk of dying.

ERNST: For me there's one thing, Tilly—nothing is left to do. Carl——?

CARL: They've killed you already.

ERNST: That's right. But you're alive. Other comrades are working. The day is coming and I'll be in the final result. That right can't be denied me. In that dizzy, dazzling structure some part of me is built. You must understand. Take the gun, Carl.

CARL (*drawing hand away*) : I won't do it.

ERNST: I couldn't do it myself. There isn't enough strength left. . . . Tilly, no tears ! (*Smiles wearily.*) Such bourgeois traits in a worker . . . What is your answer, Carl ?

CARL: That is what you must do. Do it yourself. Before you turn idiot. When you do that the world will know you were innocent. They'll see you came voluntarily, that . . . (*Suddenly*) Who am I to sit in judgment ?

ERNST: These guns are complicated pieces of machinery. (*Has picked it up.*) Our Germans make them like works of art. (*Weighs the gun in his hand.*) Tilly, Carl, our agony is real. But we live in the joy of a great coming people ! The animal kingdom is past. Day must follow the night. Now we are ready : we have been steeled in a terrible fire, but soon all the desolate places of the world must flourish with human genius. Brothers will live in the soviets of the world ! Yes, a world of security and freedom is waiting for all mankind ! (*Looks at them both deeply. Walks to door to room L.*) Do your work, comrades. (*Exits.*)

TILLY (*for a moment stands still. Then starts for room. CARL stops her*) : Carl, stop him, stop him. (*CARL holds her back.*)

CARL : Let him die. . . .

TILLY : Carl. . . . (*Shot heard within.*)

CARL : Let him live. . . .

SLOW CURTAIN